CU00709622

Palgrave Studies in Race, Inequality and Social Justice in Education

Series Editors
Jason Arday
Department of Sociology
Durham University
Durham, UK

Paul Warmington
Centre for Education Studies
University of Warwick
Coventry, UK

Vikki Boliver
Department of Sociology
Durham University
Durham, UK

Michael Peters
Wilf Malcolm Institute of Educational Research
The University of Waikato
Hamilton, New Zealand

James L. Moore III
Interim VP for Diversity & Inclusion
The Ohio State University
Columbus, OH, USA

Zeus Leonardo
Graduate School of Education
University of California, Berkeley
Berkeley, CA, USA

This series focuses on new developments in the study of race, social justice and education. Promoting theoretically-rich works, contributions include empirical and conceptual studies that advance critical analysis whilst attempting to destabilise the institutionalised racist orthodoxy that has undermined the notion of education being a tool of social mobility. The series will consider social mobility as a form of equality narrowly defined whilst also critiquing the ideology of social mobility which essentially pits individuals against one another in a sink or swim competition, entirely ignoring the reality of deep and damaging structural inequalities. A central aim of the series will be to address important current policy issues, such as social mobility, widening participation etc., while also recognising that critical studies of race are also concerned with wider, fundamental trans-formations in education, knowledge and society, i.e. the dismantling of racist structures, concern with education's role in reproducing racial inequality.

Arif Mahmud • Maisha Islam
Editors

Uncovering Islamophobia in Higher Education

Supporting the Success of Muslim Students
and Staff

Editors
Arif Mahmud
University of Roehampton
London, UK

Maisha Islam
University of Southampton
Southampton, UK

ISSN 2524-633X   ISSN 2524-6348   (electronic)
Palgrave Studies in Race, Inequality and Social Justice in Education
ISBN 978-3-031-65252-3   ISBN 978-3-031-65253-0   (eBook)
https://doi.org/10.1007/978-3-031-65253-0

Cover credit line: StellaPhotography / Alamy Stock Photo

This Palgrave Macmillan imprint is published by the registered company Springer Nature Switzerland AG.
The registered company address is: Gewerbestrasse 11, 6330 Cham, Switzerland

If disposing of this product, please recycle the paper.

To Amma and Abbu (Mum and Dad)—always wanting to make you both proud.
To Aisha, Zayd, and Layla—the apples of my eye.

FOREWORD

This timely collection offers a much needed and significant scholarly contribution. It acts as a symbol of hope in complex and confusing times as well as serving as a renewed evidence base to stimulate action to address Islamophobia as an unacknowledged form of racism.

The authors within this collection have carefully and sensitively curated the documenting of intersectional experiences and realities of Muslim staff and students within British universities unearthing the kaleidoscopic manifestations of racism. In doing so, they have catalogued our stories, past and present. The chapters establish the nexus between systemic engines of discrimination and exclusion with individual and generational harm. They write at a time when many Muslims have been effectively silenced on campus and in digital spaces (this during an apparent renaissance of academic freedom and free speech).

Since the summer of 2020 there have been more sector conversations to consider just how deeply racialised university spaces are. However, the critical analysis provided by this collection demonstrates there is significant distance to travel for institutions to authentically accept religiosity in order to evolve into inclusive organisations which can recruit, retain, and sustain diversity.

The volume sets out that the manifestations of racism go far deeper than the violent whiteness of university catering (a perfectly evocative and apt designation by Professor Kehinde Andrews), although that is a useful illustration of the wilfulness and determination of the system to insist on exclusion—keeping racial and religious minorities at the margins.

In these accounts, we are presented with the reality that staying power far too often depends on individual resilience, informal and personal support networks, and the presence of allies rather than on effective, robust systems of governance, equity practice, and positive cultures that intentionally address oppression and discrimination.

The co-editors, for whom I hold great professional respect and admiration, directed me to include personal reflections in this foreword. Alongside the honour and sense of responsibility, panic ensued. I am one of a handful of Muslims who have defied statistical probabilities to reach university senior leadership. Throughout my career, no one, I mean no one, has ever asked me what it is like being a Muslim working in UK higher education. I have been in UK higher education for 20 years. In that time, I have never been taught by, or worked for, anyone existing at a proximal intersection of race, ethnicity, religion, gender, and socio-economic background. I use the term socio-economic background deliberately here, finding the romanticisation of (permanent) working-class identity by highly remunerated university staff somewhat tenuous.

My identity as a British Pakistani woman is more obvious to see, but my religiosity may be harder to spot. Early on in my lecturing career, other academic colleagues enquired as to whether I'd had an arranged marriage and if I could explain why so many Muslims were on benefits (welfare support). I could not muster the courage to ask in return, why the bar of professional expectation and capability is set so high for non-natives. Existing in a paradox, the sector favours its Muslim and ethnic minority women to be submissive and servile. When our voice and expertise is heard we are received as argumentative, unmanageable, and a threat to institutional cultures that are simply not ready to accept the implications of 'inviting' diversity to the table.

Despite the construct of university senior staff as power wielding and omnipotent, vulnerability accompanies some of us at every level. We apply a continual assessment of when and with whom to conceal or reveal our faith. That ongoing unease has not diminished with this temporal hierarchy and positional privilege. This self-censorship is not unfounded given the findings of a 2023 study which suggested Muslims are the second-least liked group in Britain, second only to Gypsy, Roma, and Traveller communities.[1] Absorbing the chapters in this edited collection in order to

---

[1] https://www.birmingham.ac.uk/documents/college-artslaw/ptr/90172-univ73-islamophobia-in-the-uk-report-final.pdf.

provide this modest contribution, I have read the accounts of precarity, discrimination, and epistemic violence. There have been tears of knowing and familiarity.

The pages that follow should be read as an indictment on the performance of universities to adequately discharge their legal and ethical obligations, not least because increasingly it is Muslim student tuition fee income that is keeping the lights on in several institutions. On the one hand, this change in student demographics tells a proud (though not pain-free) history of generational social mobility (this because most Muslim communities are working-class communities), but, on the other hand, these statistics have not resulted in the shifting of power and voice. Muslims experience the extremes of hyper-visibility or invisibility, and in both scenarios accompanied by disenfranchisement within institutional structures where they remain on the margins of decision-making, management, and leadership.

A number of contributors suggest the intellectual climate may be changing and warming to the discussion of Islamophobia—if this is the case, then adequately resourced practical interventions must follow to disrupt systemic disparities and epistemic oppression. Institutional culture is created by those with positional power and maintained by governance boards, making the Muslim lived experience a necessary competent within those spaces. It is however impossible to ignore the growing collective of Muslim Generation Z social activists, many are women, working within our universities to make them more accountable and decolonial. These courageous individuals are organised and organising, networked, and building a new chapter for Muslims within higher education.

London South Bank University   Zainab Khan
London, UK

Praise for *Uncovering Islamophobia in Higher Education*

"This is an important and timely intervention by leading experts. The combination of data alongside personal accounts provides a deeper granular picture of the impact of campus culture on the achievements, outcomes, and lived experience of Muslims in higher education. The findings should be taken seriously by both national policy makers and sector decision makers."

—The Rt Hon Baroness Sayeeda Warsi

"The editors of this volume have brought together authors with intellectual rigour and lived experience of Islam within British Higher Education and enduring Islamophobia. The volume provides a compelling, incisive, and nuanced narrative that educators, higher education managers and civil actors can use to challenge Islamophobia and indeed all forms of societal injustice within and outside of our educational spaces."

—Professor Sariya Cheruvallil-Contractor

"*Uncovering Islamophobia in Higher Education* sheds light on the multiple battles and institutional harms that Muslim students and staff encounter daily in UK universities and the various strategies they use to mediate and resist these challenges and oppressions. This powerful and timely contribution is a must-read for anyone who is committed to promoting social justice in education. It is a call to action, urging universities to create a positive culture that intentionally addresses Islamophobia as a form of structural racism."

—Professor Farzana Shain

CONTENTS

1 Introduction: Systematic Islamophobia in UK Higher
  Education   1
  Arif Mahmud and Maisha Islam

Part I   Islamophobia in the Ivory Tower: Theoretical and
         Reflexive Framings   15

2 White Atmosphere and Pedagogic Violence: Female
  Muslim Graduate's Experiences on an Undergraduate
  Degree in a Russell Group University   17
  Yasmin Hussain and Paul Bagguley

3 *Seen but Overlooked*: Unveiling the (Counter)narratives of
  Black Muslim Women Navigating Higher Education   33
  Amira Samatar, Aida Hassan, and Ruqia Osman

4 The Rise and Decline of Muslim Representation in
  Student Unions: Motivations and Experiences of Muslim
  Sabbatical Officers in Student Unions   57
  Lila Tamea

5 The Contested Phenomenon: Intersectional Identities   77
  Fatema Khatun

6   "Never let anyone tell you that you're not good enough":
     Using Intersectionality to Reflect on Inequality in British
     Academia   97
     Afsana Faheem and Mohammed Rahman

7   Navigating British Academia as an Early Career Muslim
     Woman   121
     Amena Amer and Nihan Albayrak-Aydemir

8   Between Invisibility and Hypervisibility: Reflections on
     Being 'Permanently Precarious' as a British Muslim
     Woman Within the Ivory Towers of Academia   143
     Fauzia Ahmad

9   "This Girl is a Nation": Muslim Women's Narratives of
     Self and Survival in the Academy   161
     Heidi Safia Mirza

Part II   Institutional and Policy Change Geared Towards
          Religious Equity   179

10   Islamophobia's Past, Present, and Future: Insights and
     Reflections from Multi-generational Muslim Academics   181
     Maisha Islam and Tariq Modood

11   The Changing Landscape of Higher Education for British
     Muslims: Exclusion, Marginalisation, and Surveillance   201
     Tahir Abbas

12   Islamophobia in the Secular University: Understanding
     and Addressing the Muslim Student Awarding Gap   215
     Reza Gholami

13   Utilising the Race Equality Charter to Embed Religious
     Equity for Muslim Students and Staff in Higher
     Education   231
     Shames Maskeen

14   The 'New' Intersectionality of Disadvantage?
      British Muslim Students and the Widening
      Participation Agenda   251
      Zain Sardar

15   Conclusion: Entrenched Inequalities and Evolving
      Challenges: Harnessing Hope for Muslim Students and
      Staff in Higher Education   269
      Maisha Islam

Index   293

NOTES ON CONTRIBUTORS

Tahir Abbas is Professor of Radicalisation Studies at the Institute of Security and Global Affairs, Leiden University, The Hague, and an Honorary Professor at the Institute of Arab and Islamic Studies, University of Exeter, UK. He is currently the Scientific Coordinator of the European Commission (EC)-funded H2020 DRIVE project, which is exploring radicalisation and social exclusion in northwest Europe. He is also the Principal Investigator of the EC-funded PROTONE project, which explores ways in which to protect religious places of worship in Europe. His recent books are *Ruminations* (Beacon Books, 2022), *Islamophobia and Securitisation* (Springer, 2022, with L. Welten), *Countering Violent Extremism* (Bloomsbury, 2021), *Islamophobia and Radicalisation* (Hurst/ Oxford University Press, 2019), and *Contemporary Turkey in Conflict* (Edinburgh University Press, 2017). His recent edited books are *Global Counter-Terrorism: A Decolonial Approach* (eds., with S. Dutta and S.I. Bergh, Manchester University Press, 2024, forthcoming) and *Ethnicity, Religion, and Education in the UK* (eds., with K. Iqbal, Routledge, 2024). He is a fellow of the Academy of Social Sciences and a fellow of the Royal Society of Arts. www.tahir-abbas.com

Fauzia Ahmad is a qualitative sociologist whose work and publications have focused on British Muslim women and experiences of higher education and employment, Islamophobia, and Muslim feminist decolonial research perspectives. Her current research is exploring British Muslims and their personal relationships and partner selection. At the time of writing, she had been based for seven years in the Department of Sociology, Goldsmiths, where she has since gone through her fourth redundancy there.

Nihan Albayrak-Aydemir is an Assistant Professor of Social Psychology at Boğaziçi University, Turkey, and holds a visiting fellowship at the London School of Economics and Political Science. Her research expertise spans identity, intergroup helping, migration, and meta-science. Dedicated to addressing challenges encountered by marginalised communities in higher education and academia, she explores the impacts of intergroup power dynamics, research methodologies, and teaching practices on scientific knowledge production and the experiences of scientists. Alongside her research on other topics like supporting refugees and responses to global emergencies, she actively develops mentoring programmes and support groups aimed at empowering marginalised communities. For more information, please visit her website at www.nihanalb.com.

Amena Amer is a lecturer at University College London, UK. Her research interests broadly focus on exploring experiences of identity and belonging. More specifically, she is interested in the experiences of minority and marginalised groups, examining how members of these groups manage and negotiate their identities and positions within society in relation to boundaries of inclusion and exclusion.

Amena has previously worked in the third sector drawing connections between her academic research interests and its real-world application and impact. She has developed and facilitated workshops in schools and communities across the UK exploring issues of identity, stereotypes, intersectional experiences, and self-expression, as well as designing and delivering workshops for secondary school teachers on positionality and reflexivity.

Paul Bagguley is a distinguished academic in the field of sociology, currently serving at the University of Leeds, UK. With a robust background in sociological theory and research, Bagguley has dedicated his career to exploring themes such as social movements, race and ethnicity, and the sociology of religion. His research is widely recognised for its depth and impact, contributing significantly to academic and public discourse on these critical issues.

Throughout his tenure at the University of Leeds, Bagguley has been involved in numerous research projects, publications, and conferences, establishing himself as a leading voice in contemporary sociology. His work often intersects with pressing social concerns, providing insightful analyses and fostering a better understanding of complex social dynamics.

Afsana Faheem is an Assistant Professor at University of Birmingham, Dubai. Her teaching and research primarily focuses on clinical psychology, with particular interest in diversifying and amplifying the voices and experiences of racial/ethnic minority communities. In her previous role at the University of Bath, Afsana co-developed the mentoring programme for aspiring clinical psychologists from Black, Asian, and Minority Ethic (BAME) groups and launched the "What About Us" Podcast to help enhance the visibility of diverse clinical psychology professionals. Both initiatives received recognition for their contribution within the field.

Reza Gholami is Professor of Sociology of Education at the University of Birmingham, UK, where he is also the founding co-director of the Birmingham Research Group on Education Policy (BREP). He holds his PhD from the Department of Anthropology and Sociology at School of Oriental and African Studies (SOAS), University of London, and has held academic posts and fellowships at several universities, including the University of Wisconsin, Madison, USA; Monash University, Australia; and University College London, UK. He is a fellow of the Royal Society of Arts and senior editor of the Sociology of Education section of the *Journal of Cogent Education*.

Gholami's research is internationally recognised and focuses on community-inclusive and "diasporic" forms of education within the context of chronic educational disparities affecting racial, ethnic, and religious minorities. He uses qualitative and quantitative methods while working collaboratively with a range of educational stakeholders around the world to develop innovative educational resources to support local schools and foster intercommunal learning. His current project is funded by the Paul Hamlyn Foundation and explores issues of belonging and diversity in schools through theatre-based pedagogies. He is also working on a Leverhulme Trust-funded project that examines how young people in England engage with freedom of expression around sensitive issues of race and faith.

Gholami is the author of numerous books and articles in his field, including the forthcoming book *Knowledges that Destroy* (with Dr Danielle Tran); the monograph *Secularism and Identity*; and the co-edited volume *Education and Extremisms: Re-thinking Liberal Pedagogies in the Contemporary World*. He also regularly appears in national and international media, for example writing in *The Conversation* about the impact of COVID-19 lockdowns on refugees and asylum seekers and featuring in the BBC Radio 4 documentary *The Corrections* about the Birmingham "Trojan Horse" affair.

Aida Hassan is a PhD student at Queen Mary University of London (QMUL), UK. Her research broadly focuses on the international politics of global health. She was also a former student lead for the Global Health Anti-Racism Steering Committee at QMUL, a student-staff project invested in anti-racist and decolonial changes within the global health curriculum.

Yasmin Hussain is notable Professor of Sociology at the University of Leeds, UK, specialising in the areas of race and ethnicity, migration, and the sociology of health and illness. Hussain's academic journey is marked by a commitment to examining the complexities of identity, belonging, and the experiences of marginalised communities.

Her research has made significant contributions to understanding the sociocultural dynamics that shape health disparities and the lived experiences of ethnic minorities. Hussain's work is characterised by its interdisciplinary approach, often intersecting with fields such as cultural studies and public health. Hussain's influence extends beyond academia through her active involvement in public discourse and community engagement, making her a prominent figure in both the sociological and broader community.

Maisha Islam is the Doctoral College Research Culture Lead for Equality, Diversity, and Inclusion at the University of Southampton, UK, and recently completed a professional Doctorate in Education. Maisha's main research interests lie in the area of racially minoritised students' experience, and Muslim students' sense of belonging/student voice in higher education, where she presents, writes, and has published on these topics. Maisha is heavily invested in the areas of race and religious equality in higher education. For example, Maisha has investigated "Asian" student experience in relation to degree-awarding gaps and has sat on Universities UK staff panels which developed guidance for universities tackling racial harassment and Islamophobia on campus. Additionally, she has completed a two-year term serving on the Office for Students' Student Panel (2020–2022) and is co-chair of a Steering Group for a Research England/ Office for Students funding programme seeking to improve access and participation of racially minoritised students in postgraduate research study.

Zainab Khan is a University Pro Vice-Chancellor. She has held executive leadership roles for the past five years and has worked in Higher Education since 2007, firstly as a legal academic before moving into strategic leadership roles which have focused on education, EDI, and more recently academic resource strategy. She is Professor of Higher Education and a barrister by background. Zainab is also the Vice-Chair of the Premier League's EDI Standard and convenor of the Senior Women of Colour in Higher Education Network which she established in 2020 to raise visibility of the underrepresentation in executive leadership.

Fatema Khatun in 2023, she joined Aston as an academic support tutor, overseeing postgraduate business and management students. Her expertise lies in student engagement, particularly assisting global majority students throughout their degree programmes. Khatun gained experience in various higher education (HE) institutions in the West Midlands. With a teaching background in HE, she instructed at both undergraduate and postgraduate levels, specialising in early childhood education, diversity, and special educational needs. Currently pursuing a PhD in Education, her research focuses on exploring the correlation between the Black Asian and Ethnic Minority (BAME) attainment gap and student engagement. Khatun's writing delves into discussions on precarity in HE contracts and demanding workloads. Research interests encompass pedagogy, creative methodologies, and the intersection of religious and academic identity. As a British-born Muslim, her research predominantly centres on identity and decolonised approaches.

Arif Mahmud is a Senior Lecturer at the University of Roehampton, UK, and member of the Centre of Teaching, Learning, and Human Development. His research interests focus on social justice issues in education, mental health, and wellbeing, and exploring pertinent issues related to British Muslims. Mahmud has captured over £100k of research funding as PI and Co-I and has written extensively in national and international academic journals. He is the co-editor of the book *Mental Wellbeing in Schools: What Teachers Need to Know to Support Pupils from Diverse Backgrounds* (Routledge, 2022). Mahmud also holds numerous external roles such as Race Equity Consultant (MA Consultancy Ltd) and sits on various editorial boards such as for the *British Journal of Educational Psychology*.

Shames Maskeen is the Associate Director of The Race Institute and Lecturer in Developmental Psychology at Leeds Trinity University, UK. The Race Institute aims to improve the experiences of racialised minorities in the public, private, and voluntary sectors through research, CPD, and knowledge exchange. The Race Institute emerged from the need to keep anti-racism on the national agenda to enable sustained transformational change.

Shames is a member of the Centre for Applied Education Research steering group, co-chairs the Black, Asian, and Minoritised Ethnicities student network at Go Higher West Yorkshire, and is an associate for Race Equality at Advance HE. His research focusses on solving racial inequities and the intersection of culture, religion, and gender experienced by racialised minorities in higher education and beyond.

In his previous role as an Institutional Lead for the Race Equality Charter, he was the driving force in Leeds Trinity University, becoming the first University in Yorkshire to achieve the Bronze award. He is passionate about anti-racism leadership and more importantly in taking action to make a real difference and equitable world for young people.

Heidi Safia Mirza is Emeritus Professor of Equality Studies in Education at UCL Institute of Education, University of London, UK. A daughter of the Windrush generation from Trinidad, Heidi is known for her pioneering intersectional research on race, gender, and identity in education and championing equality and rights for Black, Asian, and Muslim women through educational reform. She is the author of several best-selling books including *Race, Gender and Educational Desire* and *Young Female and Black*, which were voted in the top 40 most influential educational studies in Britain. Mirza is one of the first and few women of colour professors in Britain and a leading voice in the global debate on decolonisation. She edited the flagship book, *Dismantling Race in Higher Education: Racism, Whiteness and Decolonising the Academy*.

Tariq Modood is Professor of Sociology, Politics, and Public Policy and founding director of the Centre for the Study of Ethnicity and Citizenship at the University of Bristol, UK, and the co-founder of the journal, *Ethnicities*. He has held 40+ grants and consultancies, has 35+ (co-) authored and (co-)edited books and reports, and 300+ articles and chapters. He was ranked #131 in the world (#19 in UK) in the Research.Com citations 2022 ranking for Law, Politics, Sociology and Social Policy. His work is frequently cited by policymakers and practitioners and on several occasions has influenced policy. He was appointed an MBE by the Queen for services to social sciences and ethnic relations in 2001, made a fellow of the Academy of Social Sciences (UK) in 2004, and elected a fellow of the British Academy in 2017. His latest books include *Essays on Secularism and Multiculturalism* (2019) and *Multiculturalism: A Civic Idea* (2nd ed; 2013); as co-editor: *Multiculturalism and Interculturalism* (2016) and *The Problem of Religious Diversity: European Problems, Asian Challenges* (2017); and co-edited Special Issues, "Multiculturalism, Religion, Secularism and Nationalism" (*Ethnicities*, 2021), "Some Forms of Racism and Anti-racism in Asia and the Middle East: Beyond the Euro-Americancentricity" (*Political Quarterly*, 2022), and "The Governance of Religious Diversity: Global Comparative Perspectives" (*Religion, State and* Society, 2022). His latest book is with Thomas Sealy, *The New Governance of Religious Diversity* (Polity, June, 2024). He has a You Tube Channel and WEBSITE.

Ruqia Osman has devoted her professional career to working with marginalised communities. She is committed to bringing people together to build socially just communities by facilitating radical change and eradicating systemic barriers. Whilst currently focusing on racial justice, mental health, and policy, Ruqia has worked across several UK universities to develop programmes to improve the experience of marginalised students and close ethnicity-awarding gaps.

Ruqia has researched topics related to race and racism, colourism, skin lightening, and health inequalities. After pursuing a postgraduate degree in Global Public Health, she was able to develop a profound understanding of the destructive ways in which systemic racism affects public health, particularly for the most marginalised individuals in the UK.

Mohammed Rahman is a Senior Lecturer at Birmingham City University, UK. He is also an Expert Network Member for the Global Initiative Against Transnational Organized Crime and the co-founder and director of CORE Consultants. His research interests focus on serious violence and organised crime, social inequalities, and the development of qualitative research methodologies. Mohammed has written extensively, including books, book chapters, and peer-reviewed journal articles. He recently co-authored *Ethics in Qualitative Criminological Research: Risks, Boundaries, Emotions, and Reflexivity* (Routledge, 2024), and regularly disseminates his research through national and international media outlets.

Amira Samatar, MA, AFHEA, is a researcher focused on the educational experiences of racially minoritised students in British universities, particularly Black women. Her work speaks to the unique challenges these students face, contributing to a deeper understanding of their academic journeys. Amira is dedicated to advancing racial literacy in higher education, and he actively supports the global majority undergraduate and master's students, striving to increase support and opportunities for racially minoritised students.

Zain Sardar is a joint Programme Manager at the Aziz Foundation. He leads on the Foundation's engagement with its university partners and higher education stakeholders. As well as completing his PhD in Law at Birkbeck, University of London, he has previously worked in higher education administration and policy. Zain also currently sits on the Yorkshire Consortium for Equity in Doctoral Education external advisory board.

Lila Tamea is a postgraduate researcher and tutor at Liverpool John Moores University, UK, where her PhD delves into the manifestations of Islamophobia and its impact on Muslim students in higher education. With a background in student activism, Lila has previously served as the president of her Student Union, as well as a panel member for the Office for Students, being a positive advocate for Muslim students and contributing her expertise to national discussions on educational policies. In addition to her academic and advocacy work, Lila hosts the "Being Muslim" podcast, a podcast which amplifies Muslim voices and experiences within the education sector.

ABBREVIATIONS

APP	Access and Participation Plans
APPG	All-Party Parliamentary Group
BAME	Black, Asian and minority ethnic
BME	Black, minority ethnic
CRT	Critical Race Theory
ECR	Early Career Researcher
EDI	Equality Diversity and Inclusion
EHRC	Equality and Human Rights Commission
FOSIS	The Federation of Student Islamic Societies
HEI	Higher Education Institution
HESA	Higher Education Statistics Agency
IHRA	International Holocaust Remembrance Alliance
MCB	Muslim Council of Britain
NESA	Network of Sisters in Academia
NUS	National Union of Students
OfS	Office for Students
REC	Race Equality Charter
STEM	Science Technology Engineering and Mathematics
SU	Student Union
WP	Widening Participation
UK HE	UK Higher Education
UKRI	UK Research and Innovation
UCU	University College Union

CHAPTER 1

Introduction: Systematic Islamophobia in UK Higher Education

Arif Mahmud and Maisha Islam

There has been a disturbing increase in Islamophobia over the last 25 years, both nationally in the UK and internationally. This has resulted in pervasive racism that has infiltrated major institutions in British society, disparaging Muslims within public and policy spheres. Higher education (HE), once seen as a space for progressive thinking and cultural inclusivity, has regrettably played a role in harbouring and perpetuating this form of racism (Aune et al., 2020; Gould, 2020; Mahmud & Islam, 2023). This persistent racism experienced by British Muslims is perpetuated by a narrative of suspicion rooted in institutional racial ascriptions, linking Islam to violent extremism and other criminal and antisocial behaviours (Awan, 2012). The discourse is often shaped by dominant right-wing media and senior government officials aiming to present Islam as a threat to freedoms, liberties, and fundamental British values (Mondon & Winter, 2017).

A. Mahmud (✉)
University of Roehampton, London, UK
e-mail: arif.mahmud@roehamtpon.ac.uk

M. Islam
University of Southampton, Southampton, UK
e-mail: m.islam@soton.ac.uk

The exploitation and amplification of Islamophobia by individuals and groups for politically motivated agendas or other unethical considerations seem to have shifted from being implicit marginalisation to an explicit one, thus further enabling exaggeration and validation of racial, xenophobic, and anti-Islamic sentiments amongst communities in the UK and beyond. This has been palpable with the most recent Palestinian Nakba, exacerbating the hostile environment for Muslims all around the world. At the time of compiling this edited collection, a catastrophic humanitarian crisis has been taking place with families, communities, and multiple generations of Palestinian people being lost over recent weeks (and decades) of atrocities. Many more millions are subsequently being injured and displaced. Nonetheless, and to contextualise the situation in Palestine with Islamophobia in the UK and internationally, there has been systematic opposition, widespread hypocrisy, and outright rejection to acknowledge the basic rights of Palestinian Muslims and simultaneously wider Muslim communities in the UK and abroad. Senior members of the UK government have branded some pro-Palestinian protests as "hate crimes" (The Guardian, 2023), and have attempted to censor the wearing of the *keffiyeh* (scarf) and waving of the Palestinian national flag—a double standard to freedom of speech and expression that many Muslims continuously endure. Manzoor-Khan (2022: 163) in her book, *Tangled in Terror: Uprooting Islamophobia*, mentions how "Islamophobia is and was never about Muslims" but an operation of power, translating to all aspects of Muslim lives. Therefore, at the beginning and centre of the discussion of Islamophobia we must acknowledge the entangled political, economic, and social narratives around racism in the UK and beyond.

The role of the media in this crisis cannot be ignored as a major contributor towards furthering the trope of Muslims as the "enemy within" either intentionally (possible political, racial, or xenophobic agendas) or due to misconceived and misinterpreted religious, social, and cultural concepts (for a meta-analysis, see Ahmed & Matthes, 2017). The Western media's continuous portrayal of Islam as a violent religion prone to terrorism has further intensified the phobia against British Muslims. Illustration of veiled women or bearded men along with the news of terrorism worked to strengthen the link between Islam and terrorism. Not only that, but this image also leads to essentialising Muslims as being backward, oppressive to women, and the uncivilised "other." Amidst these challenging social, political, and cultural conditions in contemporary Britain, individuals (of all ages) and Muslim communities are living, interacting, defending, and negotiating matters of identity, civil rights and liberties, safety, and security in multiple spheres of everyday life (Zempi & Awan, 2019).

The sphere which we have endeavoured to shed light on in this edited collection is university spaces in the UK. Universities are prime spaces where people are given the opportunity to engage with the "other" through intercultural and interreligious interaction. University campuses have the capacity to make available a safe place for students to learn and appreciate differences and diversity. The ever-increasing distrust among people of different faiths is not due to differences in ideologies; instead, it is a product of ignorance and misinformation. Knowledge gained through first-hand engagement (which this edited collection hopes to elucidate) is significantly more reliable and valuable compared to the ideas that are being fed by media or politically motivated groups. However, to understand Muslim experiences in HE, we must first recognise that two in five of all religious hate crime offences in the UK are targeted against Muslims (Home Office, 2023), making Muslims the most targeted faith group. Muslims have, in fact, remained consistently, and especially, vulnerable to religiously motivated hate crime offences and this has increased by 140% since the armed "conflict" in Palestine (Muslim Council of Britain, 2023). So, how does this translate into Islamophobia and anti-Muslim hate in UK HE? Despite many positive experiences, research shows that Islamophobia and anti-Muslim hatred exist in UK universities, affecting a significant number of Muslim students (Universities UK, 2021). A report published by the National Union of Students (2018) found that one in three Muslim students had experienced abuse or crimes related to their Muslim identity, and a similar number were worried about verbal abuse, physical attacks, and property damage. Female students wearing traditional religious garments had heightened concerns about such abuse, reflecting the often-gendered nature of Islamophobia.

These incidents often hold an intersectional dimension as they are also directed at racially minoritised students, in addition to other forms of harassment, microaggressions, stereotyping, offensive assumptions, hostility, and, of course, suspicion (Aune et al., 2020). However, Muslims are less likely to report Islamophobic incidents due to a lack of trust in institutional and organisational response, be it their university or even the wider police (Ramadan, 2021). These experiences negatively impact Muslim students' academic performance, mental health, and sense of belonging (Mahmud, 2024a, b), leading to lower degree attainment and satisfaction—less than two-thirds of Muslim students are awarded a first or 2:1 (Advance HE, 2023a; Gholami, 2021). These inequalities may also account for the under-representation of Muslim staff compared to the student population in UK higher education—with data suggesting Muslim staff account for 2.2% of the staff population (Advance HE, 2023a), whereas Muslim students account for 10.2% of the student population (Advance HE, 2023b).

Much of the discourse surrounding Muslim students and staff (in this edited collection and within wider academic literature) has been centred on the contested nature of the Prevent duty. The duty imposes a legal obligation on specified authorities, including universities and colleges, to consider the need to prevent individuals from becoming involved in terrorism and to report those who are seen as "vulnerable" to it (NUS Connect, 2016). However, this duty has faced substantial criticism within UK HE. It has been criticised for having been implemented uncritically; a racialised agenda, potentially restricting intellectual freedom; and transforming the educational environment into one of surveillance (Awan, 2012; Kyriacou et al., 2017; NUS Connect, 2016). In both policy discourse and practical implementation, Prevent seems to disproportionately target Muslim communities, leading to the racialisation of perceptions of "risk" in higher education institution's (HEI) dynamics and debates. This heightened scrutiny has resulted in many Muslim students experiencing racism on university campuses, whether intentionally or unintentionally, due to a moral panic surrounding Islamic fundamentalism. Consequently, British Muslim university students are increasingly viewed as security threats, causing self-censorship of their beliefs and opinions to avoid being labelled as "terrorists" (Saeed, 2018). This leads to the suppression of certain topics in HEI discussions, preventing critical debates and discussions from taking place, precisely like that of the events happening within Palestine. The silence on certain ideas and perspectives creates gaps or "vacuums" in critical discourse that need to be addressed urgently, as it becomes unsafe to express specific views. This contradicts the purpose of higher education and universities, a space where critical conversations are expected to happen, and this potentially stifles debates that could challenge radicalised perspectives.

The intersection of religious bias, Islamophobia, and xenophobia in the targeting of Muslims at the national level necessitates a thorough examination of the extent to which Muslim staff and students encounter prejudice and discrimination within HEIs. It is crucial that such empirical investigations and scholarly research are not only relevant to but also critical of the regulations that shape institutional policies and practices. This is essential for creating university campuses where Muslims (staff and students) can thrive (Ahmadi et al., 2019; Mahmud, 2024a, b). Without counter-narratives and a focus on combating the institutionalisation of Islamophobia, this current situation becomes ingrained in how non-Muslims perceive Muslims, especially within UK universities. Muslims have already become the primary "cultural other," and Islamophobia is arguably the most accepted form of racism in the UK. It is therefore crucial for universities to implement the necessary steps that actively address and disrupt Islamophobia, ensuring that they do not contribute to the sustenance of racism. Universities must remain vigilant in addressing racial and religious intolerance, fulfilling their moral obligation to lead in advancing diversification, inclusion, and social justice. In order to establish and promote a socially just university environment, it is essential to gain a deeper understanding of Muslim staff and students and how various forms of institutionalised Islamophobia affect them.

Therefore, this book is presented in the context of the current socio-political and socio-cultural landscape, with the aim of addressing these issues and the manifestation of institutional Islamophobia to better support the success of Muslims within the academy. Subsequently, this book attempts to examine the practices, policies, and the identity of Muslim staff and students in UK HEIs within this socio-political, socio-cultural, and geo-religious context. It also offers insights into reforming the HE landscape and the transformation of perspectives and policies into professional practice by addressing the institutionalised Islamophobia and monolithic portrayals Muslim students and staff are often subject to.

The book has three main objectives: first, to explore how Islamophobia has become ingrained in HEIs through authentic autoethnographic accounts from Muslim students and staff; second, to assess the extent to which other social identities (i.e. intersectional Muslim identities) have been overlooked by HEI senior leadership teams while shedding light on the critical intersection between Islamophobia and institutional policy; and finally, to provide recommendations for enhancing institutional policy and professional practice. In an era marked by misinformation (Giroux, 2018; Haynes et al., 2023), our focus is on highlighting contextualised lived experiences in order to facilitate meaningful analysis of institutionalised Islamophobia. The book aims to showcase a diversity of Muslim staff and student journeys in and around HE. Therefore, our audience extends to students, academics, professional service staff, and university partners including Student Unions. Each chapter delves into how HEIs can better support Muslim staff and students by reviewing perspectives, policies, and practices within and outside of learning and teaching spaces to combat Islamophobia on their campuses.

Through an intentional act of resistance, each contributor identifies as Muslim, with each chapter encompassing a range of perspectives that typically receive little recognition in academic circles, including postgraduate research students, professional service staff, sabbatical officers, and charity sector contributors. This is in addition to the full spectrum of voices and experiences of early career researchers, senior academics, and professors. Notably, the intersectional voices of Black, Asian, and Minority Ethnic female Muslim scholars are prominently featured. These unapologetically Muslim contributors possess direct experiences in UK HE and have previously contributed valuable insights to discussions on Islamophobia, anti-Muslim rhetoric, and wider anti-racism discourse and practice.

The book is structured into two parts. The first part utilises a core tenet within Critical Race Theory methodology, that of storytelling and counter-narratives (Solorzano & Yosso, 2001). This section centralises the experiential knowledge of Muslim students and staff by providing vignettes to the multiple and intersecting oppressions that are faced and confronted in the day-to-day lived experience of many Muslims within UK HE. In doing so, we set the foundation for dismantling the inequality encountered by providing perspectives which disrupt hegemonic ideologies that have portrayed Muslim students and staff through simplistic, derogatory, and limited lenses. This is with hope to reclaim our space in HE, our histories, our stories, our futures, and our joys (Gilliam & Toliver, 2021).

Having established the institutional harms and violence experienced by Muslim students and staff, the second part of this edited collection aims to address and spotlight the tangible ways in which universities and sector bodies can more meaningfully enact change both at the national and local level. In keeping with core tenets of a Critical Race Theory methodology, the stories/experiences of Muslim students and staff themselves need to be guided towards concrete change. The chapters featured here detail the limitations and opportunities presented within current UK HE policy and practice. Collectively, these chapters will challenge readers to consider how Muslim student and staff success can be championed through utilising existing channels and mechanisms (e.g.

the Race Equality Charter mark) but also widening the scope of regulatory levers within our arsenal.

To begin Part I, Chap. 2 by Hussain and Bagguley examines the "White atmosphere" of the university and how this lacks resonance with Muslim female graduates, often alienating and isolating their experiences. This is explored with reference to the pedagogical violence Muslim female graduates experienced whilst at university, mainly concerning the learning environment, curriculum, peers and teachers, and assessment. The chapter ends with calls for cultural recognition and transformation, underpinned and led at the institutional level through leadership and policies focused upon religion and belief.

Following the undergraduate journey, Samatar, Hassan and Osman in Chap. 3, using Black feminist theory and methods of storytelling, reveal intimate experiences at a "crossroad of complexity" of young, Somali, Muslim female doctoral students and early-career staff. The chapter amplifies the personal and unique experiences of three Black Muslim women as they navigate institutional politics and sheds light on the gendered Islamophobia they face within the academic setting, as well as the misogynoir they encounter as Black women in embarking professional careers in academia. At this unique intersection, many lessons are unveiled via the composite counter stories presented.

Tamea in Chap. 4 explores Muslim student experiences from a vantage point of elected Muslim student representatives—a position which provides a unique account of Muslim students navigating the terrain of Students Union politics. The chapter highlights how covert and overt Islamophobia transcend into these spaces, whereby Student Unions hold a function to ensure representation of student bodies and their interests. Interviews with Muslim student sabbatical officers reveal how "Muslim issues" stand to gain little support and invite undue hostility and harm with little to no support from their Unions.

Moving into an early-career researcher stage, Khatun, in Chap. 5, highlights the entry points into the UK HE landscape for a working-class Muslim female lecturer. Reflexively examining how her visible Muslim-ness has complicated her professional identity and her sense of belonging, the chapter examines the unnecessarily placed burden on the shoulders of Muslim female academics who, despite being told are an acceptable archetype of Muslim-ness, are still met with the colonial white male gaze.

Subsequently, Faheem and Rahman in Chap. 6 use a duo-ethnographic approach to discuss the intersectionality between race, gender, religion, and social class within the landscape of British academia. The authors critically discuss how their marginalised identities, and the lack of institutional recognition they have received, has contributed to a Eurocentric curriculum, imposter syndrome, tokenism, microaggressions, and a cold campus climate. The chapter offers poignant reflections, including having genuine regard for Muslim colleagues' wellbeing and success; the importance of reflexive safe spaces for those with hesitancy speaking about issues related religious and racial equity; and unpaid EDI labour generally carried out by minoritised staff.

Chapter 7 by Amer and Albayrak-Aydemir similarly explores the experiences of early-career Muslim women in UK HE and considers the nuanced ways in which religion, gender, and career stage interplay and intersect, particularly in having consequences for their recognition, success, progression, and retention. The authors paint a picture of internal conflict and negotiations of self, for example, proving the legitimacy of their work by combatting accusations of bias as insider researchers; constant expectation to engage in EDI work which limits capacity for academic progression; and a manifest absence of Muslim female academics of whom to provide guidance.

Such challenges emerge as progressively manifest for senior female Muslim academics. In Chap. 8, Ahmad, utilising a candid autoethnographic approach, examines the unfair treatment of a Muslim academic who identifies as "permanently precarious." The chapter openly highlights the feelings of imposter syndrome, the covert repeated experiences of microaggressions, and the academic nepotism that exists within UK HE. The chapter ends with Ahmad asking those who found the reading uncomfortable or problematic to acknowledge the source of discomfort, posing a series of questions to consider for those serious about decolonising the academy.

Strategies of self are explored in the final chapter of Part I. Mirza's research explores the narratives of self and survival of three transnational professional Muslim women who live and work in UK universities, examining the ways in which the women draw on their embodied practices and inner sense of self to negotiate and survive the postcolonial disjuncture's of racism and Islamophobia which frame their everyday lives. Utilising Black feminist methodology, Mirza astutely captures the "intersectional othering" Muslim women experience and subsequently describes the implications of this for aspiring Muslim female academics.

Part II pivots these discussions of Islamophobia into how we can enact institutional change which starts to build religious equity into our universities. In Chap. 10, Islam and Modood use a narrative interview methodology to illustrate how Islamophobia has manifested within UK HE's past, present, and what this subsequently means for its future. The chapter highlights the intellectual shift in the academic climate which is more open to acknowledging religious-based inequalities, and is an example of how Muslim staff and students re-exist within academia by using Islamic identity as a form of capital.

Further exemplifying the dynamism of Islamophobia, Abbas in Chap. 11 examines the consequences of neoliberalism on British Muslim students and the influence of the "neo-orientalist, racist, and Islamophobic counter-terrorism" Prevent programme. The chapter details evolving perceptions of British Muslims within HE over the past five decades, looking specifically at neoliberalisation which has created both favourable (albeit unintentional) and harmful conditions for Muslim students. The chapter goes on to provide an interesting assessment of how an increasingly marketised system can be of detriment to Muslim students as universities, keen on recruiting any and all students, may fail to grasp the complexity and heterogeneity of their student bodies.

Another characteristic of the current HE landscape identified by Gholami in Chap. 12 is the role of political secularism and de-theologised Christian culture. The chapter highlights the consistent demonisation of Muslims as a collective and our response to the constant public vilification. Gholami further alludes to the topical yet unaddressed issue of Muslim student degree-awarding gap which he argues needs to be more meaningfully addressed through a rigorous assessment of both racism *and* secularism.

Another approach of meaningful redressal is detailed in Chap. 13, where Maskeen's case study describes utilising the Race Equality Charter to advance racial and religious equity. Drawing upon primarily qualitative data and Maskeen's personal experiences, the chapter centres on the lived experiences of racially minoritised Muslim students and staff to argue how institutional diversity schemes can be used to serve religiously minoritised communities in HE. The chapter describes the importance of understanding the profile of student bodies, gaining senior leadership buy-in to spearhead and add legitimacy to such activity, and working in partnership with Muslim students to empower and encourage autonomy and change.

From focusing on local level policy to national, sector level directives, Sardar in Chap. 14 contextualises the widening participation and fair access agenda in relation to Islamophobia. He draws upon testimonial evidence and autoethnographies of Aziz Foundation's scholars and scholarship candidates to demonstrate the importance of recognising inequalities related to Muslim students' access, success, and progression in HE. The chapter reinforces a perspective from British Muslim students that their faith provides a "bestowing and sustaining agency" which is key to empowerment, identity, and belonging; and makes the case for Muslim students being formally recognised in widening participation efforts.

Finally, Islam in Chap. 15, summarises the ideas expressed across this edited collection through four apparent themes: gendered Islamophobia; Muslims as under-served and seen to be undeserving; the dynamic and fluid nature of Islamophobia; and hope. Islam provides recommendations from across the chapters related to institutional culture, academic knowledge, and policy provision and utilises reflexive questions for readers to consider in order to support institutional and organisational change for Muslim students and staff.

As editors, our aim here is to shed light on understanding and assisting British Muslim staff and students in the institutions of higher education for the purpose of recruiting and retaining Muslim talent. To date, we believe there is no collection of Muslim experiences which captures the wide range of student and staff voices in UK HE and this is what makes this book timely and distinctive. In doing so, the book makes a significant contribution as a Muslim collective who have historically been spoken about, rather than given a platform. Whilst this book offers accounts of lived experiences and theorised accounts related to Islamophobia in UK HE, it also offers institutional and sector-wide policy recommendations in order to tackle these manifestations of inequality and provide equitable suggestions for change that are rooted in the voices of Muslim students and staff.

Definition of Islamophobia
Following Zempi and Awan (2019), this co-edited collection welcomes the definition of Islamophobia released by the All Party Parliamentary Group on British Muslims across the UK:

Islamophobia is rooted in racism and is a type of racism that targets expressions of Muslimness or perceived Muslimness. (All Party Parliamentary Group on British Muslims, 2018, p. 11)

Whilst we acknowledge that both the term and the phenomenon it describes are contested (see Allen, 2020; Gould, 2020; Mondon & Winter, 2017), this definition reflects our own understanding of Islamophobia as a form of anti-Muslim racism which disproportionately affects the experiences and outcomes of Muslims and those with perceived Muslim identities.

References

Advance HE. (2023a). Equality + higher education Staff statistical report 2023. Retrieved November 30, 2023, from https://www.advance-he.ac.uk/ knowledge-hub/equality-higher-education-statistical-reports-2023a

Advance HE. (2023b). Equality + higher education Students statistical report 2023. Retrieved November 30, 2023, from https://www.advance-he.ac.uk/ knowledge-hub/equality-higher-education-statistical-reports-2023b

Ahmadi, S., Sanchez, M., & Cole, D. (2019). Protecting Muslim students' speech and expression and resisting Islamophobia. In *Student activism, politics, and campus climate in higher education* (pp. 97–111). Routledge. https://doi. org/10.1177/1748048516656305

Ahmed, S., & Matthes, J. (2017). Media representation of Muslims and Islam from 2000 to 2015: A meta-analysis. *International Communication Gazette, 79*(3), 219–244.

All Party Parliamentary Group on British Muslims. (2018). *Islamophobia defined: Report on the inquiry into a working definition of Islamophobia/anti-Muslim hatred. London: All Party Parliamentary Group on British Muslims.* Retrieved December 30, 2023, from https://static1.squarespace.com/static/ 599c3d2febbd1a90cffdd8a9/t/5bfd1ea3352f531a6170ceee/ 1543315109493/Islamophobia+Defined.pdf

Allen, C. (2020). *Reconfiguring Islamophobia: A radical rethinking of a contested concept.* Springer Nature.

Aune, K., Weller, P., Cheruvalil-Contractor, S., Osmond, J., & Peacock, L. (2020). *Tackling religion or belief-related harassment and hate incidents: A guide for higher education providers.* Retrieved November 30, 2023, from https://www. officeforstudents.org.uk/media/4dfc9b51-dfd7-4f02-a1f0-54ea2095cd4c/ coventry-university-research-and-evaluation-report.pdf

Awan, I. (2012). "I Am a Muslim Not an Extremist": How the prevent strategy has constructed a "suspect" community. *Politics & Policy, 40*(6). https://doi.org/10.1111/j.1747-1346.2012.00397.x

Gholami, R. (2021). Critical race theory and Islamophobia: Challenging inequity in higher education. *Race Ethnicity and Education, 24*(3), 319–337. https://doi.org/10.1080/13613324.2021.1879770

Gilliam, E., & Toliver, S. R. (2021). Black feminist wondaland: Reckoning, celebrating, and reclaiming joy in higher education. *Journal of Effective Teaching in Higher Education, 4*(2), 84–98. https://doi.org/10.36021/jethe.v4i2.167

Giroux, H. A. (2018). What is the role of higher education in the age of fake news? In *Post-truth, fake news: Viral modernity & higher education* (pp. 197–215). Springer. https://doi.org/10.1007/978-981-10-8013-5_17

Gould, R. R. (2020). The limits of liberal inclusivity: How defining Islamophobia normalizes anti-Muslim racism. *Journal of Law and Religion, 35*(2), 250–269. https://doi.org/10.1017/jlr.2020.20

Haynes, C., Ward, L. W., & Patton, L. D. (2023). Truth-telling, Black women and the pedagogy of fake news in higher education. *Pedagogy, Culture & Society, 31*(5), 899–914.

Home Office. Department for Crime, Justice and Law. (2023). *Official statistics hate crime, England and Wales, 2022 to 2023 second edition.* Retrieved December 21, 2023, from https://www.gov.uk/government/statistics/hate-crime-england-and-wales-2022-to-2023/hate-crime-england-and-wales-2022-to-2023

Kyriacou, C., Reed, B. S., Said, F., & Davies, I. (2017). British Muslim university students' perceptions of Prevent and its impact on their sense of identity. *Education, Citizenship and Social Justice, 12*(2), 97–110. https://doi.org/10.1080/14681366.2021.1955405

Mahmud, A. (2024a). Exploring the experiences of Muslim doctoral students in UK higher education: Challenges, implications, and pathways to inclusivity. *Studies in Higher Education.* https://doi.org/10.1080/03075079.2024.2357718

Mahmud, A. (2024b). Addressing Inequalities in Accessing Mental Health Services for Muslim University Students in the United Kingdom: Implications for Attainment and Wellbeing. *Journal of Beliefs & Values.* https://doi.org/10.1080/13617672.2024.2320013

Mahmud, A., & Islam, M. (2023). Intersectional oppression: A reflexive dialogue between Muslim academics and their experiences of Islamophobia and exclusion in UK Higher Education. *Sociology Compass, 17*(2), e13041. https://doi.org/10.1111/soc4.13041

Manzoor-Khan, S. (2022). *Tangled in terror: Uprooting Islamophobia.* Pluto Press.

Mondon, A., & Winter, A. (2017). Articulations of Islamophobia: From the extreme to the mainstream? *Ethnic and Racial Studies, 40*(13), 2151–2179. https://doi.org/10.1080/01419870.2017.1312008

Muslim Council of Britain. (2023). *Islamophobia awareness month 2023: Confronting hate in challenging times.* Retrieved November 15, 2023, from https://mcb.org.uk/islamophobia-awareness-month-2023-muslim-stories-confronting-hate-in-challenging-times/

National Union of Students (NUS). (2018). *The experience of Muslim students in 2017–18.* Retrieved November 30, 2023, from www.nusconnect.org.uk/resources/the-experience-of-muslim-students-in-2017-18

NUS Connect. (2016). *Preventing prevent.* Retrieved December 2, 2023, from https://www.nusconnect.org.uk/campaigns/preventing-prevent-we-are-students-not-suspects

Ramadan, I. (2021). When faith intersects with gender: The challenges and successes in the experiences of Muslim women academics. *Gender and Education, 34*(1). https://doi.org/10.1080/09540253.2021.1893664

Saeed, T. (2018). Islamophobia in higher education: Muslim students and the "Duty of Care". In J. Arday & H. Mirza (Eds.), *Dismantling race in higher education.* Palgrave Macmillan.

Solorzano, D., & Yosso, T. J. (2001). Critical race and LatCrit theory and method: Counter-storytelling Chicana and Chicano graduate school experience. *Qualitative Studies in Education, 14*(4), 471–495. https://doi.org/10.1080/09518390110063365

The Guardian. (2023). *Suella Braverman calls pro-Palestine demos 'hate marches'.* https://www.theguardian.com/politics/2023/oct/30/uk-ministers-cobra-meeting-terrorism-threat-israel-hamas-conflict-suella-braverman

Universities UK. (2021). *Tackling Islamophobia and anti-Muslim hatred: Practical guidance for UK universities.* Retrieved December 2, 2023, from https://www.universitiesuk.ac.uk/what-we-do/policy-and-research/publications/tackling-islamophobia-and-anti-muslim

Zempi, I., & Awan, I. (Eds.). (2019). *The Routledge international handbook of Islamophobia.* Routledge.

PART I

Islamophobia in the Ivory Tower:
Theoretical and Reflexive Framings

White Atmosphere and Pedagogic Violence: Female Muslim Graduate's Experiences on an Undergraduate Degree in a Russell Group University

Yasmin Hussain and Paul Bagguley

I'm not saying how staff treat 'them' just generally the atmosphere I do think that some people feel left out and isolated just because they're a bit different.
—Samiyah *(The use of pseudonyms are employed in this chapter)*

Y. Hussain • P. Bagguley (✉)
University of Leeds, Leeds, UK
e-mail: p.bagguley@leeds.ac.uk

© The Author(s), under exclusive license to Springer Nature
Switzerland AG 2024
A. Mahmud, M. Islam (eds.), *Uncovering Islamophobia in Higher Education*, Palgrave Studies in Race, Inequality and Social Justice in Education, https://doi.org/10.1007/978-3-031-65253-0_2

17

INTRODUCTION

This chapter draws upon qualitative interviews with recent Muslim graduates from one department of a Russell Group[1] university. It brings together Bohme's (2017a) theory of atmospheres as arenas with certain emotionally charged moods with Matusov and Sullivan's (2020) account of pedagogical violence to reflect upon the graduates' experience of university, its learning environment and assessment. It will show how the "White atmosphere" of the university, in learning and non-learning contexts, and its pedagogic violence in the forms of summative assessment, epistemological pedagogical violence and students' ambivalence around pedagogical violence produce isolation and disenchantment with education for Muslim students, with the potential for diverse outcomes in terms of future careers. The chapter analyses this empirical data using theoretical resources that are new to or rarely used in this area.

Principally framed by the theory of atmospheres and pedagogical violence we also draw upon discussions of the "racial economy of emotions" (Bonilla-Silva, 2019) and the pedagogical self (Harris et al., 2017). Each of these has its own scope and limitations, but we argue are complementary for the purposes of our analysis. Part of our concern here, then, is drawing critically and reflexively on these wider theoretical developments in sociology and more generally how this might contribute to giving voice to Muslim students in developing a transformative critique of the White university.

The data was generated as part of a wider project on the first degree awarding gap between ethnically minoritised students and White British students in a Russell Group social science department. Institutional data showed that the department had a persistent awarding gap over several years and the department wished to understand the underlying reasons for this in terms of the experiences of a cohort of recent graduates (i.e. those who had graduated from the 2021 academic year) from ethnically minoritised backgrounds. They were thus, part of the "COVID-19 generation" of students, but that is not an aspect that we have the space to examine here. In total, 18 out of the 22 graduates of colour participated in our interviews and these have helped us to understand the pervasive and negative impact exclusion and discrimination has on the student experience

---

[1] The Russell Group is a consortium of 24 world-class, research-intensive universities in the United Kingdom.

and their ability to achieve. Those interviewed were all UK Home students, and for the purposes of this chapter, we have focused upon the experiences of the Muslim students, who all, incidentally, happened to be women. All but one originated in the local region, and their final degree classification were bifurcated between first class and third class/pending. Recorded qualitative interviews were conducted online by the first author of this chapter, all data have been anonymised, and the interviewees have been given pseudonyms. The interviews were semi-structured focusing upon school experiences, academic experiences and wider social lives at university. The data were analysed and coded thematically. Whilst much of what the female Muslim graduates experienced is discussed in this chapter, they framed it in more general terms of being religiously minoritised as Muslims along with other minorities. Some of this, specifically around alcohol or issues such as protests around Palestine and how some White non-Muslim graduates responded to these, were specifically Islamophobic. This raises an important theme of a sense of solidarity across different groups of ethnically minoritised students, whilst still recognising the specificities of the experiences of Muslim women.

THE "WHITE ATMOSPHERE" OF THE UNIVERSITY

The concept of atmospheres has in recent years become the focus of extended debate and elaboration (e.g. see Bohme, 2016, 2017a, 2017b; Griffero, 2014, 2017; Griffero & Moretti, 2018; Julmi, 2017; Low, 2016). These contributors and others obviously all begin from a recognition of the commonplace metaphor of the atmosphere of a place as communicating something real yet intangible to people, a mood that has an emotional impact on people (e.g. Bohme, 2017a); yet, there are divergences between them. They also have quite diverse origins and applications in critiques of ecological sciences (Bohme, 2017a), aesthetics, architecture, organisation studies (e.g. Julmi, 2017) and urban sociology (Low, 2016). For our purposes here, it seems a very useful way for thinking about the sense of intangible racism, sexism and Islamophobia that many feel in certain places and times and the emotional states that this produces in minoritised subjects (e.g. see Anderson, 2011; Bonilla-Silva, 2019; Tate, 2016). Bohme's discussions have been criticised for suggesting a universal response to atmospheres (Low, 2016) and therefore being Eurocentric. However, some using the concept have noted how the effectivity of atmospheres is dependent upon structural inequalities such as racism (e.g. Low, 2016: 177; Del Gurcio et al., 2018), and we would add, in this instance, Islamophobia.

Atmospheres are produced by the co-presence of people and things, and Bohme (2016, 2017a, 2017b) in his various publications has emphasised how, although atmospheres are "intangible", they have an emotional impact that people experience and are often capable of articulating this impact in some form. This is where we would like to draw out a connection between the debates around the concept of atmospheres with discussions of the "racial economy of emotions" (Bonilla-Silva, 2019: 1). The White atmosphere of a university, such as the one where this study took place where Black, South Asian and Muslim students are visibly ethnically minoritised, resides not just in the "difference" of the majority of students and staff, but also the everyday images, that is, on the walls of departments and other public areas. There are some exceptions to this such as the recent development of large cohorts of taught postgraduate students from China, and the predominance of Black, South Asian, Muslim and East European support staff such as cleaners. Thus, the racialised and secular atmosphere of the university from our perspective impacts upon ethnically minoritised Muslim students emotionally. It enables "race" to "come to life" as Bonilla-Silva has expressed it: "… race cannot come to life without being infused with emotions, thus, racialized actors feel the emotional weight of their categorical location" (Bonilla-Silva, 2019: 2).

His discussion here is especially insightful for our argument as, although he does not reference the contemporary debates about atmospheres, he argues that racialised emotions: "… need not be the product of social interactions, [and] can surface from looking at a picture, reading a newspaper, watching a movie, or walking into—or even thinking about—a location" (Bonilla-Silva, 2019: 2). The White atmosphere of the university, or even just recalling it in an online interview context, may generate racialised emotions, which in this context also have a religious aspect. Hence the discomfort felt and expressed (Bonilla-Silva, 2019: 12). A final theme of his discussion of the racialised economy of emotions that we explore below is how racialised emotions are ambivalent (Bonilla-Silva, 2019). Whilst the emotions that the Muslim female graduates described to us were feelings of alienation, loneliness and disengagement from the curriculum, their White and non-Muslim peers, the university, the academic staff and their department, they also praised certain aspects of all of these and their enjoyment of them.

THE PEDAGOGICAL SELF AND PEDAGOGICAL VIOLENCE

The Muslim female graduates referred to a range of themes that might be identified as constituting the pedagogical self that included: the central role of the lecturers; dialogical encounters with peers and inter-subjective recognition of the self in the "other"; earlier educational experiences and a new (academic) literacy to name past and current experiences (Harris et al., 2017). On the other hand, they also referred to a range of "psycho-social and relational harms" that others have analysed as pedagogical violence (Matusov & Sullivan, 2020: 439).

In their research, Harris et al. (2017) found that Black and Muslim students in their study had the opportunity to "reinvent themselves" in the context of a youth and community work course. We find the concept of a pedagogical self a valuable way of conceptualising student experiences. However, whereas Harris et al. (2017) found an instance of the pedagogical self being positive and providing opportunities for self-reinvention, what we want to suggest is that the pedagogical self is caught between contradictory logics. Primarily, these are the desire for education on the part of ethnic and religious minorities and the White institution of the university. For each of the themes identified by Harris et al. (2017), we can identify parallel but contradictory logics. For example, encounters with peers might be dialogical but also involve micro-aggressions. Furthermore, the inter-subjective sense of the self of the "other" might be experienced as more alienating in the context of a Eurocentric curriculum in a White university. Rather, the pedagogical selves that we encounter here might be best thought of as the product of a site of friction between the structural racism and Islamophobia of the Eurocentric White university and anti-racist and anti-Islamophobia resistance.

Although principally concerned with compulsory education, many of the themes of pedagogical violence (e.g. Bourdieu & Passerson, 1990; Foucault, 1995) are visible within the university context. Central to the idea of pedagogical violence is a lack of student choice and voice with respect to the curriculum, assessment, peers and teachers, time and location, forms of communication, and assessment. Consequently, students "... are expected to submit their will, desire, heart, mind, feelings, behaviour and attitudes for non-conditional cooperation..." (Matusov & Sullivan, 2020: 440), and the racialised, secular Eurocentric character of this is what comes through in our interviewees experiences of the university.

Although both students and lecturers may be motivated by a "love of their subject", they are hemmed in by bureaucratic rules on the one hand (Matusov & Sullivan, 2020: 441) and Eurocentric epistemological violence on the other. Whilst recent writers such as Matusov and Sullivan (2020) have pointed to a broad range of pedagogical violences, we wish to highlight their necessarily racialised and secular forms. Summative assessment by ranking students in ways that have implications for their future careers is often picked as a powerful form of pedagogical violence as it encapsulates the non-negotiable character of Eurocentric educational demands and may have the effect of discouraging students from expressing ideas that do not fit these assumptions.

NAVIGATING THE WHITE ATMOSPHERE OF A RUSSELL GROUP UNIVERSITY

The Muslim female graduates told us about their reactions on first arriving at the university. For example, Halima Ali came from North West London and was very complimentary about the area she was brought up and completed her schooling in:

> I've always been brought up in an ethnically diverse area so, I'm from [London borough] ... so, that's very diverse as in there's loads of people that live here from different backgrounds. South Asian, Somali, people from all around. And so I'm very used to a diverse background especially because, being in London, you're very used to that on a day to day basis. So, my schools were mainly Somali, and Bengali and then my college was mainly just West African and East African and then some South Asian....

She contrasted the university with the area she came from. Although she expected the academic staff and the students to be predominantly White, she still found this a shock:

> I didn't expect it to be as white as it was, honestly. I think that was something that kind of shocked me, I thought because it's [a Russell group university] maybe there would be like a more diverse group of people. But I didn't actually process that it would be as white as it was, the whole university.

Over time, this became progressively more of an issue for them as students, as they became more conscious about their skin colour, their religious identity markers and the lack of diversity within the classroom which became problematic for them fitting in. It was at this point that pedagogical violence began to make itself felt more explicitly. For example, according to Sana Rashid:

> Honestly, I don't think I enjoyed university as a whole just because, I don't know, I feel like I never really fitted in. I just feel like it was a very predominantly white university. And not even just that it was a predominantly white university, I feel people were from very different [ethnic] backgrounds to myself. So, I always just kind of felt out of place and never really wanted to contribute in certain classes and lectures and stuff just because I always felt, what if my answer's not right, what if I sound stupid.…

This final point about "feeling stupid" illustrates how the White atmosphere structures the pedagogical violence of the forms of communication (Matusov & Sullivan, 2020: 440), where Sana self-reflexively modified her pedagogical self (Harris et al., 2017) initially in a negative way considering leaving the university. For Sana, this alienation from the department and the university reached such an intensity that she was going to leave because it got too much for her, but then she spoke to an ethnically minoritised male member of staff, who incidentally was not a Muslim:

> … at one point I felt like I didn't want to be there anymore…I spoke to [lecturer X] about that and they obviously opened up about … being a lecturer of colour and how their experience has been. And then it made me realise it's not just me that feels like this. And, you know, you could be someone that works at this institution and still feel like that … was very, very helpful.

This encounter demonstrates the critical importance of the role of ethnically minoritised and Muslim academic staff in overcoming crises for students of colour. The resonance (Rosa, 2019), the responsiveness and mutual recognition of a shared alienation, described here is almost palpable, and what is even more positive is how this reached across differences of gender, religion and ethnicity.

Samiyah had a similar experience with a different male member of staff and talked about knocking on their door just because he was Asian and a Muslim,

[Lecturer's name], I met in first year and I didn't know who he was … I just knocked on his door once and I spoke to him, and we just had a conversation and I remember since the first conversation I ever had, ever since I struggled in uni with my personal circumstances, he always pushed me and he believed in me. I'll never ever, ever forget that, and he encouraged me to take on opportunities. He always wanted me to be, you know do, do the best. He told me to never quit [university]. …If I didn't have someone like that from the beginning, I would probably have quit [university].

The Muslim female graduates had concerns about their programme being predominantly of White middle-class girls. This created a challenge for them in terms of not feeling they really belonged in the department, difficulties making friends and raised questions in their minds about whether they could continue with their degree. Samiyah, for example, talked about trying hard not be seen as another "Asian girl" (e.g. Ahmad, 2001; Bagguley & Hussain, 2016) on the course, so her proactivity was designed by her to dispel the stereotypes people had:

I would probably not have been recognised for my talent. I'd probably just be seen oh as that Asian girl just doing her work, just I guess a number on their statistics. I had to showcase my talent and showcase my potential to prove, … but I had to kind of do what I had to do for my own sake, if that makes sense, to increase my own prospects.

AMBIVALENCE

The diverse racialised and religious identities of the academic staff in the department were also one of the sources of emotional ambivalence for the graduates. One of the main things that Halima Ali, for example, liked about the university was being taught by "non-White" academics. She contrasted this with her other negative experiences, as well as the experiences of her friends at other universities:

Although there were things which were negative it was like, at the end of the day, I still had lecturers who weren't White you know? And that's something that's different. Because I know a lot of people who went to university and they are shocked when I tell them, "Oh I have a lecturer who is black, oh I have a lecturer who is Pakistani, oh I have a lecturer that's actually Muslim". People are shocked because their lecturers are all White, they have never had someone that was different…, they've always had the same kind of lecturers, the same men, always men that are White and older. That's something that I'm proud that I had, because I had people from all different backgrounds actually teaching me.

Ambivalence is one of the main themes of Bonilla-Silva's (2019) analysis of the racial economy of emotions, and it is one of the main ways in which the White atmosphere of the university makes its presence felt. For example, Sana Rashid touched upon the lack of diversity within the department and the university, despite praising the campus and her degree programme:

> Sometimes, I think most times, the uni is amazing as in obviously it's a really nice campus, it's amazing. And the actual course, the ... degree, I feel it's really good. But as a whole I just feel it's not, it's not diverse enough. And I feel that played a really big part in my experience. So overall I feel like I had more of a negative experience than positive....

THE EXCLUSIONARY NATURE OF SOCIAL ACTIVITIES

For Muslim students, the normative practice of social activities amongst students was experienced as exclusionary. This is an important often neglected aspect of what we are here referring to as the White atmosphere of the university. It is not just a pedagogical experience, but also a wider social experience that is frequently overlooked (for exceptions relevant to this chapter, see, for example: Islam et al., 2019; Islam & Mercer-Mapstone, 2021) in discussion of racism and Islamophobia in higher education. The university has for many years employed a Muslim chaplain, and prayer rooms have been available in several buildings across the campus since at least the 1970s. In contrast to this quite good provision, according to Sana Rashid, the majority of social activities at university are mainly centred around "going out" (i.e. clubbing and partying) and drinking. This was especially exclusionary for the Muslim female graduates, particularly during welcome activities that are typically organised at the beginning of the academic year (i.e. commonly known as Freshers week):

> ... the fresher's week, I didn't really get involved because I felt it all revolved around going out, drinking, and that's all stuff that I don't do.... There was so much pressure on fresher's being all about socialising through going out and drinking it kind of, once again, excluded you ... it kind of limits how much of a friendship you can make with people. And then it just kind of makes you think well, what is the point of trying to make friends because it

gets to a point where there's, well no I can't do this, or I don't do this. And it's like trying to explain your beliefs to someone.

Samiyah Iqbal also described how she felt excluded by the dominant "drink and drugs" culture and talked about one White woman who did not drink with whom she, therefore, formed the only friendship from her first year:

> I think she's middle class, so she obviously used to go out, but she didn't drink so she had similar issues to me because I didn't drink, and she didn't drink... I don't want to talk about drink and drugs. I'm not interested in that. I want to talk about you know, "Are you okay? How is your family doing?" We talk about what we like, we go out to eat but doesn't have to revolve around drinking, going clubs etc.

Anaya did not go to social events organised by students in the department again because they were organised around alcohol, "the [social events] ... were mainly at a pub, and I don't think I went to much ... I'll just feel uncomfortable". In this way, we can see how the atmosphere of events revolving around alcohol produced racialised and Islamophobic emotions for the students.

Epistemological Violence in Pedagogical Spaces

For Muslim female graduates of colour, discussions within tutorials were dominated by a secular White lens and this was difficult in several ways for students who felt they were seen as experts on race, ethnicity or religion, in the case of Muslim students. This created a different dynamic in the tutorials and needed to be paid more attention to when allocating tutorial classes from the perspective of our graduates. According to Mariya Khan, for example:

> I was one of the very few people of colour in the class. ... having all White students, they're going to have a very set or very White experience of the world ... tutorials need to have inclusivity and understanding I guess people from different backgrounds, but unless they [the White students] actually talk about it or are interested in learning about it, they're not really going to know our perspective.

In a series of episodes that illustrate not just the racialised atmosphere of the university, but also its Islamophobic atmosphere and how this translates into forms of pedagogical violence, Amara Jackson felt that she was treated differently by some academic staff because she started wearing the hijab during the first year of starting university:

> … they wouldn't take me as seriously as someone else, such as a White student. I don't think they would really ask me to answer questions in a classroom … I don't know if it was malicious or anything, I think I just wasn't taken as seriously for when to answer questions or things like that. No one would really ask me to do anything, I was left out most of the time.

She also felt marginalised by the other students:

> If I was in an all-White class, no one would speak to me, honestly, I'm not even going to lie, but I don't know if that was me or because I wear the hijab, I don't know. So, in group work, no one really engaged with me, no one would take me seriously, but I don't know how I would change that … People reacted as if I wasn't someone they could be friends with.

A particular theme that illustrates the dilemmas of epistemological violence and the racialised, Islamophobic character of the pedagogical violence of the university relates to teaching about race and who teaches these topics. For instance, according to Halima Ali:

> When it comes to race modules and lectures on race, I don't know if this is a far stretch but I feel like if it's only possible for it to be taught by a person of colour…. It's more comfortable for people of colour in the room. Because I've been in slavery modules where it's been a White person telling me about slavery, and I don't know why but it just makes me really uncomfortable. Already, you're having looks because you're talking about black people and you know, people look around, oh, there's a couple of black people in the room. So, I feel like that needs to be a thing where the person who's delivering this module is someone of colour because it does make me feel comfortable having certain histories spoken about by certain people.

ISOLATION

The isolation that the Muslim female graduates experienced directly arose from the White atmosphere of the university more generally as well as the pedagogical violences of their programme of study. Indeed, this White atmosphere may be argued to be something specific to certain subjects and disciplines within Russell Group universities, whilst some degree programmes and disciplines may have significantly higher proportions of Muslim students and academic staff of colour. Sana Rashid's experiences illustrate this point well, where she suggested her university's faculty should be more diverse in order to create a more positive experience for students of colour:

> Just kind of making it a bit more diverse and inclusive because although, like I said, there is more minority students going to these universities, I feel like a lot of them have very similar experiences to myself where you always kind of feel like the outsider or not fully included within the university … because of the social events and stuff. So, I feel like doing more to kind of include everyone. I was left out most of the time.

Muslim female graduates also discussed how they "got on" with their peers, and most of the interviewees talked about having few friends in the university or in their own department. There were a few who had a number of friends and who were from different backgrounds. These students often remained connected with friends from home rather than developing new friendships on their course or more widely across the university. For students still living at home, they socialised up to a point but had more connections with friends from home. Students did comment, however, on how there were very few social events that they felt comfortable attending, and also students preferring to keep themselves to themselves which made it difficult to make friends, according to Samiyah Iqbal:

> There was a lack of community … like with the students. Everyone was doing their own thing, the lack of support.

She goes on to argue:

> I used to speak to everyone, socialise but I never connected and clicked with anyone. I used to just do my work, stay focused, help people when they

need, talk to them when I need to, but I didn't really want to build anything just if I didn't click with them because that's just not me.

Amara Jackson did not enjoy her time at university because she largely spent the three years at the university on her own, and she particularly highlighted her negative experience of living in university halls of residence which are normally the hub of students' social lives:

> I didn't enjoy my university experience; I don't want to lie. That is not solely because of the university, I think that is because I'm quite an introvert, so, I didn't really make any friends except for one. So, I didn't really enjoy myself…., I just didn't get along—Not that I didn't—with the people that I lived with, we had nothing in common, let's say. I didn't have anything in common with anybody near me in my halls, even on other blocks, so, I didn't really want to make friends with anybody.

Career Ambition

Despite their many negative experiences of university, the Muslim female graduates in our study retained powerful senses of ambition for their own futures reflecting findings from the literature of the past 20 years or so (e.g. Ahmad, 2001; Bagguley & Hussain, 2016). In a comment that almost expresses how she "survived" university, Amara Jackson expressed great optimism for the future and was going to start work in the new year (2022), "I start work in January … I'm going to work for refugees in London". Sana Rashid was also waiting to start her job in central government. Most of the Muslim women who were interviewed in this work had clear and highly ambitious career plans:

> I found a job in the civil service … which I'm still waiting on a start date for because the actual security clearances take forever. So, I'm still currently just working at my part time job until I get a start date. …I wasn't too sure exactly what I wanted to do. But then when I came across this role, I was like, oh this sounds like something I'd be quite interested in because it's research so it's a research analyst.

There were however some of our graduates who were undecided on the jobs they wanted to do resulting in various kinds of temporary employment. These kinds of temporary routine jobs before establishing a more "middle-class" career are commonly found amongst humanities and social science graduates more generally, but ethnic minority students in the United Kingdom have been found to struggle more than White students to establish themselves in the labour market (Lessard-Phillips et al., 2018). For instance, Anaya Habib was still working to fill in the time whilst she was looking for a job.

> I'm just working in [retail shop] as a Christmas temp … I'm hoping to go into research or policy … Before I wanted to go mainly into research. But now I'm open to both research and policy.

In another example illustrating this issue, Mariya Khan is currently undergoing "Kickstart"[2] training with the aim to secure full time employment in the NHS:

> I am doing a Kickstart training. A Kickstart employment for six months at the NHS doing admin … I do like working for the NHS and yes, that's basically it, answer phones and stuff like that.

In a similar fashion Halima Ali went into an internship, and in the longer term has plans for doing a Master's and PhD in education to work with children, but following her graduating:

> … I did a theatre marketing course like an internship and then trying to figure out what I want to do. So now I'm trying to get into a role which is a housing officer role through a graduate scheme so, the housing officer role is based in London and so, I've applied for that recently.

CONCLUSION

To summarise, our Muslim female graduates can be described as having an alienating experience of university in the sense as recently theorised by Rosa (2019: 178–179) where social interactions are experienced as: "…external, unconnected, non-responsive, in a word: <u>mute</u>" (emphasis in the original). This he contrasts with "resonance" where social relations are responsive, where "each speaks with their own voice" (Rosa, 2019: 175). What we hope to have demonstrated through this discussion of our research exploring Muslim female graduates' experiences is that the

---

[2] Kickstart was a scheme aimed at unemployed 18–24-year-olds at risk of long-term unemployment and has now closed.

atmosphere of the White university lacks resonance for them. Its racialised and often Islamophobic atmosphere is alienating for them along several dimensions. The White atmosphere of the university could be transformed through cultural recognition where there is less emphasis on cultural practices involving alcohol, and this would have to be at all levels of the institution down to departmental level. The university would also have to be much more proactive in the recruitment of staff and students in all departments at all levels of staff from non-White backgrounds. This should be underpinned and led at the institutional level through leadership and policies focused upon religion and belief and inequalities related to them. The pedagogical violences (Matusov & Sullivan, 2020) of the curriculum, assessment, peers and teachers, time and location, forms of communication, and assessment produced alienating effects for the Muslim female graduates. However, these were experienced with a degree of ambivalence. The Muslim female graduates retained their valuing of education, despite often almost overwhelming negative experiences and this is evident in terms of the additional training and careers that they were embarking upon. Whilst ongoing debates about the decolonisation of the curriculum are currently centre stage, pedagogy and assessment need to take a more negotiated and student led form. University rhetoric makes much of the themes of belonging and community, yet within this, institutions need to increasingly recognise and act upon the recognition that they are not singular universal communities, but each university is a community of communities.

REFERENCES

Ahmad, F. (2001). Modern traditions? British Muslim women and academic achievement. *Gender and Education, 13*(2), 137–152. https://doi.org/10.1080/09540250120051169

Anderson, E. (2011). *The cosmopolitan canopy: Race and civility in everyday life.* W.W. Norton.

Bagguley, P., & Hussain, Y. (2016). Negotiating mobility: South Asian women and higher education. *Sociology, 50*(1), 43–59. https://doi.org/10.1177/0038038514554329

Bohme, G. (2016). *Atmospheric architectures: The aesthetics of felt spaces.* Bloomsbury.

Bohme, G. (2017a). *The aesthetics of atmospheres.* Routledge.

Bohme, G. (2017b). *Critique of aesthetic capitalism.* Surhkamp Verlag.

Bonilla-Silva, E. (2019). Feeling race: Theorizing the racial economy of emotions. *American Sociological Review, 84*(1), 1–25. https://doi.org/10.1177/0003122418816958

Bourdieu, P., & Passerson, J.-C. (1990). *Reproduction in education, society and culture*. Sage.

Del Gurcio, A., Di Palma, M. A., & Terranova, T. (2018). Technosocial atmospheres: Migration, institutional racism and Twitter. In T. Griffero & G. Moretti (Eds.), *Atmosphere/Atmospheres: Testing a new paradigm* (pp. 47–62). Mimesis International.

Foucault, M. (1995). *Discipline and punish: The birth of the prison*. Vintage Books.

Griffero, T. (2014). *Atmospheres: Aesthetics of emotional spaces*. Routledge.

Griffero, T. (2017). *Quasi-Things: The paradigm of atmospheres*. SUNY.

Griffero, T., & Moretti, G. (Eds.). (2018). *Atmosphere/Atmospheres: Testing a new paradigm*. Mimesis International.

Harris, P., Haywood, C., & Mac an Ghaill, M. (2017). Higher education, decentred subjectivities and the emergence of a pedagogical self among Black and Muslim students. *Race Ethnicity and Education, 20*(3), 358–371.

Islam, M., Lowe, T., & Jones, G. (2019). A "satisfied settling"? Investigating a sense of belonging for Muslim students', in a UK small-medium Higher Education Institution. *Student Engagement in Higher Education Journal, 2*(2), 79–104.

Islam, M., & Mercer-Mapstone, L. (2021). "University is a non-Muslim experience, you know? The experience is as good as it can be": Satisfied settling in Muslim students' experiences and implications for Muslim student voice. *British Educational Research Journal, 47*, 1388–1415. https://doi.org/10.1002/berj.3733

Julmi, C. (2017). *Situations and atmospheres in organizations: A (new) phenomenology of being-in-the-organization*. Mimesis International.

Lessard-Phillips, L., Boliver, V., Pampaka, M., & Swain, D. (2018). Exploring ethnic differences in the post-university destinations of Russell Group graduates. *Ethnicities, 18*(4), 496–517. https://doi.org/10.1177/1468796818777543

Low, M. (2016). *The sociology of space: Materiality, social structures and action*. Palgrave Macmillan.

Matusov, E., & Sullivan, P. W. (2020). Pedagogical violence. *Integrative Psychological & Behavioral Science, 54*, 438–464. https://doi.org/10.1007/s12124-019-09512-4

Rosa, H. (2019). *Resonance: A sociology of our relationship to the world*. Polity Press.

Tate, S. A. (2016). 'I can't quite put my finger on it': Racism's touch. *Ethnicities, 16*(1), 68–85. https://doi.org/10.1177/1468796814564626

Seen but Overlooked: Unveiling the (Counter)narratives of Black Muslim Women Navigating Higher Education

Amira Samatar, Aida Hassan, and Ruqia Osman

INTRODUCTION

The experiences of Black Muslim women across the world are deeply influenced by a complex interplay of cultural, social, and political dynamics. These layered dynamics, which shape their realities, are also mirrored within academic spheres, including in the United Kingdom (UK) and similar geographical contexts. By examining the intersections of race, gender, religion, and academia, this chapter explores how the unique experiences of Black Muslim women resonate within the educational landscape, shedding light on the challenges, barriers, and the ongoing struggle for recognition and inclusivity.

The lived experiences and voices of Black Muslim women are not only multifaceted but remain starkly absent from the current discourse centring

A. Samatar (✉)
Sheffield Hallam University, Sheffield, UK

A. Hassan • R. Osman
Queen Mary University of London, London, UK

© The Author(s), under exclusive license to Springer Nature Switzerland AG 2024
A. Mahmud, M. Islam (eds.), *Uncovering Islamophobia in Higher Education*, Palgrave Studies in Race, Inequality and Social Justice in Education, https://doi.org/10.1007/978-3-031-65253-0_3

33

race and gender in higher education (HE) (Nurein & Iqbal, 2021; Stevenson, 2014). While not exclusively resonating with either Black or Muslim communities, Black Muslim women exist at a crossroads of complexity, which has often been overlooked and under-researched (Samatar & Sardar, 2023; Sardar, 2021; Johnson, 2020). The intersectionality of Black Muslim women is central to this chapter, as this concept provides a way of thinking about identity and its relationship to power being utilised as an "analytic sensibility" (see Choo & Ferree, 2010). Essentially, intersectionality studies the overlapping or intersecting social identities and related systems of oppression, domination, or discrimination (Carastathis, 2014). The usefulness of intersectionality here is how it connects different aspects of the self and other systems of power to explore the complexity of disadvantage and oppression (Choo & Ferree, 2010; Crenshaw, 2013). Considering their intersecting identities of race, gender, and religion, this chapter acknowledges and explores Black Muslim women's specific vulnerabilities in academic environments (Nurein & Iqbal, 2021; Johnson, 2020; Jones, 2006).

In this chapter, co-authored by three Black visibly Muslim women of Somali heritage, we utilise a critical race theory (CRT) counter-narrative method to explore our experiences of Islamophobia, misogynoir and anti-Blackness in HE spaces. The value of CRT lies in its recognition of systemic racism and power structures on individual and structural levels, which significantly impact those racialised outside of whiteness (Riccucci, 2022; Johnson, 2020). Lived experience as a criterion for meaning and knowledge-making is a central canon within CRT and can include approaches such as counter-storytelling, which this chapter will adopt (Solórzano & Yosso, 2002). The utilisation of critical race counter-stories by other scholars (Doharty et al., 2021; Jenkins et al., 2021; Shimomura, 2023) to explore the experiences of people of colour in academic spaces resonates with and strengthens our approach to sharing our narratives. Clemons (2019) asserts that Black women have historically utilised alternative ways of producing and validating knowledge. Therefore, we embrace a counter-storytelling approach using composite characters to authentically share our unique perspectives and insights.

This chapter aims to shed light on the experiences of three Black Muslim women by sharing our own personal and intimate experiences in academia and, as such, can be considered auto-ethnographic (Ellis et al., 2011; West et al., 2021). To achieve this, we will utilise the framework of intersectionality and draw upon the principles of CRT. Our goal is to present our stories to convey and connect to the authentic lived experiences of marginalised individuals within HE, both in the UK and globally. Therefore, our chapter centres our voices as marginalised individuals in academia and acknowledges the complex dimensions of our identities that are often seen but overlooked.

The variety of the authors' educational journeys contributes to the richness of their narratives, which are shared under pseudonyms to protect against potential academic whitelash.[1] Khadija, Farida, and Layla's stories critically explore important themes of invisibility, microaggressions, and belonging unapologetically as Black Muslim women navigating HE. The subsequent sections of this chapter showcase their stories to resonate with individuals who have experienced marginalisation within academic spaces. Our *niyyah* (intention) is to foster a sense of connection and understanding among those who have faced or are currently facing similar struggles.

THE FORGOTTEN OTHER: KHADIJA'S STORY

To be a Black Muslim woman means you may be subject to your experience and your identity being disregarded in a variety of ways. You may experience marginalisation in spaces supposedly at the forefront of liberation, freedom of expression, and equality of opportunity in society. And yet, it appears that the combination of your gender, your choice of religious garment, and the abundance of melanin expressed in your skin acts like a cloak of invisibility in spaces you are qualified to be in or spaces intricately linked to part of your identity. Therefore, you should feel like you should belong, whether this is in predominantly "Black spaces", "Muslim" spaces, and places of worship or within broader society. A survey conducted by *The Black Muslim Forum* demonstrates this; "63.41% of Black Muslims felt they did not belong in the UK Muslim community; 53.95% felt they did not belong to their local Mosque and 84% felt they did not belong in Islamic societies at their university" (Nurein & Iqbal, 2021).

The existence of Muslims has been heavily politicised by national and international discourse that has shaped public perception. Moreover, opting to be "visibly Muslim" by wearing a hijab has implications for how one is perceived and treated by society. By using the framework of

---

[1] Whitelash (a derivative of backlash) is a term used to describe a hostile response, typically driven by racism, to preserve and reinforce white supremacist patriarchal norms.

intersectionality, the interplay of race, gender, and faith can be comprehended. The forthcoming section will delve into Khadija's narrative, aiming to elucidate the intricate experiences of Black Muslim women in HE, focusing on the perspective of professional services.

THE DATA GAP

Since embarking on her professional career in HE immediately after graduation, Khadija has been tirelessly dedicated to addressing ethnicity awarding gaps[2] in HE. Her involvement in this work began with releasing the ethnicity awarding gap report by Universities UK and the National Union of Students in 2019. Recognising the desire for change, Khadija became acutely aware of the lack of concrete actions and institution-wide commitment required to effect meaningful transformations (UUK, 2019).

On a typical day, Khadija spends considerable effort persuading her academic colleagues to actively engage with the student partnership programmes she oversees, designed to close the awarding gap in academic departments. Despite some colleagues expressing their support and championing her work, she continually struggles with limited resources, a lack of willingness from colleagues to participate, and exclusion from crucial discussions and spaces to drive the necessary changes.

The year 2020 seemed to offer a glimmer of hope for transformative change, at least in Khadija's perception. The international response following the murder of George Floyd in 2020 and the subsequent pledges for anti-racist actions and reforms within HE were seen as promising developments (Advance HE, 2021). Khadija recollects contributing to a few of these statements, albeit with a certain degree of scepticism, having personally experienced dismissive responses when reporting racist incidents at these very institutions that now claimed to stand in solidarity with their Black communities and pledged to address racism on their campuses.

We are committed to building a culture of anti-racism and inclusion.
  This University has a zero-tolerance approach to racism, harassment and discrimination.[3]

---

[2] "The ethnicity degree awarding gap at universities means that white students are more likely to be awarded top grades in their degrees than Black, Asian and Minority Ethnic (BAME) students" (Universities UK, 2022).

[3] These are a couple of examples of the types of statements that were included in universities' responses to the murder of George Floyd and the numerous Black Lives Matter protests that were happening across the country at the time.

Acknowledging that institutional change is a gradual process, Khadija recognised the importance of celebrating progress, regardless of its form. Witnessing the shift in discourse from the "BAME"[4] awarding gap to disaggregated ethnicity gaps across the HE sector was considered a significant achievement for Khadija. She found the term "BAME" deeply problematic due to its usage as an umbrella term encompassing individuals of non-white ethnicities. By grouping people in this manner, the distinct experiences within various ethnic groups are overlooked (Fakim & Macaulay, 2020). This becomes particularly concerning when examining ethnicity awarding gaps and student experiences.

Khadija firmly believes that the lack of disaggregated data reporting can be detrimental as it allows the reality of on-campus situations to remain obscured. For instance, data from University UK's 2022 Ethnicity awarding gap report indicates an 8.8% awarding gap for BAME students, while the gap for Black students is 18.4% (UUK, 2022). The same reasoning used in conversations referencing Black versus BAME can be used when looking at Black as a racialised category alone. Not all Black individuals share a homogeneous experience, as factors such as ethnicity, faith, class, gender, and sexuality can influence outcomes and student experience. However, if we are not collecting or analysing data in this way, how can we truly understand the experience of students with multiple identities? How can we truly appreciate the experience of Black Muslim women in a data-driven sector that is not quite there yet with intersectional data analysis and reporting?

SEEN BUT NOT HEARD

After a demanding week at work, marked by frustrating meetings and interactions, Khadija returned to her desk, thinking deeply about the recent meeting she had just attended. A familiar sense of discomfort pervaded her, a feeling she had grown accustomed to throughout her professional career in HE, especially in her work with marginalised students, student experiences, and awarding gaps. The source of her frustration stemmed from being unexpectedly called upon to present at a meeting at the last minute while other colleagues had been afforded ample time to prepare. In this instance, Khadija was asked to present her ongoing *underfunded* and *unrecognised* efforts to reduce the ethnicity awarding gap to a

---

[4] Black, Asian, and Minority Ethnic.

committee responsible for discussing learning and teaching-related matters at the university.

Khadija commenced her presentation by providing the necessary context, outlining the significant barriers and challenges she had encountered while implementing her work across various university departments. While her endeavours were initially acknowledged and commended, she was swiftly dismissed without adequately addressing the remaining challenges. To her dismay, certain colleagues voiced deeply problematic views and showed reluctance to engage with Khadija directly. Instead, they turned their attention to her white colleague, questioning the necessity of such initiatives and casting doubt on the data she presented.

As Khadija often does, she wondered if she would have experienced the same microaggressions if she were a cis-gendered white woman or man, and upon realising this would not have been the case, she starts drafting an email to raise her concerns. As the only person of colour and visibly Muslim woman in the space, Khadija felt undermined. Was the English she was speaking not "English enough"? Were her words evaporating into thin air? Why were her calls to action ignored? Why did it take for her white colleague to repeat the exact statistics for others to feel reassured? These are all questions that Khadija had been asking herself for years and will continue to ask for many years.

> *To: Jonathan Smith*
> *From: Khadija Mohamoud*
> *Subject: RE: Ethnicity Awarding Gap*
> *Dear Jonathan,*
> *Whilst I appreciated the opportunity to present, being asked to present merely a few hours before felt tokenistic. I am concerned that closing the ethnicity awarding gap is not a priority for the institution, and I feel the hesitance to discuss and address my concerns needs to be addressed.*
> *I feel the discussion drifted into an unproductive space where inappropriate comments were made to avoid taking accountability and shifting the blame onto students. For instance, Judith's comment about raising entry requirements as an additional measure to close the awarding gap was misplaced.*
> *I feel there is a lack of understanding among committee members, a barrier to progression. Please consider reviewing membership and ensuring the proper training is provided to committee members so that we can start having more productive conversations.*
> *I hope we can find a way forward.*
> *Kind regards,*
> *Khadija*

Regarding policies and service provision, UK HE is a data-driven sector; if it is not evidence-based or data-informed, people do not want to hear it. Khadija dedicated a significant portion of her work to supporting Black students. However, from a policy and research standpoint, she observed a tendency to categorise all Black students into a singular box, disregarding the vast diversity of experiences within that racial category. This categorisation served as a barrier, as it failed to recognise the distinct experiences of Black Muslim women. In the realm of UK HE, there remains a notable lack of understanding about Black Muslim individuals, and this gap is perpetuated by the failure to analyse the intersection of faith, gender, and ethnicity in data analysis. As a result, the existence and experiences of Black Muslim women are effectively erased from the data.

"How can you be Muslim? You're Black!"[5]

The world in which we live has been significantly influenced by imperialism. As a result of that, we live in a world where racialised social hierarchies have been embedded into the fabric of our globalised society (Rehman & Laybourn-Langton, 2020). When whiteness is understood as a desirable commodity, we can begin to understand the phenomenon of colourism and the preferential treatment of individuals based on the shade of their skin (Fabrizi, 2015). This means that despite two people belonging to the same "race" or "ethnic group", they may have access to differing levels of privilege and economic and political opportunities based on the shade of their skin (Nix & Quan, 2015; The Black Story, 2021). This phenomenon manifests in HE and adds further nuance to the experiences of Black Muslim women.

---

[5] The subheading "How can you be Muslim? You're Black" refers to the numerous times in which Black Muslims may have had their faith or "Blackness" questioned. These kinds of experiences may be more common in towns and cities where there is not a large Black Muslim population.

The authors appreciate that the categories of race and faith are not binary, and there is no universal Black or Muslim experience. It is more elaborate than that. For instance, a woman who is "visibly Muslim", and has a lighter shade of skin, may have a very different experience from someone who is "darker" and less "visibly Muslim". Additionally, anti-Black discrimination and colourism are major problems in Muslim communities, with 48.98% of Black Muslims reporting they have experienced this type of discrimination in religious settings (Nurein & Iqbal, 2021).

"A Symbol of Oppression": Visibility of Muslimhood

As Layla will describe in her story "The Harsh Politics of Belonging", the racialisation of Muslims has contributed to the marginalisation experienced by Black Muslims in the UK. The "British Muslim" identity has become analogous with South Asian or Arab ethnic groups (Nurein & Iqbal, 2021). The assumed homogeneity of the "Muslim race" is one of the major factors contributing to the erasure and undermining of Black Muslims in the UK.[6] In recent years, discourse around Muslim women has grown exponentially. Particularly peaking after major "Jihadi" terrorist incidents and anti-Muslim propaganda driven by the far right (Allen, 2014; ENAR, 2016). This has played into EU and international policy-making with the introduction of legislation banning Islamic veils that cover the face, hijab, and modest swimwear to clamp down on extremism, aid "integration", and create "public spheres" that are culture-free, neutral, and universal (Grillo & Shah, 2012; Dearden, 2017; Weaver, 2018).

The single-story narrative that has been superimposed onto Muslim women in Western media is that of being submissive, financially oppressed, terrorists, extremists, uneducated, housewives, and sexual objects for men who are in need of liberation, facilitated by more "progressive" and Westernised legislation and people (Kasirye, 2021). This directly contradicts the "liberal" notion of freedom of expression and providing women with the choice to wear what they want.

Khadija's narrative represents the experiences of individuals in HE, explicitly addressing the challenges faced by Black Muslim women and women of colour, including othering, unequal access to opportunities, racism, and discrimination due to systemic inequalities (Samatar, 2024; Zewodle, 2021). Crenshaw (2013) emphasises the complexity of identifying the root cause of oppression when it arises from the intersection of multiple identities. These forms of oppression can manifest as microaggressions or direct or indirect discrimination. Recognising the unique challenges marginalised groups face is essential in addressing systemic

---

[6] Note: When considering the ways in which people choose to practice their faith and wear religious garments, it is important to consider that context matters. While wearing religious garments is considered to be a decision that an individual chooses to make, there are some instances where this element of choice is removed. This next section is centred around the perspective of Muslim communities that are based in Western countries, like the UK, where they may be* afforded more liberty and protection around their decision to wear or not wear religious garments.

barriers in HE. Layla's narrative further explores race, identity, and belonging themes, providing additional insights into these issues.

Unmasking Microaggressions: Farida's Story

As Farida settles back into her designated desk in the shared office space for PhD students on campus, the echoes of the morning's student-staff meeting held by her graduate school continue reverberating in her mind, occupying what feels like a substantial amount of mental space. Being in her second year as a law PhD student, Farida had grown accustomed to feeling disheartened after such meetings. However, today's gathering had an intensified effect, leaving a lingering impact that surpassed her usual threshold of tolerance. Farida reflects on past naivety from her first year when she believed these meetings could provide her with support and a sense of community. However, with a tinge of embarrassment, she now realises just how mistaken she was in her expectations.

Today's meeting brought to the forefront an agenda frequently touted but often inadequately addressed by many HE institutions: equality and diversity. Farida, the sole Black and hijabi PhD student in her department, found herself under the scrutiny of both conscious and unconscious gazes, which further heightened the sense of surveillance she felt in an already vulnerable and exposed environment. Within academia, a continuous discourse exists on the burden and tax imposed upon individuals from underrepresented groups to address equality, diversity, and inclusion (Trejo, 2020). This anticipation was palpable for Farida, particularly in the context of the meeting, where the following remarks made by one senior academic were difficult to overlook:

> *While we all value equality and diversity, we must also stress the importance of student quality and academic rigour. Even when students experience challenges, it is vital to avoid a victim mentality as it does not provide effective solutions. In our upcoming meetings, our main focus is highlighting positive student engagement. Pursuing a PhD is a privilege, and every individual must comprehend and appreciate this opportunity.*

Throughout the meeting, Farida couldn't forget the phrases "victimhood mindset", "PhD privilege", and "student quality". She wondered if the senior academic knew the issues she had raised regarding cultural competence and inclusion within her department. She suspected the comments were a less-than-subtle response, made more apparent by the lack of eye contact from others, leaving her feeling exposed as the only melanin-rich student in the room. After the meeting, Farida received an email from the senior academic that evening:

> *Dear Farida*
> *Following today's meeting, I'm sharing a link: 'Top 10 Strategies for PhD Student Resilience.' I hope it proves helpful and anticipate your feedback at the next meeting; best wishes.*

Farida let out a deep sigh. The email she received removed any chance of interpreting the meeting neutrally. Farida was undeniably facing microaggressions, a recurring experience that she knew would likely continue. However, this familiarity didn't make it any less painful to cope with. The scholarship of Dr Chester Pierce, a Black American psychiatrist, can be attributed to the development of microaggressions as a term used to describe the subtle 'everyday' occurrences of racism that African Americans frequently experienced (1970). These actions can be verbal, non-verbal, or environmental and are directed towards people of colour, sometimes intentionally or unconsciously (Solórzano et al., 2000; Sue et al., 2007). Pierce's work used (1970) microaggressions and the concept of an "offensive mechanism" to address the mental health needs of African American communities, as he believed existing theories lacked a comprehensive framework for considering the impact of race and racism in the experiences of these communities (Pérez Huber & Solorzano, 2015). Since then, the term microaggressions has entered the popular lexicon, a wealth of scholarly literature on racialised microaggressions in higher education has emerged (see Grier-Reed, 2010; Pittman, 2012; Pérez Huber & Solorzano, 2015; Franklin, 2016; Johnson & Joseph-Salisbury, 2018; Doharty, 2019; Morales, 2021). Farida's experiences with microaggressions in academia echo Pierce's sentiments that the "*most offensive actions are not gross and crippling, but rather they are subtle and stunning [...] blows delivered incessantly*" (1970, p. 265).

This situation was undeniably stunning. It wasn't just the words but also the subtle cues, like the lack of eye contact in the meeting and the condescending email offering advice on resilience. These actions created an uncomfortable atmosphere that, for Farida, felt close to crossing the boundaries of appropriateness. While some might dismiss these incidents as over-analysis stemming from a hypersensitive perspective, those attuned to the politics of microaggressions understand that their significance extends beyond explicit statements (Sue et al., 2007, 2019). It resides in the subtler, unspoken messages that quietly simmer beneath the surface (Joseph-Salisbury, 2019). The capacity to perceive these implicit undercurrents and to interpret what remains unsaid constitutes a taxing yet indispensable skill Farida has had to cultivate to navigate her path in academia, especially as a Black Muslim woman (Trejo, 2020; Morales, 2021; Samatar et al., 2021).

Scholars such as Henry and Glenn (2009) and West (2019) provide insights into the exceptional and unconventional strategies employed by Black women as they traverse the complex terrain of higher education and its myriad of challenges. In this context, Black women often face covert marginalisation and overt acts of violence, ranging from being rendered "visibly invisible" (Collins, 1986) to experiencing verbal, physical, and digital forms of policing (Pittman, 2012; Johnson & Joseph-Salisbury, 2018; Jenkins et al., 2021). As articulated by Porter (2022), Black women must navigate institutional spaces that, on one hand, tokenistically celebrate them as symbols of equality, diversity, and inclusion, while, on the other hand, perpetuate their marginalisation and erasure. This sentiment also extends to the surveillance of Muslims in campus spaces and the critical scrutiny experienced by Muslim women (Mir, 2006; Chaudry, 2021).

In this context, Farida finds herself entangled in a complex balancing act where she must preserve her composure to survive this marginalisation and erasure. This intricate dynamic requires her to navigate microaggressions, including the one described earlier carefully, and to select responses that shield her from further unwarranted stigmatisation, including the "angry Black woman"[7] trope often applied to many Black Muslim women (Henry & Glenn, 2009; Doharty, 2019; Nurein & Iqbal, 2021). This does not mean Farida silences herself as, in the words of Audre Lorde (2017), this, too, will not protect her. The opposite is true, she fully acknowledges the critical role self-advocacy plays as a defence mechanism in her context. However, this, too, is colour-coded and presents its own set of challenges, particularly when the silhouette of her hijab is misconstrued as a sign of vulnerability, and her agency is at times disempowered without her consent (ENAR, 2016; Chaudry, 2021). This balancing act

---

[7] The angry Black woman trope is a pervasive stereotype rooted in misogynoir that characterises Black women as hostile, aggressive, overbearing, illogical, ill-tempered, and bitter for displaying human emotions that are accepted in other social groups (Ashley, 2014).

can impose a substantial burden, as articulated by Sue et al. (2019), and is a common experience for students of colour who are often compelled to risk assess their movements constantly (Franklin, 2016). It is important to note that this emotional and intellectual labour goes mostly unacknowledged and rarely, if ever, compensated.

Farida is acutely aware of the challenging circumstances faced by Black Muslim women in academia, characterised by high workloads, constrained career prospects, pervasive feelings of exclusion, and inadequate support from academic hierarchies (Henry & Glenn, 2009; Sue et al., 2019). The socio-economic and racial inequalities, emotional strains, and concealed burdens within educational environments magnify and unveil the vulnerability of Black Muslim women within these contexts (Mir, 2006; Joseph-Salisbury, 2019; Morales, 2021; Chaudry, 2021). Given these harsh realities, Farida acknowledges the importance of preserving her well-being, understanding that she cannot compromise this for academic status. This does not imply that pursuing an academic career is futile; instead, it underscores her need to be vigilant in setting and maintaining personal boundaries. One of these boundaries involves Farida's choice to assume a protective persona, symbolised by the metaphorical "mask".

The symbolic "mask", inspired by Maya Angelou's rendition of the poem "Masks" (2020), speaks to Farida's strategy for self-protection within the academic spaces. This protective persona is characterised by a set of boundaries that encompass self-care practices. It is important to note that these boundaries are not defined through a neoliberal perspective but are instead centred on the value of recuperation after resisting the systemic impact of whiteness, enduring microaggressions, and confronting the racial dynamics that are prevalent within the higher education sphere (Franklin, 2016; Doharty, 2019; Morales, 2021; Porter, 2022; Hersey, 2022). Additionally, part of Farida's protective strategy includes connecting with like-minded communities and maintaining a clear sense of her purpose. With these foundational values in mind, Farida ceases her participation in the student-staff meetings after a contemplative evening following the day's events. She no longer regards these meetings as conducive to fostering meaningful change. Instead, she will redirect her efforts towards spaces that align with her values and shared objectives for progress and equity in academia.

HARSH POLITICS OF BELONGING: LAYLA'S STORY

Layla thought she would have an easy morning today: she woke up on time to pray *fajr*,[8] did the laundry, and made an early start to the library before her doctoral supervision meeting at noon. Somehow, the day went south before it even began. Layla briefly wondered for a moment what sparked the horrible start to her day. Could it have been the train delays, as commuters shoved past her on the platform, or the possibility she could lose her favourite but oversubscribed spot in the library? Or perhaps this negative feeling could have stemmed from the email she received while on the crowded train:

> *Dear Layla,*
>
> *Thank you for your email. We appreciate your interest in involving the Race Equality Network in Islamophobia Awareness Month and campaign against anti-Muslim discrimination.*
>
> *We understand that individuals may be subjected to intolerant views because of their religion or culture. However, as a network, we mainly focus on race-related issues that affect students and staff and strive to improve their experiences at our university. We also want to ensure we respect everyone from different backgrounds and faith, even those from non-faith backgrounds.*
>
> *At this moment, we will not be able to take on this initiative. Please contact the Student Association if you wish to plan an open forum around this subject.*
>
> *Kind regards,*
> *Brenda (Chair of the Race Equity Network)*

After a couple of weeks of waiting, Layla finally received a response from the Chair of the Race Equity Network in her faculty about a proposal for an Islamophobia Awareness Month event. Though much to her dismay, the Network rejected her proposal and refused to participate in this initiative, as stated in the email above. Layla exalted a sigh, failing to hide her disappointment on a train carriage filled with commuters. She glossed over the email again, sitting idle on her phone screen, as her frustration grew with every sentence. Although disappointed, Layla was not entirely surprised by the response, as she knew there was reluctance by the Network to address issues of Islamophobia as racism.

Following the murder of George Floyd and the resurgence of Black Lives Matter in June 2020, Layla joined the Network at a time when

---

[8] One of the compulsory prayers for Muslims which starts at dawn.

anti-racist and decolonial movements were becoming mainstream in the HE sector. Although many movements such as Rhodes Must Fall and "Why Is My Curriculum White" were forming and growing internationally before June 2020 (see Mirza, 2018; Esson, 2020; Hall et al., 2021), the resurgence of Black Lives Matter almost solidified the case for race and racism to be taken seriously by many Global North institutions. Upon joining the network, Layla initially found the efforts of the Race Equity Network admirable and felt somewhat hopeful about the future experience of Black and Brown students and staff on campus. Although there were a few non-white and all-women members in the Network, she was the only Black and Muslim member. Over time, however, her opinion of the Network changed. As the claims of anti-racist change felt nothing short of virtue signalling and performative, Layla became subsumed with disappointment and betrayal. She also noticed how her role as the "Black student voice" became a cheap source of labour for the staff members of the Network, often relying on her for menial tasks such as emailing potential speakers and taking minutes in monthly meetings. Feeling like her voice was hijacked by the senior members of the Network, Layla felt her only role was to be the hollow face of "transformative anti-racist change", even though there was nothing transformative nor anti-racist about the Network. The final nail in the coffin was their dismissal of Islamophobia as an issue of racism, as the Chair spells out in her email above.

For Layla, this was the disappointing reality of being a Black and Muslim woman and the everyday feelings of being ignored, misplaced, and misunderstood (Nurein & Iqbal, 2021). As a Black and Muslim student at a British institution, Layla knew she was under the watchful eye of Prevent, a counter-radicalisation apparatus that could easily label her anti-racist activism as a "potential sign of extremism" (see Saeed, 2021; Hassan, 2021). She was always conscious of how she was dressed, expressed her religion, or even what books or sources she accessed online could somehow be flagged up by her university[9] (Sabir, 2022; Choudhury, 2017). The reality of over-policing and criminalisation of Black students was not lost on her, as students could even be arrested for something innocuous as

---

[9] This was the case for Dr Rizwaan Sabir, who was unfairly charged with suspected terrorism for looking up Al Qaeda training documents as part of his doctoral research (see Sabir, 2022).

wearing a hoodie[10] by campus security and police officers (Meley, 2022). Layla foolishly believed that the Race Equity Network would stand in solidarity with Black and Muslim students subjected to these racist forms of state securitisation. Instead, it became clear to Layla that she was never going to be able to escape these harsh politics of belonging, even by spaces she thought would advocate for someone like herself.

Feeling frustrated by the email, Layla finally reached the campus library. Although she was relieved to find her usual spot still empty, she was too frustrated to get started on her list of tasks. Instead, Layla read through the email again, this time on her laptop. As she grimaced over the response by the Network Chair, Layla took stock of what was meant by "race-related issues". How is it possible to address Islamophobia as a form of racism when Islam is not a race? Is it really racism when the notion of Islam remains an existential threat to British values (Meer & Modood, 2009, 2019)? Edward Said (1978) has notably identified in Orientalism how the West has produced a powerful, moralised picture of Islam and the "Arab world" through an imaginative construct that platforms white European values of the world (i.e. "liberal" and "progressive") over the non-European Other (i.e. "autocratic" and "backwards"). Equally, the obfuscation of Islamophobia as a form of racism by progressive, liberal, and even anti-racist spaces can instead promote a liberal form of racism that is acceptable and in line with the status quo of British society (Mondon & Winter, 2017). According to Mondon and Winter (2017), illiberal forms of racism are expressed or embodied in extreme, unacceptable hate due to exclusivist ideologies (i.e. white supremacy), exemplified by far-right groups in Western societies. However, liberal forms of racism, in contrast to illiberal racism, are not obvious at first but more likely to be accepted because of its "proclaimed allegiance to fantasised liberal and democratic principles" (i.e. more mainstream due to progressive politics) (Mondon & Winter, 2017: 2162). For instance, "woke"[11] academics may

---

[10] In November 2020, a Black student at the University of Manchester was racially profiled and demanded to present his ID by campus security, with footage online showing that the student was held up against a wall by the security guards. The student said he was accused of "looking like a drug dealer" for simply wearing a hoodie (see Meley, 2022).

[11] The phrase "stay woke" emerged by Black activists in the USA as a means of consciousness and vigilance to forms of racial injustice and white supremacy, namely, racial violence by police and state authority. However, the term "woke" has grown into a narrow, one-word distillation of progressive ideologies and political correctness, often used to describe individuals or ideas that advocate for a performative sense of social justice (see Bunyasi & Smith, 2019).

refuse to stand in solidarity with Palestinian causes because, unlike Israel, Palestine is not a democratic or secular state, and their struggles of living under settler colonialism can be justified. Likewise, liberal racism can also explain why progressive spaces dedicated to equality, diversity, and inclusion may distance themselves from addressing Islamophobia because of the mainstream narrative that acceptance of Islam contests the progressive ideals in Western society, such as free speech, human rights, and gender equality (Mondon & Winter, 2017; Cervi, 2020). Returning to the email once more, she noticed the Network also wished to respect students and staff from non-faith backgrounds. For Layla, she recognised this hesitancy to address the real plights of Islamophobia as a form of liberal racism, which was ironic for a Network focused on achieving race equity and inclusion for students and staff of colour.

By obscuring and erasing Islamophobia as a form of racism, the Race Equity Network ignored the complex intersectionality of Black Muslim women and their racialised experiences. As Black students are subjected to excessive policing, Muslim students are forced to exist in a surveillance state in a post-9/11 world (Kundnani, 2014; Hopkins, 2011). Layla firmly believed that universities should seek to address these structural forces as issues of racism. However, she instead questioned whether these anti-racist initiatives by British and Western academic institutions actually seek to tackle racism or amplify it. All the while, racialised students are expected to shoulder this burden by maintaining an illusory image of anti-racist change, so universities can absolve their own racial anxieties and present themselves anew as an institution inclusive of BAME students. "What a joke", Layla scoffed at the thought. Layla knew well the impact of anti-Blackness and Islamophobia had on her life from a young age, from her school years to university. From when one of her classmates "jokingly" inspected her hijab for a hidden bomb in secondary school, to being labelled as "the troublesome Black woman" by her non-Black professors for speaking her mind in class. The intersectionality of Layla's identity confounded her ability to find meaning and belonging in the world around her, and painfully so in anti-racist spaces that she commonsensically believed would understand her lived experiences of anti-Black racism and Islamophobia. For Layla, belonging was a contested and elusive concept for Black and Muslim students at British universities and beyond.

CONCLUSION

This chapter delved into the experiences of three Black Muslim women navigating HE, revealing the complex interplay of race, religion, and gender in shaping their identities and experiences. While existing literature has started to unravel the experiences of individuals in HE through a gendered and racialised lens, the voices of Black Muslim individuals (especially women) remain largely absent (Hopkins, 2011; Stevenson, 2014; Mondon & Winter, 2017; Johnson, 2020; Samatar et al., 2021). In light of this gap, this chapter has brought attention to the overlooked experiences of Black Muslim women in HE. This has been achieved by recognising and centring the unique challenges they face at the intersections of multiple systems of oppression and by presenting their narratives through a counter-storytelling method (Doharty et al., 2021; Jenkins et al., 2021; Shimomura, 2023).

Khadija, Farida, and Layla's narratives highlighted the various barriers they encounter as they navigate HE in pursuit of their educational and professional goals. Khadija's narrative delved into the systematic neglect of Black Muslim women within HE and data analyses. Khadija contends that this neglect arises from the absence of intersectional examination concerning essential aspects of student experiences, attainment, retention, and graduate outcomes. Farida's narrative examined the toxic interplay of microaggressions and the rhetoric of resilience often weaponised against marginalised individuals in academic spaces (Trejo, 2020; Morales, 2021). Similarly, Layla's narrative highlighted the divisive but stark reality of Black and Muslim women on campus: simultaneously ignored and policed, as well as invisible and hyper-visible. All three of these narratives raise essential doubts about whether academic spaces, policies, and committees under the guise of "equality, diversity and inclusion" genuinely intend to meaningfully challenge racism and Islamophobia across the sector in the UK and globally (Hall et al., 2021; Esson, 2020).

We hope the counter-stories shared by the authors of this chapter serve as a compelling call to action, urging researchers to continue shining a light on the unique experiences and perspectives of Black Muslim students. Notably, we advocate this through engaging in meaningful and ethical research that amplifies the voices and narratives of Black Muslims in HE. Ultimately, we hope this will foster greater knowledge, awareness, and change towards more equitable practices and policies.

In light of the Office for Students' focus on access and participation plans,[12] as well as efforts to address ethnicity awarding gaps and enhance the overall experience of Muslim and racially minoritised students, it is crucial to consider the engagement of Black Muslim students in these initiatives. Examining their experiences and identifying potential disparities in degree outcomes within this group is paramount. Therefore, we advocate for further intersectional analysis to ensure that universities have a comprehensive understanding of the experiences and challenges these marginalised students face, as well as to develop effective interventions.

However, this can only be achieved by acknowledging that Black Muslim students' experiences are not monolithic and, therefore, recognising that a standardised approach may not always be suitable. We encourage universities to conduct tailored research and analysis to determine the most appropriate interventions for supporting Black Muslim students and staff on their campuses. By doing so, universities can better design and implement strategies that address this particular student population's specific needs and circumstances. This approach will contribute to creating a more inclusive and equitable environment for Black Muslim students, Muslim students, and racially minoritised students, fostering their academic success and overall well-being within the university setting.

As three Black Muslim women authoring this chapter, we are deeply aware of how challenging navigating academic environments can be and that constantly advocating for yourself and others in university spaces can take a considerable toll on physical health and mental health, potentially leading to burnout and increased stress levels. For this reason, it is critical that Black and Muslim staff and students practise self-care and prioritise their mental and physical well-being (Hersey, 2022). This may entail setting limits, having breaks, disengaging from university "life", and solely focusing on their academic and professional goals, prioritising their physical and mental health. In the end, HE institutions must ensure that a climate of equity and inclusion exists, which both values and proactively seeks to improve the experiences of their most marginalised student groups and staff.

In conclusion, this chapter's exploration of the counter-stories of three Black Muslim women in HE shed light on the intersectionality of their

---

[12] These plans apply to all English higher education providers who charge above the basic tuition fee cap. They set out how providers will improve equality of opportunity for underrepresented groups to access, succeed in, and progress from higher education.

identities and the unique challenges that they face. Throughout this chapter, we explored the multifaceted nature of their journeys, highlighting the various barriers they encounter and their perseverance. Their stories serve as reminders of the importance of creating inclusive spaces that value diversity and empower individuals from all backgrounds to thrive. By embracing and uplifting the experiences of Black Muslim women, we can foster a more equitable and inclusive HE landscape for all.

References

Advance HE. (2021). Black Lives Matter and the student voice. *Advance HE*. Retrieved February 27, 2023, from https://blogs.shu.ac.uk/narrowing-thegaps/files/2021/07/Advance-HE-BLM-and-the-student-voice-June-2021.pdf

Allen, F. (2014). *Islamophobia in the UK: The role of British newspapers in shaping attitudes towards Islam and Muslims*. Master's thesis, University of Wales, Trinity St David. https://repository.uwtsd.ac.uk/id/eprint/413/

Angelou, M. (2020). The mask. *Facinghistory.org*.

Ashley, W. (2014). The angry black woman: The impact of pejorative stereotypes on psychotherapy with black women. *Social Work in Public Health, 29*(1), 27–34.

Bunyasi, T. L., & Smith, C. W. (2019). *Stay woke: A people's guide to making all Black Lives Matter*. NYU Press.

Carastathis, A. (2014). The concept of intersectionality in feminist theory. *Philosophy Compass, 9*(5), 304–314.

Cervi, L. (2020). Exclusionary populism and Islamophobia: A comparative analysis of Italy and Spain. *Religion, 11*(10), 516. https://doi.org/10.3390/rel11100516

Chaudry, I. (2021). "I felt like I was being watched": The hypervisibility of Muslim students in higher education. *Educational Philosophy and Theory, 53*(3), 257–269. https://doi.org/10.1080/00131857.2020.1769603

Choo, H. Y., & Ferree, M. M. (2010). Practicing intersectionality in sociological research: A critical analysis of inclusions, interactions, and institutions in the study of inequalities. *Sociological Theory, 28*(2), 129–149.

Choudhury, T. (2017). Campaigning on campus: Student Islamic societies and counterterrorism. *Studies in Conflict & Terrorism, 40*(12), 1004–1022.

Clemons, K. M. (2019). *Black feminist thought and qualitative research in education*. Virginia State University.

Collins, P. H. (1986). Learning from the outsider within: The sociological significance of Black feminist thought. *Social Problems, 33*(6), 14–32. https://doi.org/10.2307/800672

Crenshaw, K. W. (2013). Mapping the margins: Intersectionality, identity politics, and violence against women of color. In *The public nature of private violence* (pp. 93–118). Routledge.

Dearden, L. (2017). China bans burqas and 'abnormal' beards in Muslim province of Xinjiang. *Independent*. Retrieved February 13, 2023, from https://www.independent.co.uk/news/world/asia/china-burqa-abnormal-beards-ban-muslim-province-xinjiang-veils-province-extremism-crackdown-freedom-a7657826.html

Doharty, N. (2019). 'I FELT DEAD': Applying a racial microaggressions framework to Black students' experiences of Black History Month and Black History. *Race Ethnicity and Education, 22*(1), 110–129. https://doi.org/10.1080/13613324.2017.1417253

Doharty, N., Madriaga, M., & Joseph-Salisbury, R. (2021). The university went to 'decolonise' and all they brought back was lousy diversity doublespeak! Critical race counter-stories from faculty of colour in 'decolonial' times. *Educational Philosophy and Theory, 53*(3), 233–244.

Ellis, C., Adams, T. E., & Bochner, A. P. (2011). Autoethnography: An overview. *Historical Social Research/Historische Sozialforschung*, 273–290.

ENAR. (2016). Forgotten women: The impact of Islamophobia on Muslim women in the United Kingdom. *European Network Against Racism*. Retrieved December 27, 2022, from https://www.enar-eu.org/forgotten-women-the-impact-of-islamophobia-on-muslim-women/

Esson, J. (2020). "The why and the white": Racism and curriculum reform in British geography. *Area, 52*(4), 708–715. https://doi.org/10.1111/area.12475

Fabrizi, D. (2015). Fanon and Hooks. *The facts of Whiteness: Examining Whiteness through the Black gaze*. Retrieved January 3, 2023, from https://thefactsofwhiteness.org/fanon-and-hooks/

Fakim, N., & Macaulay, C. (2020). 'Dont call me BAME': Why some people are rejecting the term. *BBC*. Retrieved February 19, 2023, from https://www.bbc.co.uk/news/uk-53194376

Franklin, J. (2016). Racial microaggressions, racial battle fatigue, and racism-related stress in higher education. *Journal of Student Affairs at New York University, 12*(44), 44–55.

Grier-Reed, T. L. (2010). The African American student network: Creating sanctuaries and counterspaces for coping with racial microaggressions in higher education settings. *The Journal of Humanistic Counseling, Education and Development, 49*(2), 181–188. https://doi.org/10.1002/j.2161-1939.2010.tb00096.x

Grillo, R., & Shah, P. (2012). *Reasons to ban? The anti-burqa movement in Western Europe*. MMG Working Paper 12-05. Max Planck Institute for the Study of Religious and Ethnic Diversity.

Hall, R., Ansley, L., Connolly, P., Loonat, S., Patel, K., & Whitham, B. (2021). Struggling for the anti-racist university: Learning from an institution-wide response to curriculum decolonisation. *Teaching in Higher Education, 26*(7–8), 902–919. https://doi.org/10.1080/13562517.2021.1911987

Hassan, A. (2021). Government policy is feeding campus Islamophobia [Online]. *Tribune*. Retrieved November 18, 2022, from https://tribunemag.co. uk/2021/11/islamophobia-awareness-month-students-prevent-securitisation-state-surveillance

Henry, W. J., & Glenn, N. M. (2009). Black women employed in the ivory tower: Connecting for success. *Advancing Women in Leadership Journal, 29*, 10.21423/awlj-v29.a271.

Hersey, T. (2022). *Rest is resistance: A manifesto*. Hachette UK.

Hopkins, P. (2011). Towards critical geographies of the university campus: Understanding the contested experiences of Muslim students. *Transactions of the Institute of British Geographers, 36*(1), 157–169. https://doi.org/10.1111/j.1475-5661.2010.00407.x

Jenkins, D. A., Tichavakunda, A. A., & Coles, J. A. (2021). The second ID: Critical race counterstories of campus police interactions with Black men at Historically White Institutions. *Race Ethnicity and Education, 24*(2), 149–166. https://doi.org/10.1080/13613324.2020.1753672

Johnson, A. (2020). Throwing our bodies against the white background of academia. *Area, 52*(1), 89–96.

Johnson, A., & Joseph-Salisbury, R. (2018). 'Are you supposed to be in here?' Racial microaggressions and knowledge production. In J. Arday & H. S. Mirza (Eds.), *Dismantling race in higher education: Racism, whiteness and decolonising the academy*. Palgrave.

Jones, C. (2006). Falling between the cracks: What diversity means for black women in higher education. *Policy Futures in Education, 4*(2), 145–159.

Joseph-Salisbury, R. (2019). Institutionalised whiteness, racial microaggressions and black bodies out of place in higher education. *Whiteness and Education, 4*(1), 1–17. https://doi.org/10.1080/23793406.2019.1620629

Kasirye, F. (2021). The portrayal of Muslim women in Western media. A content analysis of the New York Times and The Guardian. *Advance*. Preprint.

Kundnani, A. (2014). *The Muslims are coming! Islamophobia, extremism, and the domestic war on terror*. Verso.

Lorde, A. (2017). *Your silence will not protect you*. Silver Press.

Meer, N., & Modood, T. (2009). Refutations of racism in the 'Muslim question'. *Patterns of Prejudice, 43*(3–4), 335–354. https://doi.org/10.1080/003132 20903109250

Meer, N., & Modood, T. (2019). Islamophobia as the Racialisation of Muslims. In I. A. Irene Zempi (Ed.), *The Routledge international handbook of Islamophobia*. Routledge.

Meley, C. (2022). The students fighting to keep cops off campus [Online]. *Huck Magazine*. Retrieved June 22, 2023, from https://www.huckmag.com/article/body-worn-cameras-are-quietly-taking-over-london

Mir, S. (2006). *Constructing third spaces: American Muslim undergraduate women's hybrid identity construction*. Indiana University.

Mirza, H. S. (2018). What then, can be done? In J. Arday & H. S. Mirza (Eds.), *Dismantling race in higher education: Racism, whiteness and decolonising the academy*. Palgrave.

Mondon, A., & Winter, A. (2017). Articulations of Islamophobia: From the extreme to the mainstream? *Ethnic and Racial Studies, 40*(13), 2151–2179. https://doi.org/10.1080/01419870.2017.1312008

Morales, E. (2021). "Beasting" at the battleground: Black students responding to racial microaggressions in higher education. *Journal of Diversity in Higher Education, 14*(1), 72. https://doi.org/10.1037/dhe0000168

Nix, E., & Quan, N. (2015). *The fluidity of race: "Passing" in the United States, 1880–1940*. NBER working papers series, National Bureau of Economic Research.

Nurein, S. A., & Iqbal, H. (2021). Identifying a space for young Black Muslim women in contemporary Britain. *Ethnicities, 21*(3), 433–453. https://doi.org/10.1177/14687968211001899

Pérez Huber, L., & Solorzano, D. G. (2015). Racial microaggressions as a tool for critical race research. *Race Ethnicity and Education, 18*(3), 297–320. https://doi.org/10.1080/13613324.2014.994173

Pierce, C. (1970). Offensive mechanisms. In F. B. Barbour (Ed.), *The Black seventies* (pp. 265–282). Porter Sargeant.

Pittman, C. T. (2012). Racial microaggressions: The narratives of African American faculty at a predominantly White university. *Journal of Negro Education, 81*(1), 82–92.

Porter, C. J. (2022). (Re)imagining belonging: Black women want more than survival in predominantly White institutions. *Journal of College Student Development, 63*(1), 106–110. https://doi.org/10.1353/csd.2022.0002

Rehman, A., & Laybourn-Langton, L. (2020). *The relationship between imperialism, racism, and the environmental crisis*. Post Carbon Institute. https://www.postcarbon.org/great-unraveling/imperialism/

Riccucci, N. M. (2022). *Critical race theory: Exploring its application to public administration*. Cambridge University Press.

Sabir, R. (2022). *The suspect: Counterterrorism, Islam and the security state*. Pluto Press.

Saeed, T. (2021). Resisting Islamophobia: Muslim youth activism in the UK. In P. Morey, A. Yaqin, & A. Forte (Eds.), *Contesting Islamophobia*. Bloomsbury.

Said, E. W. (1978). *Orientalism*. Pantheon Books.

Samatar, A. (2024). Through, around or over the gate? Navigating academia from a Black Muslim woman's perspective. In *The Black PhD experience* (pp. 57–62). Policy Press.

Samatar, A., & Sardar, Z. (2023). *Transitions: British Muslims between undergraduate and PGT studies contents.* https://www.azizfoundation.org.uk/wp-content/uploads/2024/02/British-Muslims-UPGT-FINAL-2.pdf

Samatar, A., Madriaga, M., & McGrath, L. (2021). No love found: How female students of colour negotiate and repurpose university spaces. *British Journal of Sociology of Education, 42*(5–6), 717–732. https://doi.org/10.1080/0142569 2.2021.1914548

Sardar, Z. (2021). *Intersectionality of race and religion.* [online] *Aziz Foundation.* Available at: https://www.azizfoundation.org.uk/wp-content/uploads/2024/05/Intersectionality-of-Race-Religion-Widening-Participation-Report-Zain-Sardar-final.pdf [Accessed 28 Sep. 2024].

Shimomura, F. (2023). The voice of the other in a 'liberal' ivory tower: Exploring the counterstory of an Asian international student on structural racism in US academia. *Whiteness and Education.* Ahead of print.

Solórzano, D. G., & Yosso, T. J. (2002). Critical race methodology: Counter-storytelling as an analytical framework for education research. *Qualitative Inquiry, 8*(1), 23–44.

Solorzano, D., Ceja, M., & Yosso, T. (2000). Critical race theory, racial microaggressions, and campus racial climate: The experiences of African American college students. *Journal of Negro Education,* 60–73.

Stevenson, J. (2014). Internationalisation and religious inclusion in United Kingdom higher education. *Higher Education Quarterly, 68*(1), 46–64. https://doi.org/10.1111/hequ.12033

Sue, D. W., Capodilupo, C. M., Torino, G. C., Bucceri, J. M., Holder, A., Nadal, K. L., & Esquilin, M. (2007). Racial microaggressions in everyday life: implications for clinical practice. *American Psychologist, 62*(4). https://doi.org/10.1037/0003-066X.62.4.271

Sue, D. W., Alsaidi, S., Awad, M. N., Glaeser, E., Calle, C. Z., & Mendez, N. (2019). Disarming racial microaggressions: Microintervention strategies for targets, White allies, and bystanders. *American Psychologist, 74*(1). https://doi.org/10.1037/amp0000296

The Black Story. (2021). Texturism & featurism: The nasty cousins of colourism. *The Black Story: Virtual Interactive Exhibition.* Retrieved December 29, 2023, from https://theblackstory.com/public/Resources/details/66

Trejo, J. (2020). The burden of service for faculty of colour to achieve diversity and inclusion: the minority tax. *Molecular Biology of the Cell, 31*(25), 2752–2754. https://doi.org/10.1091/mbc.E20-08-0567

UUK. (2019). Black, Asian and Minority Ethnic student attainment at UK universities: Closing the gap. *Universities UK.* Retrieved December 29, 2022, from https://www.universitiesuk.ac.uk/what-we-do/policy-and-research/publications/black-asian-and-minority-ethnic-student

UUK. (2022). Closing the gap: Three years on. *Universities UK*. Retrieved December 29, 2022, from https://www.universitiesuk.ac.uk/what-we-do/policy-and-research/publications/features/closing-gap-three-years

Weaver, M. (2018). Burqa bans, headscarves and veils: A timeline of legislation in the West. *The Guardian*. Retrieved January 5, 2023, from https://www.theguardian.com/world/2017/mar/14/headscarves-and-muslim-veil-ban-debate-timeline

West, N. M. (2019). By us, for us: The impact of a professional counterspace on African American women in student affairs. *Journal of Negro Education, 88*(2), 159–180.

West, N. M., Payne, A. N., Smith, M. D., Bonds, N. T., Alston, A. D., & Akalugwu, W. N. (2021). A collaborative autoethnography of six Black women walking tightropes in higher education. *Negro Educational Review, 72*.

Zewodle, S. (2021). Racism and othering in international higher education: Experiences of Black Africans in England. *Centre for Global Higher Education*. https://www.researchcghe.org/perch/resources/publications/working-paper-62.pdf

The Rise and Decline of Muslim Representation in Student Unions: Motivations and Experiences of Muslim Sabbatical Officers in Student Unions

Lila Tamea

INTRODUCTION AND CONTEXT

Between the academic years 2019–2021, I had the privilege of representing students as an SU sabbatical officer at a large post-92 university in the north-west of England, with a student body of over 27,000. I faced a number of challenges at that time, some relating to the intense nature of the role—particularly during the COVID-19 pandemic—but mostly due to the complexities of navigating my identity as a hijabi[1] Muslim woman in this space. It was comforting but unsurprising to discover that I was not the first, nor the last, both in my SU or nationally, to experience these

[1] The term "hijabi" refers to a hijab-wearing woman. The *hijab* is a headscarf which covers the hair and neck of the wearer.

L. Tamea (✉)
Liverpool John Moores University, Liverpool, UK
e-mail: l.a.tamea@ljmu.ac.uk

© The Author(s), under exclusive license to Springer Nature
Switzerland AG 2024
A. Mahmud, M. Islam (eds.), *Uncovering Islamophobia in Higher Education*, Palgrave Studies in Race, Inequality and Social Justice in Education, https://doi.org/10.1007/978-3-031-65253-0_4

challenges. This chapter will give an insight into these unique but shared experiences of Muslim sabbatical officers and leaders in SUs and higher education (HE).

SUs are "an association of the generality of students whose principal purposes include promoting the general interests of its members as students" (Education Act 1994, Part II, s.20). Whilst most universities in England and Wales have an SU, they are an entirely independent body to the institution. Their size and impact vary, but the majority of SUs offer between three and five full-time paid sabbatical officer roles, with a team of full and part-time staff (Smith, 2020). SUs serve a variety of functions, including facilitating student voice and representation, offering independent advice and representation, and student-led liberation and welfare campaigns (Brooks, 2014; Day & Dickinson, 2018; Smith, 2020). They also play an integral role in representing student communities through student groups, sports, societies, and voluntary liberation officers (often referred to as part-time officers) (Day & Dickinson, 2018). Sabbatical officers (also referred to as Student Officers) are full-time paid student representatives who lead an SU and are democratically elected year-on-year by the student body. Elected officer teams may look different across unions, but generally, they include a President, Vice President for Education, Vice President for Activities (often split into separate roles of Sports and Societies in some larger SUs), and Vice President for Community/Welfare (Smith, 2020). In more recent years, some SUs have introduced Liberation or Diversity officers (Smith, 2020). Most SUs are also affiliated with the National Union of Students, representing 95% of SUs and seven million students collectively (NUS, 2022).

From the start of their role, sabbatical officers are catapulted into and expected to navigate complex university systems and bureaucratic structures, learning on the job how to make positive change through diplomatic and effective leadership. By working in partnership with the university, they act as the student voice in committees and boards, locally and nationally, and are often referred to as a "critical friend" (Islam et al., 2021). However, it is common that student leaders report feelings of imposter syndrome, intimidation, and pressure from senior staff in these environments (Liyanage, 2020; Raaper, 2019; Lowe & Lowe, 2022).

EXPERIENCES OF MUSLIM SABBATICAL OFFICERS IN HIGHER EDUCATION

In this section, I will examine the key barriers facing Muslim sabbatical officers. The themes highlighted are not unique to Muslim sabbatical officers, but are also experienced by Muslim leaders and academics across institutions. Eight former sabbatical officers across seven SUs participated in semi-structured interviews for this research. In total, there were seven female and one male participant, with six out of the seven female participants wearing *Hijab*. Each interview lasted between 20–40 minutes, with three core themes:

- **Motivations**: What motivated you to nominate yourself for the role?
- **Experience**: What was your experience in the role?
- **Challenges**: Did you face any challenges in the role? If you did, what were they and how did you navigate them?

Participants came from universities across England; however, the sample was predominantly London-based, with three from outside of London—this included one from north-west and another from north-east England. This is important in understanding the context and demography of the student body, where London-based universities have a significantly higher proportion of Muslim students, which Mubarak (2007) suggests provides ethnically diverse students with more cultural affiliation and belonging. All participants were involved in other forms of student activism prior or during their role, such as the Federation of Student Islamic Societies (FOSIS) or within NUS as a delegate to a national conference or scrutiny panel. One of the participants was also previously a two-term sabbatical officer at a Further Education College. Within the sample, there was representation from Russell Group and post-92 institutions, with each sabbatical officer representing 15,000–32,000 students. Participants were assigned pseudonyms in this chapter to protect their anonymity.

Using thematic analysis (Braun & Clarke, 2022), significant common challenges were reported by all participants. This included Islamophobia—covert and overt; unfounded allegations of homophobia and/or antisemitism; disproportionate scrutiny and challenge—both during elections and in the role; and self-censorship, isolation, loneliness, lack of support, and mental health challenges as a result. A notable and unique challenge for some officers was the COVID-19 pandemic (Hedlund, 2020), but additional challenges such as poor support structures, burnout, and imposter syndrome are also known to be common amongst sabbatical officers widely (Dickenson, 2021; Scott, 2022). Imposter syndrome is a feeling of self-doubt and perceived fraudulence whilst operating in a specific context which one may be unfamiliar to (Breeze, 2018; Kennedy, 2021), where the individual doubts their legitimacy, competency, or accomplishments in that space (Pákozdy et al., 2023). For sabbatical officers, this could look like being afraid to challenge or scrutinise new or existing university policy or use a critical voice in boards or committees dominated by career academics or senior leaders. Participants also believed that these challenges were amplified due to their Muslim or racial identity.

INTERSECTIONALITY: THE MULTI-LAYERED IDENTITY OF A MUSLIM SABBATICAL OFFICER

Recognising participants' intersectional identities is important when considering the complex challenges they may face, particularly when taking into account their ethnicity, class, or gender (Crenshaw, 1991). In addition to race, gender, and class, Muslims also navigate further intersectional identities such as whether they are veiled, are considered more practising, or follow a specific sect of Islam. For Muslim veiled women, this may be seen through the "Hijab Effect", termed by Asmar et al. (2004), who found that veiled Muslim women experience more challenges at university and are less likely to feel valued or satisfied with their experience. Collin's theory of the Matrix of Domination (Collins, 2000) also allows us to understand the nature in which these institutions are increasingly more difficult to navigate when one belongs to multiple marginalised groups. The framework highlights that there is a matrix of oppression which individuals may navigate, whilst also recognising that those facing oppression can also still hold elements of privilege.

At university, it is reported that less than two-thirds of Muslim students graduate with a 2:1 or first-degree outcome (McMaster, 2020); and that they are less likely to achieve a professional job after graduating (Shaffait, 2019). In this study, *Zara*, who was a Black, first-generation hijabi from a working-class background explained that it was this stark reality that motivated her to engage in extracurricular activities as a student, where she was reticent of the challenge of potential racism, Islamophobia, or bias during graduate recruitment processes.

Thus, Day and Dickinson (2018) propose that SUs have a critical role in enhancing students' social capital, and thus, social mobility, and this was consistently recognised as one of the motivating factors for Muslim sabbatical officers nominating themselves for the role. *Lena*, another working-class Pakistani sabbatical officer, from a north-east-based post-92 University shared:

People from where I am don't go to university, that's not a thing.

She shared that witnessing the lack of representation was a key motivation for engaging in student politics:

Having people who look like you and sound like you is important. That's why I went for sabb [sabbatical officer]. There was never anyone who looked like me. There was never a South Asian—there was definitely no Muslim sabb. There was no one who represented me... They [the SU] just didn't care.

The participants shared how they feel, as a result of their time representing students, that they "*paved the way for other students from marginalised backgrounds to run for office*", demonstrating the significant positive impact of representation in these roles.

In the context of sabbatical officers, gender was cited by multiple women sabbaticals as an additional identity to navigate in the role, where most find themselves in spaces dominated by older, white middle-class men. Many experienced imposter syndrome, particularly at the start of their term, but shared that as they got more comfortable in taking up the space, this diminished. Having other Muslim colleagues or women of colour in senior management roles supporting and empowering them made a significant impact on their self-efficacy, which refers to the "judgement of one's capabilities to organise and execute courses to attain designated goals" (Bandura, 1977 in Zimmerman, 2000). In the interviews, one hijabi South Asian participant made positive reflections, referring to her relationship with her Muslim Chief Executive Officer (CEO), who played a critical and pivotal role in understanding her challenges, helping guide her, affirming her legitimacy, and empowering her through the process.

Muslims Versus "Secular" Institutions

Critical Race Theory provides a framework for analysing the systems of power and privilege in relation to race, class, and gender, but also faith in this context. It suggests that underlying assumptions, structures, and practices perpetuate racial inequality and discrimination, where we find Muslims, in particular, navigating multi-layered barriers and systems of oppression (Hiraldo, 2010).

Despite advocating for social justice and equity, universities can often further exasperate divides by failing to acknowledge the differences amongst their students. Further to this, the *habitus* of institutions show how there is a deeply embedded and dominant social culture which affects how we behave and perceive particular social circumstances (Bourdieu & Passeron, 1990). In this context, for Muslims in HE, the idea and insistence of secular campuses is one which presents a unique challenge (Stevenson, 2014; Aune & Stevenson, 2016; McMaster, 2020), where despite the positive influence faith provisions have on Muslim students and indeed the wider student body students, institutions have been historically tentative about establishing such spaces and places for discussions (Aune & Stevenson, 2016; Stevenson, 2018). Aune and Stevenson (2018) suggest it is for fear of endorsing "oppressive practices" as a result of stereotypical beliefs of Muslims—such as Islam oppressing women or that Muslims are homophobic.

In the interviews for this study, many Muslim officers reported that they felt as though, in order to push through campaigns, they had to "secularise" the ideas, principles, and rationale behind them. One such example was a Muslim officer sharing how she brought about women-only swimming sessions at her university. Instead of justifying it with the rationale that there is a large Muslim student body, and it would encourage more Muslim women to participate, she avoided labelling it as a "Muslim issue" and instead a "women's issue". This meant when it was implemented, she had to navigate additional challenges when the windows were see-through to the public. Another key example would be the way in which Muslims navigate the provision of faith spaces, where they often secularise it to "quiet spaces" as they believe universities may be more willing to accommodate other groups, such as those who are neurodiverse. This reinforces the "Good Muslim/Bad Muslim" trope termed by Mamdani (2002), whereby Muslims portray themselves as "good civilians" by minimising aspects of their faith to be accepted by the Western, secular white society. However, this only further perpetuates negative stereotypes or beliefs about Muslims, where they disguise their needs amongst secular "norms". Manzoor-Khan (2022) interestingly describes this idea of secularism as an alternative to white supremacy.

University drinking culture is also a common recurring barrier which has adverse impacts on the Muslim student experience (Hopkins, 2010; Islam et al., 2019; Tamea, 2022), where the presence of alcohol in a range of social and university environments often leads to students missing out or compromising their religious beliefs. Being a Muslim leader in an organisation which promotes drinking culture, then, was cited as a challenge by two of the Muslim sabbaticals. One talked about how her SU had "partner bars" which were agreements offering exclusive discounts for students at her university. She was asked to engage in a promotional video for them as a sabbatical officer team and despite facing no issues for declining, she described how it meant she missed out on a team activity which added to the feeling of exclusion.

Ahmad (2001) describes how this also makes students feel isolated when they prioritise aspects of their religious identity or make requests for alternative provisions. Sabbatical officers often described that it was easier to gain support for campaign ideas when they were predicated on Western, Eurocentric ideas of student wellbeing, safety, or sobriety, rather than religious belief.

Islamophobic Tropes and Identity Politics as a Muslim Sabbatical Officer

The presumption that Muslims are inherently homophobic is a common Islamophobic trope, and this is regularly weaponised to justify structural and imperial violence (Safdari, 2019). In this study, all of the sabbatical officers referenced this as a challenge, whether it was by direct allegations, or feeling singled out or watched by colleagues in and around LGBTQ+ circles and conversations for simply belonging to the faith.

Two of the participants in this study referred to their experience during SU elections. One shared how she was approached by a student who said, "*You're Muslim so you're homophobic!*" Another participant, again during the election period, was asked, "*What is your opinion on the LGBTQ+ community?*" Others described how they felt they were expected to proactively participate in festivals such as Pride, conforming to the use of pronouns or wearing rainbow laces/lanyards which they believed undermined their religious beliefs. In these kinds of liberal or progressive spaces, Muslim officers felt by not proactively participating, they were singled-out, treated differently, and/or accused of being homophobic. Many of them described feeling like they were under a "*watchful eye*", navigating a climate of suspicion, particularly in and around discussions on LGBTQ+ campaigns. They felt as though some colleagues were waiting for an opportunity to "*catch them out*".

One participant specifically shared how in her role, she was accused of homophobia by an LGBTQ+ colleague after they had expressed concerns about their performance. Prior to the accusation, the sabbatical officer and staff member had a great relationship, and the sabbatical officer described them as a trusted colleague; however, the concern was interpreted as the sabbatical officer being homophobic. The exercise of this Islamophobic trope demonstrates how easily complaints can be weaponised to reverse the scrutiny on to Muslim colleagues, who are then left vulnerable in that environment.

Similarly, a perception that Muslims cannot work on "Muslim campaigns" is something many Muslim officers were often reticent and paranoid over. Reem said, "*I've always been conscious of what I do in a position of leadership because I don't want to be always lobbying just for Muslims*"; she added, "*But if I don't work on this, who will?!*", adding, "*someone who is LGBTQ+ or has a disability would not worry if it's coming across like they're supporting their community—this would be encouraged and valued*". This perceived favouritism of secular and liberal ideas is rooted in white supremacy, as Manzoor-Khan (2022) suggests, where sabbatical officer campaigns that cater predominantly to white, non-Muslim audiences pass through with less scrutiny or challenge than a campaign for Muslim students.

Muslim students often feel compelled to compromise or negotiate their faith and identity to fit into Students' Union (SU) spaces (Mubarak, 2007; Islam et al., 2019; Islam & Mercer-Mapstone, 2021; Tamea, 2022). This is particularly evident in relation to the SU's drinking culture and the promotion of liberal secular values, which frequently clash with the religious beliefs of Muslim students. For example, Zac, a former sabbatical officer turned SU leader, pointed out that "identity politics" is a significant issue in student unions today. He observed that Muslim students, along with other religious groups, often feel uncomfortable engaging in SU activities, particularly when invited to participate in campaigns that conflict with their religious values, such as LGBTQ+ initiatives. Zac noted that students of faith frequently feel disempowered to express their beliefs, fearing accusations of homophobia or transphobia. As a result, many feel pressured to engage in activities that contradict their religious convictions. Zac's reflections suggest a perceived "hierarchy of oppression" within SUs, where, because of their religious and cultural incompetence, the rights and perspectives of religious students are not afforded the same consideration and protection as those of other marginalised groups. This was further evidenced by Reem, who was unsure how to decline an invitation to partake in a Pride campaign out of fear of being labelled homophobic. She was then photographed where she described feeling *"used as a token by the SU in future materials as the progressive Muslim woman"*.

Pro-Palestine Activism and the IHRA Definition of Antisemitism in Student Unions

Similarly, pro-Palestine activism—whether through campaigns to reject the International Holocaust Remembrance Alliance (IHRA) definition of antisemitism, Boycott, Divestment, and Sanctions (BDS) movements, or public statements—remains a contentious issue within SU spaces. Prolific Muslim activists commonly report being targeted by Zionist lobby groups, where they face intense scrutiny for their position. We can see this in the experience of Shaima Dallali, who, in November 2022, was the first NUS President to be dismissed (Shearing, 2022) after intense scrutiny from the Union of Jewish Students (UJS), NUS, and the media for comments she had made and apologised for over 10 years prior to election. After what was likely an already agonising process and investigation, Dallali learnt of her dismissal through Twitter (Dallali, 2022), after an insider of NUS had allegedly leaked it to the *Jewish Chronicle*—the largest Jewish community newspaper in the United Kingdom. Dallali was then accused by reporters of lying about not having known earlier, where she has since legally challenged and had this rectified (Dallali, 2023). This demonstrates the targeting and scrutinous climate of suspicion Muslims must endure as public representatives of their faith; another example of the perceived hierarchy of oppression whereby Muslim activists' dignity and wellbeing is compromised in favour of other protected groups.

Furthermore, the IHRA Working Definition of Antisemitism (IHRA, 2016) is a "hot topic" in HE and SU spaces (Lukman et al., 2021; Gould, 2018, 2020). Despite the author of the definition himself expressing concerns of its impact on free speech and academic freedom (Stern, 2019; Gould, 2020), many universities adopted it after the then Education Secretary, Gavin Williamson, mandated Vice Chancellors to recognise it within their institutions (Sherwood, 2021). Thus, with its adoption across many universities and SUs, pro-Palestinian sabbaticals and academics have come under investigation as a result. Throughout the interviews, Muslim sabbatical officers reportedly felt uncomfortable and unequipped to challenge the definition and were worried about being targeted or accused of antisemitism by Zionist lobby groups for their stances.

The case of Shahd Abusalama, formerly an academic at Sheffield Hallam, who faced an online smear campaign for her criticism of Israel is a notable example of the pacifying nature of the definition but also the incompetence of institutions on how to navigate it (Charrett, 2022). Zionist media targeted Abusalama, which prompted an investigation by her university. She was initially suspended but reinstated. Similarly, one of the sabbatical officers in this study faced accusations of antisemitism by another sector organisation, where they cited breach of the IHRA definition to accuse them of "unlawful antisemitism" from three historic tweets criticising Israel. This student legally challenged the organisation for its misuse of the definition, where they were successful and later reinstated into the role. Like Abusalama's case, it demonstrated that HE spaces are not equipped with the political or legal awareness to navigate the definition.

Increased Scrutiny and Hostile Environments for Muslim Sabbatical Officers

As visible representations of our faith, participants described the hostile environment they were often subjected to. This was apparent from their election to the end of their terms. Elections were noted as particularly challenging for female participants.

One participant, Zara;

Elections are twice as harder because we have to prove twice as much that we're trustworthy.

You kind of noticed the differences in how you're treated compared to white counterparts.

She then shared that she had to endure a re-election due to the number of complaints she received for having a sophisticated campaign. In the re-election, paper ballots had to be introduced and when she went to cast her vote in the box, one SU staff member said to her

[Zara]... you're not going to make us organise another re-election, are you?

Sarah also shared how she had complaints that she was "terrorising" and being "sarcastic and intimidating" to another candidate for wishing them good luck during elections, whilst no complaint was made to another white male candidate standing who also wished the same candidate "good luck". This further demonstrates the climate of scrutiny and suspicion that Muslim students navigate in this role.

In one of the interviews, Zac, who was also an advisor to NUS Presidents said:

"Muslims are expected to hold a stronger level of resilience", sharing how former female Muslim NUS President, Zamzam Ibrahim, received hate mail from America labelling her a terrorist.

In 2019, during office, she tweeted:

It doesn't matter how frequent it happens, what the context is, where it happens or who the perpetrators are. I will always be racially profiled and discriminated against. Who you are, what you've achieved and what you do will never matter.... (Ibrahim, 2019)

In another tweet, she added

The pain of being hit w/ [with] discrimination hits as hard today, as it did to 12yr old me who had her hijab ripped off! (Ibrahim, 2019)

Similar sentiments were experienced by SU sabbatical officers, who often received death threats and intimidation for their stance on wider political topics. Lena shared how she had to be escorted to and from her campus by security after campaigning for faith spaces at her union.

Sabbatical officers also shared that SU staff could not understand or navigate issues or experiences related to the Muslim student body. One participant, who previously delivered Islamophobia Awareness Training to

SUs, shared that often there was a lack of awareness or understanding from SU staff on the realities of being Muslim in HE. She shared:

> *When I delivered this training, staff were like 'what? That's what they go through?...I feel so sad. This is shocking'. I feel staff are often just ignorant to the issues we face.*

Another participant, Aleyah, shared that she felt "*pushed out*" from her SU. She said the support for Muslims is "*non-existent*", describing that this led her to resign from the role.

Many officers also reflected on the "internal politics" they had to face in their student unions. In referencing the challenges faced navigating handling both Muslim students and internal staff complexities, Zara put:

> *it's like you're fighting more within your own group than you are the actual cause.*

The Rise and Decline of Muslims in SUs

Undoubtedly, the COVID-19 pandemic, coupled with the intense scrutiny and the unprecedented suspension of a NUS President, has caused a ripple effect on Muslim engagement with SUs and the NUS.

Zac, now a deputy CEO at a London-based SU, has been active in SU spaces since 2014 and spoke about the rise and decline of Muslims engaging in leadership roles over the years. He reflected upon how, in his time as a sabbatical officer, there were only a handful of Muslims taking up sabbatical officer positions, and over the years, with the election of visible Muslim representatives at NUS, more Muslims felt empowered to engage:

> *There were only a handful of Muslims in 2013–15—very few of us. There wasn't a national body representing us or fighting for Muslim issues. Then, you had a suddenly constant presence of Muslim leaders in these national leadership roles at NUS. These guys understood us, it went from 10 to 30 to like 60–75 [Muslims sabbaticals nationally] at one point.*

He added:

> *There isn't that kind of national framework that was there when I was there. [The] COVID[-19 pandemic] interrupted national organising which encouraged Muslims to run for office....*

Reflecting on Dallali's treatment at NUS, he suggested that:

> *It's not as attractive as a role unfortunately. There's no one going 'hey, you should replicate my experience'. They don't have a national body to kind of give them the advice and support on how to navigate that. That's a huge shame.*

This highlights the positive impact of visibility and representation, but also how the opposite can have the same reverse impact.

RECOMMENDATIONS

As part of the interviews, participants made recommendations on multiple aspects of their role, both to their current and future Muslim sabbatical counterparts, and institutions like SUs and the NUS. The experience of Muslim sabbatical officers is a complex one, but by implementing some of the recommendations below, a more harmonious experience can be achieved for both Muslim sabbaticals and sector organisations.

For SUs and NUS

Implementation of Islamophobia training
Johnson and Lollar (2002) suggest that diversity education plays a foundational role in a democracy by equipping students for meaningful participation. The implementation of Islamophobia Awareness Training as well as other types of Racial Literacy training are essential in creating safe spaces for staff to engage in often contentious issues. In this chapter, it was noted how one of the barriers for Muslims in SUs is how staff are often unaware of the exclusionary effects of their lack of awareness or competence on "Muslim" issues. Linking to this, many Muslim students often felt excluded or as if they did not feel part of a team because their colleagues did not understand them, so encouraging safe spaces for dialogue and debate for Muslims and non-Muslims in SUs via training is key to bridging this.

Culturally Sensitive and Mental Health and Wellbeing Support
SUs need to be aware of the often isolating experience of being a Muslim or racialised minority in this space. Many Muslim officers reported feeling lonely and excluded due to a lack of understanding of how faith impacts their role. SUs should consider recommending and resourcing

appropriate mental health support such as counselling or therapy for officers with Muslim professionals in these fields.

Facilitate or establish Muslim Sabbatical Officer Networks
Many officers also reported the therapeutic effect of being part of Muslim sabbatical officer networks due to the collective solidarity and understanding they felt. There were feelings that since COVID-19, the presence of these officer networks had diminished. SUs and NUS should be aware of or support the facilitation of Muslim Sabbatical Officer Networks, as well as other student community networks.

Listen to your sabbatical officers
Many participants reported feeling "gaslit" by various colleagues who often denied their lived experiences. Often, they described situations escalating and impacting their mental health, which could have been preventable if their SU leadership had taken action earlier. A common example is when they receive false complaints of homophobia or antisemitism or feel as though they are dealing with disproportionate amounts of scrutiny and challenge from students or colleagues on their campaigns. Listening to them, validating their challenges, and working with them to resolve these issues is key to facilitating a safe space for them.

Muslim representation in SU Senior Leadership
One of the key challenges reported was how Muslims are often fighting internal battles within their SUs. However, where Muslim sabbatical officers had Muslim senior leaders in their teams, they shared more optimistic reflections in their role. This was due to feeling understood, not having to explain barriers or ask for advice on how to deal with "Muslim issues". Whilst it would be unrealistic to suggest recruiting Muslims into senior leadership at every SU, the sentiment of culturally and religiously competent leaders and having safe spaces for dialogue creates a more positive experience for those in SUs.

For Muslim Sabbatical Officers

Communicate your boundaries early
Many participants expressed the importance of Muslim officers having the space to be their full authentic "Muslim self" and not compromise on their core beliefs to fit into the role. This meant communicating their boundaries early on, such as needing to pray during the work day or that they will not plan or attend social events which revolve around drinking.

Find your network

One participant noted that *"if there isn't a group, make one—don't wait for a national body like NUS or FOSIS to organise it"*. Other ways could be engaging in internal staff networks at your university, for example, ethnically diverse staff networks.

Practising self-care

Participants reflected on the pressure they felt from various stakeholders in their roles—the student body, the university, their SU staff, but also the Muslim community and themselves. Many participants, particularly Muslim veiled women, had a desire to "prove" themselves in the role, smash glass ceilings, and break the stereotypes. Participants were generally aware of the time constraints in the role—being in office for 12–24 months, which meant they worked themselves until burnout. Ultimately to be effective in the role, you need to take the time to recharge and refocus.

CONCLUSION

The role of a sabbatical officer is an incredible opportunity but a challenging one—it provides students with the ability to gain unique new skills and develop their careers. However, for Muslim sabbaticals, it can also be a time of isolation and trauma, with minimal support. Whilst the opportunities within universities are "open to all", it does not mean that they are accessible to all (Mercer-Mapstone & Bovill, 2019), and we have seen that in the context of SUs. This suggests further work is needed to level the playing field for Muslim students.

Whilst this chapter reveals inequalities for Muslims in SUs, many who have engaged with SUs recognise the benefits on their development and career prospects. Muslim representation over the years has had a significant impact in empowering other marginalised communities to run for office, but we have seen how the reverse can also have the same effect, with the decline of Muslim students taking up these elected sabbatical officer positions. Whilst a number of factors have contributed to this, recent events only illustrate the hostile environment Muslim sabbatical officers have to endure, where the role is no longer seen as attractive. By committing to tackling Islamophobia, challenging this (perceived) hierarchy of racism, and listening to Muslim students and sabbatical officers' experiences, universities and sector representative bodies can create a more inclusive and positive space for Muslims to engage and thrive.

References

Ahmad, F. (2001). Modern traditions? British Muslim women and academic achievement. *Gender and Education*, *13*(2), 137–152. https://doi.org/10.1080/09540250120051169

Asmar, C., Proude, E., & Inge, L. (2004). 'Unwelcome Sisters?' An analysis of findings from a study of how Muslim women (and Muslim Men) experience University. *Australian Journal of Education*, *48*(1), 47–63. https://doi.org/10.1177/000494410404800104

Aune, K., & Stevenson, J. (2016). How religion or belief frame participation and access in UK higher education. In *Religion and higher education in Europe and North America* (pp. 39–54). Routledge.

Bandura, A. (1977). Self-efficacy: Toward a unifying theory of behavioral change. *Psychological Review*, *84*(2), 191–215. https://doi.org/10.1037/0033-295X.84.2.191

Bourdieu, P., & Passeron, J. C. (1990). *Reproduction in education, society and culture*. Sage Publications.

Braun, V., & Clarke, V. (2022). Conceptual and design thinking for thematic analysis. *Qualitative Psychology*, *9*(1), 3–26. https://doi.org/10.1037/qup0000196

Breeze, M. (2018). Imposter Syndrome as a Public Feeling. Feeling Academic in the Neoliberal University, [online] pp. 191–219. https://doi.org/10.1007/978-3-319-64224-6_9.

Brooks, R. (2014). What role do students' unions play in today's HE system? *What role do students' unions play in today's HE system?* Retrieved June 10, 2023, from https://blogs.surrey.ac.uk/sociology/2014/08/20/what-role-do-students-unions-play-in-todays-he-system/

Charrett, C. C. (2022). *How a Palestinian academic defeated a campaign to silence her*. [Online] www.aljazeera.com. Retrieved June 20, 2023, from https://www.aljazeera.com/opinions/2022/2/10/how-a-palestinian-academic-defeated-a-campaign-to-silence-her

Collins, P. H. (2000). *Black feminist thought: Knowledge, consciousness, and the politics of empowerment*. Routledge.

Crenshaw, K. (1991). Mapping the Margins: Intersectionality, Identity Politics, and Violence against Women of Color. Stanford Law Review, [online] 43(6), pp. 1241–1299. Available at: https://www.jstor.org/stable/1229039.

Dallali, S. (2022). *NUS President dismissed via Twitter*. [online] Twitter. Retrieved March 10, 2023, from https://twitter.com/ShaimaDallali/status/1587498159357427712?ref_src=twsrc%5Etfw%7Ctwcamp%5Etweetembed%7Ctwterm%5E1587498159357427712%7Ctwgr%5E4c684944c07db9b360a3eacfb54580088be640e5%7Ctwcon%5Es1_&ref_url=https%3A%2F%2Fwww.lbc.co.uk%2Fnews%2Fshaima-dallali-nus-sacked-anti-semitism-investigation%2F

Dallali, S. (2023). *Jewish Chronicle corrected their article and removed a quote from a NUS source*. [Online] Twitter. Retrieved March 10, 2023, from https://twitter.com/ShaimaDallali/status/1616480734058774538

Day, M., & Dickinson, J. (2018). *David versus Goliath: The past, present and future of students' unions in the UK*. [Online]. https://www.hepi.ac.uk/wp-content/uploads/2018/09/HEPI-Students-Unions-Report-111-FINAL-EMBARGOED1-1.pdf

Dickenson, J. (2021). We need to talk about sabbatical burnout. Retrieved June 7, 2023, from https://wonkhe.com/blogs-sus/we-need-to-talk-about-sabbatical-burnout/

Education Act 1994 (Part II). https://www.legislation.gov.uk/ukpga/1994/30/part/II

Gould, R. R. (2018). Legal form and legal legitimacy: The IHRA definition of antisemitism as a case study in censored speech. *Law, Culture and the Humanities, 18*(1), 153–186. https://doi.org/10.1177/1743872118780660

Gould, R. R. (2020). The IHRA definition of antisemitism: Defining antisemitism by erasing palestinians. *The Political Quarterly, 91*(4). https://doi.org/10.1111/1467-923x.12883

Hailu, M., Collins, L., & Stanton, A. (2018). Inclusion and safe-spaces for dialogue: Analysis of Muslim students. *Journal of Comparative and International Higher Education*. [Online] 10. https://files.eric.ed.gov/fulltext/EJ1233249.pdf

Hedlund, A. (2020). *Induction in disruption – Becoming a sabbatical officer in 2020*. [Online]. www.qaa.ac.uk. Retrieved June 16, 2023, from https://www.qaa.ac.uk/scotland/news-events/blog/induction-in-disruption-becoming-a-sabbatical-officer-in-2020

Hiraldo, P. (2010). The role of critical race theory in higher education. *The Vermont Connection* [Online] *31*(7): 7. https://scholarworks.uvm.edu/cgi/viewcontent.cgi?article=1092&context=tvc

Hopkins, P. (2010). Towards critical geographies of the university campus: understanding the contested experiences of Muslim students. *Transactions of the Institute of British Geographers, 36*(1), pp. 157–169. https://doi.org/10.1111/j.1475-5661.2010.00407.x.

Ibrahim, Z. (2019). *It doesn't matter how frequent it happens, what the context is, where it happens or who the perpetrators are...* [Online] Twitter. Retrieved June 23, 2023, from https://twitter.com/ZamzamMCR/status/1159087704275116032

International Holocaust Remembrance Alliance (IHRA). (2016). *Working definition of antisemitism*. [Online] IHRA. https://www.holocaustremembrance.com/resources/working-definitions-charters/working-definition-antisemitism

Islam, M., Burnett, T.-L., & Collins, S.-L. (2021). Trilateral partnership: An institution and students' union collaborative partnership project to support underrepresented student groups. *International Journal for Students as Partners*, 5(1), 76–85. https://doi.org/10.15173/ijsap.v5i1.4455

Islam, M., Lowe, T., & Jones, G. (2019). A 'satisfied settling'? Investigating a sense of belonging for Muslim students in a UK small-medium Higher Education Institution. *Student Engagement in Higher Education Journal*, 2(2).

Islam, M., & Mercer-Mapstone, L. (2021). 'University is a non-Muslim experience, you know? The experience is as good as it can be': Satisfied settling in Muslim students' experiences and implications for Muslim student voice. *British Educational Research Journal*, 47(5), 1388–1415. https://doi.org/10.1002/berj.3733

Johnson, S. M., & Lollar, X. L. (2002). Diversity policy in higher education: The impact of college students' exposure to diversity on cultural awareness and political participation. *Journal of Education Policy*, 17(3), 305–320. https://doi.org/10.1080/02680930210127577

Kennedy, C. (2021). *An interpretive approach to understanding the impostor phenomenon over time – ProQuest*. [Online]. www.proquest.com. Retrieved June 10, 2023, from https://www.proquest.com/openview/91861cc33d5b38473 df0c1f26f6c7b3d/1?pq-origsite=gscholar&cbl=18750&diss=y&casa_token=-5zcolFNWBwAAAAA:7wpENiouBDUa69UVYITkHjSCETohtMKm6NatXA 6oCR0PWz3pYJOjJqfl0KLvKanrVfD_frhRJA

Liyanage, M. (2020). *Miseducation: Decolonising curricula, culture and pedagogy in UK universities*. [Online] HEPI. Retrieved February 8, 2023, from https://www.hepi.ac.uk/2020/07/23/miseducation-decolonising-curricula-culture-and-pedagogy-in-uk-universities/

Lowe, C., & Lowe, T. (2022). All Ireland Journal of Teaching and Learning in Higher Education (AISHE-J) Creative Commons Attribution-NonCommercial-ShareAlike 3.0. *AISHE-J*, [Online] 14(1). Retrieved June 16, 2023, from https://api.repository.cam.ac.uk/server/api/core/bitstreams/1f176b83-3801-4082-ac50-82b466661d97/content

Lukman, G. A., Sharif, O., Scott-Cracknell, M., Smith, S., & Walton, J. (2021). *Defining antisemitism on UK campuses: Lived experiences of the IHRA definition Defining antisemitism on UK campuses: lived experiences of the IHRA definition ACKNOWLEDGEMENTS*. [Online] Balfour Project. https://balfourproject.org/bp/wp-content/uploads/2021/10/BR-IHRA-Report-2021-NEW-FINAL.pdf

Mamdani, M. (2002). Good Muslim, Bad Muslim: A political perspective on culture and terrorism. *American Anthropologist*, 104(3), 766–775. https://doi.org/10.1525/aa.2002.104.3.766

Manzoor-Khan, S. (2022). *Tangled in terror: Uprooting Islamophobia*. Pluto Press.

McMaster, C. N. (2020). *Research insight: Religion and belief in UK higher education.* [Online] *Advance-HE.* www.advance-he.ac.uk/knowledge-hub/research-insight-religion-and-belief-ukhigher-education

Mercer-Mapstone, L., & Bovill, C. (2019). Equity and diversity in institutional approaches to student–staff partnership schemes in higher education. *Studies in Higher Education, 45*(2), 1–17. https://doi.org/10.1080/03075079.2019.1620721

Mubarak, H. (2007). How Muslim students negotiate their religious identity and practices in an undergraduate setting. *Social Science Research Council.*

National Union of Students (NUS). (2018). *The experience of Muslim students in 2017–18.* [Online]. www.nusconnect.org.uk/resources/the-experience-of-muslim-students-in-2017-18

NUS. (2022). *Become a member.* [Online] NUS UK. Retrieved June 20, 2023, from https://www.nus.org.uk/members#:~:text=NUS%20is%20a%20confederate%20association

Pákozdy, C., Askew, J., Dyer, J., Gately, P., Martin, L., Mavor, K. I., & Brown, G. R. (2023). The imposter phenomenon and its relationship with self-efficacy, perfectionism and happiness in university students. *Current Psychology.* https://doi.org/10.1007/s12144-023-04672-4

Raaper, R. (2019). Constructing political subjectivity: The perspectives of sabbatical officers from English students' unions. *Higher Education, 79*(1), 141–157. https://doi.org/10.1007/s10734-019-00400-9

Safdari, N. (2019). The sensationalization of the 'Homophobic Muslim': Tracing the roots of islamophobia and homophobia. *Oregon Undergraduate Research Journal, 15*(1), 34–42. https://doi.org/10.5399/uo/ourj.15.1.5

Scott, L. (2022). A practical guide to handling sabbatical officer burnout. Retrieved June 7, 2023, from https://wonkhe.com/blogs-sus/a-practical-guide-to-handling-sabbatical-officer-burnout/

Shaffait, H. (2019). *Inclusivity at university Muslim student experiences.* [Online]. https://www.kcl.ac.uk/geography/assets/kcl-sspp-muslim-policy-report-digital-aw.pdf

Shearing, H. (2022). NUS president dismissed over anti-Semitism claims. *BBC News.* [Online], November 1. Retrieved March 10, 2023, from https://www.bbc.co.uk/news/education-63477692

Sherwood, H. (2021). Williamson wrong to force universities to abide by anti-semitism definition, say lawyers. *The Guardian.* [Online], January 7. Retrieved March 10, 2023, from https://www.theguardian.com/politics/2021/jan/07/williamson-wrong-to-force-universities-to-abide-by-antisemitism-definition-say-lawyers

Smith, N. (2020). *SU officer roles research.* https://wonkhe.com/wp-content/wonkhe-uploads/2020/10/SU-Officer-Roles-Research-2020.pdf, Wonkhe, pp. 1–12.

Stern, K. (2019). I drafted the definition of antisemitism. Rightwing Jews are weaponizing it. *The Guardian*. [Online], December 13.

Stevenson, J. (2013). Discourses of inclusion and exclusion: Religious students in UK higher education. *Widening Participation and Lifelong Learning, 14*(3), 27–43.

Stevenson, J. (2014). Internationalisation and religious inclusion in United Kingdom higher education. *Higher Education Quarterly, 68*(1), 46–64. https://doi.org/10.1111/hequ.12033

Stevenson, J. (2018). Report: Muslim Students in UK Higher Education: Inequality and Inequity. Muslim Students in UK Higher Education. [online] Available at: https://www.azizfoundation.org.uk/wp-content/uploads/2024/03/Bridge-Higher-Education-report-2.pdf.

Tamea, L. (2022). *The Muslim student experience: How Muslims negotiate barriers in higher education*. Masters dissertation.

Zimmerman, B. J. (2000). Self-efficacy: An essential motive to learn. *Contemporary Educational Psychology, 25*(1), 82–91. https://doi.org/10.1006/ceps.1999.1016

CHAPTER 5

The Contested Phenomenon: Intersectional Identities

Fatema Khatun

BISMILLAH (بسم الله) THE BEGINNINGS

This Arabic phrasing means "in the name of Allah", which is also the first word in the Qur'an, and refers to the Qur'an's opening phrase, the Basmala. More frequently, it is used as an invocation used by Muslims at the beginning of an undertaking. Thus, I start my chapter in a similar fashion under the guidance of Allah. I attempt to present, in sometimes painfully polemic coherency, how Islamophobia inhabits UK Higher Education (HE) through the particular lens of being a British Asian female Muslim lecturer, researcher, and student.

Since starting my PhD in late 2019, I have become concerned, obsessed even, with "arrivals". Ahmed (2019) explores arrivals as pivotal points in our narrations. To fully comprehend our experiences, one must attempt to understand their arrival during journeys and the discourse of "choices" which has brought them to supposedly unfamiliar institutions of higher learning. Therefore, using a reflexive approach, this chapter will discuss

F. Khatun (✉)
Aston University, Birmingham, UK
e-mail: khatunf1@aston.ac.uk

A. Mahmud, M. Islam (eds.), *Uncovering Islamophobia in Higher Education*, Palgrave Studies in Race, Inequality and Social Justice in Education, https://doi.org/10.1007/978-3-031-65253-0_5

77

how my entry into different parts of HE has been shaped by constrained choices. In this chapter, I will include excerpts from one of my entry points into the UK HE landscape as a Muslim lecturer, examining how visible Muslim-ness has complicated my professional identity and reflecting upon the increased marketisation of identity to explore my sense of belonging. Using Lather's (1991a, 1991b) notion of reflexivity as requiring a sincere attempt to deconstruct one's own work and the motives behind it, I start this chapter with an exploration of such an arrival into the HE system; not my first, not my last, but a significant arrival, nonetheless.

But first, I must preface the significance of this arrival by stating I am a British-born, third-generation Asian, Muslim woman, hijab-wearing, first of my immediate family to go to university, first in the extended family to successfully complete a Master's degree and the first to explain to my grandmother what a Doctor of Philosophy means. In this exploration, I discuss my positionality as a working-class British Muslim woman researcher who is affiliated with an inner-city university, teaching and researching British Muslim female students. Leistyna (2004, p. 21) argues that "my locality necessarily conditions me to ask certain questions .... However, even within the limits of my position, and under historical and cultural influences, my job as a learner is to connect it to the rest of the world". As Manzoor-Khan (2022, p. 1) effectively points out Islamophobia "does not exist because of the lack of laws against it, or the lack of Muslim MPs and peers", rather, Islamophobia continues to haunt global believers of Islam because superficial solutions such as the focus on banal numerical data keep conversations about Islamophobia away from addressing its historical roots and structural causes in the UK HE landscape.

For example, former Prime Minister Boris Johnson, during his time as Foreign Secretary made a jibe referring to Muslim women (2018). He claimed that Muslim students who wear burkas were letterboxes, stating universities should be entitled to tell students to remove a veil if a student "turns up ... looking like a bank robber" (Zempi, 2019). An organisation which provides support against Islamophobia and anti-Muslim crimes reported "a significant spike in anti-Muslim attacks ... and recorded a total of 57 incidents in the three weeks following the comment, of which 22 were directed at visibly identifiable Muslim women" (Tell MAMA, 2018). The overarching representations of Muslim women in media and politics have created images evoking either pity or a sense of impending danger and, consequently, any middle space between these extremes is not acknowledged. Mainstream Western media creates an image of perpetually distressed and suffering women, leaving behind a discouraging narrative regarding the agency of women who practice Islam (Mastro, 2016). Muslim women of all races are continually targeted, especially those who display visible markers of faith such as the hijab. One can state that discrimination against Muslim women operates in numerous domains, and it targets our religious and racialised belonging (Mescoli, 2020).

I present in this chapter, a view of an insider position of Islamophobia as the outcome of colonial histories dominated by "unseen and unrecognised white supremacy" (Dyer, 1997). This chapter highlights the complicated transactional quality of diverse identities in a space of global capitalism which is mirrored in the HE space. In the following sections, I will explore how the neoliberalised UK HE system has changed expectations regarding equality, diversity, and inclusion (EDI) policies and practices with direct emphasis on Islamophobia and visible Muslim-ness which are reflective of other globalisation movements which have effectively sought to position Islam and its believers as "the other" (Said, 1978). Through personal reflections, I seek to explore how "a racialised episteme" of Islamophobia is interrupted or disorientated (Puwar, 2004, p. 42) by my very presence in a HE institution.

With all this in mind, I return to my arrival into a new higher education space. As a newly qualified teacher and now researcher, I look forward to my interview at the local university. Through various established networks, word of mouth, and what I still believe to be a stroke of good fortune, I sat in front of the department head. They lean forward, their glasses now resting precariously on the bridge of their nose,

" *I've heard good things about you*". I beam with a sense of pride at the praise.
    "*It will be good for our students to have someone who looks like them at the front of the class*".

This became a pivotal point in understanding my sense of belonging in a higher education institution.

On Being a Role Model: Performing the Perfect Muslim

While initially excited by the prospect of a "real" lecturing job, I found myself sitting on the periphery, as something which is radically outside of the normalised experience of higher education; invariably continuing to position me as exceptional in the institution. While the world moves on and new ideas develop, the discourse in relation to Islam and Muslim women is reminiscent of ideas from 20 years ago (Törnberg & Törnberg, 2016). Scholarship on young Muslim women in higher education in Western countries has concentrated on the educational achievements and career aspirations of young British Muslim women of South Asian backgrounds (see: Ahmad, 2001; Bagguley & Hussain, 2007; Bhopal, 2016, 2017; Dwyer & Shah, 2009; Mellor, 2011; Takhar, 2016). While these studies highlight an increasing number of young South Asian women in HE and demonstrate that they have invested heavily in education and shown determination to overcome institutional and cultural obstacles to realise their educational achievements, there are little explorations of the space these Muslim women occupy in HE or how the transition to other roles in academia have played out.

Going forward, I will draw an analysis of my understanding of the reflexivity of discomfort (Hamdan, 2010), which has multiple and intersecting facets. The arguments I present do not exist as separate entities, rather a complicated nexus of historical, geographical, and financial structures that interact with my identity as a Muslim woman in different intersectional ways. For example, the Muslim population is 3.87 million, or 6.5% of the total in England and Wales. About 5% of 16–24-year-old Muslims are British-born and 76% are UK citizens. The majority of the Muslim population identifies as "South Asian", consisting predominantly of Bangladeshi, Pakistani, Afghani, and Indian second-generation citizens; however, diversity amongst Muslim ethnicities in the United Kingdom is said to be rising (Muslim Council of Britain, 2022).

Despite the rising population, there are four persistent stereotypes that crop up in discussions around the Muslim communities of the United Kingdom, which collectively view the community as misogynistic, violent/cruel, strange, or different (Whitaker, 2002), and, most importantly, male. For female believers of Islam, identity has always been riddled with a greater sense of confusion often brought on by other people's ideas of what a Muslim woman is supposed to be (Jussawalla et al., 2023). Assumptions about the presupposed constrictions of tradition, culture, and faith intermingled with the expectations of greater society to integrate and assimilate have created varying stereotypes of the Muslim woman. Indeed, as noted by many scholars, the position of Muslim women in a given society is used as a barometer to establish the stark difference between the alleged orthodoxy of Muslim societies and the democratic practices of the West (Bano, 2017; Seedat, 2013). In order to be taken seriously in either sphere (as a feminist or as a Muslim), many in Western audiences require that she reject one of the two as unjust (Mastro, 2016). Working in such contentious entanglements, I feel that my students and I are being coerced into cohabiting cooperatively in UK HE.

While exploring intersectional Islamophobia, my aim is not to demystify the rationale or the expectations of Muslim women in HE who choose to wear the hijab, rather, I attempt to offer a more nuanced approach of how marketised diversity and the colonial white male gaze pigeonholes identities of a working-class Muslim female lecturer.

Contrary to what we are presented with, there is not one type of Muslim woman but there is a certain visibility attached to "uber-cool, trendy Hijabis" (Bakkar, 2019) of which I discovered I embodied when I became a lecturer. It became apparent during my arrival into HE spaces as a lecturer I was considered to represent a specific version of the Muslim woman which was desirable for the department. This trendy Hijabi is presented as an identity encompassing both faith and capitalist modernity, with little to no conflict in this amalgamation. With this accepted archetype of what an acceptable Muslim woman in HE embodies, our choices and voices are reduced to perpetuate the same narrative presented to us. This presented narrative is not from the point of view of Muslim women but from the point of view of the somatic norm. The "somatic norm", defined by Puwar (2001) is the body which is separate from the mind and considered universally neutral and professional—oftentimes the domain for white middle-class men. Thus, our choices become reduced, including how we are expected to navigate the HE space and the very ways we discuss our faith. As a member of a minority in UK HE, I have "terms and conditions" attached to my free speech (Abdel-Magied, 2017). Rendered as the educated "liberated", feminist Muslim role model remains beneficial in a marketised system which I will discuss further but for now I want to draw attention to why she, the trendy Hijabi, became such an important figure in HE.

At the time of writing, the Black, Asian and minority ethnic (BAME) degree awarding gap in UK HE institutions remains between 13% and 20% which means minoritised students, including Muslim students, are less likely to achieve a first- or upper-second-class degree when compared to their white counterparts (OfS, 2018). The potential explanatory factors identified by HEFCE, now Office for Students (the regulator of English higher education), include "curricula and learning", "staff and student relationships", and "social, economic and cultural capital" (Wong et al., 2021; Arday & Mirza, 2018).

Furthermore, Stevenson (2014) observes that there is a scarcity of academic literature exploring the experiences of religious students in HE, despite data highlighting a need to examine different parts of student identity. She argues that even though religion plays a large part in forming culture, it is rarely ascribed any value (Stevenson, 2014). So as part of a wider EDI initiative, some institutions began exploring possibilities of hiring non-white staff in the hopes it would mitigate and improve inter-staff–student relationships, particularly in post-92 universities with higher proportions of BAME students (Noden et al., 2014). The idea of representation, through visible bodies, is sold to students as the holy grail of acceptance, solidifying this notion of "if they can do it, I can". Thus, my role as lecturer becomes more about creating a greater sense of belonging while still adhering to the marketised terms and conditions of representing a very specific university experience.

Additionally, what this approach has done is effectively placed a greater burden upon the shoulders of non-white lecturers to perform additional duties. Staff involvement with minority students falls into three main behavioural categories: mentoring, role modelling, and advocating for minority students (Arment et al., 2013; Cole, 2008). As a result, my role becomes a position of entering into personal pastoral relationships with students to serve as a "positive" role model and also attempting to interact with other staff and administrators to work on improving the support and resources for my students. To summarise, despite the growing support available for Muslim and minoritised students, universities have failed to provide students with substantive experiences for people like them (Khatun et al., 2021). Oftentimes relying on carefully curated marketised imagery and certain appearances such as the hijab to promote diversity, universities have rendered Muslim women and their actual needs invisible.

This brings me to my next problem. Although I was considered the embodiment of acceptable archetype of Muslim-ness and a proud wearer of the hijab, I was still met by "the look". Puwar (2004) explains that the white gaze often referred innocuously as "the look" by global majority students is in fact the direct result of being space invaders. This means that certain places such as HE institutions, with all their privileges, have often remained reserved for the heteronormative middle-class white male academic, including the very lecture rooms I now occupy. In addition to previous years of physical reservations, we now find ourselves moving into a psycho-social reservation of spaces which are often more tacit in their approach; sometimes only tangible through "a look". The claim Muslim women make on institutions by occupying spaces they are not expected to be in is constantly challenged by "a look" which abnormalises their presence and locates them using racialised frameworks as belonging elsewhere. Therefore, despite my legitimate invitation into the HE space as an "equal" (Puwar, 2004), the expectations remain of those bodies to take up alternative rhythms of occupation in this space. This challenges the ways Muslim women have been categorised, fixed, and rendered hyper-visible yet invisible.

Whiteness, as it seems, is inescapable. It seems to be everywhere (Ahmed, 2007). It has become commonplace for whiteness to be represented as invisible, unmarked, or the unmarked against which all other colours are marked and measured as forms of "deviance" (Ahmed, 2007). Puwar (2004) notes that as different identities are fixed by the white gaze, the white gaze is also disorientated by the close proximity of these foreign bodies. Most importantly, the construction of "other" has been fixed in opposition to the self and this image is disturbed with black/brown bodies; order becomes chaos. "A racialised episteme is interrupted" or disorientated (Puwar, 2004, p. 42). By the very nature of our being, myself and other Muslim women in the HE space are deviant in every sense of the way. However, this deviancy has not gone unnoticed, and in the following section I will explore how "neoliberal brand culture that authorises a commodification and marketing of 'diversity' has … heightened popular visibility" in HE (Banet-Weiser & Glatt, 2023).

MARKETISATION OF MULTICULTURALISM

EDI initiatives, by and large, have been reduced to performative measures. EDI is treated as a selling point for institutions and quality markers such as Teaching Excellence Framework (TEF) and Research Excellence Framework (REF) which reflect how educational policies in the United Kingdom have focused on marketisation, new public managerialism, and performativity (see: Ball, 2012). Despite strong rhetorical commitments for equality and diversity, there is a prevalence of deficit labels such as "BAME" and "minority students" which has created marginalised rhetoric that removes Muslim students from the traditional experience.

The government has made claims that there are aims to increase the numbers of students from BAME backgrounds entering HE by 20% (Connell-Smith & Hubble, 2018). However, as the literature has demonstrated previously, minority ethnic students are better represented in the post-92 HE institutions, in more vocationally oriented courses (Brennan & Shah, 2003). The deficit model attached to minoritised students is further consolidated by student choice fallacy (Callender & Dougherty, 2018; Ball et al., 2002). As part of the marketing mechanism, students are enticed by a wealth of choices; however, in reality only a select few of those choices are recognisably suitable for different students (see: Ball et al., 2002). Neoliberal marketisation in higher education has encouraged universities to embrace a particular version of diversity. Archer (2007) also argues that these constructions of diversity derive an important element of their symbolic power from an association with notions of "democratisation", "equality", and "fairness". However, I argue that in practice, marketised EDI has been used to increase numbers with little thought given to the different pedagogical and learner support a diverse student body might bring with it (French, 2013) and one that is emptied of political and cultural significance and made palatable for a consumer marketplace (Banet-Weiser & Glatt, 2023).

A central critique of this chapter is how the term "diversity" operates within institutions. Ahmed (2012) explains how the attention to diversity has led to the term "diversity" being used on its own or with the term "equality", such that people increasingly talk about doing "E & D" work. EDI work becomes embodied through paperwork and policies. Thus, our bodies become a performance indicator, a tick in a box. The nature of diversity data as a means of becoming more marketable becomes an arduous process for different bodies. Universities and other regulatory bodies are apt at collecting EDI data; however, the process for committing to change or policies are often too slow. The enactment of policy making works to enhance the reputation of HEIs and provides a smokescreen of conformity which gives the illusion of addressing racial disadvantages (Bhopal & Pitkin, 2020). As a result, sluggish top-down approaches to bureaucracy overshadow the lived experiences of different minoritised students, making it harder to express any ideas regarding change.

Furthermore, marketing campaigns with visual images of "happy colourful faces as a visual translation of the multicultural mosaic" (Ahmed & Swan, 2006) often forget the work and difficulties required to fit all the pieces of the mosaic together. Multiculturalism features in scholarly work and political commentaries as a contested and blurred term. It has been referred to as a state or ideological concept that includes top-down policies and political spin (Andreouli & Howarth, 2013) and cultural plurality itself (Gilroy, 2005). However, multiculturalism is generally referred to as a political and policy response to govern and manage multi-ethnicity created by immigrant populations, an issue of "managing" and responding to diversity (Ahmed, 2009). This consolidates Puwar's (2004) observations that the inclusion of people who look different, or "diverse", is a mechanism which allows whiteness of the institution to remain concealed. Multicultural marketing has at best created a sense of "satisfied settling" (Islam et al., 2018), whereby students have (unconsciously) accepted not having access to a richer and more fulfilled university experience in relation to religious needs despite other Muslim bodies being represented in marketing campaigns. As a result, intersectional identities become reductive—a dangerous mechanism of being seen but not heard. "My feminism will be intersectional, or it will be bullshit" (Dzodan, 2011)—the central component of this chapter and popularised internet catchphrase begins to illuminate some of the issues faced when identity and EDI becomes a marketing metric. Ironically, the catchphrase allowed global capitalism and marketised diversity to erase the very thing Dzodan was fighting for—the voices of marginalised female communities. Janmohamed (2016, p. 11) offers the perspective of the modernised Muslim—Generation M who "engage in all aspects of modernity through the lens of faith", drawing on experiences such as readily available halal food to designer brand hijabs. According to this interpretation, despite increased scrutiny of Islam, there is minimal conflict of identity in this approach. However, the increased popularity of modernised Muslim believers conceals much of the hard work required in creating a more just society. In this interpretation, Generation M is a relatively elite group, but disproportionately influential. They are generally young, middle-class and—crucial to Janmohammed's (Janmohamed, 2016) argument—wield huge spending power, contributing greatly to the global economy. One could argue that Muslim-ness is accepted in HE, but only when it offers large sums of financial contribution, which effectively marginalises the working-class students in inner-city universities.

THE CONTESTED PHENOMENON: AN OBSCENE DEVIANT

In this section, I explore some of the philosophical underpinnings of space and highlight the importance to the Muslim woman in HE. For Lefebvre (2001), "representations of space" are the means by which ideology and knowledge are combined in a social-spatial practice which locates and reinforces a culture's social power. In de Certeau's (1984) social geography, power relations define these social spaces, while social places are where these power relations have been settled in favour of one way of viewing the world. In HE, spaces are governed and defined by the somatic norm/white man. Even without the physical presence of the somatic norm, lecture spaces are constructed with this default in mind. This means that even in lecture rooms, spaces with a far higher concentration of minoritised or Muslim students still remain marginalised or on the periphery. Therefore, despite UK policies to widen access and participation (see: Crawford et al., 2016; Boliver, 2013; Bowes et al., 2015; Broecke & Hamed, 2008) for Muslim students, the tacit psycho-social reservation provides some students with a hidden legitimacy that me and my students simply cannot afford. In addition to this lack of affordance, there is a keen awareness amongst Muslim students that this form of belonging and legitimacy is not provided to them (Stevenson, 2014). As noted by Reay et al. (2009), there is a general distrust of hegemonic constructions of knowledge by disenfranchised groups. Despite this, students often feel a desire to fit into an institutional habitus. Ahmed (2006, p. 3) further points out, for some, being a student at a university feels as comfortable as a pair of slippers—it is not "just that bodies are moved by the orientation they have; the orientations we have towards others shape the contours of space" by affecting relations of proximity and distance between bodies which changes our sense of belonging drastically. Lefebvre (2001) also states that monumental space offers each member of a society an image of that membership, an image of his or her social visage, for example, through student marketing materials or statues. Puwar (2004) expands on Lefebvre's thinking by "suggesting that monumental spaces operate as a means of separating the sacred from the profane and repressing those ... Which are not prescribed by monumental space" (Lefebvre, 2001, p. 226). This brings us to a contradiction—it is evident that universities have spent time and money on marketing material that monuments or showcases different identities but in the sacred spaces of HE learning they are to be repressed or "in short ... banished as the obscene" (Lefebvre, 2001, p. 226). While students of different minority ethnic backgrounds are encouraged to partake in HE, their identity as a Muslim believer is considered obscene in this seemingly secular system, evidenced in the pathologising of Islam and their Muslim identity (Husain & Howard, 2017).

The term "obscene" which I have borrowed from Lefebvre, can be adapted further to explain the uncomfortableness felt when a racialised episteme is disturbed. Bakhtin (1984) in *Rabelais and His World* explores notions of grotesque realism as degradation and the lowering of all that is abstract, spiritual, and noble to the material level. Using this philosophical mechanism, if we were to bring abstract space into the corporal level, the Muslim woman becomes a figure of unruly biological and social exchange (Harpold, 1990), and, most importantly, unfitting or unyielding to the spaces in which they have been invited into. To further this notion of the grotesque or obscene, Bakhtin (1984) employs exaggerations and hyperbole. In my interpretation, there is a specific focus on certain aspects of the body which are exaggerated. If I were to extend this to myself—the obscene feature becomes the hijab I often wear. I draw attention to the hijab because, physically, it is a single piece of cloth worn over my head, but the abstract and social symbolism is far more amplified. "Hijab" is a word which has been deeply politicised and "has become synonymous with Muslim female identity" (Khan, 2019, p. 1). This instrument of interpreted modesty has been perceived as a tool of injustice and outdated misogyny, while others have argued vehemently it is an integral part of their identity as Muslim women and expressions of personal choice. Such powerful seesaw of sliding perceptions is precisely what makes the hijab such an obscene feature in the HE space. My hijab has become a symbol of power against common Western political discourse and colonialised notions of freedom. The choice to wear my hijab means becoming the visible Muslim woman in a reserved, privileged institution and also forcing others to grapple with multi-layered complicated individual rather than relying on somatic privileges to put us into neat boxes.

What Next? The New Face of Faith

In the United Kingdom, calls for a "British Islam" have been cited in several government-issued documents (Manzoor-Khan, 2022). Under such scrutiny, it can be assumed that Islam, in its current forms, is a result of migrating foreign bodies and the import of dangerous ideologies. On a personal level, as a believer of faith, Morsi (2017, p. 194) eloquently captures my struggles: "What happens when I come to realise the way I speak is more a result of the War on Terror than the Quran?" One of the overlooked and under-acknowledged impacts of Islamophobia on Muslim people is their own relationship to Islam. The policies and processes attached to Islamophobia in HE impact the ability for staff and students to practise and narrate Islam, to participate in politics or even impact knowledge for fear of it being misconstrued. The impact of having your beliefs, and by extension your identity, called into question or described as an archaic mechanism incompatible with the modern world can be traumatic for students to sit through. The Prevent duty (2015) with the numerous criticisms levelled at it (Lowe, 2017; Revell, 2019; Jerome & Elwick, 2019) has created an HE space whereby visible Muslim-ness makes staff and students who practice their faith vulnerable to suspicion by heavily implying Muslim students and staff are predisposed to extremism.

A recent government report on integration and extremism highlights the parallel lives amongst different ethnic and religious communities, suggesting that minoritised groups should be encouraged to embrace "British values" (Wintour, 2011). There is evidence from the UK HE sector (Scott-Baumann, 2018) that Muslim students perceive themselves to be under Prevent surveillance which is said to have a "chilling effect" on the speech and behaviour of students. Stevenson (2014) found that several participants felt they were "let down" by their university. For example, one participant stopped trying to make new friends and within a few months was socialising only with other Muslims, commenting that: "*In the end, you just want to be with people who accept you for what you are, so that you don't have to pretend any more. I haven't been through everything I've been through just to end up being someone else than who I really am*". Unfortunately, it is clear how Islamophobia in academia has taken root, thus shaping how students engage with their degrees—negotiating, strategising, and navigating fear (Akel, 2021).

As a result, living as a contested phenomenon in the HE space, the terrain traversed can be traumatic, and cause mental fatigue, which can often reveal itself in the form of lower attainment, increased anxieties, and lower levels of belonging (Mirza, 2017). With a growing number of students from increasingly diverse backgrounds now entering higher education (Ilieva & Killingley, 2023), the "university" represents a distinctive space where the inclusion agenda is becoming more influential. It has been suggested that university leaders feel under increased pressure to demonstrate inclusivity and improve the nature of educational provision so that all students can feel welcome and be successful on equality grounds (Basit & Tomlinson, 2012). However, through a marketised approach, Islamophobia risks becoming a complex issue which is "expected to be resolved with superficial solutions in the name of valuing diversity" (Koutsouris et al., 2019, p. 1). The solutions to overcome such deeply rooted colonial inequalities are neither simple nor short-term. Moving forward in HE institutions, stronger reflexive practices need to be embedded at all levels. I am advocating for notions of "third space" (Soja, 1996) where identities are negotiated and continuously re-negotiated in an educational context to be co-created through the use of shared realities and genuine empathy. Opening the HE space to become "the trusting and supportive environment advocated through critical pedagogy" (Khatun et al., 2021), third space offers possibility of transformation through teachable moments to create a self that sits amidst contradictory cultural practices of HE. Takhar (2016) frames the possibility of a third space as a site of resistance, a resistance to a fixed identity, but I argue to overcome the simplistic binary reflections of Islamophobia, we must actively seek to legitimise different students—not through a deficit perspective of reluctant acceptance but one which values their experiences in our pedagogies. At its core, we must allow agency in occupying HE spaces for Muslim female lecturers through greater means than their visible appearance. In summary, this chapter sought to highlight how from EDI neoliberal marketisation to Generation M, the Muslim female staff/student population is often fixed by the white gaze. I brought to attention the inhabiting of different spaces in HE under the commercialised lens of EDI and Islamophobia through accounts of a brown Muslim student-lecturer in a modern university in the hope we can move away from marketised and performance-based reviews of structural inequalities to create meaningful belonging in HE.

REFERENCES

Abdel-Magied, Y. (2017). *I tried to fight racism by being a "Model minority"—and then it backfired.* Retrieved February 21, 2023, from https://www.teenvogue.com/story/fight-racism-model-minority-yassmin-abdel-magied.

Ahmad, F. (2001). Modern traditions? British Muslim women and academic achievement. *Gender and Education, 13*(2), 137–152. https://doi.org/10.1080/09540250120051169

Ahmed, S. (2006). *Queer phenomenology: Orientations, objects, others.* Duke University Press.

Ahmed, S. (2007). A phenomenology of whiteness. *Feminist Theory, 8*(2), 149–168. https://doi.org/10.1177/1464700107078139

Ahmed, S. (2009). Embodying diversity: problems and paradoxes for Black feminists. *Race Ethnicity and Education, 12*(1): 41–52. https://doi.org/10.1080/13613320802650931.

Ahmed, S. (2012). *On being included: Racism and diversity in institutional life.* Duke University Press.

Ahmed, S. (2019). *What's the use?: On the uses of use.* Duke University Press.

Ahmed, S., & Swan, E. (2006). Doing diversity. *Policy Futures in Education, 4*(2), 96–100. https://doi.org/10.2304/pfie.2006.4.2.96

Akel, S. (2021). *Institutionalised: The rise of Islamophobia in higher education.* London Metropolitan University.

Andreouli, E., & Howarth, C. (2013). National identity, citizenship and immigration: Putting identity in context. *Journal for the Theory of Social Behaviour, 43*(3), 361–382. https://doi.org/10.1111/j.1468-5914.2012.00501.x

Archer, L. (2007). Diversity, equality and higher education: a critical reflection on the ab/uses of equity discourse within widening participation. *Teaching in Higher Education, 12*(5–6), 635–653. https://doi.org/10.1080/13562510701595325

Arday, J., & Mirza, H. S. (2018). *Dismantling race in higher education: Racism, whiteness and decolonising the academy.* Palgrave Macmillan. (ERIC Number: ED610553).

Arment, A. R., Kendricks, K. D., & Nedunuri, K. V. (2013). Minority student perceptionsof the impact of mentoring to enhance academic performance in STEM disciplines. *Journal of STEM Education: Innovations and Research, 14*(2), 38–46.

Bagguley, P., & Hussain, Y. (2007). *The role of higher education in providing opportunities for South Asian women.* Retrieved September 13, 2022, from https://www.jrf.org.uk/report/role-higher-education-providing-opportunities-south-asian-women

Bakhtin, M. M. (1984). *Rabelais and His World.* Indiana University Press.

Bakkar. (2019). On the representation of Muslims. In Khan, M. (ed). *It's not about the burqa: Muslim women on faith, feminism, sexuality and race.* Palgrave Macmillan.

Ball, S., Reay, D., & David, M. (2002). "Ethnic choosing": Minority ethnic students, social class and higher education choice. *Race Ethnicity and Education, 5*, 333–357. https://doi.org/10.1080/1361332022000030879

Ball, S. J. (2012). Performativity, commodification and commitment: An I-Spy guide to the Neoliberal University. *British Journal of Educational Studies, 60*(1), 17–28. https://doi.org/10.1080/00071005.2011.650940

Banet-Weiser, S., & Glatt, Z. (2023). 'Stop treating BLM like Coachella: The branding of intersectionality. In *The Routledge companion to intersectionalities.* Routledge.

Bano, M. (2017). *Female Islamic education movements: The re-democratisation of Islamic knowledge.* Cambridge University Press. https://doi.org/10.1017/9781316986721

Basit, T. N., & Tomlinson, S. (2012). *Social inclusion and higher education.* Policy Press.

Bhopal, K. (2016). British Asian women and the costs of higher education in England. *British Journal of Sociology of Education, 37*(4), 501–519. https://doi.org/10.1080/01425692.2014.952811

Bhopal, K. (2017). Addressing racial inequalities in higher education: equity, inclusion and social justice. *Ethnic and Racial Studies, 40*(13), 2293–2299. https://doi.org/10.1080/01419870.2017.1344267

Bhopal, K., & Pitkin, C. (2020). 'Same old story, just a different policy': race and policy making in higher education in the UK. *Race Ethnicity and Education, 23*(4), 530–547. https://doi.org/10.1080/13613324.2020.1718082

Boliver, V. (2013). How fair is access to more prestigious UK universities? *British Journal of Sociology 64*(2): 344–364. https://doi.org/10.1111/1468-4446.12021

Bowes, L., Evans, J., Nathwani, T., Birkin, G., Boyd, A., Holmes, C., Jones, S. (2015). *Understanding progression into higher education for disadvantaged and under-represented groups.* Retrieved from https://www.gov.uk/government/publications/progression-into-higher-education-for-disadvantaged-and-under-represented-groups

Brennan, J., & Shah, T. (2003). *Access to what? Converting education opportunity into employment opportunity [Final report].* Retrieved July 23, 2021, from http://www.open.ac.uk/cheri/index.htm

Broecke, S., & J. Hamed. (2008). *Gender gaps in higher education participation: An analysis of the relationship between prior attainment and young participation by gender, socio-economic class and ethnicity.* Department for Innovation, Universities and Skills.

Callender, C., & Dougherty, K. J. (2018). Student choice in higher education—Reducing or reproducing social inequalities? *Social Sciences, 7*(10), 189. https://doi.org/10.3390/socsci7100189

Cole, D. (2008). Constructive criticism: The role of student-faculty interactions on African American and Hispanic students' educational gains. *Journal of College Student Development, 49,* 587–605. https://doi.org/10.1353/csd.0.0040

Connell-Smith, A., & Hubble, S. (2018). *Widening participation strategy in higher education in England.* Retrieved September 28, 2021, from https://commonslibrary.parliament.uk/research-briefings/cbp-8204/.

Crawford, C., Gregg, P., Macmillan, L., Vignoles, A., & Wyness, G. (2016). Higher education, career opportunities, and intergenerational inequality. *Oxford Review of Economic Policy 32*(4): 553–575. https://doi.org/10.1093/oxrep/grw030

de Certeau, M. (1984). *The Practice of Everyday Life*. Berkeley, University of California Press.

Dwyer, C., & Shah, B. (2009). Rethinking the identities of young british muslim women. In P. Hopkins & R. Gale (Eds.), *Muslims in britain: Race, place and identities* (pp. 55–73). Edinburgh University Press.

Dyer, R. (1997). *White: Essays on race and culture*. Routledge. https://doi.org/10.4324/9781315003603

Dzodan, F. (2011). My feminism will be intersectional or it will be bullshit! tiger beatdown. Available at: https://web.archive.org/web/20240829045825/; http://tigerbeatdown.com/ (Accessed: 1 October 2024).

French, A. (2013). 'Let the Right Ones In!': Widening Participation, academic writing and the standards debate in higher education. *Power and Education, 5*(3), 236–247. https://doi.org/10.2304/power.2013.5.3.236

Gilroy, P. (2005). Multiculture, double consciousness and the 'war on terror'. *Patterns of Prejudice, 39*, 431–443. https://doi.org/10.1080/00313220500347899

Hamdan, A. K. (2010). Reflexivity of discomfort in insider-outsider educational research. *McGill Journal of Education, 44*(3), 377–404. https://doi.org/10.7202/039946ar

Harpold, T. (1990). *Grotesque corpus: Hypertext as carnival;* In Texas, 1990. Retrieved July 26, 2023, from http://www.pd.org/Perforations/perf3/grotesque_corpus.html

Husain, A., & Howard, S. (2017). Religious microaggressions: A case study of Muslim Americans. *Journal of Ethnic & Cultural Diversity in Social Work, 26*(1–2), 139–152. https://doi.org/10.1080/15313204.2016.1269710

Ilieva, J. B., & Killingley, P. (2023). *International higher education strategy 2.0:Targeted growth for resilience*. Oxford International Education Group: International Higher Education Commission. Retrieved July 26, 2023, from https://ihecommission.uk/wp-content/uploads/2023/05/INTERIM-Report-Final-May-2023.pdf

Islam, M., Lowe, T., & Jones, G. (2018). A 'satisfied settling'? Investigating a sense of belonging for Muslim students in a UK small-medium Higher Education Institution. *Student Engagement in Higher Education Journal, 2*(2), 79–104.

Janmohamed, S. Z. (2016). *Generation M: Young muslims changing the world*. I.B. Tauris.

Jerome, L., & Elwick, A. (2019). Identifying an Educational response to the prevent policy: Student perspectives on learning about terrorism, Extremism and radicalisation. *British Journal of Educational Studies, 67*(1), 97–114. https://doi.org/10.1080/00071005.2017.1415295

Jussawalla, F. F., Omran, D., & Abd el-Aziz, H. (2023). *Muslim women's writing from across South and Southeast Asia*. Routledge, Taylor and Francis Group.

Khan, M. (2019). *It's not about the Burqa: Muslim women on faith, feminism, sexuality and race.* Pan Macmillan.

Khatun, F., French, A., & Smith, R. (2021). Reconceptualising student experiences: exploring embodiment and identity through differential HE space. *The Journal of Educational Innovation, Partnership and Change, 7*(1). https://doi.org/10.21100/jeipc.v7i1.1021

Koutsouris, G., Anglin-Jaffe, H., & Stentiford, L. (2019). How do we understand social inclusion in education? *British Journal of Educational Studies, 68*(2), 179–196. https://doi.org/10.1080/00071005.2019.1658861

Lather, P. (1991a). *Feminist research in education: Within/against.* Deakin University.

Lather, P. (1991b). *Getting smart: Feminist research and pedagogy with/in the postmodern.* Routledge.

Lefebvre, H. (2001). *The production of space.* Wiley.

Leistyna, P. (2004). Presence of mind in the process of learning and knowing.

Lowe, D. (2017). Prevent strategies: The problems associated in defining extremism: The case of the United Kingdom. *Studies in Conflict & Terrorism, 40*(11), 917–933. https://doi.org/10.1080/1057610X.2016.1253941

Manzoor-Khan, S. (2022). *Tangled in terror: Uprooting Islamophobia.* Pluto Press.

Mastro, M. A. (2016). The mainstream misrepresentation of Muslim women in the media. *The Cupola Scholarship at Gettysburg College,* p. 13.

Mellor, J. (2011). "I really couldn't think of being married, having a family with nothing behind me": Empowerment, education, and british pakistani women. In Bolognani, M., & Lyon, S. M. (Eds.), *Pakistan and its diaspora: Multidisciplinary approaches* (pp. 217–237). Palgrave Macmillan US. https://doi.org/10.1057/9780230119079_9.

Mescoli, E. (2020). Intersectionality and Muslim women in Belgium. In N. Fernandez, & K. Nelson, (Eds.), *Gendered lives: Global issues.* Retrieved July 21, 2023, from https://orbi.uliege.be/handle/2268/253902

Mirza, H. S. (2017). 'One in a million': A journey of a post-colonial woman of colour in the white academy. In D. Gabriel & S. Tate (Eds.), *Inside the ivory tower, narratives of women of colour surviving and thriving in British Academia.* Trentham Press.

Morsi, Y. (2017). *Radical skin, moderate masks: De-radicalising the Muslim and Racism in post-racial societies.* Rowman & Littlefield Publishers. Retrieved July 26, 2023, from https://rowman.com/ISBN/9781783489121/Radical-Skin-Moderate-Masks-De-radicalising-the-Muslim-and-Racism-in-Post-racial-Societies

Muslim Council of Britain. (2022). *2021 census: As UK population grows, so do British Muslim communities | Muslim Council of Britain.* Retrieved July 10, 2023, from https://mcb.org.uk/2021-census-as-uk-population-grows-so-do-british-muslim-communities/.

Noden, P., Shiner, M., & Modood, T. (2014). University offer rates for candidates from different ethnic categories. *Oxford Review of Education, 40*. https://doi. org/10.1080/03054985.2014.911724

Office for Students (OfS). (2018). How do student outcomes vary by ethnicity?– Office for students. Available at: https://www.officeforstudents.org.uk/ (Accessed: 30 September 2024).

Puwar, N. (2001). The racialised Somatic norm and the senior civil service. *Sociology, 35*(3), 651–670.

Puwar, N. (2004). *Space invaders: Race, gender and bodies out of place*. Berg Publishers.

Reay, D., Crozier, G., & Clayton, J. (2009). 'Fitting in' or 'standing out': Working-class students in UK higher education. *British Educational Research Journal, 36*(1), 107–124. https://doi.org/10.1080/01411920902878925

Revell, L. (2019). Teacher practice and the pre-crime space: prevent, safeguarding and teacher engagement with extremism and radicalisation. *PRACTICE, 1*(1), 21–36. https://doi.org/10.1080/25783858.2019.1591765

Said, E.W. (1978). *Orientalism*. Wolfgang Laade Music of Man Archive. Routledge & Kegan.

Scott-Baumann, A. (2018). 'Dual use research of concern' and 'select agents'. *Journal of Muslims in Europe, 7*(2): 237–261. https://doi.org/10.1163/22117954-12341373.

Seedat, F. (2013). When islam and feminism converge. *The Muslim World, 103*(3): 404–420. https://doi.org/10.1111/muwo.12022.

Soja, E.W. (1996). *Thirdspace: Journeys to Los Angeles and Other real-and-imagined places*. Wiley. (Google-Books-ID: BGbszAEACAAJ).

Stevenson, J. (2014). Internationalisation and Religious Inclusion in United Kingdom Higher Education. *Higher Education Quarterly, 68*(1), 46–64. https://doi.org/10.1111/hequ.12033

Takhar, S. (2016). Bangladeshi female students in higher education: 'Agentic Autonomy' at the race/gender trajectory. In Takhar, S. (Ed.), *Advances in Gender Research* (pp. 41–62). Emerald Group Publishing Limited. https://doi.org/10.1108/S1529-212620160000021004.

Tell MAMA. (2018). *Tell MAMA annual report 2018 normalising hate*. London: Faith Matters. Retrieved July 5, 2022, from https://tellmamauk.org/wp-content/uploads/2019/09/Tell%20MAMA%20Annual%20Report%20 2018%20_%20Normalising%20Hate.pdf

Törnberg, A., & Törnberg, P. (2016). Muslims in social media discourse: Combining topic modeling and critical discourse analysis. *Discourse, Context & Media, 13*, 132–142. https://doi.org/10.1016/j.dcm.2016.04.003

Whitaker, B. (2002). *Worst impressions.* The Guardian, 24 June. Available at: https://www.theguardian.com/world/2002/jun/24/worlddispatch.pressandpublishing (Accessed: 30 September 2024).

Wintour, P. (2011, February 5). David Cameron tells Muslim Britain: Stop tolerating extremists. *The Guardian.* Retrieved July 26, 2023, from https://www.theguardian.com/politics/2011/feb/05/david-cameron-muslim-extremism

Wong, B., ElMorally, R., & Copsey-Blake, M. (2021). 'Fair and square': what do students think about the ethnicity degree awarding gap? *Journal of Further and Higher Education, 45*(8), 1147–1161. https://doi.org/10.1080/0309877X.2021.1932773

Zempi, I. (2019). Veiled Muslim women's views on law banning the wearing of the niqab (face veil) in public. *Ethnic and Racial Studies, 42*(15), 2585–2602. https://doi.org/10.1080/01419870.2019.1588985

"Never let anyone tell you that you're not good enough": Using Intersectionality to Reflect on Inequality in British Academia

Afsana Faheem and Mohammed Rahman

Our Approach and Positionalities

We believe that the most organic approach to challenge and interrogate what we intend to explore is through duoethnography and scholastic reflexivity. Ellis et al. (2010) posit that duoethnography is critically framed for qualitative research methods based on personal experiences. However, Given (2008) summarises duoethnography to be a literary style that provides stories of insights containing theses and antitheses of two or more individuals between which readers can form their own synthesis. Traditionally, ethnographic modes of research are facilitated by reflexivity. Reflexivity is often used as a tool in social sciences to establish the role of researchers during research and the consequences that their inputs may

A. Faheem (✉)
University of Bath, Bath, UK
e-mail: af890@bath.ac.uk

M. Rahman
Birmingham City University, Birmingham, UK

A. Mahmud, M. Islam (eds.), *Uncovering Islamophobia in Higher Education*, Palgrave Studies in Race, Inequality and Social Justice in Education, https://doi.org/10.1007/978-3-031-65253-0_6

97

have on the setting and the subjects under investigation, questions being asked, data being generated, and its interpretation (Rahman & Abdulkader, 2022). As Dunier (2006) reminds us, those submerged in scholarship should become authors of their own lives, and in doing so, should experience some dignity with the research process. Emirbayer and Desmond's (2012) work on race and reflexivity offers visceral meanings of scholarly reflexivity, as the authors argue that we must go beyond the understanding that reflexive thinking entails more than how one's social position affects the scientific analysis. Rahman and Deuchar (2024) have deemed reflexivity to be a continuous ethical exercise as it allows us to integrate ethical, social, and political judgements within research, therefore, increasing the accountability for the knowledge that is produced. Like Mahmud and Islam (2022), we share our positionalities at the forefront of this chapter so that we can both reflect and be transparent about how our social, political, and historical contexts may have influenced our experiences as researchers and academics. We recognise that the terms Black, Asian, and Minority Ethnic (BAME) and people of colour are imperfect, however, we use them interchangeably when referring to individuals from minority ethnic backgrounds.

Dr Afsana Faheem: Afsana is a second-generation Muslim British Pakistani female, who comes from a working-class background in the West Midlands. Afsana pursued higher education (HE) as a mature student after deciding to change her career path, albeit without certainty. Afsana is the first to study and complete a professional doctorate in her family. Afsana has a longstanding passion for working with disadvantaged communities, with particular interests in inequalities, mental health, and cultural competency. For her recent post, Afsana relocated to an affluent, predominantly White, and middle-class city in Somerset. This presented new challenges and experiences that forced Afsana to reflect on her own identity, race, religion, and culture—something she was consciously unaware of beforehand.

Dr Mohammed Rahman: Mohammed is a second-generation Muslim British Bangladeshi, who comes from a racially minoritised background. He has experienced implicit and explicit modes of racism and Islamophobia in most of his 10+ years in academia, having majored in four degrees (BSc, MA, MEd, PhD), studied two postgraduate courses, and taught from visiting lecturer to his current role as a Senior Lecturer. As a result of his own injustices combined with his passion to elevate those that he educates, he is keen on enhancing the experiences of young people in higher education, especially those from minoritised groups that like him are often the first in their families to study at university at undergraduate and postgraduate levels.

INTRODUCTION

The negative portrayal of Muslims in the mass media has led to increased discrimination, racism, exclusion, and harassment towards Muslim staff and students in HE settings (Pilkington, 2013; Stevenson, 2018). Muslim students represent the second largest religious group in HE, yet statistics show that the percentage of Muslim staff is comparatively low across the United Kingdom (3.2% compared to 8.9%) (Advance HE, 2019, 2020). These disparities widen for Muslim staff in senior positions, particularly Muslim women (Almaki et al., 2016; Madsen et al., 2012; Ramadan, 2017). In her study about racism in higher education, Mirza (2018) states that in comparison to 3895 White female and 12,455 White male professors in the United Kingdom, there were only 345 British women of colour professors. The statistics are also disturbing for men of colour. The theoretical basis of what we intend to discuss is grounded within the analytical framework of intersectionality. Crenshaw's (1989) seminal work on intersectionality drew upon how legislation reacts to issues that consist of gender and racial discrimination. Since then, intersectionality has provided novel perspectives within studies in social psychology (Cole, 2009; Macey & Carling, 2011), education (Nichols & Stahl, 2019), and workplace practice (Bloch et al., 2021; Rosette et al., 2018). Over time, some have challenged the methodological aspects of intersectional scholarship due to its interpretivist nature (Bilge, 2013; Carbin & Edenheim, 2013), whilst others have praised how intersectional philosophy through qualitative investigations has helped make sense of individuals' multiple identities and how this creates unique patterns of oppression (Jibrin & Salem, 2015).

Our social science disciplines have been historically rooted in White rhetoric that favours theories, practices, concepts, and ideologies from a Eurocentric gaze (Adams et al., 2015; Guthrie, 2004; Tauri, 2018), thus limiting diverse perspectives and thinkers in education and scholarship (Patton et al., 2007). To "decolonise the curriculum", universities are encouraged to respect and include diverse narratives and worldviews in order to enrich the student learning experience (Advance HE, 2020; Gusa, 2010). However, to gain credibility, decolonisation needs to not only consider the curriculum, but also the recruitment, promotion, and scholarship of people of colour (Begum & Saini, 2019). Given the inherent Whiteness of HE settings, Patton and Haynes (2020) challenge the commitment towards racial equality that continues to maintain and serve the interests of White individuals. Whiteness is described as the "...*location of structural advantage, or race privilege... it is a 'standpoint', a place from which White people look at ourselves, at others, and at society.... a set of cultural practices that are usually unmarked and unnamed*" (Frankenburg, 1993, p. 1). Both implicit and explicit, conscious and unconscious biases create monocultural environments that favour the recruitment of White academics, particularly in positions of seniority (Ramadan, 2017). While attempts are made to make teaching teams more inclusive, these efforts are often seen as tokenistic in order to avoid criticism (Sherrer, 2022).

Discriminatory and exclusionary practices have a negative impact on the careers of BAME academics, yet this is seldom acknowledged by senior management (Bhopal & Jackson, 2013). Incidences of microaggressions send negative and disparaging messages that have detrimental consequences on the well-being of marginalised groups (Nadal et al., 2010; Sue, 2010). Microaggressions are typically defined as "*brief and commonplace daily verbal, behavioural, and environmental indignities, whether intentional or unintentional, that communicate hostile, derogatory, or negative racial slights and insults to the target person or group*" (Sue et al., 2007, p. 273). However, microaggressions are not always overt, they can be subtle, and often unrecognised by the victim (Nadal et al., 2011; Sue, 2010). The so-called glass ceiling of academia tends to prevent individuals from minority backgrounds from pursuing leadership positions and fosters bouts of imposter syndrome (Arday, 2018). Imposter syndrome creates a strong sense of self-doubt for not being intelligent enough or being discovered as a fraud and is particularly observed in high-achieving women (Clance & Imes, 1978) and academics from BAME backgrounds (Allen-Ramdial & Campbell, 2014; Chrousos & Mentis, 2020; Khatun et al., 2021). Research indicates that the "class ceiling" can also widen pay disparities between those from working-class backgrounds, women, ethnic minorities, and those educated at non-Russell group universities (Friedman et al., 2015). As such, individuals may sabotage their careers by minimising their own accomplishments (Parkman, 2016).

Not only this but some academic spaces can foster cold campus climates and create feelings of un-belonging and exclusion. The intersectionality between race, religion, ethnicity, and social class tends to marginalise students [and staff], particularly those studying or working in prestigious and inherently White institutions (Pilkington, 2011; Reay et al., 2009). Minority students report that such environments can be "anxiety inducing", especially when the student does not share similar demographics as the majority group (Reay, 2018). For example, interviews with Muslim students' found that they often felt invisible, unheard, unrepresented, and misunderstood by other White staff and students (Stevenson, 2018). Although universities are likely to incorporate spaces and events that are considerate of religion (e.g. prayer rooms, Islamic Society events), they often fail to understand the responsibilities that religious observations such as Ramadan can present (e.g. prayer times, breaking fasts) (Tyrer & Ahmad, 2006). During such periods, Muslim students may require additional support and flexibility in attending taught sessions and completing assessments. These oversights are further experienced by Muslim staff, who receive inadequate support or opportunities that are considerate towards their religious needs and practices. For example, during Ramadan 2022, after waiting for a sufficient period, both authors had to reach out to their respective institutions as they failed to acknowledge the holy month. Only one institution responded immediately and subsequently offered provisions for students and staff.

To note, we recognise that universities have invested in diversity; however, the preservation of policies does not ensure an inclusive and equitable environment (Hurtado et al., 1998). To remove the institutional barriers that BAME individuals face, our institutions have signed up to the Race Equality Charter (REC). Set up by AdvanceHE, the REC provides a framework for institutions to identify and consider institutional and cultural barriers for BAME staff and students (for further discussion on the REC, see Chap. 13). However, these policies need to be implemented strategically, otherwise, they create unequal opportunities and serve no other purpose than to guise commitment towards making academia more inclusive (Ahmed, 2012; Woodall, 2013). We want to stress that this needs to be a shared endeavour. Unlike White academics who are held in high esteem for their engagement with matters relating to equality, diversity, and inclusion (EDI), such efforts are merely seen as a "hobby" for BAME staff (Wright et al., 2007). This can lead to increased burn-out, frustration, and exclusion.

Our Contribution

We aim to contribute to the literature by sharing our lived experiences as academics teaching at two very different British HE institutes. Afsana teaches at a campus university in Somerset, whereas Mohammed teaches at a university in the West Midlands. Through an intersectional lens, we intend to bring to the fore some of our experiences and discuss how these have affected our workplace practice. This includes both implicit and explicit modes of oppression that we have encountered in relation to our minority statuses of race, class, gender, and religious observances. Through intersectionality, we are better positioned to critically discuss how our marginalised identities, and the lack of institutional recognition they receive, have contributed to a Eurocentric curriculum, imposter syndrome, tokenism, microaggressions, and created a cold campus climate. We also aim to share some of the novel pedagogical approaches that we have embedded within our teaching practices to help diversify the curriculum and make it more inclusive. We will discuss how institutions can learn through our experiences and take action to help change the landscape of HE for the future.

Our Experiences

We are of the opinion that most make a judgement on whether a person is a Muslim based on physical attributes as opposed to objectively probing their beliefs and practices. Of note, we are both practising Muslims, observing our faith-based beliefs such as upholding the profession of faith (Shahada), praying five times a day (Salah), donating 2.5% of our overall wealth every year (Zakat), fasting consecutively for one month (Ramadan), and undertaking the pilgrimage to Makkah, in Saudi Arabia (Hajj). Afsana wears a hijab (religious headscarf), which is a symbolic female Muslim garment. Along with this, we are both from British-Asian backgrounds, who are working class, and who happen to be working in academia full-time. We feel it is important to note our positionality within this chapter as well as how we both view ourselves beyond it. As such, we present our experiences across three themes: (1) learning through reflection, (2) learning through experiences, and (3) learning through action.

Learning Through Reflection

In the first theme, we reflect on our lived experiences as Muslim academics by discussing how the intersectionality between our race, religion, gender, and social contexts have shaped and influenced our academic journeys. By being vulnerable and transparent, we hope to offer an insight into how we have navigated through British academia in order for others to learn and consider ways to create spaces that are more inclusive to the needs of marginalised groups.

Afsana – I am a proud Muslim, cherishing my hijab as a sign of independence and empowerment. I have never questioned my identity as a Muslim, primarily due to my former institute being situated in an ethnically diverse city. The West Midlands is multicultural, inhibiting over 507,500 (8.6%) of the Muslim population alone (Office for National Statistics, 2019). As such, the university generally attracted a large Muslim student body, although this was less visible in the Muslim staff-to-student ratio. Having worked in a number of different roles at the university, I was well versed in the common practices, challenges, and complexities that were experienced at all levels of seniority. That is, from the lens of a student, researcher, administrator, graduate manager, and academic. Narratives relating to discriminatory and exclusionary practices were frequently discussed across different departments. It was a systemic issue. BAME staff often felt isolated, were forced to question their own abilities, and were expected to work twice as hard as their White colleagues to be promoted into senior positions. This preferential treatment became more evident during my doctoral studies. White counterparts were often offered more favourable research and funding opportunities, as well as lectureship positions with similar (or fewer) qualifications or experiences. One senior White academic recommended I should visit a "food bank" if I was struggling financially rather than suggesting opportunities for growth, which he had done with other White doctoral researchers. Having experienced such exclusionary practices, I decided to seek opportunities elsewhere. To my naivety, what I did not envisage was the drastic shift in behaviours and attitudes towards me once the new position was accepted. Given the "high ranking" of the new institute, flippant comments were made about why I had been selected for this role. One White academic questioned, "How did you get that? I've applied there before and never got it!", whilst the other jested "You're *just* the poster brown girl". Whilst these comments were taken lightly at the time, it was not until later that they began to make an impact. Being consciously unaware of incidences of microaggressions whilst experiencing them is not uncommon (Nadal et al., 2011; Sue, 2010). Regardless, I decided to pursue this opportunity, as it was the natural progression to what I loved doing the most—teaching.

The move to Somerset was vastly different to what I was used to. Unlike the Midlands, only 1.1% (60,000) of the residents in the South West are Muslim (Office for National Statistics, 2019). The stark contrast was evident, in both the city and campus. As I walked through the corridors of my new institution, I was greeted by a wall of staff photos and digital images of students, who were predominately all White. I began to ask myself … was I *really* just a "poster brown girl"? That is when it emerged, imposter syndrome. Admittedly, at times, it was difficult to navigate through these unfamiliar feelings, often overshadowed by a sense of unworthiness and less accomplished than my colleagues. Not just this, but being the only visible Muslim academic, from working-class roots, intensified feelings of self-doubt and displacement. Comments from my former institution replayed in my mind, leading me to believe that the sole reason for my role was tokenistic. One day, I decided to share my concerns with my line manager and questioned why I was recruited. She replied, "You were hired because you were brilliant, and you stood out from all of the other candidates that we interviewed. Never let anyone tell you that you're not good enough". Those words never left me. Upon reflection, it is a shame that I needed validation to recognise my worth as an academic. I recognise that other Muslim staff in HE seldom have opportunities or the space to have these conversations (Ahmed, 2001; Mahmud & Islam, 2022; Ramadan, 2021). I was fortunate to have a line manager and team that were incredibly supportive when those bouts of imposter syndrome emerged. They helped me recognise that I *deserved* to be here, just like anyone else. This highlighted the importance of advocates, particularly White colleagues in predominantly White institutions, who are nurturing, encouraging, and sensitive to the needs of diverse staff (Harris & Lee, 2019).

As time went on, I became more consciously aware of the campus climate and began to notice the lack of representation around shared spaces. For example, during my first week, I attended an event organised by the university's Islamic Society and was astonished to see no Muslim academics and only a handful of Muslim students. After speaking to the local Imam [faith leader] who was delivering a talk that day, I was alarmed to learn that I was the second Muslim academic he had met in over 10 years of visiting the university. At this very moment, I realised that this transition was going to be more than just an academic one, but rather a social, cultural, and religious one too. Often departmental social events were organised around "going to the pub" or "having a drink", which I avoided as a practising Muslim. Whilst I do not believe that this was intentional, those subtle omissions have the capability of "othering" individuals. However, my team understood and respected my choice and often planned course events that were considerate of my needs (e.g. picnics and eating at halal restaurants). Such inclusive practices were immensely appreciated as they fostered a sense of belonging (Tyrer & Ahmed, 2006). However, at a university level, there was seldom any acknowledgement of religious events, such as Ramadan (Mcmaster, 2020; Weller et al., 2011). Living away from home, particularly during the pandemic, was an incredibly isolating period. After speaking to Muslim students, I realised that the lack of support during the holy month was experienced more widely. Having raised concerns, I was pleased to see the university take action by offering support to Muslim staff and students during this period. Whilst this is a small step in the right direction, I hope that this practice is embedded within the fabric of the institution to become more inclusive to the needs of its Muslim population.

Mohammed – Imposter syndrome is something that I experienced extensively a few months into my current position. I became a Senior Lecturer after 1.5 years of full-time Lectureship. This was picked up by some of my colleagues, with some making remarks explicitly and most implicitly on my progression, and how my minority status played a role in being promoted. Prior to the promotion and during my time as a lecturer, I experienced imposter syndrome due to the actions of a senior White female colleague. She would often remind me that she played a pivotal role in my appointment. As such, I started to experience a sense of self-doubt relating to work achievements (Dahlvig, 2013). It was only after a period of reflection that I came to realise the copious amount of work that I achieved before my current position, which my peers have very limited knowledge of. I had to remind myself that as a doctoral student, I had published consistently over three years in several internationally recognised peer-reviewed journals, as well as leading final-year core modules that consisted of 200 students. Alongside research and teaching, I was heavily engaged with community work, thus creating contacts and networks that my department benefitted from and still does by way of scholarship and enterprise. Some of the core responsibilities that I had as a PhD student were that of a Lecturer and even a Senior Lecturer's role. My feeling of imposter syndrome made me think critically about my family background (Castro et al., 2004; King & Cooley, 1995; Sakulku & Alexander, 2011). It made me question, and to a certain extent, I felt guilty for excelling in some of my background norms in the context of HE. For my generation in the Bangladeshi community, it is widely accepted that undergraduate education is the pinnacle and anything beyond that is a bonus. Harvey and Katz (1985) note how individuals who are the first in their family to exceed norms or expectations tend to demonstrate imposter behaviour. As the first in my family to complete a PhD, there was a lack of academic family mentorship.

Important here is to note that my feeling of being an imposter and combining it with the critical thinking of my background (i.e. ethnicity, class, and religion) from an intersectional perspective has also affected my relationship with family, especially my parents. I believe that feeling like an imposter in academia and combining this as an only child from a South Asian background has contributed extensively to my experience of parentification (Castro et al., 2004). Parentification is known as a process of role reversal, whereby a child is obliged to act as a parent to their parents. Culturally, parentification is far more prevalent in BAME communities, namely, within the South Asian diaspora, and it is also viewed to be a form of social capital (Bourdieu, 1984). Parentification is something that I am happy to embrace, but only through reflection have I learned the impact that academia has had on its acceleration.

I resonate with Afsana's experiences of being invited to the pub for a drink. This seems to be a default expectation of British culture, which unashamedly disregards the values and cultures of those who do not drink alcohol, be it because of their faith or otherwise, or those who do not wish to occupy a space that primarily sells alcohol. An example of this is the uproar in England leading up to the 2022 FIFA World Cup because of Qatari officials banning the buying of alcohol inside football stadiums (Ingle, 2022). Because of this, British media outlets were saturated with news stories of Qatar's "oppressive" regime, with few acknowledging how the banning of alcohol reduced hooliganism, violence, and even sexual assaults against women (MEMO, 2022). This is a global example of the blatant disregard and forceful nature that Britain largely has about the cultures, values, and practices of other nations as well as the contradiction of its own fundamental values—respect and tolerance—which states that we all do not share the same beliefs and values. Coming back to my own experiences, over the years, I have had to experience a cold campus climate and the subsequent microaggressions associated with it because of my unwillingness to partake in alcohol-dominated work-related socials (Piacentini & Banister, 2009).

One of the most disturbing alcohol-related encounters I have had within academia was during my PhD studies. In front of several junior and senior colleagues, a colleague at that time remarked how I should celebrate my PhD success in the future in his words by "drinking champagne" because "there's nothing in the Quran that specifically states champagne". Although I made clear reference to how all forms of intoxication are prohibited in Islam, he rebutted by stating "I've read the Quran cover to cover, and there's nothing in it that says that champagne is prohibited". I made a note of this in one of my PhD reflexive entries, dated 19 February 2015. The relevance of this date is of extreme importance, as I was only five months into my studies. According to my reflexive entry, I felt it was "...unreasonable for him to think about me celebrating my PhD with champagne, rather his focus should be getting me through my first semester".

Towards the end of 2015, I removed this academic, a White—upper middle-class—professor, as my supervisor, and it was only later that I was able to fully comprehend the microaggression associated with me pushing back on his comments of me drinking champagne and removing him as a supervisor. In the summer of 2016 at a graduation social, which also served as a leaving function for a colleague, this academic took it a step further. They offered to pour me a glass of champagne in front of several colleagues even though he was fully aware by now that I was a practising Muslim. For me, this encounter reaffirmed the ignorance and privilege that some White senior colleagues have, who openly disrespect the beliefs and values of minority staff, without any worry of the consequences (Bhopal, 2018).

Learning Through Experience

This theme considers the novel pedagogical approaches that we have embedded within our teaching to encourage students to learn through experience—ours and others like us. Given the Eurocentric nature of the curriculum, we consider our intersectionalities as academics, as well as our students, and our respective disciplines to enhance the student learning experience.

Afsana – As I moved into my teaching role during my doctoral studies, I saw the difference representation made, particularly for Muslim students. Comments were made about the lack of knowledge about Islam among staff, and how being taught by a Muslim academic made students feel inspired, understood, and motivated (Gusa, 2010; Stevenson, 2018). Given the inherent lack of representation in clinical psychology (Lang, 2020), a conference was planned to feature clinical practitioners from various religious and cultural backgrounds. However, given the toll of the global pandemic, the event was cancelled. This subsequently led to the development of a novel technology-enhanced pedagogical approach—a podcast. In the digital age, initiatives such as podcasts have been shown to enhance the student learning experience, increase motivation, and respect for diverse talents (Evans, 2008; Fernandez et al., 2009). Enabling a digital platform allowed us to bring voices from seldom-heard groups, such as Muslim practitioners, to areas predominantly catered towards White academics, students, and practitioners. The podcast, titled "*What About Us? Cultural Awareness in Clinical Psychology* featured a diverse range of mental health professionals who shared their lived experiences working in the sector and offered examples of real-world clinical practice. Topics included "Mental health barriers for British Bangladeshi men" with clinical psychologist Dr Shah Alam; "Autism awareness in the Somali community" with PhD researcher Nura Aabe; and "Adapting therapy for Muslim communities" with clinical psychologist Dr Nadia Sadique. The first-hand narratives revealed new and often unheard experiences from guest speakers and allowed students to reflect on their own cultural competency needs (Bhui et al., 2007). Alarmingly, for most White students, this was the first time that they were taught such topics throughout their entire education. For example, one student from a White background commented:

> I found the podcasts extremely interesting and useful. It was great hearing first-hand what the struggles of BAME practitioners are and how they went about tackling them. It was also good to hear about cultural adaptations in real-world clinical practice....

Through such inclusive practices, universities can attract diverse narratives and experiences that can help develop and enhance student knowledge and learning. From continual feedback, these initiatives are greatly valued across the sector as well as clinical training programmes.

Mohammed – Similarly to Afsana, I have also utilised techno-pedagogical approaches through my own research-informed teaching experiences. The curriculum that I teach is extremely Eurocentric and so are the teaching approaches (Arday et al., 2022). Therefore, to give students a transformative learning experience and one that will equip them with some of the cultural nuances within the discipline of criminology, I have previously employed digital technology as a tool that facilitates an in-depth investigation of a crime through the observation of environments, peoples, and cultures. For example, through several cases, my PhD explored serious violence within organised crime in the West Midlands, England. The majority of my research was street-level and certain aspects of my ethnography were captured through the use of digital technology, namely, a car dash-cam (Rahman, 2016; Rahman, 2017; Rahman, 2019). Across several modules, I have been able to use captured research information through the use of digital technology. In recent student feedback, one student commented on how they were able to "relate to some of [my] real life examples", as well as me "understanding the cultural significance of what [they] are studying". My experiences of using techno-pedagogical approaches in my teaching and wider scholarship have allowed me to connect with inner-city community students from various backgrounds, with some within this cohort seeing me as a role model figure, as well as students that are from middle-class rural backgrounds that have, what I call, "secondary knowledge" of urban street life.

Learning Through Action

This final theme stresses the importance of HE institutions to not only learn from our experiences but to actively consider our suggestions and put them into action. We believe that without appropriate implementation, our experiences, like many others, will be left unseen, unheard, and unappreciated.

Afsana – One of the fundamental features of developing an inclusive environment is being surrounded by individuals who have genuine positive regard for your well-being and success. Sadly, conversations with other Muslim academics have made it clear that this is a privilege rather than a common practice. In predominantly White institutes, White advocates have the power to shape the experiences of BAME staff (Park & Denson, 2009). As such, advocate-mentoring may be a useful way to help encourage and develop the careers of minoritised staff (Harris & Lee,

2019). However, this can only be achieved in spaces that promote opportunities to actively and openly share stories, experiences, and challenges within HE. But this needs to be a two-way process. From conversations with White colleagues, it is apparent that there is a sense of uneasiness and hesitation in talking about matters relating to race, ethnicity, and culture. Often concerns are expressed about feeling discomfort in discussing such matters given their own position of power, privilege, and White guilt (Iyer et al., 2003). White staff often fear getting it wrong or causing offence. However, through my personal experience, I have found that without having reflexive and safe spaces, where such conversations can be shared, there is little that can be done to address and improve inclusive practice.

Moreover, initiatives to diversify the sector should be shared by all staff and not reliant on the motivation and determination of BAME individuals (Ahmed, 2006). Often, BAME staff are expected to incorporate and adopt roles to enhance EDI within HE without appropriate recognition and reward. Having completed the leadership programme for BAME women in academia, I realised that these expectations are common within academia. Attendees on the programme overwhelmingly shared their experiences of tokenistic gestures, and inconsiderate policies and practices within their respective institutions. In addition, obstacles to their career progression were made due to vagueness in promotion guidelines, and the lack of acknowledgement of their contributions to EDI work (Bhopal & Jackson, 2013; Park & Denson, 2009). This led to several individuals leaving their positions altogether following the scheme. I believe that without appropriate support, agency, curiosity, and genuine positive regard, initiatives such as leadership programmes will fail to make a long-term impact or improvements to the weathered landscape of HE.

Mohammed – Representation in my department among staff is bleak and this has been the case for several years. Based on my impressionistic observations, discussions on representation tend to make colleagues uncomfortable and often the microaggressions that come with the discussions are embraced with narratives of implicatory denial (Cohen, 2001). Out of 30 full-time permanent staff members in my subject area, three are from BAME backgrounds. The majority are White, with an even blend of gender. Traditionally, I have taught undergraduate (level 6) and postgraduate (level 7) modules. I teach on one of the biggest cohorts of a core final-year undergraduate module that consists of over 200 students, and this has been the case since I was a PhD student. The module in question offers the most accurate representation of the overall student demographic of the course that I mainly teach. In my recent cohort, the ethnic makeup consisted of 51.3% BAME (14.95% Black, 28.35% Asian and 7.73% Mixed), 47.4% White, 0.52% Other, and 1.03% Not Declared. The statistics offer the understanding that the course that I deliver consists of a BAME majority population, with the Asian background being the most dominant ethnic background. Yet, this shockingly fails to mirror staff representation. While my institution embraces ethnicity and diversity within the student population, it has consistently failed to address this diversity within the academic staff population. Below is a recent excerpt from a student who was able to relate to some of my scholarly activities:

> I was able to use their research for my module assessment and as a result, I have taken a further interest by volunteering for a charity. I have been inspired by their work, especially as I am from a minority background. Their research has been used in teaching sessions for students like me to get a better understanding of some of the key theories and concepts which I have found difficult to understand through other examples.

Given the disparity between staff and student ethnic backgrounds in my discipline and the subsequent lack of relatability that most students in my cohort have with my colleagues, I have decided to take proactive measures rather than waiting for my institution to sufficiently address these inequalities. For instance, in recent years, I have elected to teach core undergraduate modules across all year groups so that minority students, who paradoxically are a majority in the population, can at the very least access and relate to an academic that is of similar kind regarding ethnicity, race, religion, and class throughout their studies. Admittedly, while this is not a sustainable solution for most minoritised academics, institutions must recognise that representation matters in HE across all provisions to appropriately connect with cultures and reduce implicit bias (Walker, 2020).

OUR RECOMMENDATIONS

Based on this chapter, the following recommendations are offered:

- *To carry out bespoke intersectional training:* As opposed to merely acknowledging it as a phenomenon that concerns inequalities, higher education institutions need to undertake bespoke sustainable intersectional work to fully comprehend the issues within their establishments. Any work will need to consist of staff consultation and participation at all levels, a robust methodology, and an evaluation by an external agency of practices that are implemented.

• *Higher education institutions need to be consistent when tackling inequalities:* Most universities are at the very least committed to Athena SWAN, Stonewall, and the Race Equality Charter. These initiatives are typically embedded within UK higher education institutes to improve equality for protected characteristics such as gender, sexuality, and race within the student and staff body (Henderson & Bhopal, 2022). However, there is nothing of a similar kind available nationally about religion and beliefs. Although the Census (2021) data suggests a decline in the Christian population in England and Wales, there have been sizable increases in the recording of religion of minority populations (namely, those identifying themselves as Muslim and Hindu). Therefore, there is an urgent need for universities to commit towards religion and belief as part of their equality, diversity, and inclusionary work, especially given that religion-based hate crime in England and Wales is on the rise (GOV.UK, 2022).

• *Address imposter syndrome:* Institutions should address imposter syndrome by developing training that increases the visibility of the problem and the negative consequences for staff. This may include experiences of microaggressions, discriminatory, and exclusionary practices. Staff should be made aware of and have access to initiatives such as mental health support and mentoring, especially for those from minoritised backgrounds (Chrousos & Mentis, 2020).

• *Inclusive spaces to talk about Whiteness:* Whilst this is a difficult topic to discuss, all staff must be able to openly discuss, share, and engage in constructive conversations about the inherent Whiteness within the curriculum, workforce, and campus climates. This needs to be a two-way process, with active engagement from all stakeholders to help improve the university landscape (Ahmed, 2012).

CONCLUSION

Through an intersectional lens, we have shared our experiences of academia as Muslim academics which incorporated feelings of imposter syndrome, microaggressions, tokenism, and cold campus climates. We reflected on the inherent Eurocentric landscape of HE and discussed ways in which we have embedded novel techno-pedagogical approaches to enhance the student learning experience. We also considered ways in which the sector can learn through our experiences by taking action to make the academic environment more inclusive. Finally, we make recommendations that may be considered as part of university policies, plans, and training to minimise exclusionary practices for individuals from ethnic minority backgrounds. We were able to largely achieve the above through years of reflexive practice. Therefore, we encourage other Muslim minority academics to objectively and unashamedly reflect continuously and consistently on their own learning, experiences, and actions, so as to be able to advance knowledge and help mitigate inequality within British HE and beyond.

REFERENCES

Adams, G., Dobles, I., Gómez, L. H., Kurtiş, T., & Molina, L. E. (2015). Decolonizing psychological science: Introduction to the special thematic section. *Journal of Social and Political Psychology, 3*(1), 213–238. https://doi.org/10.5964/jspp.v3i1.564

Advance Higher Education. (2019). Equality in higher education: staff statistical report 2019. Retrieved February 12, 2023, from www.advance-he.ac.uk/knowledge-hub/equality-higher-education-statistical-report-2019

Advance Higher Education. (2020). Equality in higher education: staff statistical report 2020. Retrieved February 12, 2023, from https://www.advance-he.ac.uk/knowledge-hub/equality-higher-education-statistical-report-2020

Ahmed, S. (2006). Doing diversity work in higher education in Australia. *Educational Philosophy and Theory, 38*(6), 745–768. https://doi.org/10.1111/j.1469-5812.2006.00228.x

Ahmed, S. (2012). *On being included: Racism and diversity in institutional life.* Duke University Press.

Allen-Ramdial, S. A. A., & Campbell, A. G. (2014). Reimagining the pipeline: Advancing STEM diversity, persistence, and success. *BioScience, 64*(7), 612–618. https://doi.org/10.1093/biosci/biu076

Almaki, S. H., Silong, A. D., Idris, K., & Wahat, N. W. A. (2016). Challenges faced Muslim women leaders in higher education. *Journal of Educational and Social Research, 6*(3), 75–75. https://doi.org/10.5901/jesr.2016.v6n3p75

Arday, J. (2018). Understanding race and educational leadership in higher education: Exploring the Black and ethnic minority (BME) experience. *Management in Education, 32*(4), 192–200. https://doi.org/10.5040/9781350068629.ch-008

Arday, J., Branchu, C., & Boliver, V. (2022). State of the art: What do we know about Black and Minority Ethnic (BAME) participation in UK higher education? *Social Policy and Society*, *21*(1), 12–25. https://doi.org/10.1017/s1474746421000579

Begum, N., & Saini, R. (2019). Decolonising the curriculum. *Political Studies Review*, *17*(2), 196–201. https://doi.org/10.1177/1478929918808459

Bhopal, K. (2018). *White Privilege: The myth of a post racial society*. Policy Press.

Bhopal, K., & Jackson, J. (2013). The experiences of Black and minority ethnic academics: Multiple identities and career progression. University of Southampton: EPSRC Report. Retrieved February 12, 2023, from https://eprints.soton.ac.uk/374244/1/__userfiles.soton.ac.uk_Users_slb1_mydesktop_Aiming%2520Higher.pdf

Bhui, K., Warfa, N., Edonya, P., McKenzie, K., & Bhugra, D. (2007). Cultural competence in mental health care: A review of model evaluations. *BMC Health Services Research*, *7*(1), 1–10. Available at:. https://doi.org/10.1186/1472-6963-7-15

Bilge, S. (2013). Intersectionality undone: Saving intersectionality from feminist intersectionality. *Du Bois Review: Social Science Research on Race*, *10*(2), 405–424. https://doi.org/10.1017/s1742058x13000283

Bloch, K. R., Taylor, T., Church, J., & Buck, A. (2021). An intersectional approach to the glass ceiling: Gender, race and share of middle and senior management in U.S. workplaces. *Sex Roles*, *84*, 312–325. https://doi.org/10.1007/s11199-020-01168-4

Bourdieu, P. (1984). *Distinction: A social critique of the judgement of taste*. Routledge.

Carbin, M., & Edenheim, S. (2013). The intersectional turn in feminist theory: A dream of a common language? *European Journal of Women's Studies*, *20*(3), 233–248. https://doi.org/10.1177/1350506813484723

Castro, D., Jones, R., & Mirsalimi, H. (2004). Parentification and the impostor phenomenon: An empirical investigation. *American Journal of Family Therapy*, *32*, 205–216. https://doi.org/10.1080/01926180490425676

Census. (2021). Religion, England and Wales: Census 2021. Retrieved February 11, 2023, from https://www.ons.gov.uk/peoplepopulationandcommunity/culturalidentity/religion/bulletins/religionenglandandwales/census2021

Chrousos, G. P., & Mentis, A. A. (2020). Imposter syndrome threatens diversity. *Science*, *367*(6479), 749–750. https://doi.org/10.1126/science.aba8039

Clance, P. R., & Imes, S. A. (1978). The imposter phenomenon in high achieving women: Dynamics and therapeutic intervention. *Psychotherapy: Theory, Research & Practice*, *15*(3), 241. https://doi.org/10.1037/h0086006

Cohen, S. (2001). *States of Denial: Knowing about atrocities and suffering*. Polity Press.

Cole, E. R. (2009). Intersectionality and research in psychology. *American Psychological Association, 6*(3), 170–180. https://doi.org/10.1037/a0014564

Crenshaw, K. (1989). Demarginalizing the intersection of race and sex: A black feminist critique of antidiscrimination doctrine, feminist theory and antiracist politics. *University of Chicago Legal Forum, 8*, 57–80. https://doi.org/10.4324/9780429500480-5

Dahlvig, J. E. (2013). A narrative study of women leading within the Council for Christian Colleges & Universities. *Christian Higher Education, 12*(1/2), 93–109. https://doi.org/10.1080/15363759.2013.739435

Dunier, M. (2006). Voices from the sidewalk: Ethnography and writing race. *Ethnic and Racial Studies, 29*(3), 543–565. https://doi.org/10.1080/01419870600598113

Ellis, C., Adams, T. E., & Bochner, A. P. (2010). Autoethnography: An overview. qualitative Sozialforschung/forum. *Qualitative Social Research, 12*(1).

Emirbayer, M., & Desmond, M. (2012). Race and reflexivity. *Ethnic and Racial Studies, 35*(4), 574–599. https://doi.org/10.1080/01419870.2011.606910

Evans, C. (2008). The effectiveness of m-learning in the form of podcast revision lectures in higher education. *Computers and Education, 50*, 491–498. https://doi.org/10.1016/j.compedu.2007.09.016

Fernandez, V., Simo, P., & Sallan, J. M. (2009). Podcasting: A new technological tool to facilitate good practice in higher education. *Computers and Education, 53*, 385–392. https://doi.org/10.1016/j.compedu.2009.02.014

Frankenburg, R. (1993). *White women, race matters: The social construction of whiteness*. Routledge.

Friedman, S., Laurison, D., & Miles, A. (2015). Breaking the 'class' ceiling? Social mobility into Britain's elite occupations. *The Sociological Review, 63*(2), 259–289. https://doi.org/10.1111/1467-954x.12283

Given, L. M. (2008). *The SAGE encyclopedia of qualitative research methods*. Sage.

GOV.UK. (2022). *Hate crime, England and Wales, 2021 to 2022*. Retrieved February 11, 2023, from https://www.gov.uk/government/statistics/hate-crime-england-and-wales-2021-to-2022/hate-crime-england-and-wales-2021-to-2022

Gusa, D. L. (2010). White institutional presence: The impact of Whiteness on campus climate. *Harvard Educational Review, 80*(4), 464–490. https://doi.org/10.17763/haer.80.4.p5j483825u110002

Guthrie, R. V. (2004). *Even the rat was white: A historical view of psychology*. Pearson Education.

Harris, T. M., & Lee, C. N. (2019). Advocate-mentoring: A communicative response to diversity in higher education. *Communication Education, 68*(1), 103–113. https://doi.org/10.1080/03634523.2018.1536272

Harvey, J., & Katz, C. (1985). *If I'm so successful, why do I feel like a fake? The imposter phenomenon*. St. Martin's Press.

Henderson, H., & Bhopal, K. (2022). Narratives of academic staff involvement in Athena SWAN and race equality charter marks in UK higher education institutions. *Journal of Education Policy, 37*(5), 781–797. https://doi.org/10.1080/02680939.2021.1891576

Hurtado, S., Milem, J. F., Clayton-Pedersen, A. R., & Allen, W. R. (1998). Enhancing campus climates for racial/ethnic diversity: Educational policy and practice. *The Review of Higher Education, 21*(3), 279–302. https://doi.org/10.1353/rhe.1998.0003

Ingle, S. (2022). *Beer ban is show of strength and an almighty two fingers up to Qatar's critics.* https://www.theguardian.com/football/blog/2022/nov/18/qatar-beer-ban-a-show-of-strength-and-an-almighty-two-fingers-up-to-its-critics

Iyer, A., Leach, C. W., & Crosby, F. J. (2003). White guilt and racial compensation: The benefits and limits of self-focus. *Personality and Social Psychology Bulletin, 29*(1), 117–129. https://doi.org/10.1177/0146167202238377

Jibrin, R., & Salem, S. (2015). Revisiting intersectionality: Reflections on theory and praxis. *An Interdisciplinary Journal in the Humanities and Sciences, 5,* 7–24. https://doi.org/10.4324/9781315210810-8

Khatun, R., Saleh, Z., Adnan, S., Boukerche, F., & Cooper, A. (2021). Covered, but not sterile: Reflections on being a hijabi in medicine and surgery. *Annals of Surgery, 273*(3), 83–84. https://doi.org/10.1097/sla.0000000000004655

King, J. E., & Cooley, E. L. (1995). Achievement orientation and the impostor phenomenon among college students. *Contemporary, Educational Psychology, 20*(3), 304–312. https://doi.org/10.1006/ceps.1995.1019

Lang, J. (2020). Analysis and recommendations on diversity of the mental health workforce. Retrieved February 12, 2023, from https://dleith.co.uk/tavistock-andportman.nhs.uk/documents/2099/Analysis_and_recommendations_on_diversity_of_the_mental_health_workforce.pdf

Macey, M., & Carling, A. (2011). *Ethnic, racial and religious inequalities: The perils of subjectivity.* Palgrave.

Madsen, S. R., Longman, K. A., & Daniels, J. R. (2012). Women's leadership development in higher education: Conclusion and implications for HRD. *Advances in Developing Human Resources, 14*(1), 113–128. https://doi.org/10.1177/1523422311429734

Mahmud, A., & Islam, M. (2022). Intersectional oppression: A reflexive dialogue between Muslim academics and their experiences of Islamophobia and exclusion in UK Higher Education. *Sociology Compass, 17*(2). https://doi.org/10.1111/soc4.13041

Mcmaster, N. C. (2020). Research insight: Religion and belief in UK higher education. Retrieved May 5, 2023, from https://s3.eu-west-2.amazonaws.com/assets.creode.advancehe-document-manager/documents/advance-he/AdvHE_Religion%20and%20belief_1606302802.pdf

MEMO. (2022). *Female fans feel safe at Qatar World Cup, thanks to reduced alcohol consumption.* https://www.middleeastmonitor.com/20221206-female-fans-feel-safe-at-qatar-world-cup-thanks-to-reduced-alcohol-consumption/

Mirza, H. S. (2018). Racism in higher education: "What then, can be done?". In H. S. Mirza & J. Arday (Eds.), *Dismantling race in higher education: Racism, whiteness and decolonising the academy* (pp. 3–23). Palgrave Macmillan.

Nadal, K. L., Issa, M., Griffin, K. E., Hamit, S., & Lyons, O. B. (2010). Religious microaggressions in the United States: Mental health implications for religious minority groups. In D. Sue (Ed.), *Microaggressions and marginality: Manifestation, dynamics, and impact.* John Wiley & Sons.

Nadal, K. L., Wong, Y., Griffin, K., Sriken, J., Vargas, V., Wideman, M., & Kolawole, A. (2011). Microaggressions and the multiracial experience. *International Journal of Humanities and Social Sciences, 1*(7), 36–44.

Nichols, S., & Stahl, G. (2019). Intersectionality in higher education research: A systematic literature review. *Higher Education Research & Development, 38*(6), 1255–1268. https://doi.org/10.1080/07294360.2019.1638348

Office for National Statistics. (2019). Population estimates by ethnic group and religion, England and Wales: 2019. Retrieved February 12, 2023, from https://www.ons.gov.uk/peoplepopulationandcommunity/populationandmigration/populationestimates/articles/populationestimatesbyethnicgroupandreligionenglandandwales/2019

Park, J. J., & Denson, N. (2009). Attitudes and advocacy: Understanding faculty views on racial/ethnic diversity. *The Journal of Higher Education, 80*(4), 415–438. https://doi.org/10.1353/jhe.0.0054

Parkman, A. (2016). The imposter phenomenon in higher education: Incidence and impact. *Journal of Higher Education Theory & Practice, 16*(1).

Patton, L. D., & Haynes, C. (2020). Dear white people: Reimagining whiteness in the struggle for racial equity. *Change: The Magazine of Higher Learning, 52*(2), 41–45. https://doi.org/10.1080/00091383.2020.1732775

Patton, L. D., McEwen, M., Rendón, L. I., & Howard-Hamilton, M. F. (2007). Critical race perspectives on theory in student affairs. *New Directions for Student Services, 120*, 39–53. https://doi.org/10.1002/ss.256

Piacentini, M. G., & Banister, E. N. (2009). Managing anti-consumption in an excessive drinking culture. *Journal of Business Research, 62*(2), 279–288. https://doi.org/10.1016/j.jbusres.2008.01.035

Pilkington, A. (2011). *Institutional racism in the academy: A UK case study.* Trentham Books.

Pilkington, A. (2013). The interacting dynamics of institutional racism in higher education. *Race, Ethnicity and Education, 16*(2), 225–245. https://doi.org/10.1080/13613324.2011.646255

Rahman, M. (2016). *Understanding organised crime in Birmingham: A case study of the 2003 new year shootings.* British Society of Criminology Conference Paper.

Rahman, M. (2017). *Ballers and Killers: Making sense of homicide in the context of organised crime within the West Midlands, England*. Unpublished doctoral thesis, Birmingham City University.

Rahman, M. (2019). *Homicide and organised crime: Ethnographic narratives of serious violence in the criminal underworld*. Palgrave.

Rahman, M., & Abdulkader, M. (2022). Living Rough: The vulnerabilities of rough sleepers in Birmingham, UK. *Abuse: An International Journal, 3*(1), 22–42. https://doi.org/10.37576/abuse.2022.029

Rahman, M., & Deuchar, R. (2024). *Ethics in qualitative criminological research*. Routledge.

Ramadan, I. (2017). Experiences of Muslim academics in UK higher education institutions. Retrieved February 12, 2023, from https://era.ed.ac.uk/bitstream/handle/1842/31350/Ramadan2017.pdf?sequence=1&isAllowed=y

Ramadan, I. (2021). When faith intersects with gender: The challenges and successes in the experiences of Muslim women academics. *Gender and Education, 34*(1), 33–48. https://doi.org/10.1080/09540253.2021.1893664

Reay, D. (2018). Race and Elite Universities in the UK. In J. Arday & H. S. Mirza (Eds.), *Dismantling race in higher education: Racism, whiteness and decolonising the academy*. Palgrave Macmillan.

Reay, D., Crozier, G., & Clayton, J. (2009). Strangers in paradise: Working class students in Elite Universities. *Sociology, 43*(6), 1103–1121. Available at:. https://doi.org/10.1177/0038038509345700

Rosette, A. S., de Leon, R. P., Koval, C. Z., & Harrison, D. A. (2018). Intersectionality: Connecting experiences of gender with race at work. *Research in Organizational Behavior, 38*, 1–22. https://doi.org/10.1016/j.riob.2018.12.002

Sakulku, J., & Alexander, J. (2011). The imposter phenomenon. *International Journal of Behavioral Science, 6*(1), 73–92.

Sherrer, K. (2022). What is Tokenism, and why does it matter in the workplace?. Retrieved February 12, 2023, from https://business.vanderbilt.edu/news/2018/02/26/tokenism-in-the-workplace/

Stevenson, J. (2018). Muslim students in UK higher education: Issues of inequality and inequity. Retrieved February 12, 2023, from https://www.azizfoundation.org.uk/wp-content/uploads/2021/01/Bridge-Higher-Education-report-2.pdf

Sue, D. W. (2010). *Microaggressions in everyday life: Race, gender, and sexual orientation*. John Wiley & Sons.

Sue, D. W., Capodilupo, C. M., Torino, G. C., Bucceri, J. M., Holder, A., Nadal, K. L., & Esquilin, M. (2007). Racial microaggressions in everyday life: Implications for clinical practice. *American Psychologist, 62*(4), 271–286. https://doi.org/10.1037/0003-066x.62.4.271

Tauri, J. M. (2018). The master's tool will never dismantle the Master's house: An indigenous critique of criminology. *Journal of Global Indigeneity, 3*(1), 37–40. https://doi.org/10.4324/9780203825235-7

Tyrer, D., & Ahmad, F. (2006). Muslim women and higher education: Identities, experiences and prospects: A Summary Report. Retrieved February 12, 2023, from http://image.guardian.co.uk/sys-files/Education/documents/2006/08/02/muslimwomen.pdf

Walker, A. (2020). Traditional white spaces why all-inclusive representation matters. *Journal of Dance Education, 20*(1), 157–167. https://doi.org/10.1080/15290824.2020.1795179

Weller, P., Hooley, T., & Moore, N. (2011). Religion and belief in higher education: The experiences of staff and students. Retrieved May 5, 2023, from https://repository.derby.ac.uk/item/94422/religion-and-belief-in-higher-education-the-experiences-of-staff-and-students

Woodall, D. (2013). Challenging whiteness in higher education classrooms: Context, content, and classroom dynamics. *The Journal of Public and Professional Sociology, 5*(2), 8. https://doi.org/10.1057/9781137471130.0012

Wright, C., Thompson, S., & Channer, Y. (2007). Out of place: Black women academics in British universities. *Women's History Review, 16*(2), 145–162. https://doi.org/10.1080/09612020601048704

Navigating British Academia as an Early Career Muslim Woman

Amena Amer and Nihan Albayrak-Aydemir

SETTING THE SCENE

The higher education sector, together with the working conditions of academics, has become very different compared to what it was a generation ago (Kenny, 2017), changing globally and particularly intensely in the last decade (see Afonso, 2014; Cannella & Koro-Ljungberg, 2017; Lynch & Ivancheva, 2015). As a result, academics are now facing greater levels of

---

Both authors contributed equally to this work.

A. Amer (✉)
University College London, London, UK
e-mail: a.amer@ucl.ac.uk

N. Albayrak-Aydemir
Boğaziçi University, Istanbul, Türkiye

London School of Economics and Political Science, London, UK
e-mail: nihan.albayrakaydemir@bogazici.edu.tr

A. Mahmud, M. Islam (eds.), *Uncovering Islamophobia in Higher Education*, Palgrave Studies in Race, Inequality and Social Justice in Education, https://doi.org/10.1007/978-3-031-65253-0_7

121

scrutiny, higher expectations, fewer opportunities, and lower job security—which altogether result in a condition of academic precarity (Albayrak-Aydemir & Gleibs, 2023). This has significantly impacted career development, work satisfaction, wellbeing, and the likelihood of remaining in the profession (Hollywood et al., 2020). In addition, mental health problems have gained increased attention and focus within the academic community in the last decade (Eleftheriades et al., 2020), with academics reported to experience significantly higher levels of mental health conditions compared to other professional groups (Goodwin et al., 2013). A wide range of factors are found to impact the mental health and wellbeing of academics, including workload (Darabi et al., 2017), job security (Simons et al., 2019), and support of employers and peers (Guthrie et al., 2017).

To add to the serious concerns about conditions within the higher education sector, further challenges come to the fore when considering the experiences of people of colour (staff and students). Indeed, while universities frame themselves as open and inclusive spaces, students and staff of colour often report feelings of disconnect, isolation, and a general lack of belonging (Ahmet, 2020; Stockfelt, 2018; Wright et al., 2007). Campaigns such as #MyRacistCampus and calls to decolonise the curriculum have aimed to not only highlight these concerns but also invite and work towards active and sustainable change (Bonam et al., 2017). Addressing these issues is in institutions' best interests, particularly given the negative implications such experiences have on student retention and success (Malik & Wykes, 2018; Stevenson, 2012). Despite there being limited research available beyond the experience of undergraduate students of colour (Samatar et al., 2021), this undoubtedly also has consequences on decisions to undertake postgraduate studies—a particularly worrying point given the increase in requirements for postgraduate qualifications in the job market more generally (Samatar et al., 2021), not least when considering the lack of representation of people of colour in academic jobs, which often require PhDs.

In effect, only 17% of academic staff within academic institutions are Black, Minority Ethnic (BME) and they face a 9% pay gap compared to their white counterparts (HESA, 2020). To add to this shocking statistic, they not only express similar experiences in relation to the lack of belongingness to those of minoritised students but also face additional issues, such as their expertise and seniority being questioned (Bhopal, 2016; Mirza & Arday, 2018; Wright et al., 2007). Such experiences bring to the fore the gravity of the situation within the UK higher education sector and beyond. This is before considering the intersections of other identities, such as gender or faith—a category widely overlooked (Ramadan, 2017). When considering the experiences of women of colour, for instance, we see a 'double penalty' against them (Bhopal, 2016), with their experiences going unnoticed and unacknowledged (Mirza, 2009). As such, these findings highlight important considerations for universities with regard to the retention and progression of minoritised and marginalised students and staff and emphasise that true care, recognition, and support must be provided, which will undoubtedly lead to more positive outcomes for all, staff and students alike (Samatar et al., 2021; Universities UK and National Union of Students, 2019).

Drawing on our own experiences as the foundation for our narrative within this chapter, we take stock of some of the challenges we have faced alongside others like us, as minoritised and marginalised academics, in our journeys within academia against the backdrop of the context only briefly painted above. More specifically, we consider our experiences as early career scholars of colour who are also visibly Muslim women, reflecting on the spaces in which we have studied and worked (both elite and modern post-92 institutions in the UK), and how our research expertise, knowledge, and approaches have been received by our peers. We also highlight significant differences which emerge through our ways of visibly expressing our Muslim identities, which bring in yet more layers and levels of detail to the picture when presenting the experiences of early career Muslim women researchers in British academia.

REFLEXIVITY: OUR POSITIONS AND EXPERIENCES

To begin, we must foreground our narrative with a clear stipulation of the positions from which we write and contextualise our experiences in important ways. Amena is a London-born British Muslim. Her ethnic background is of mixed North African and European heritage and while she is, and has been, visibly Muslim for a significant portion of her life through wearing the *hijab*, she now does so in 'turban' style—a style that can be described as 'less traditional' (not wrapped under the chin covering the neck). She has lived in London all her life, completing her entire education journey from nursery through to PhD in this city. Nihan is Turkish and grew up in Türkiye. She came to London after completing her undergraduate degree in Istanbul and completed two master's degrees and a PhD at three different elite and Russell Group British universities in

London. She is also visibly Muslim—wearing the hijab in a more 'traditional' style, which can readily be recognised by other Muslims as a 'Turkish-style'.[1]

Thus, our articulation of these positions become important for understanding many of the similarities and perhaps more significantly, the differences in our experiences. For example, for Amena, like many British Muslims, her experience of growing up in the UK has been shadowed by a reality of exclusionary language often peddled by politicians and an atmosphere of suspicion and surveillance, particularly since 9/11 and 7/7 (Guest et al., 2020; Ramadan, 2017). It framed so much of her experience that British Muslim identities, in the wake of 7/7, became the focus of her undergraduate dissertation at a modern (post-92) university she attended and became the catalyst for her passion in research which eventually culminated in completing a master's and PhD at an elite Russell Group institution. Although Nihan grew up and studied in a predominantly Muslim country, her experiences of exclusion and discrimination resemble (or sometimes even exceed) Amena's. In Türkiye, wearing hijab in schools was forbidden. So, she had to change her high school three times to be able to wear a hijab in disguise and she intentionally chose a university where the hijab ban would be taken less seriously. In all the places where she could wear a hijab to pursue an education, however, she was treated as if she was given a favour and should be grateful to be 'allowed to enter' schools. Even after the hijab ban has been practically revoked for several years, there is still a big backlash and resistance to the acceptance of 'hijab' in elite academic spaces. Compared to such experiences, she finds it more comfortable and easier to exist and claim spaces in UK Higher Education, where she is (and feels) more easily accepted as an individual, mostly due to the diversity efforts—regardless of these efforts being sincere or tokenistic.

What Does Being an Early Career Academic Mean?

Although there is variation in who is considered an early career academic, in general, academics who completed their PhD (or equivalent qualification) within the last five to eight years are called early career academics

---

[1] This distinction in style is important to note as it is different to styles readily worn by Muslim women, British, or otherwise, and is generally understood to be unique to Turkish Muslim women who wear the hijab.

(McKay & Monk, 2017; UK Research and Innovation, 2022). They are a broad group, whose employment status can vary depending on the type of contract (e.g. fixed-term or permanent), employment focus (e.g. research or teaching only), and level of expertise. Regardless of these differences in contracts, however, all are at the initial stage of their careers where they try to follow individual professional aspirations while handling institutional performance targets (Hollywood et al., 2020). The first five years of an academic job are a crucial indicator of both future academic progress and overall happiness (Laudel & Gläser, 2008), as well as leaving academia (Austin et al., 2007). In effect, what academics experience in the early years of their career can shape their perceptions of academia, their vision for teaching and learning, and their professional identity development (Nicholls, 2005; Remmik et al., 2011). When the experiences of being an early career academic are coupled with being a member of a minoritised community (e.g. religious or ethnic) and being a woman, they only further aggravate the challenges faced.

WHAT DOES BEING A MUSLIM ACADEMIC MEAN?

Muslim students and staff have come under increasing scrutiny over the years, with the Prevent Strategy and other such UK government-led security policies having added to their struggles to belong and be accepted. Within emergent research looking at religious identities on campus, it has been noted that many Muslims feel unsafe and under constant surveillance (Shaffait, 2019; Stevenson, 2018). Thus, navigating religious identities in these spaces can become a challenge, exemplified in findings illustrating that Muslim students are more likely to leave university before finishing their degrees and, if they do complete, do less well than their peers (Stevenson, 2018). In effect, a recent report notes that in 2017/2018, the proportion of Muslim students graduating with a 2:1 or first degree was less than all other students belonging to other religious groups and students with no religion (Codiroli Mcmaster, 2020). Hence, these gaps in completion and attainment rates make it less likely that these students have the qualifications to pursue further studies, let alone an academic career. To add, while we may be able to speculate about the experience of Muslim academics based on research findings examining the experiences of Muslim students as well as an awareness of the broader context for Muslims in the UK as noted above, there is in fact little research about Muslim academics specifically, with most research focusing on the category BME (e.g. Arday, 2018; Bhopal et al., 2016; Harris & Ogbonna, 2023; Ramadan, 2017). As such, important nuances become missed. Indeed, being visibly Muslim, through markers of religious identity (such as keeping a beard or a hijab), may further accentuate experiences of exclusion and play a significant role in experiences of belonging (Amer, 2020; Blackwood et al., 2015; Hopkins & Greenwood, 2013). This is particularly the case for women, for whom markers are often more common, more visible, and more recognisable. As such, Muslim women (the majority of whom will also be women of colour) have a lot to contend with in academia.

What Does Being a Woman Academic Mean?

Being a woman academic entails not only navigating various challenges but also advocating for change in academia. To date, extensive research has shed light on the experiences of women academics. Traditionally, most of these studies have explored the experiences and perceptions of women academics who survived to exist within the academic system (Bagilhole, 1993), addressed structural and systemic discriminatory practices within academia as key contributors to the gender gap (Aiston & Jung, 2015), acknowledged the rates of sexual harassment within academia and the use of non-disclosure agreements to silence staff and students (Weale & Batty, 2016), and highlighted the marginality and vulnerability of women academics while emphasising their potential for making positive contributions through feminist scholarship (Acker, 1983, 1992). While these studies have played a significant role in underlying the specific conditions in which women try to exist in academia, intersectional approaches have brought to the fore the experiences of minoritised groups among women academics (e.g. Joseph et al., 2021; Mirza, 2014). These studies are especially important as they highlight the systemic barriers at the marginalised intersections faced by minoritised women academics and their efforts to improve educational equity for all. For instance, recent research focusing on the politics of publishing research about Black women and intersectionality in higher education reveals that this type of research was usually published in journals with low impact factors (Joseph et al., 2021), indicating a lack of recognition and value for this important research. Similarly, through an exploration of the experiences of postcolonial diasporic Black and ethnicised women academics in higher education, Mirza (2014) underlines the embodiment of gendered and racialised differences as well as the erasure of these academics' presence in mainstream educational institutions. These realities are all in conjunction with experiences of systemic racism and bullying faced by minoritised women academics (see Rollock, 2019). Hence, marginalised women academics face significant additional challenges in occupying a historically white and male-dominated space, such as the issues of marginalisation, lack of belonging, survival strategies, excessive scrutiny, lack of progression, workload management, limited opportunities, lack of support, and inadequate access to resources (Wright et al., 2007). Recognising the intersectionality in women academics' experiences within academia is therefore of great importance to challenge and subvert the power dynamics that perpetuate inequality in academia and ultimately, to advocate for institutional changes in higher education. Thus, while being a woman academic, and indeed one of a minoritised background, involves navigating a variety of obstacles and challenges including a lack of due attention and acknowledgment given for their work (Readsura Decolonial Editorial Collective et al., 2022; Reddy & Amer, 2023), through their research and activism, women academics make important contributions to critical discussions and work towards a more inclusive and equitable academic environment.

LIVING AT THE INTERSECTIONS OF BEING AN EARLY CAREER ACADEMIC, A MUSLIM, AND A WOMAN

For us, as early career Muslim women academics, living at the intersections has consequences in numerous aspects of our lives. Navigating our identities can create a sense of internal conflict and a need to constantly negotiate different aspects of ourselves in different spaces and contexts. Below, we comment on the aspects we find to be critical based on both research evidence and our own experiences, which are (1) professional identity development, (2) representation and role models, (3) support mechanisms, and (4) mental health and wellbeing.

Professional Identity Development

Professional identity development, and its recognition by others, plays a critical role in not only how academics decide on their professional values and academic activities, but also their success in doing so. Moreover, identity performance—the extent to which one accentuates or minimises certain aspects of their identities (Klein et al., 2007)—plays an interesting role in these dynamics. For example, the extent to which one expresses their religious identity (such as by wearing the hijab, in the case of Muslim women) can have consequences on professional identity development given the climate of scrutiny, surveillance, and suspicion, as previously highlighted. Our own experiences echo findings from a plethora of previous research which demonstrates the extent to which minoritised academics need to work harder to achieve recognition and success, compared to their non-minoritised peers (Lukate, 2022; Reddy & Amer, 2023).

A particular experience which stands out is the consistent need to justify our own positions and declare our identities, as early career Muslim women, in relation to our research and researcher identity. This is not something we can readily avoid given the visibility of our Muslim identity. Questions of bias and overinterpretation have been directed to us in ways that forefront our Muslimness over and above our ability to engage in critical and rigorous research practices. Moreover, our ability to engage in research as 'insiders', bringing richness and depth to the work that we do is overlooked, denying us recognition as equal contributors to knowledge production (Reddy & Amer, 2023). It is this exact ability as 'insiders' that allows us to bring an original perspective to a mainstream topic or discover an original topic in our fields. Thus, in denying the recognition of knowledge contributions and contributors, it pushes us to the margins, maintaining a status quo of hegemonic knowledge production that is embedded in colonial power structures related to 'whose knowledge counts' (Bou Zeineddine et al., 2022; Readsura Decolonial Editorial Collective et al., 2022; Reddy & Amer, 2023). We, nevertheless, endeavour to continue to remain true to the research we undertake; however, if we want to establish ourselves within our fields, we, as early career researchers, feel pressured to travel the roads that are travelled by 'mainstream'[2] researchers until we receive the slightest recognition for our work (Reddy & Amer, 2023). Only after this recognition, may many of us feel free to follow original insights deriving from the uniqueness of our identities.

Other examples include the consistent narrowing of the framing of our research and knowledge contribution by others because of our overarching community of focus (e.g. questions about how our research on Muslim identities is connected to views on terrorism and extremism) or indeed

---

[2] This can include the use of particular methods, theories, and topics that do not disrupt the status quo within one's specific discipline.

persistent expectations to engage in professional citizenship activities around diversity, equality, and inclusion simply because of our visible Muslim identities. While there may be a desire to play an active role in our institutions as early career academics in order to build stronger professional identities for ourselves, our wishes to do so often feel exploited when our institutions reach out to us more with opportunities related to diversity and less with research, teaching, and other activities that are considered essential for an academic. Such experiences are frustrating to say the least, stripping us from a sense of control over how we develop our academic identity and the activities we engage in when doing so.

Representation and Role Models

Muslim academics, especially when considering the additional intersection of being a woman, are underrepresented in the UK academic system, particularly in leadership and more senior roles (Ahmet, 2020; Bhopal & Pitkin, 2018). This can make it difficult to find role models and mentors who share their experiences and can provide support and guidance in their career development. Indeed, early career academics, in general, have been reported to have inadequate academic support and mentoring (Hardwick, 2005) while having to navigate academia's many demands and high workloads (Austin et al., 2007). Thus, the chances of receiving such support decrease further for minoritised academics.

In our own experience, we have struggled to find Muslim women academics in our institutions and in our disciplines. The few that are there are honest about the challenges and barriers they have and continue to face trying to remain in academia and be recognised for the work they do on a level playing field. This is before taking into account the hurdles faced when considering successful promotion and acquiring leadership roles. A lack of representation, institutional racism, and cultural bias is often cited to explain the barriers we face, which have serious consequences on our futures and those of others like us in a space that is made up predominantly of, and for, those that are elite, male, and middle class (Bhopal, 2016; Bhopal & Pitkin, 2018). This can limit opportunities for career advancement and may prevent us from influencing policy and decision-making in our fields. Thus, the lack of minority representation and role models in academia continues the cycle of the struggle faced by scholars from minoritised backgrounds and causes another layer of burden on those who are in the early stages of their careers (McGee, 2020).

Unfortunately, such lack of representation is something many early career scholars from minoritised backgrounds face from the beginning of their higher education experience well before becoming academics themselves. Whilst the number of students from minoritised backgrounds attending university continues to increase, there are clear disparities in the types of universities they attend with a clear underrepresentation in the elite[3] universities but an overrepresentation in post-1992[4] universities (Alexander & Ardy, 2015; Boliver, 2016; Sundorph et al., 2017). Furthermore, students have little opportunity to engage with and be taught by faculty from minoritised backgrounds, with those who are present often being on fixed-term or other forms of precarious contracts (Bhopal & Pitkin, 2018). In our own experiences as students (and indeed as staff), we have been acutely aware of this disparity in who makes up the student body and academic faculty within different institutions. Having attended and worked in modern (post-92) as well as elite UK universities, one cannot escape the stark difference in the student bodies in these institutions highlighted above, and the absence of academic staff from minoritised backgrounds. Staff from minoritised backgrounds tend to fill roles in professional services instead, bringing up concerns about the consequences on minoritised students' future aspirations given the limited access to, and opportunities to see, people 'like us' in academic positions (Ahmet, 2020). We have seen the power of our own presence as Muslim women academics in universities where Muslim women students (as well as other students of minoritised backgrounds) have actively sought to seek support, engage, and work with us, giving us the opportunity to mentor them as they navigate their university life. Such support can be invaluable, regardless of academic aspirations but requires a change in the academic environment to ensure we stay.

Support Mechanisms

The culture of academic spaces is important for all researchers and academics, not least for those who are early career and of minoritised

---

[3] In the UK, this typically refers to high-ranking institutions that accept students with the highest grades and also draw a substantial amount of money from externally funded research projects.

[4] Also known as modern or new universities. In the UK, these institutions typically gained university status in 1992 through the Further and Higher Education Act 1992.

backgrounds. This is because it is these places where they not only face barriers but also find means to navigate these barriers in order to rightly claim and take up space within academia even if on the margins. For instance, departmental culture and support play a key role in how early career academics adapt to academia (Trowler & Knight, 1999). The extent to which they feel isolated can impact the development of research careers in academia (Smith, 2010), with more supportive academic departments making it more likely for early career researchers to have an easier integration into the profession, feel less isolated, and develop stronger research careers. It is, however, critical to note here that what a department does to support people does not necessarily equate to how much people *feel* supported by the department. A lack of connection between these two, therefore, does more harm than good for both the institution and the people.

A potential reason why support mechanisms do not end up supporting people is that most support mechanisms are top-down and do not factor in the unique individual challenges early career academics go through (McKay & Monk, 2017). This becomes especially relevant when these academics come from minoritised backgrounds, as in the case of Muslim women academics. Our experiences so far have shown us that the unique challenges we go through are rarely recognised, let alone supported. A challenge, for example, is how we are approached and treated by others and how our 'atypical' appearance as an academic is used to evaluate the work we do. As with every other early career researcher, we try to network and make connections inside and outside our institutions (such as through professional organisations), but we also expect others who are at later stages of their career to approach us as they approach other early career academics. However, we often notice how people seem reluctant to engage with us, perhaps in an attempt to avoid 'the unknown' until they recognise a sign of elitism (e.g. through our universities, countries, or accents). To add to this, the ways in which we differently express and perform our Muslim identities through different styles of hijab and dress add another rather stark layer to these interactions. In Amena's experience, the dramatic overnight change in experiences of interactions when choosing to adopt a less traditional style of hijab a few years ago was shocking, with colleagues being far more forthcoming than previously, engaging in small talk and being active in fostering collegial relationships. In managing these experiences, we have sought to carve out spaces for ourselves along with other minoritised academics, to support and nurture each other as best we can, echoing the attempts of many other academics of minoritised or marginalised backgrounds (Bhopal, 2022).

Such interpersonal relations in academia are not only important for how we currently function, but also important for how we think we will function in the future (see, e.g., Stevenson & Clegg, 2011). In effect, recent evidence demonstrates that even though departmental culture, quality of work relationships, and perceived respect of colleagues towards oneself are not related to academics' intention to stay in academia, they are connected to how positively academics imagine their future in academia (Hollywood et al., 2020). Indeed, the challenges early career and visibly Muslim women academics go through are often unrecognised, yet their visible identities are all too often taken advantage of to showcase diversity. As such, these contradictions portray a completely different (and potentially a darker) picture for these academics compared to their peers who may not have to contend with these same issues, resulting in significant consequences on mental health and wellbeing.

Mental Health and Wellbeing

The current academic system puts many academics at risk for poor mental health and wellbeing and although much of this can be managed by providing academics with peer support, career advancement, and mentorship, these resources of support are not equally accessible to minorities (Nicholls et al., 2022). Thus, the current state of academia puts minorities at a higher risk for mental health issues. For example, students from racially minoritised backgrounds are more likely to experience mental health issues, compared to those from majority backgrounds—even when the ratio of minoritised students at the university increase (Smith et al., 2014). Indeed, these issues are echoed among the experiences of minoritised academic staff, where discrimination, marginalisation, and the lack of appropriate support systems within academia have serious consequences on their mental health and wellbeing (Arday, 2022). Moreover, as is the case in all sectors, those within academia are also susceptible to prejudices experienced more broadly in everyday life. For example, Muslim academics may be affected by negative media portrayals of Muslims and Islam as well as the broader political marginalising narratives and stereotypes (see, e.g., King & Ahmad, 2010; Saleem et al., 2017; Unkelbach et al., 2008). These can filter into the workplace creating a hostile work environment, which can, then, lead to feelings of isolation and insecurity as well as a sense of being constantly on guard. These issues can be further exacerbated by a lack of cultural connection between minoritised academics and the spaces and communities they navigate in academia as well as identity confusion due to having to deal with two separate identities (inside vs. outside academia). This can then result in further social, academic, and financial challenges, especially for early career researchers (Albayrak & Okoroji, 2019) and decrease wellbeing.

Early career academics are also at a higher risk of mental health issues because of precarious working conditions (Woolston, 2020). The instability of contracts, the increasing pressure to do more, and the need to prove oneself can be listed as some of the many factors that impact the wellbeing of early career researchers. Indeed, locus of control affects how happy and stressed academics feel and how positively they think about their future career in academia (Hollywood et al., 2020). More specifically, the more academics lose control of the work they do, the less happy and the more stressed they feel and the more pessimistic they get about their future academic career. This no doubt applies to academics across the sector, but particularly impacts those early in their career when we note the increasingly competitive and hostile working environment that is so prevalent within higher education today (Albayrak-Aydemir & Gleibs, 2023).

Early career academics are often left to deal with such problems themselves, with a general lack of adequate support and mentorship (Hollywood et al., 2020), as well as a prevalent culture of competition such as 'publish or perish' which leads to further feeling of isolation (Obradović, 2019). Without the constructive support system coupled with the constant self-doubt, early career academics can barely take the time to cope with mental health problems and to improve their wellbeing. This is even harder for early career Muslim academics, and minoritised academics in general, as they may face further challenges through discrimination, racism, bias, and stereotyping based on their religion, race, and ethnicity, all of which can limit their career prospects and hinder their wellbeing and ability to advance in their field (see, e.g., Ahmad, 2001; Barlow & Awan, 2016; Mahmud & Islam, 2023; Ramadan, 2022). It is thus no surprise that the pressures of academia such as the widely acknowledged norm to 'publish or perish' and inadequate support mechanisms have pushed many to leave the sector (University College Union, 2022), not least academics of minoritised backgrounds who contend with additional obstacles and challenges (Valentine, 2020). As such, this brings to the fore serious questions about the future of the sector and what this means for subsequent generations of students.

CONCLUSION

Navigating British academia as an early career Muslim woman is a complex journey that requires resilience, adaptability, and a strong sense of self. Throughout this chapter, we have explored the unique challenges faced by early career Muslim women in their pursuit of academic success. Despite academia's claim for being an inclusive, stimulating, and enriching space, in emphasising some of the conditions within UK higher education in which early career Muslim women academics, including ourselves, have to navigate, we hope to have highlighted some of the particular barriers that are encountered on an almost daily basis as we endeavour to find our path. Specifically, we have engaged in four areas we find critical in having shaped and continue to shape both our own experiences, and the experiences of those like us, these being (1) professional identity development, (2) representation and role models, (3) support mechanisms, and (4) mental health and wellbeing. We make no claim in stating that these are the only areas that are important as we confront the lack of inclusivity in academic spaces in the UK. Instead, we use these areas as a launch pad, drawing on research and examples of our own to add to the many calls for addressing the hurdles, barriers, and hostility experienced by early career Muslim women academics and minoritised academics alike, which has resulted in the erasure of their narratives and an absence of their critical knowledge contributions.

We have also highlighted the ways in which we find solace and support in our almost daily fight to remain within academia, even if this existence is on its very margins. We have seen how cultural, religious, and gender dynamics intersect within academic context. Being a Muslim woman in academia often means juggling multiple identities and expectations. However, the power of embracing intersecting identities can enable Muslim women to bring their diverse perspectives and experiences to enrich academic discourse. Building supportive networks and finding mentors who can provide guidance and encouragement along the way becomes especially important at this point. Muslim women face unique barriers, such as stereotypes, biases, and limited representation, but by connecting with others who have navigated similar paths, they can find solidarity and strength. Establishing strong relationships with allies within academia can foster an inclusive and diverse academic environment where Muslim women feel empowered to thrive. We have emphasised the need for institutions to actively address the unique barriers faced by early career Muslim women. By fostering a culture of inclusivity, diversity, and equal opportunity, universities and research institutions can create an environment where Muslim women can flourish and reach their full potential. Implementing policies that promote diversity in hiring, offering mentorship programmes, and accommodating religious needs are essential steps towards creating an equitable academic landscape. As such, it is high time that UK academia take these calls seriously and faces up to not only how it can be a debilitating place for minoritised researchers but to also understand, acknowledge, and take action to address the nuanced experiences within this group. Indeed, while there are some claims by institutions to be working towards change, the inclusion and recognition of experiences through religious identities, the prevalence of Islamophobia both within academia and more widely in society, and the intersections with other identities such as being a woman and an early career researcher are still widely absent. This silence only adds to the violence and harm experienced. Thus, to echo Reddy and Amer's (2023) call for making space for complaint, we hope that in being vulnerable by directly sharing our own experiences through the medium of this book chapter, our voices and critical contributions, along with those of other Muslim women early career academics on the margins, are recognised and taken seriously in a bid towards making academia more inclusive and equal.

References

Acker, S. (1983, January). Women, the other academics. *Women's Studies International Forum, 6*(2): 191–201. Pergamon. https://doi.org/10.1016/0277-5395(83)90010-9

Acker, S. (1992). New perspectives on an old problem: The position of women academics in British higher education. *Higher Education, 24*(1), 57–75. https://doi.org/10.1007/BF00138618

Afonso, A. (2014). How academia resembles a drug gang. *SSRN Electronic Journal*. Retrieved May 5, 2023, from https://doi.org/10.2139/ssrn.2407748

Ahmad, F. (2001). Modern traditions? British Muslim women and academic achievement. *Gender and Education, 13*(2), 137–152. https://doi.org/10.1080/09540250120051169

Ahmet, A. (2020). Who is worthy of a place on these walls? Postgraduate students, UK universities, and institutional racism. *Area, 52*(4), 678–686. https://doi.org/10.1111/area.12627

Aiston, S. J., & Jung, J. (2015). Women academics and research productivity: An international comparison. *Gender and Education, 27*(3), 205–220. https://doi.org/10.1080/09540253.2015.1024617

Albayrak, N., & Okoroji, C. (2019). Facing the challenges of postgraduate study as a minority student. In H. Walton (Ed.), *A Guide for Psychology Postgraduates* (2nd ed., pp. 63–66). The British Psychological Society.

Albayrak-Aydemir, N., & Gleibs, I. H. (2023). A social-psychological examination of academic precarity as an organizational practice and subjective experience. *British Journal of Social Psychology, 62*(S1), 95–110. https://doi.org/10.1111/bjso.12607

Alexander, C., & Ardy, J. (2015). Introduction: Race and higher education. In *Runnymede trust aiming higher: Race, inequality and diversity in the academy.* Runnymede Trust. http://www.runnymedetrust.org/uploads/Aiming%20Higher.pdf

Amer, A. (2020). Between recognition and mis/nonrecognition: Strategies of negotiating and performing identities among white Muslims in the United Kingdom. *Political Psychology, 41*(3), 533–548. https://doi.org/10.1111/pops.12637

Arday, J. (2018). Understanding race and educational leadership in higher education: Exploring the Black and ethnic minority (BME) experience. *Management in Education, 32*(4), 192–200. https://doi.org/10.1177/0892020618791002

Arday, J. (2022). No one can see me cry: Understanding mental health issues for black and ethnic minority academic staff in higher education. *Higher Education., 83*(1), 79–102. https://doi.org/10.1007/s10734-020-00636-w

Austin, A. E., Sorcinelli, M. D., & McDaniels, M. (2007). Understanding new faculty background, aspirations, challenges, and growth. In R. P. Perry & J. C. Smart (Eds.), *The scholarship of teaching and learning in higher education: An evidence-based perspective* (pp. 39–89). Springer.

Bagilhole, B. (1993). How to keep a good woman down: An investigation of the role of institutional factors in the process of discrimination against women academics. *British Journal of Sociology of Education, 14*(3), 261–274. https://doi.org/10.1080/0142569930140303

Barlow, C., & Awan, I. (2016). "You need to be sorted out with a knife": The attempted online silencing of women and people of Muslim faith within academia. *Social Media+ Society, 2*(4), 1–11. https://doi.org/10.1177/2056305116678896

Bhopal, K. (2016). *The experiences of Black and minority ethnic academics: A comparative study of the unequal academy.* Routledge.

Bhopal, K. (2022). Academics of colour in elite universities in the UK and the USA: The 'unspoken system of exclusion'. *Studies in Higher Education, 47*(11), 2127–2137. https://doi.org/10.1080/03075079.2021.2020746

Bhopal, K., Brown, H., & Jackson, J. (2016). BME academic flight from UK to overseas higher education: Aspects of marginalisation and exclusion. *British Educational Research Journal, 42*(2), 240–257. https://doi.org/10.1002/berj.3204

Bhopal, K., & Pitkin, C. (2018). *Investigating higher education institutions and their views on the Race Equality Charter.* University and Colleges Union. Retrieved April 15, 2023, from https://www.ucu.org.uk/media/9535/Investigating-higher-education-institutions-and-their-views-on-the-Race-Equality-Charter-Sept-18/pdf/REC_report_Sep18_fp.pdf

Blackwood, L., Hopkins, N., & Reicher, S. D. (2015). 'Flying while Muslim': Citizenship and misrecognition in the airport. *Journal of Social and Political Psychology, 3*(2), 148–170. https://doi.org/10.5964/jspp.v3i2.375

Boliver, V. (2016). Exploring ethnic inequalities in admission to Russell group universities. *Sociology, 50,* 247–266. https://doi.org/10.1177/0038038515 75859

Bonam, C. M., Taylor, V. J., & Yantis, C. (2017). Racialized physical space as cultural product. *Social and Personality Psychology Compass, 11*(9), 1–12. https://doi.org/10.1111/spc3.12340

Bou Zeineddine, B., Saab, R., Lášticová, B., Kende, A., & Ayanian, A. H. (2022). "Some uninteresting data from a faraway country": Inequity and coloniality in international social psychological publications. *Journal of Social Issues., 73*(2), 320–345. https://doi.org/10.1017/9781108779104.040 [Opens in a new window]

Cannella, G. S., & Koro-Ljungberg, M. (2017). Neoliberalism in higher education: Can we understand? Can we resist and survive? Can we become without neoliberalism? *Cultural Studies – Critical Methodologies, 17*(3), 155–162. https://doi.org/10.1177/1532708617706117

Codiroli Mcmaster, N. (2020). *Research insight: Religion and belief in UK higher education analysis of Higher Education Statistics Agency (HESA) student data for 2017/18.* Advanced HE. Retrieved April 15, 2023, from https://s3.eu-west-2.amazonaws.com/assets.creode.advancehe-document-manager/documents/advance-he/AdvHE_Religionandbelief_1606302802.pdf

Darabi, M., Macaskill, A., & Reidy, L. (2017). Stress among UK academics: Identifying who copes best. *Journal of further and Higher Education, 41*(3), 393–412. https://doi.org/10.1080/0309877X.2015.1117598

Eleftheriades, R., Fiala, C., & Pasic, M. D. (2020). The challenges and mental health issues of academic trainees. *F1000Research, 9,* 104. https://doi.org/10.12688/f1000research.21066.1

Goodwin, L., Ben-Zion, I., Fear, N. T., Hotopf, M., Stansfeld, S. A., & Wessely, S. (2013). Are reports of psychological stress higher in occupational studies? A systematic review across occupational and population based studies. *PLoS ONE*, *8*(11), e78693. https://doi.org/10.1371/journal.pone.0078693

Guest, M., Scott-Baumann, A., Cheruvallil-Contractor, S., Naguib, S., Phoenix, A., Lee, Y., & Al Baghal, T. (2020). *Islam and Muslims on UK university campuses: Perceptions and challenges*. Durham University; SOAS; Coventry University and Lancaster; Lancaster University. Retrieved April 2, 2023, from https://eprints.soas.ac.uk/33345/1/file148310.pdf

Guthrie, S., Lichten, C., van Belle, J., Ball, S., Knack, A., & Hofman, J. (2017). *Understanding mental health in the research environment: A rapid evidence assessment*. RAND Europe. Retrieved May 19, 2023, from https://doi.org/10.7249/RR2022

Hardwick, S. W. (2005). Mentoring early career faculty in geography: Issues and strategies. *The Professional Geographer*, *57*(1), 21–27. https://doi.org/10.1111/j.0033-0124.2005.00456.x

Harris, L. C., & Ogbonna, E. (2023). Equal opportunities but unequal mentoring? The perceptions of mentoring by Black and minority ethnic academics in the UK university sector. *Human Resource Management Journal*. Advance online publication. https://doi.org/10.1111/1748-8583.12492

HESA. (2020). *Higher education staff statistics: UK, 2018/19*. Higher Education Statistics Agency. Retrieved May 10, 2023, from https://www.hesa.ac.uk/news/23-01-2020/sb256-higher-education-staff-statistics

Hollywood, A., McCarthy, D., Spencely, C., & Winstone, N. (2020). 'Overwhelmed at first': The experience of career development in early career academics. *Journal of Further and Higher Education*, *44*(7), 998–1012. https://doi.org/10.1080/0309877X.2019.1636213

Hopkins, N., & Greenwood, R. M. (2013). Hijab, visibility and the performance of identity. *European Journal of Social Psychology*, *43*(5), 438–447. https://doi.org/10.1002/ejsp.1955

Joseph, N. M., Haynes, C., & Patton, L. D. (2021). The politics of publishing: A national conversation with scholars who use their research about Black women to address intersectionality. *Educational Researcher*, *50*(2), 115–126. https://doi.org/10.3102/0013189X20985460

Kenny, J. (2017). Academic work and performativity. *Higher Education*, *74*(5), 897–913. https://doi.org/10.1007/s10734-016-0084-y

King, E. B., & Ahmad, A. S. (2010). An experimental field study of interpersonal discrimination toward Muslim job applicants. *Personnel Psychology*, *63*(4), 881–906. https://doi.org/10.1111/j.1744-6570.2010.01199.x

Klein, O., Spears, R., & Reicher, S. (2007). Social identity performance: Extending the strategic side of SIDE. *Personality and Social Psychology Review*, *11*(1), 28–45. https://doi.org/10.1177/1088868306294588

Laudel, G., & Gläser, J. (2008). From apprentice to colleague: The metamorphosis of early career researchers. *Higher Education, 55*(3), 387–406. https://doi.org/10.1007/s10734-007-9063-7

Lukate, J. M. (2022). Space, race and identity: An ethnographic study of the black hair care and beauty landscape and black women's racial identity constructions in England. *Journal of Social Issues, 78*(1), 107–125. https://doi.org/10.1111/josi.12433

Lynch, K., & Ivancheva, M. (2015). Academic freedom and the commercialisation of universities: A critical ethical analysis. *Ethics in Science and Environmental Politics, 15*(1), 71–85. https://doi.org/10.3354/esep00160

Mahmud, A., & Islam, M. (2023). Intersectional oppression: A reflexive dialogue between Muslim academics and their experiences of Islamophobia and exclusion in UK Higher Education. *Sociology Compass, 17*(2), e13041. https://doi.org/10.1111/soc4.13041

Malik, A., & Wykes, E. (2018). *British Muslims in UK higher education: Socio-political, religious and policy considerations.* Bridge Institute. https://www.azizfoundation.org.uk/wp-content/uploads/2021/01/Bridge-Higher-Education-report.pdf

McGee, E. O. (2020). Interrogating structural racism in STEM higher education. *Educational Researcher, 49*(9), 633–644. https://doi.org/10.3102/0013189X20972718

McKay, L., & Monk, S. (2017). Early career academics learning the game in Whackademia. *Higher Education Research and Development, 36*(6), 1251–1263. https://doi.org/10.1080/07294360.2017.1303460

Mirza, H. S. (2009). *Race, gender and educational desire: Why black women succeed and fail.* Routledge.

Mirza, H. S. (2014). Decolonizing higher education: Black feminism and the intersectionality of race and gender. *Journal of Feminist Scholarship, 7*(7), 1–12. https://digitalcommons.uri.edu/jfs/vol7/iss7/3

Mirza, H. S., & Arday, J. (2018). *Dismantling race in higher education: Racism, whiteness and decolonising the academy.* Palgrave Macmillan.

Nicholls, G. (2005). New lecturers' constructions of learning, teaching and research in higher education. *Studies in Higher Education, 30*(5), 611–625. https://doi.org/10.1080/03075070500249328

Nicholls, H., Nicholls, M., Tekin, S., Lamb, D., & Billings, J. (2022). The impact of working in academia on researchers' mental health and wellbeing: A systematic review and qualitative metasynthesis. *PLoS ONE, 17*(5), e0268890. https://doi.org/10.1371/journal.pone.0268890

Obradović, S. (2019). Publication pressures create knowledge silos. *Nature Human Behaviour, 3*, 1028. https://doi.org/10.1038/s41562-019-0674-7

Ramadan, I. (2017). *Experiences of Muslim academics in UK Higher Education Institutions.* Doctoral dissertation, the University of Edinburgh. Edinburgh Research Archive. Retrieved May 12, 2023, from https://era.ed.ac.uk/handle/1842/31350

Ramadan, I. (2022). When faith intersects with gender: The challenges and successes in the experiences of Muslim women academics. *Gender and Education,* *34*(1), 33–48. https://doi.org/10.1080/09540253.2021.1893664

Readsura Decolonial Editorial Collective (in random order), Ratele, K., Reddy, G., Adams, G., & Suffla, S. (2022). Decoloniality as a social issue for psychological study. *Journal of Social Issues,* *78*(1): 7–26. https://doi.org/10.1111/josi.12502

Reddy, G., & Amer, A. (2023). Precarious engagements and the politics of knowledge production: Listening to calls for reorienting hegemonic social psychology. *British Journal of Social Psychology,* *62*(S1), 71–94. https://doi.org/10.1111/bjso.12609

Remmik, M., Karm, M., Haamer, A., & Lepp, L. (2011). Early career academics' learning in academic communities. *International Journal for Academic Development,* *16*(3), 187–199. https://doi.org/10.1080/1360144X.2011.596702

Rollock, N. (2019). *Staying power: The career experiences and strategies of UK black female professors.* University and College Union. Retrieved May 17, 2023, from https://www.ucu.org.uk/media/10075/Staying-Power/pdf/UCU_Rollock_February_2019.pdf

Saleem, M., Prot, S., Anderson, C. A., & Lemieux, A. F. (2017). Exposure to Muslims in media and support for public policies harming Muslims. *Communication Research,* *44*(6), 841–869. https://doi.org/10.1177/0093650215619214

Samatar, A., Madriaga, M., & McGrath, L. (2021). No love found: How female students of colour negotiate and repurpose university spaces. *British Journal of Sociology of Education,* *42*(5–6), 717–732. https://doi.org/10.1080/01425692.2021.1914548

Shaffait, H. (2019). *Inclusivity at university: Muslim student experiences.* King's College London. https://www.kcl.ac.uk/geography/assets/kcl-sspp-muslim-policy-report-digital-aw.pdf

Simons, A., Munnik, E., Frantz, J., & Smith, M. (2019). The profile of occupational stress in a sample of health profession academics at a historically disadvantaged university in South Africa. *South African Journal of Higher Education,* *33*(3), 132–154. https://doi.org/10.20853/33-3-3199

Smith, J. (2010). Forging identities: The experiences of probationary lecturers in the UK. *Studies in Higher Education,* *35*(5), 577–591. https://doi.org/10.1080/03075070903216650

Smith, K. M., Chesin, M. S., & Jeglic, E. L. (2014). Minority college student mental health: Does majority status matter? Implications for college counseling services. *Journal of Multicultural Counseling and Development, 42*(2), 77–92. https://doi.org/10.1002/j.2161-1912.2014.00046.x

Stevenson, J. (2012). *Black and minority ethnic student degree retention and attainment.* The Higher Education Academy. https://www.advance-he.ac.uk/knowledge-hub/black-and-minority-ethnic-student-degree-retention-and-attainment

Stevenson, J. (2018). *Muslim students in UK higher education: issues of inequality and inequity.* Bridge Institute for Research and Policy. https://www.azizfoundation.org.uk/wp-content/uploads/2021/01/Bridge-Higher-Education-report-2.pdf

Stevenson, J., & Clegg, S. (2011). Possible selves: Students orientating themselves towards the future through extracurricular activity. *British Educational Research Journal, 37*(2), 231–246. https://doi.org/10.1080/01411920903540672

Stockfelt, S. (2018). We the minority-of-minorities: A narrative inquiry of black female academics in the United Kingdom. *British Journal of Sociology of Education, 39*(7), 1012–1029. https://doi.org/10.1080/01425692.2018.1454297

Sundorph, E., Vasilev, D., & Coiffait, L. (2017). *Joining the elite: How top universities can enhance social mobility.* Reform. https://reform.uk/wp-content/uploads/2018/10/Joining-The-Elite-final.pdf

Trowler, P., & Knight, P. (1999). Organizational socialization and induction in universities: Reconceptualizing theory and practice. *Higher Education, 37*(2), 177–195. https://doi.org/10.1023/A:1003594512521

UK Research and Innovation. (2022). *Early career researchers: career and skills development.* https://www.ukri.org/what-we-offer/developing-people-and-skills/ahrc/early-career-researchers-career-and-skills-development/

Universities and Colleges Union. (2022). *UK higher education: a workforce in crisis.* https://www.ucu.org.uk/media/12532/UK-higher-education%2D%2D2D-a-workforce-in-crisis/pdf/UK_HE_Report_24_Mar22.pdf

Universities UK and National Union of Students. (2019). *Black, Asian and Minority Ethnic Student Attainment at UK Universities: #closing the gap.* Universities UK. https://www.universitiesuk.ac.uk/sites/default/files/field/downloads/2021-07/bame-student-attainment.pdf

Unkelbach, C., Forgas, J. P., & Denson, T. F. (2008). The turban effect: The influence of Muslim headgear and induced affect on aggressive responses in the shooter bias paradigm. *Journal of Experimental Social Psychology, 44*(5), 1409–1413. https://doi.org/10.1016/j.jesp.2008.04.003

Valentine, S. (2020). Time for Black women to leave academia? [Blog post]. https://medium.com/the-faculty/time-for-black-women-to-leave-academia-4a97dcf3ed2f

Weale, S., & Batty, D. (2016). Sexual harassment of students by University staff hidden by non-disclosure agreements. *The Guardian*, August 26. Retrieved May 16, 2023, from https://www.theguardian.com/education/2016/aug/26/sexual-harassment-of-students-by-university-staff-hidden-by-non-disclosure-agreements

Woolston, C. (2020). Postdocs under pressure: 'Can I even do this any more?'. *Nature, 587*, 689–692. https://doi.org/10.1038/d41586-020-03235-y

Wright, C., Thompson, S., & Channer, Y. (2007). Out of place: Black women academics in British universities. *Women's History Review, 16*(2), 145–167. https://doi.org/10.1080/09612020601048704

Between Invisibility and Hypervisibility: Reflections on Being 'Permanently Precarious' as a British Muslim Woman Within the Ivory Towers of Academia

Fauzia Ahmad

INTRODUCTION: THE PERMANENTLY PRECARIOUS ACADEMIC

When you have to fight for an existence, fighting can become an existence.
— Sara Ahmed (2017, p. 175)

I begin with a confession: this chapter was submitted *very, very* late. This in itself may not surprise many academics, especially in current climates within higher education institutions (HEIs) where increasing workloads are becoming normalised, and where rising precarity, increasing disparities in gender and ethnic pay gaps, and the real prospects of lower pensions add significantly to a sense of 'overwhelm' and a lack of agency and hopelessness (Loveday, 2023).

F. Ahmad (✉)
Goldsmiths, University of London, London, UK
e-mail: f.ahmad@gold.ac.uk

143

Securing time for personal academic development—the increasingly precious 'mental headspace', in order to conduct research, publish, and disseminate—is fast becoming an ideal that is unrealistic and unachievable especially within working hours as workplace pressures bleed into the safe spaces that should be our minds. Some of us experience burn out and torment ourselves for not being 'productive' while the institutions we work for gaslight us with offers of 'well-being' sessions aimed at 'managing change', implying that we are at fault for not managing redundancies and higher workloads better (Loveday, 2018). Although these are now common contexts to academic life, how are our intersectional subjectivities, in terms of race, ethnicity, gender and faith, etc., implicated in the ways these pressures within HEIs manifest themselves onto our lives?

In this chapter, I adopt an autoethnographic perspective (Ellis & Bochner, 2000; Custer, 2014) to share my reflections navigating the past 30 years through the white, secularised spaces of academia that position people of colour, people of faith, of working-class backgrounds, people with impairments, etc., as the 'Other'—as non-conforming oddballs, as disruptors, or as Nirmal Puwar (2004) describes, as 'space invaders'. My reflections here must be considered alongside the rapidly changing goal posts academics are expected to reach as a result of neoliberalism and the marketisation of HEIs. These experiences achieve a certain particularity when considered through the intersectional lens of a mid-50s British-born Muslim woman sociologist from an Indian Pakistani family who identifies as a *'permanently precarious academic'*. My research is very much embedded within the cultural and religious communities that I identify with, focusing on Muslim women in higher education and employment, in social welfare, and more recently exploring British Muslim relationships—getting married and staying married.

I entered academia with my first job in 1993, but it has taken me 29 years to achieve my first permanent post within academia—as a Senior Lecturer in Sociology—although this is only a half-time post. The past five years has been a battle, comprising many fights, enduring three redundancy processes and seven contract extensions before my institution was forced to accept my right to permanency based on four years continuous service. As I go on to demonstrate, there are structural and racialised dimensions at departmental and institutional levels behind my particular experiences here, but these are indicative of broader experiences of academia for Muslim academics and academics of colour. Our physical and mental health suffer as a result of long-term precarity (Arday, 2022), which takes on additional layers of pain when we perceive our precarity and discrimination to be deeply intertwined with our religious and cultural identities, especially when we also know that our academic areas of expertise are subject to hegemonic and colonialist assertions of authority. At the time of writing, I had recently discovered, via a random health check, that the extreme fatigue, dizzy spells, palpitations, breathlessness, headaches, difficulty focusing and sleeping—symptoms that I had dismissed as either 'normal' tiredness or symptoms of the menopause—were in fact indicative of dangerously high blood pressure and was told by my General Practitioner that I was on the verge of having an imminent heart attack or a stroke and should have been admitted to Accident and Emergency. I believed I was in relatively good shape, so I am certain that this is a manifestation of years of cumulative work-related stress borne out through long-term precarity and the anxiety and powerlessness it brings, lack of financial security, inability to plan ahead, and the exhaustion working a second academic job in order to cope with the cost of living crisis. I am, however, relatively lucky; I know some colleagues have suffered with worse health problems exacerbated by work-related stress.

My parents encouraged me to study so that I would be able to gain good employment and, to use a phrase from my earlier research on Muslim South Asian women, higher education and employment, so that I could '*stand on my own two feet*' (Ahmad, 2001; Ahmad et al., 2003). However, I am still unsteady on my feet and just about managing to stand up.

Adopting an autoethnographic approach means exposing my vulnerabilities, failings, feelings of discrimination and frustrations (Griffin, 2012). It means wondering how much I reveal here will have a bearing on my future prospects and engagements with colleagues. There will, no doubt, be aspects of what I share that will make for uncomfortable reading for some, especially those who are beneficiaries of hegemonic whiteness within HE. I know that in 'naming certain problems, I will become the problem' to paraphrase Sara Ahmed (2017, p. 34). These are decisions I am making cognisant of the ways my gendered, racialised and Muslim identity is already disadvantaged. Being precarious and financially insecure at my age and stage in my career is also embarrassing and anxiety-inducing, but this is not a victim narrative. It is an acknowledgement that precarity and unfair treatment is widespread across the sector and experienced by many excellent scholars who also feel that they are strategically disadvantaged in various ways.

Writing this chapter has been hard, traumatic even—not least because so much of my personal history is reflected in my employment history, and for the ways in which I am deeply embedded within my research. Part of my history from around 2004–2011 involved being a full-time carer to my parents, both of whom needed 24/7 care. I was only able to do occasional small projects from home, which allowed me to produce a few publications; my PhD viva occurred while my father was in hospital in a critical condition, and my mother had just been released from hospital after her first main coronary event. This period of caring was not just an act of love, and a need to return the care that I had grown up with, it was also an act that was deeply ingrained both culturally and religiously as a Muslim woman. When I began to apply for posts following my parents passing in 2009 and then 2011, I was in the early stages of grieving their loss. Applying for positions that would literally allow me to start my life again held a much deeper significance than gaining a step on the career ladder or looking for a promotion or a new institution. Now that I am in employment, albeit fractional, I continue to carry an awareness that the only reason I am *here*, is because *they*—my parents—are *not*.

Explaining this career gap in job applications and then to be faced with mostly blanket rejections, was painful. The absence of compassion from selecting panels to value my earlier teaching and research experience and appreciate that I had still managed to publish academic papers as an unemployed carer outside academia was telling. I doubt that the significance of the caring role for women from Black, ethnic minority and Muslim backgrounds, was even considered. These intersections have only recently been acknowledged within COVID-19 contexts (Hussein & Hussain, 2020) and within intersectional analysis of University and College Union (UCU)[1] data on staff on zero-hour contracts (Arday, 2022). Despite HR statements claiming to welcome candidates from diverse backgrounds, in practice, hiring processes within academia are designed to exclude. On the rare occasions that HR disclosed why my applications were rejected outright, it was because I did not bring in research money—the 'dowry'—as I call it. I was effectively rejected for being unemployed and outside academia and so clearly unable to access internal and external funding opportunities. So precarity also means that the criteria used in promotions such as the

[1] The University and College Union is a British trade union in further and higher education representing casualised researchers and teaching staff, 'permanent' lecturers, and academic-related professional services staff.

numbers of PhD students supervised to completion, or research funds won are out of reach because we are never around long enough to follow through.

So, in what ways can I, as a non-hijabi Muslim woman but one who identifies as practicing, make any claims to having experienced anti-Muslim discrimination or bias? My lack of an openly visible signifier of faith means that experiences of discrimination are racialised. My 'Muslimness' becomes manifest within the secular spaces of academia, through the open refusal of alcohol, request for Halal options, references to taking time out for prayers during the day, fasting during Ramadan, and finally through the research I do—refusing to pander to research on 'hot topics' that pathologise and stigmatise Muslims such as terrorism, forced marriages, or 'honour-based' violence, and the importance I place on centring Muslim voices.

For the rest of this chapter, I aim to share some key themes borne out of my experiences outside and inside the Ivory Tower—such as the 'imposter syndrome'. I play with the idea of 'lateness' as a metaphor for a career that feels it is always behind; I reference the 'Othering' I have experienced along with academic nepotism, patronising attitudes and microaggressions, erasure and extractive practices that I have witnessed. For me, these define how I have experienced racism and anti-Muslim sentiments which may resonate with others. There are two texts that have helped me in feeling validated and need special thanks—Saba Fatima's (2017, 2020) work on microaggressions within the academy experienced as a Muslim woman, and Aisha Ahmad's (2020) blog post, 'A Survival Guide for Black, Indigenous, and Other Women of Color in Academe'. But I dedicate this chapter to the late Jackie West who sadly and suddenly passed away while I was writing this chapter; as one of my PhD Supervisors she helped me find my voice.

ON BEING 'LATE', PRECARITY, AND IMPOSTER SYNDROME

If we are fortunate enough to gain a coveted lectureship, working overtime, well into evenings and over weekends is now normalised to the extent that, we are penalised for resisting and sticking to contracted hours when attempting to fight for better pay and conditions, including challenging widespread precarity in the sector (UCU, 2019, 2021). Within this, I further recognise that what I regard as my *lateness* in terms of career trajectory contributes to a huge sense of 'imposter syndrome' (Clance &

Imes, 1978; Wilkinson, 2020). This creates anxiety and excessive procrastination that paralyses when one tries to complete a job application, write a paper, a review, or a funding application. 'Lateness' becomes a personalised metaphor that is intimately connected to 30 years of struggle comprised of long-term precarity and insecurity, multiple redundancies, and lengthy periods of unemployment. These all feed into the sense that the failure to secure an interview or gain permanency for so long is the sole product of my own inadequacy. Wardrop and Withers (2014) articulate this sense of helplessness and desperation in writing about the 'para-academic' as one who is easily 'dispensable' and as someone who is "subjected to the callous mediocracy of temporary contracts that offer absolutely nothing in terms of 'career development'" (p. 7).

Imposter syndrome becomes further embedded while observing how junior colleagues with less experience, with fewer, less impactful publications, sometimes straight after being awarded their PhD, get the interviews and jobs for which I also applied, but was not shortlisted for. There is additional pain on learning that many of these posts were awarded to early career white women academics whose PhDs were 'on' Muslim or South Asian diasporas or Muslim or South Asian women. It is highly likely that they will have drawn on my publications for their PhDs or cited others that have, forcing me to question why my applications are rejected, knowing that I hold significantly more experience and expertise than they do. It is the realisation borne out of actual experience, that on the odd occasions where I have secured a temporary post within these departments, I have been positioned as junior to these colleagues. I know that I am not alone in these experiences.

Prior to joining my current institution, I had been unemployed for two years, after being made redundant from a Teaching Fellow post at a Russell Group institution. Although this was a position normally taken up by early career academics, after two years of unemployment following my mother's passing at the end of 2011, I was desperate for anything. My experiences here encapsulated everything that the unions have been challenging in terms of precarity and racialised precarity—extreme exploitation and casualisation of mostly ECR all desperate to secure lectureships (UCU, 2021; Arday, 2022). I spent two years here earning less that £8000 per year on a 0.4fte (a contract representing 40% of full-time hours) temporary contract for seven months of the year but with an unrealistic workload for the hours paid. When this was increased to *0.45fte (representing an additional half a day's work)* the following year, it represented almost a *doubling* in workload as it meant taking on a second teaching module. Academic nepotism was also rife here. I saw how an inexperienced white female internal candidate was hired and fast-tracked into a senior position after one year post-PhD through the allocation of senior-level teaching and administrative roles to facilitate their promotion over, and at the expense of, experienced staff of colour.

There are now numerous qualitative studies that demonstrate the realities of racial discrimination in higher education (Sian, 2019), and point to a privileging of gender over race (Bhopal & Henderson, 2019; Arday, 2022), with various sources of statistical evidence revealing stark disparities based on ethnicity in hiring and promotion practices within the higher education sector. For example, within sociology, data from the Higher Education Statistics Agency (HESA) alongside a survey of sociologists in UK higher education, revealed that 85.7% of staff are white, compared with only 14.3% from Black and Minority Ethnic (BME) backgrounds (Joseph-Salisbury et al., 2020). Women from BME backgrounds make up only 8.5% of total staff and men even less, at 5.8%. At the professorial level, there are only 25 Black, Asian, Mixed, and Other sociology professors, making up 9.8% of the total number of professors (Joseph-Salisbury et al., 2020). Given that data on Muslim staff in UK higher education is not collected, inferences can be made based on ethnicity, and it is clear that the numbers of Muslim sociology/social science academics are low.

Imposter syndrome makes us forget that our personal experiences and suspicions of discrimination are given reality in these statistics and qualitative research. For those of us who exist across the intersections of ethnicity, gender, and religion, living with precarity and frequent, long-term unemployment, we become the 'case study'; for Muslim women academics, when we are unemployed, we inhabit the stereotyped space of the victim—the (presumed) uneducated, oppressed Muslim woman.

The sense that there are opaque structural forces and unspoken biases based on our race, faith, or both, forms a suspicion, a feeling of injustice, that we only speak of in private, or not at all, and where we only feel validated if we hear someone else with the courage to articulate similar experiences. This sense of injustice links to a wider and much discussed issue of the ways in which white privilege operates and re-circulates within the academy (Arday & Mirza, 2018; Bhambra et al., 2018; Bhopal, 2016; Johnson et al., 2018), and to questions of *whose* knowledge is valued especially within the already confined field of Muslim/Islamic studies. It is a pattern that we see replicated in the lived experiences of other Muslim academics (Akel, 2021; Mahmud & Islam, 2022; Ramadan, 2021) and one that is the product of racialised regimes of power that dominate the lived realities of gendered, racially, and religiously marked academics within these Ivory Towers.

Imposter syndrome *almost* prevented me from applying to the post that I currently hold (as a Senior Lecturer), after being unemployed for two years following redundancy from the Teaching Fellow role above. Despite the 'Senior' in my title, this sense of 'imposterism' lingers as it dictates that any success is down to luck and not because it was earned, or I was the best candidate (Loveday, 2023). Imposter syndrome has become further reinforced as a result of being subjected to three redundancies within five years at my current institution, before having my legal permanency based on four years continuous service recognised in July 2022; but even this had to be fought for. Imposter syndrome continues as there is little hope of seeing an increase in my paid hours despite nearly a third of departmental colleagues having left in recent years. My institution and my department are in a dire financial situation due to a significant decrease in student numbers. After my last reinstatement, teaching that I had developed over five years was re-allocated (for no good reason) and I am now relegated to covering for staff on leave and with no discernible role of my own. This places me once again, as the low-hanging fruit that can be the easiest to dispense, should there be a need for departmental redundancies. This is why I still refer to myself as a 'permanently precarious academic'.

As marginalised academics, we are often used as gatekeepers to our communities but not recognised for our contributions while our own research is often dismissed as irrelevant or 'too close' (Ahmad, 2003). We are mined for our ideas and our contacts by colleagues who temporarily befriend us, or take ideas from our publications, for us to later discover that large research grants and multiple publications have been delivered by those colleagues without ever having invited us to act as joint grant holders or co-authors. Our collegiality is further abused, and our labour erased when our lecture slides are appropriated and false claims of intellectual copyright are asserted over our work, with no acknowledgement to ourselves.

We are viewed through 'deficit models' where our work, even when we teach core modules, is systematically and routinely devalued and viewed as something that 'anyone can do', yet when white members of staff take on the same roles, the work acquires a new level of significance and value. In our research, the appropriation of the decolonising movement by white academics is a prime example of this on a wider scale (Tuck & Yang, 2012;

Bhambra et al., 2020; Moosavi, 2020; Rai & Campion, 2022). Research 'on' Muslims has until recently, been largely dominated by non-Muslim academics whose research interests and agendas have often reflected the 'Western gaze'. They have asserted authority over Muslim and Islamic studies determining what is, and what is not, worthy of research (Said, 1979; Qureshi, 2020; Massoumi et al., 2019), and produced studies 'on' Muslim women that continue to present essentialised tropes of us as perpetually relegated to the domestic sphere within highly patriarchal family structures, an obsession with 'arranged' and 'forced marriages', and honour-based domestic violence (Abu-Lughod, 2002, 2013; Ahmad, 2003, 2017; Ahmed, 1992; Cheruvallil-Contractor, 2012; Lazreg, 1988). Numerous conversations with other Muslim women social researchers over the years highlight a collective desire to move away from these research perspectives seeking, instead, to redefine and re-claim this academic space. However, we are often met with resistance from non-Muslim academic gatekeepers demanding that we yield to essentialising frameworks that do not reflect *our* subjectivities. Additionally, our publications only seem to achieve validity if we co-publish with non-Muslims.

As Muslim women academics, we also perform additional roles of unseen and un-valued emotional labour in supporting students, especially Muslim, other minority students and female students who turn to us as they note the absence of academic staff who 'look like them' (Bhopal, 2016). We often invest extra hours in our students, especially those from disadvantaged backgrounds, because we understand what it feels like to struggle academically within secularised white spaces, where they enter already disadvantaged, only to feel 'Othered' by the curricula as well as the institutions. We understand some of the additional pressures Muslim students carry such as caring for family or needing to work. We are also acutely aware of how it feels to be surveilled and labelled as 'suspect communities' (Brown & Saeed, 2015), not just as a result of the imposition of the Prevent duty across campuses (Awan, 2012), but for how we 'present' ourselves; being aware of the stereotypes that follow us. For those of us who are precariously employed, the question also becomes one of survival and temporality; we are never around long enough to be promoted. When we ask for the same considerations in terms of parity for opportunities that we see extended to other colleagues, we are again subjected to this deficit model—we are 'not qualified' to take on particular roles, or are 'not ready' for promotion, while our white colleagues' career ambitions will be supported.

While my 'mini rant' can be interpreted as anecdotal, as one-off personalised observations borne out of sour grapes, excessive sensitivity and ego, and weaknesses within my own applications, CV, and ability to perform well at interview, it does not explain why the relatively same approach has produced the odd interview that led to a job. It still does not explain why having decades of experience teaching and researching are viewed less favourably than newly qualified white applicants researching in the same field, where they are positioned as 'outsider researchers'. And it does not explain why so many Black, Brown, and Muslim colleagues have also reported being hurt in similar ways.

Redundancies, Redundancies, Redundancies

Redundancies are brutal processes. They tear away at your self-esteem and sense of worth. There is no dignity in the redundancy process, no jubilant farewell email to colleagues, no leaving party or card, there is barely a thanks. Instead, you are told in the coldest of terms, why you are no longer required, why there is no longer a role for you, why any other member of staff can do what you do. Redundancies also reveal who your allies are among your colleagues as you witness how your existence and your contributions are easily erased by colleagues as they prepare for the next academic year without you.

I have been through my fair share of redundancies; each one has hurt emotionally, mentally, and financially. The cycle of being on fixed-term contracts is particularly pronounced among Black and minority ethnic staff within British academia (Arday, 2022), and this will include Muslim staff. Data collected by my institution's UCU branch mirrors data collected by a wider UCU (2021) study that documented how people of colour, and especially women, are more likely to be on precarious contracts and thus disproportionately subjected to redundancies. For instance, it was found that while 32% of white academic female staff were on fixed-term contracts, for Asian women, this figure was at 44%. Even more shockingly, Black staff were 50% more likely to be on zero hours contracts compared to white staff.

As Muslim women, and as women of colour, we are recognised as having protected characteristics under the Equalities Act (2010) in reference to our religion, ethnicities, and gender. This means that our institutions—as public bodies—are duty bound to ensure that we are not treated less favourably as a result of our characteristics.[2] When initiating redundancy proceedings, HEI's are therefore, expected to conduct Equalities Impact Assessments (EIA) in order to ensure that employees holding protected characteristics are not unduly targeted. However, in my redundancy experiences, this has meant little in practice. When my institution went through two periods of mass redundancies in order to recoup financial losses, the majority of these redundancies fell on staff on fixed-term contracts; over 60% were from minority backgrounds. Within my department, on both these occasions, the only lecturers remaining on fixed-term contracts, and so targeted for redundancy, were myself and one other South Asian Muslim woman; white staff who joined at the same time (also on fixed-term contracts) had been all been made permanent. No EIA's were conducted across the institution, which also failed to follow its own guidelines on best practice in managing fixed-term contracts, as well as their own racial justice strategies. We are left relying on change to happen from within the institutions that continue to discriminate against us. There exists then, a clear dissonance between the public face of diversity universities want to present, and the experiences of students and staff of colour and Muslim backgrounds.

"I DIDN'T REALISE YOU WERE A 'REAL' MUSLIM": EVERYDAY MICROAGGRESSIONS

To be repeatedly marginalised and devalued in varying ways is exhausting. While I cannot claim any direct experiences of overt Islamophobia, there are certainly racialised contexts at play and these are deeply connected to my open identification as a Muslim woman and the Muslimness of my research. My non-hijabed appearance means that some colleagues will presume I hold a secular identity—one borne from earlier stereotypes of educated Asian Muslim women as de facto rebels against religion and culture. The disappointment on realising that I define as a practising Muslim among some colleagues has been barely disguised. There have been multiple iterations of the '*I didn't realise you were a real Muslim*' (Ahmad, 2003) over the years.

My first academic role after completing a Masters, and after spending a year unemployed, was in 1993, as a research assistant in a college affiliated to a large university and based within the social work department. I spent

---

[2] Equality Act 2010, https://www.legislation.gov.uk/ukpga/2010/15/contents

seven years here, first as a research assistant, and then as a lecturer, on successive one-year temporary contracts. Social work at that time did not recognise faith-based identities and certainly did not recognise Islamophobia (Ahmad & Sheriff, 2001). This was a source of tension while I worked on a project on Black social workers career trajectories with two women who identified as Black feminists. The feminist solidarity and respect I hoped for was distinctly lacking however. For instance, one colleague would frequently call my home during Friday prayer times after I had specifically highlighted that this was one time I would be unavailable to take calls. If one of my parents answered the phone, she would ask them to confirm that I was in fact, doing my prayers. Although I remained polite about her phone calls, I viewed this as bullying and disrespectful behaviour.

There were other instances of micro and macroaggressions from other staff in that department, from being mistaken for an older South Asian woman in the department (because we all look alike), or presumed to be her daughter (we are all related); that my parents must have been cousins, married young and that I came from a large family (both untrue), to assumptions that I was 'obviously' a rebel against my religion and culture as I had been to university (this little gem has since featured prominently in my work with British Muslim women students). My non-drinking, Halal-only diet was a source of ridicule—mostly from the only other South Asian woman in the department who was a non-observant Muslim. I felt my presence must have unsettled her and other members of staff. When I got married, because it was arranged, the comments and questions from some colleagues focused on whether the marriage was forced or, how I, as an educated independent woman, could engage in something that was such an old fashioned (primitive) practice. It is indeed ironic that most of these microaggressions (Fatima, 2020) were from social work educators—who taught students to recognise their biases in order to challenge them yet were unable to recognise their own racially and religiously biased interactions with me.

Writing from a US context, Fatima (2017) highlights the microaggressions she experienced as a South Asian Muslim woman faculty member and the ways these force us into questioning ourselves on a daily basis, noting how the "epistemic border of thinking of oneself as paranoid and of being secure in one's perception of reality" (p. 148) can be so subtle and ambiguous that it acts to question our own abilities to accurately discern when behaviours acted upon us are racially and religiously charged and/or sexist or discriminatory in nature. We can sense when they are present, but the difficulty lies in convincing others, especially white colleagues, that we have been subjected to racist, Islamophobic and sexist microaggressions, or in this case a combination of all three. We then 'lose epistemic ground' because of the difficulty of quantifying actions such microaggressions, which are defined as:

> Brief and commonplace daily verbal, behavioural, and environmental indignities, whether intentional or unintentional, that communicate hostile, derogatory, or negative racial, gender, and sexual orientation, and religious slights and insults to the target person or group. (Sue, 2010, p. 5 cited in Fatima, 2017, p. 147)

I am personally tired of (often younger) white academics asking me 'who are you?' in ways that suggest that I don't belong in the academic space. As Muslim academics, we work within socio-cultural contexts that replicate the discriminations and marginalisations we experience in our everyday lives. Several employment studies document how practising Muslims feel disadvantaged in their workplaces because informal networking events centre around 'going for a drink' (Arifeen & Gatrell, 2020). Social and professional events within academia typically centre around wine receptions (including many events on Muslims and Islam) or drinks in the pub, but this obviously creates a tension for practising Muslim academics and non-drinkers. If we choose to not attend, we become excluded from the networking and bonding opportunities that these events aim to foster. If we do attend, we still remain awkward outsiders, with our fruit juices and soft drinks while we internally deal with the guilt of entering an event that centres around alcohol, and having to explain why we are not drinking (if not visibly Muslim). Muslim students feel this acutely and is one of the reasons Muslim students feel uncomfortable and excluded at university. They, and we as staff, are being reminded that we are the outsiders within these white, middle-class secular spaces.

Given that there is no legally accepted definition of Islamophobia, and that the Prevent duty exists as an Islamophobic tool for the Government to monitor Muslim staff and students in both schools and universities (Awan, 2012; Brown & Saeed, 2015; Qureshi, 2020), challenging institutionalised racism[3] and Islamophobia is difficult. As Muslim members of staff, with public profiles, world events such as the Israeli onslaught on Gaza (at the time of writing), means that we know that our public comments are monitored for signs of antisemitism or sympathy with designated terror groups. Similarly, our students tell us of their fears of 'saying the wrong thing'. Rather than coming to university to find their voice and gain confidence and experience debating alternative views, our Muslim students feel silenced and nervous. Like academic staff, they also have limited confidence in our HEI's caring as much about Islamophobia as they do antisemitism.

I fear for my visibly Muslim female and male colleagues who are subjected to the additional indignities of overt Islamophobia both inside and outside the academy, while it simultaneously seeks to profit from their images in order to gain diversity points that mean nothing in practice.

Final Thoughts

Some of what I will have voiced here will make for uncomfortable reading, and some will perceive it as deeply problematic. I accept this as long as those feeling uncomfortable acknowledge the source of their discomfort. They may not know me or be part of my life trajectory, but I would ask them to consider if there have been any points in their lives where they may have benefited from secularised, racialised, and gendered structural inequalities that privilege their identities over women who are racial, faith, and ethnic minorities within the academy. There are a series of questions that might be worth considering if one is serious about decolonising the academy. Did you receive a promotion or permanency that was not also offered to a woman of colour? Are you in a position of seniority with respect to Muslim women and women of colour who hold more experience than you? Are you a beneficiary of academic nepotism that has been denied to marginalised academics? If you research 'on', and write 'about' Muslims, how thorough are your literature reviews? Are you consciously or sub-consciously deciding not to cite original sources written by Muslim

---

[3] A recent example was the case of Dr Kajal Sharma, a University of Portsmouth academic who successfully brought a case of racial discrimination against the university and her Head of Department after she was only 1 of 12 senior academics not to be re-appointed to her post, which she had been doing for five years, and was replaced with a white candidate with no experience of the role (Weale, 2022).

women of colour? Are you parachuting into research areas that Muslim women are already working on, or jumping onto their ideas for your own research without inviting them as equal collaborators?

For those who sit on recruitment panels, think about why Muslim academics and academics of colour might be applying for positions they are over-qualified and over-experienced for. Remember that they will already have gone through hoops to get to where they are. They will have had more than average rejections but are desperate for employment. Show them due respect by not trying to exploit them through placing them at the bottom of the scale or forcing them into accepting lower grades of salary. Would you want this for yourself? Fight for their dignity as if it were your own and value them the way you would want to be valued.

To end on a note of hope, the numbers of Muslim academics within the social sciences is increasing, and many of these are visibly Muslim women. Support groups such as the Network of Sisters in Academia (NeSA)[4] indicate a need for safe spaces but also point towards a new set of emerging role models with the fresh energy needed to effect positive change within the Ivory Towers.

References

Abu-Lughod, L. (2002). Do Muslim Women Really Need Saving? Anthropological Reflections on Cultural Relativism and Its Others. *American Anthropologist, 104*(3), 783–790.

Abu-Lughod, L. (2013). *Do Muslim women need saving?* Harvard University Press.

Ahmad, F. (2001). Modern Traditions? British Muslim Women and Academic Achievement. *Gender and Education, 13*(2), 137–152. https://doi.org/10.1080/09540250120051169

Ahmad, F. (2003). Still "in progress?" – Methodological dilemmas, tensions and contradictions in theorizing South Asian Muslim women. In N. Puwar & R. Raghuram (Eds.), *South Asian women in the diaspora*. Berg.

Ahmad, F. (2017). Do young British Muslim women need rescuing? In S. Hamid (Ed.), *British Muslim Youth: Between Rhetoric and Real Lives*. London: Ashgate.

Ahmed, L. (1992). *Women and Gender in Islam: Historical Roots of a Modern Debate*. New Haven: Yale University Press.

Ahmed, S. (2017). *Living a feminist life*. Duke University Press.

---

[4] NeSA: https://www.nesaonline.com/#:~:text=ABOUT%20US,scholars%20in%20their%20respective%20fields

Ahmad, A. S. (2020). A Survival Guide for Black, Indigenous, and Other Women of Color in Academe. *The Chronicle of Higher Education*, September 18. https://www.chronicle.com/article/a-survival-guide-for-black-indigenous-and-other-women-of-color-in-academe (Accessed June 2020).

Ahmad, F., & Sheriff, S. (2001). Muslim women of Europe: Welfare needs and responses. *Social Work in Europe, 8*(1), 2–11. https://docs.scie-socialcareonline.org.uk/fulltext/0071480.pdf

Ahmad, F., Modood, T., & Lissenburgh, S. (2003). *South Asian Women and Employment in Britain: Diversity and Social Change.* Policy Studies Institute.

Akel, S. (2021). *Institutionalised. The rise of Islamophobia in higher education.* Centre for Equity and Inclusion, London Metropolitan University.

Arday, J. (2022). 'More to prove and more to lose' Race, Racism and Precarious Employment in Higher Education. *British Journal of Sociology of Education, 43*(4), 513–533.

Arday, J., & Mirza, H. (2018). *Dismantling Race in Higher Education. Racism, Whiteness and Decolonising the Academy.* London: Palgrave Macmillan.

Arifeen, S. A., & Gatrell, C. (2020). Those glass chains that bind you: How British Muslim women professionals experience career, faith and family. *British Journal of Management, 31*(1), 221–236. https://doi.org/10.1111/1467-8551.12387

Awan, I. (2012). "I am a Muslim not an extremist": How the prevent strategy has constructed a "suspect" community. *Politics and Policy, 40*(6), 1158–1185. https://doi.org/10.1111/j.1747-1346.2012.00397.x

Bhambra, G., Nişancıoğlu, K., & Gebrial, D. (2020). Decolonising the university in 2020. *Identities, 27*(4), 509–516. https://doi.org/10.1080/1070289X.2020.1753415

Bhambra, G. K., Gebrial, D., & Nişancıoğlu, K. (Eds.). (2018). *Decolonising the university.* Pluto Press.

Bhopal, K. (2016). *The experiences of black and minority ethnic academics: A comparative study of the unequal academy.* Routledge.

Bhopal, K., & Henderson, H. (2019). Competing inequalities: Gender versus race in higher education institutions in the UK. *Educational Review, 73*(2), 153–169. https://doi.org/10.1080/00131911.2019.1642305

Brown, K. E., & Saeed, T. (2015). Radicalization and counter-radicalization at British universities: Encounters and alternatives. *Ethnic and Racial Studies., 38*(11), 1952–1968.

Cheruvallil-Contractor, S. (2012). *Muslim Women in Britain: De-Mystifying the Muslimah.* London: Routledge.

Clance, P. R., & Imes, S. A. (1978). The imposter phenomenon in high achieving women: Dynamics and therapeutic intervention. *Psychotherapy: Theory, Research & Practice, 15*(3), 241–247. https://doi.org/10.1037/h0086006

Custer, D. (2014). Autoethnography as a transformative research method. *The Qualitative Report, 19*(37), 1–13. http://nsuworks.nova.edu/tqr/vol19/iss37/3

Ellis, C., & Bochner, A. P. (2000). Autoethnography, personal narrative, reflexivity: Research as subject. In N. Denzin & Y. Lincoln (Eds.), *Handbook of qualitative research* (2nd ed., pp. 733–768). Sage.

Fatima, S. (2017). On the edge of knowing. microaggression and epistemic uncertainty as a woman of color. In K. Cole & H. Hassel (Eds.), *Surviving sexism in academia: Feminist strategies for leadership* (Routledge) (pp. 147–154).

Fatima, S. (2020). I know what happened to me: The Epistemic Harms of Microaggression. In Lauren Freeman & Jeanine Weekes Schroer (Eds.), *Microaggression and Philosophy*. New York: Routledge.

Griffin, R. A. (2012). I am an angry black woman: Black feminist autoethnography, voice, and resistance. *Women's Studies in Communication, 35*, 138–157. https://doi.org/10.1080/07491409.2012.724524

Hussein, N., & Hussain, S. (2020). Migrant ethnic minority women in academia during the twin pandemics of COVID-19 and racism, transforming society. https://www.transformingsociety.co.uk/2020/07/31/migrant-ethnic-minority-women-in-academia-during-the-twin-pandemics-of-covid-19-and-racism/

Johnson, A., Joseph-Salisbury, R., & Kamunge, B. (Eds). (2018). *The Fire Now. Anti-Racist Scholarship in Times of Explicit Racial Violence*. London: Zed Books.

Joseph-Salisbury, R., Ashe, S., Alexander, C., & Campion, K. (2020). *Race and Ethnicity in British Sociology*. British Sociological Association. https://britsoc.co.uk/media/25345/bsa_race_and_ethnicity_in_british_sociology_report.pdf

Lazreg, M. (1988). Feminism and difference: The perils of writing as a woman on women in Algeria. *Feminist Studies, 14*(1), 81–107.

Loveday, V. (2018). Luck, chance, and happenstance? Perceptions of success and failure amongst fixed-term academic staff in UK higher education. *British Journal of Sociology, 69*(3), 758–775.

Loveday, V. (2023). Luck and precarity: Contextualising fixed-term academics' perceptions of success and failure. In Eric Lybeck & Catherine O'Connell (Eds.), *Universities in Crisis: Academic Professionalism in Uncertain Times* (pp. 73–92). London: Bloomsbury Academic.

Mahmud, A., & Islam, M. (2022). Intersectional oppression: A reflexive dialogue between Muslim academics and their experiences of Islamophobia and exclusion in UK Higher Education. *Sociology Compass, 17*(2). https://doi.org/10.1111/soc4.13041

Massoumi, N., Mills, T., & Miller, D. (2019). Secrecy, Coercion and deception in research on "terrorism" and "extremism". *Contemporary Social Science., 15*(2), 134–152. https://doi.org/10.1080/21582041.2019.1616107

Moosavi, L. (2020). The decolonial bandwagon and the dangers of intellectual decolonisation. *International Review of Sociology, 30*(2), 332–354. https://doi.org/10.1080/03906701.2020.1776919

Puwar, N. (2004). *Space invaders: Race, gender and bodies out of place.* Berg.

Qureshi, A. (2020). *I refuse to condemn. Resisting racism in times of national security.* Manchester University Press.

Rai, R., & Campion, K. (2022). Decoding "decoloniality" in the academy: Tensions and challenges in "decolonising" as a "new" language and praxis in British history and geography. *Ethnic and Racial Studies, 45*(16), 478–500. https://doi.org/10.1080/01419870.2022.2099750

Ramadan, I. (2021). When faith intersects with gender: The challenges and successes in the experiences of Muslim women academics. *Gender and Education, 34*(1), 33–48. https://doi.org/10.1080/09540253.2021.1893664

Said, E. (1979). *Orientalism.* Pantheon.

Sian, K. P. (2019). *Navigating institutional racism in British universities.* Palgrave Macmillan.

Tuck, E., & Yang, K. (2012). Decolonization is not a metaphor, *Decolonization: Indigeneity. Education & Society, 1*(1), 1–40. https://doi.org/10.25058/20112742.n38.04

Universities and Colleges Union (UCU). (2019). Counting the costs of casualisation in higher education. https://www.ucu.org.uk/media/10336/Counting-the-costs-of-casualisation-in-higher-education-Jun19/pdf/ucu_casualisation_in_HE_survey_report_Jun19.pdf (Accessed June 2020).

University College Union (UCU). (2021). Precarious Work in Higher Education: Insecure Contracts and How They Have Changed over Time: October 2021. https://ucu.org.uk/media/10899/Precarious-work-in-higher-education-May-20/pdf/ucu_he-precarity-report_may20.pdf (Accessed December 2021).

Wardrop, A., & Withers, D. (2014). Para-academia: Reclaiming What Has Been Devastated. In *The Para-Academic Handbook A Toolkit for Making-Learning-Creating-Acting.* Bristol: Intellect Press.

Weale, S. (2022). Portsmouth University loses discrimination case against Indian lecturer. *The Guardian.* https://www.theguardian.com/education/2022/dec/12/portsmouth-university-loses-discrimination-case-against-indian-lecturer-kajal-sharma.

Wilkinson, C. (2020). Imposter syndrome and the accidental academic: An auto-ethnographic account. *International Journal for Academic Development, 25*(4), 363–374. https://doi.org/10.1080/1360144X.2020.1762087

"This Girl is a Nation": Muslim Women's Narratives of Self and Survival in the Academy

Heidi Safia Mirza

INTRODUCTION: SITUATING THE FEMALE MUSLIM ACADEMIC

This chapter examines the personal costs and consequences for Muslim women working and studying in higher education in the Islamophobic spaces occupied by the postcolonial Muslim diaspora in Britain. Analysing the personal narratives of three transnational professional Muslim women of Turkish, Pakistani and Indian heritage in British universities, I explore how the intersection of race, gender and religion is written on and experienced within the Muslim female body.

As an Indo-Caribbean woman of Muslim heritage living and working in Britain, I am particularly interested in how the internal subjective world of Muslim women is produced by, and performed through, the external

H. S. Mirza (✉)
IOE Faculty of Education and Society, UCL, University of London, London, UK
e-mail: Heidi.Mirza@ucl.ac.uk

© The Author(s), under exclusive license to Springer Nature Switzerland AG 2024
A. Mahmud, M. Islam (eds.), *Uncovering Islamophobia in Higher Education*, Palgrave Studies in Race, Inequality and Social Justice in Education, https://doi.org/10.1007/978-3-031-65253-0_9

161

affective Islamophobic discourses that circulate in the West. Thus, in this chapter I seek to explore how Muslim women who are 'seen' as embodying a 'dangerous' or 'oppressed' religious gendered identity, subjectively 'live out' being a 'Muslim woman' in the hostile spaces of whiteness in higher education.

Drawing on my Black feminist framework of embodied intersectionality (Mirza, 2008, 2009) I examine the women's narratives of self and survival which reveal multiple layers of power, both seen and unseen, in the making of the female Muslim self. In particular, I focus on her religious, racial and ethnic identity as manifested through their subjective expressions of faith, home and belonging.

THE COLLISION OF DISCOURSES: MUSLIM WOMEN AT THE INTERSECTIONS

The personal and academic journeys of the three Muslim women in this study comes at a time of growing national concern over the Muslim presence in the 'West' in general, and in Britain in particular. There are now three generations of British born Muslims who make up 6.5% of the British population (MCB, 2022). They are now the youngest and fastest growing group in Britain. Muslim young women are now entering higher education in larger numbers than ever, especially from the Bangladeshi community (Mirza & Warwick, 2024). Their increasing presence in higher education raises the question, 'how does anti-Islamic hostility play out on the Muslim female body in university settings in post-colonial Britain?'

Since the 2001 bombing of the Twin Towers on 9/11 in New York there has been an overwhelming preoccupation with the embodied Muslim woman in British public spaces (Meetoo & Mirza, 2007). The scholarly interventions of Muslim postcolonial and critical race feminists show how the Muslim female body has become a battlefield in the symbolic war against Islam and the perceived Muslim enemy 'within' (Jiwani, 2006; Razack, 2008). In the West's ideological 'War Against Terror' the Muslim woman has come to symbolise the 'barbaric Muslim other' in our midst. This is often articulated through Muslim women being pathologised as voiceless victims of their 'backward' communities who are in need of 'saving' by the enlightened 'West' (Abu-Lughod, 2002; Zahedi, 2011). Muslim women's private reasons for wearing the headscarf (hijab) or niqab (full face veil) has become public property, a 'weapon' used by many different competing interests, from male politicians in Britain and France to white feminists in Belgium and the Netherlands to argue their cases for and against assimilation, multiculturalism, secularism and human rights (Abbas, 2019; Khan, 2019; EHRC, 2016; Coene & Longman, 2008; Scott, 2007; Killian, 2003).

The embodiment of power and disempowerment written through and within the sexed, raced and classed body is particularly important if we are to understand how religious identity is performed, experienced and articulated through Muslim women's sense of self in the context of the all-consuming hegemonic racist and sexist discourses of Western Islamophobia (Abbas, 2019) and patriarchal Islamic dominance (Patel & Siddiqui, 2010; Balzani, 2010). Thus, for the Muslim women in this study, their dress, religious disposition (piety), cultural attachments—such as food, ethnic pride, speech and style—show not only their ethnic identity (as performed) but how such embodied practices need to be understood as meaningful signs and expressions of a reflexive and resistant female Muslim agency which they 'live out' while navigating, on one hand, the wider political, religious discourses, but on the other the white privilege that lies at the heart of the elite institutional academic culture.

Unequal opportunities and outcomes for people of colour in British universities is well documented (Alexander & Arday, 2015; Mirza, 2018b). Those who manage to navigate the perilous journey into a career in the academy disproportionately find themselves on insecure fixed term contracts and lower pay. There are only 18% Black, Asian and minority ethnic academics compared with 82% who were white (Advance HE, 2021). The most shocking evidence of a 'crisis of race' in British higher education is the dearth of senior Black and minority ethnic academics. In professorial roles the share of white academics is nearly double that of Black, Asian and minority ethnic academics with 11.2% compared with 6.2%. Emejulu (2017) poignantly sums up the state of play in the British academy when she says, "To speak of universities is to recognise them as spaces of exclusion and discrimination which hide their epistemic violence behind a rhetoric of meritocracy, collegiality and the 'free exchange of ideas'".

THEORISING MUSLIM WOMEN: EMBODIED INTERSECTIONALITY IN UNIVERSITY SETTINGS

The theory of embodied intersectionality enables an understanding of how power comes to be written through and within the raced and sexed body as the Muslim woman moves through her career in higher education

(Mirza, 2014). Moreover, it provides a theoretical framework illuminating Muslim women's agency which, as the women's narratives reveal in this study, continually challenges and transforms the hegemonic discourses of race, gender and religion as it plays out in the institutional settings of the university.

The concept of embodied intersectionality theorises the complexities of race, gender, class and other 'positional' social divisions not only as lived realities (i.e. how the women in this study experience the university space holistically as Muslim, middle-class, heterosexual women) but also how this experience is affectively mediated by the body and lived through Muslim female subjectivity (Mirza, 2008, 2009). That is, it looks at how the external materiality of their situatedness (the political, economic and social structures that produce inequality in higher education) is constituted, reconfigured and lived through their corporeal representation (i.e. as racialised 'dangerous' or 'oppressed' others in the classroom). It seeks to demonstrate how intersectional 'othering' which arises at unique historical moments (i.e. when the category 'Muslim woman' is invested with a particular affective and linguistic meaning), is organised into systematic social relations and practices.

At the intersection of the material external world and the embodied interior world, the identity of the Muslim female marginal subject comes into being. As Butler (1993) argues, it is through the repetition of norms on the surface of bodies that the boundaries and fixity of social worlds materialise. The notion of an embodied intersectionality thus enables us to see how, through the articulation of their identities, Muslim women in elite patriarchal spaces of whiteness, such as the university continually resist and rename the regulatory effects of hegemonic gendered, raced and classed discourses of inequity and subjugation in their daily lives. Such resistance is played out in the subjecthood of racialised Muslim women in higher education, whose agency ultimately challenges and transcends such dominance.

INTERVIEWING MUSLIM WOMEN: NARRATIVE RESEARCH AND METHOD

The interviews with the three Muslim women whose narratives inform this chapter were part of the larger study for the cognitive testing for the ethnicity boost of the UK Longitudinal Household Survey, *Understanding*

Society.[1] For this larger study, in-depth semi structured interviews were conducted to help inform the design of the main survey questions for the ethnicity strand of the survey (Nandi & Platt, 2012). The Muslim female interviewees were in their 30s, educated to at least Masters level and were in professional occupations in higher education or studying for a higher degree. They were of Turkish, Pakistani and Indian heritage which raised interesting issues about the complexity of race, gender, religion and transnational identity while navigating their careers in higher education. The in-depth autobiographical narrative interviews interrogating 'group belonging' and 'sense of self' brought to the fore issues of religious identity, subjectivity and the body for Muslim women (Mirza, 2013; Ludhra & Chappell, 2011).

As a Muslim postcolonial woman of colour from Trinidad and an established Professor in higher education, I felt compelled to look deeper and unravel the 'identity affects' emerging within the women's narratives. I recognised the autobiographical stories they told as academics of border-crossing, journeys of the 'self' and their relationship to the wider Muslim female diaspora. Moreover, the Muslim female voices revealed the ways in which regulatory discursive power and privilege are performed or exercised in the everyday material world of the socially constructed 'Muslim woman' in the 'West'. Drawing on my own personalised embodied experience in higher education allowed me to immerse myself in the data. Analysing the accounts of the Muslim women in the study enabled me to reveal the processes of 'being and becoming' a gendered, raced and classed subject of discourse and how it is experienced and 'lived out' in the particular social field of higher education.

As this study shows, the three transnational academic Muslim women had developed strategies for survival in hostile higher educational spaces where white western male and female identity and class privilege prevailed. They did so by engaging in embodied practices of contingent and reconfigured 'Muslimness' such as the wearing or not of the hijab, going to the Mosque, eating halal food, and other acts of gendered safety, resistance, and accommodation. For example, while all three women were highly educated professionals with strong cross-national affiliations, they all

---

[1] *Understanding Society* is a world leading study of the socio-economic circumstances and attitudes of 100,000 individuals in 40,000 British households. It is funded by the Economic and Social Research Council (ESRC) at the Institute for Social and Economic Research (ISER), University of Essex. See http://www.understandingsociety.org.uk/

expressed a strong sense of being rooted in their ethnic cultures and religious identity through attachments to place, which was expressed through language, dialect, food, memories and family. For ethical purposes, the use of pseudonyms is employed in this chapter.

Mehrunissa is in her 30s and a lawyer from Bombay in India. She came to Britain in 2006, and works as a project researcher at a University in a major city in the southeast of England. For her, place and nation is very important to her sense of self which is simultaneously articulated, as she explains, *"Bombay is very important because I was born and brought up there and if I go somewhere (in India) then people would say, 'Oh you're from Bombay, not India', that's very important, your language, your dialect".*

Fatima is a lecturer in a university in a major city in the southeast of England. Born in Turkey, she is the daughter of a migrant worker who came to live in the Netherlands thirty years ago. She is a Dutch Citizen with the right to work in the UK. She is in her mid-30s and sees herself as *"very international"*, and a *"new European"*. She feels between two cultures, symbolised by train tracks, *"We bought our house where I grew up. The neighbourhood was between two rails, one train rail going to (my hometown) and the other going to Utrecht".*

Amina is in her mid-30s, and a researcher in a large metropolitan university in southeast England. She describes herself as South Asian of Indian heritage and has Dual citizenship- Canadian and British. Though born in Britain, she left the UK aged four but home for her and her family is still Toronto. She is emphatic that she is not British. She describes herself to others as a Canadian, or British Canadian if she is in other places like Nigeria. *"I'd probably have more in common with a white Canadian than I would with a South Asian Indian. I mean I think you know, basically, I'm Canadian, I'm not Indian".*

Turning to the analysis of the Muslim women's narratives in the following section, three themes emerged revealing how the women survived and thrived in everyday situations in higher education. First was how they navigated everyday racism in the corridors and classrooms and in particular how they experienced their embodied reality as raced and gendered Muslim women in Britain post 9/11. Second was the ways in which their religious disposition was central to surviving and thriving in higher education. Here the theme of the veil and embodied modesty was articulated through the women's religious agency and negotiating the heightened gendered discourse of the hijab. Third was their 'sense of belonging' and the ways in which being rooted in transnational diasporic Muslim communities gave them an embodied sense of difference that sustained them and gave them strength when navigating the loneliness of being in an alienating university space, which universally they experienced as a place of unbelonging.

NAVIGATING EVERYDAY RACISM

Both Amina and Fatima managed their racialised experiences in British higher education by expressing nostalgia for 'home'. In the countries where they grew up, Canada and Netherlands, they see racism as less rife than in Britain. The embodied experience of being a transnational woman 'out of place' is articulated by the postcolonial feminist writer Lata Mani. She writes, 'The disjunctions between how I saw myself and the kind of knowledge about me that I kept bumping into in the West opened up new questions for social and political inquiry' (Mani, 1989, p. 11). The women in the study were conscious of the 'disjunction' between how they saw themselves as Muslim women and how they were racially constructed as a 'female Muslim other' in British universities. As Mehrunissa explains:

> A *white person may call us Black, but I would never call myself Black. I'm Indian but when I go for an interview at a university, they look at me as a nation. They will say 'This girl is a nation'! So, my character, physical appearance, my skin affects how others see me. Discrimination always comes from the other.* (Mehrunissa)

Mehrunissa talks about being seen as a "*girl who is a nation*". As a 'raced' transnational Indian Muslim migrant she is knowingly no longer just an 'I'—an individual, Mehrunissa—but a homogeneous, collective 'Us'—that is a representation of a '*Black*' alien invader Muslim 'nation'. She describes the way in which her "*character, physical appearance, my skin will affect others*". The Muslim female body, like the Black body in Franz Fanon classic analysis of racialisation is "*sealed into the crushing object hood of the skin*" (Fanon, 1986, p. 11). However, in this case for the Muslim woman the veil becomes the 'second skin'.

Mehrunissa examines her relationship with her body when understanding the world as an embodied 'other'. As an Indian middle-class Muslim woman, her identifiable dress (the veil) and national markers (colour and accent) becomes an extension of her skin. Her embodied intersectional identity is both chosen (in the context of her habitus as a Muslim female

Indian) and imposed (she is 'known' and racialised as a Muslim female Indian). Her multi-layered habitus is thus 'given and given off' through her skin colour, speech, dress and bodily disposition. Bourdieu suggests that one's habitus—that is, ways of standing, speaking, walking, feeling and thinking—shows how the body is *in* the social world but also how the social world is *in* the body (Bourdieu, 1990). Habitus, as a personalised embodied experience is not only classed but also deeply racialised. Simmonds, the Black feminist writer explains,

> *As a Black woman, I know myself inside and outside myself. My relation to this knowledge is conditioned by the social reality of my habitus. But my socialised subjectivity is that of a Black woman and it is at odds with the social world of which I am a product, for this social world is a white world ... in this white world I am a fresh water fish that swims in sea water. I feel the weight of the water on my body.* (Simmonds, 1997, pp. 226–7)

Like Mehrunissa, Amina was also conscious of her body being encountered as a racialised object in the university. Amina also talks of the weight of the heavy 'gauze' of racism which she has to "*work through*" in Britain but feels the lightness of "*nothing*" in her hometown of Toronto where she feels accepted.

> *I feel more 'raced' here than I felt in Canada. It's like a kind of gauze you're trying to work through when you meet people—it's just heavy—it's just not there in Toronto I can just walk around, it's just nothing. Here there are different layers of it too. I've been told that I need to specifically say certain things in an interview because my accent is going to put them off. So, if I'm speaking on my research on race and gender on the radio I need to make a point that I'm 'of colour' so that they'll know otherwise they're going to think I'm American and think I'm white and therefore not an authority on my topic.* (Amina)

In her narrative Amina describes being 'seen' and 'not seen' through different layers in different places. In Britain she has to actively make adjustments to accommodate others. Amina feels she must do this to legitimate her authority over her academic research topic (minority women's rights). She is asked to prove her 'authentic' credentials to speak on behalf of her own when she cannot be visibly seen on the radio when talking about her research. Sara Ahmed (2009) talks eloquently on the way Black subjects are expected to 'happily' perform essentialised otherness in white organisations such as the university so these places can claim to be diverse through embodying the 'diversity' of others. She writes, "What does diversity mean for those of us who look different, and who come, in the very terms of our appearance, to embody diversity? Through diversity, the organisation is represented 'happily' as 'getting along', as committed to equality, as anti-racist. But you must smile, you must express gratitude for having been received. If your arrival is a sign of diversity, then you are a success story" (Ahmed, 2009, p. 46).

Like Amina, Fatima was also a 'success story'. 'Success', as Bradford and Hey (2007, p. 600) explain, is a neoliberal discourse of our time in which a person's psychological capital, "is constituted in practices of self-esteem, confidence and self-belief producing desires and emotions including rage, shame, resentment and pain as well as power and pleasure". As a sociologist and lecturer in a high-status university, Fatima understood her success was predicated upon her psychological capital to negotiate the markers of her difference in her professional life, such as skin colour, language and her headscarf. She talks here about the visual and social 'disjunctions' her presence creates in the racialised space of the campus.

I see myself different because I have a different religion than the majority religion and I have a different culture. I use different languages. They see me as different, but I do not see myself as different. I would think well they didn't offer me the job because of discrimination because I'm wearing a headscarf. I won't know what I would think if I were not wearing a headscarf. I was surprised, as a sociologist, I was studying race and colour and when I came to the UK I felt skin colour is very important here. (Fatima)

BEING 'FAITHFUL': VISIBILITY AND THE VEIL ON CAMPUS

For the women in the study, being a Muslim and wearing the hijab on the university campus was a crucial aspect of their sense of self and ethnic belonging in higher education. In contrast to the more outwardly collective masculine expressions of Muslimness, in which Islam has been mobilised as a site of political and nationalistic power in civil society (Abbas, 2019; Werbner, 2007; Balzani, 2010), the women expressed their faith as a private transcendental spiritual space from which they derived an inner strength. As Fatima explains, being a Muslim is very important to her sense of who she is. She describes her belief as a 'second skin' which extends to her veil and dress. She cannot imagine not having a headscarf, which is as much about her inner spiritual life as well as a naturalised external way of being. She explains:

> *Being religious or a Muslim is very important for me, it shapes and gives me power and when I feel weak, I'm not a weak person but I could feel weak, then religion is very important for me. I pray and I take time for myself. I have this feeling that a power bigger than me protects me. Having this religious feeling and this religious belief gives you the look to life. I mean the very thin line through life, you connect things with each other, and you make sense of everything and that's why religion is so important for me.* (Fatima)

Saba Mahmood (2005) seeks to explain this form of embodied gendered religious agency through the understanding of acts of piety or taqwa. She argues Muslim women's religious disposition, such as obedience to God brings spiritual rewards in and of itself to the women. The Egyptian women she studied in the mosque movement produced 'virtuous selves' through conscious acts of 'shyness' in which the female body is used as an instrument to attain a state of embodied piety. Mahmood (2005) suggests that to understand Islamic female forms of moral subjectivity and embodied spiritual interiority, we must move beyond Western imperialist and feminist notions of liberatory emancipation and the deterministic binaries of resistance/subordination by which Muslim female subjectivity and agency is so often judged. Thus, rather than seeing Fatima's practices and beliefs through the Western normative assumptions about Muslim female docility, complicity and resistance to patriarchal conservative cultural values, we must understand her agency and acts of faith within the broader political and social environment.

While it has been shown that some Muslim women chose to wear the veil on university campus in order to reassert their Muslimness as a political statement in the wake of 9/11 (Killian, 2003; Housee, 2004; Buitelaar, 2006), Amina and Mehrunissa still articulated a strong sense of 'Muslimness' though they themselves did not wear a headscarf. In her study of Pakistani Muslim women in Glasgow, Siraj (2011) shows how Muslim conservative ideology pervasively produced an idealised view of Muslim femininity even among those who chose not to wear the hijab. This commitment to modesty and the 'idea' of the hijab needs to be understood in relation to the identity choices that are available for Muslim women in Islamophobic contexts (Afshar, 2008; Mirza & Meetoo, 2018). Thus Amina, who also saw herself as primarily a South Asian Canadian, still expressed a strong affinity with other Muslims, going to festivals and celebrations in the Mosque, which she talked about as being an 'unconscious and innate' experience.

As educated professional academic women, Amina, Mehrunissa and Fatima all distanced themselves from 'the imagined' other Muslims who were 'not like them'. Fatima explains, "*[T]here are many Muslims which I do not want to belong to. But I am a religious person which is a very important part of my life*". Mehrunissa talks about Muslims having different ideologies which for her would bring about '*conflicts of interest*'. While religion was important to Amina's sense of self she does not want to be '*paralysed or suffer guilt* 'about being a Muslim. Killian (2003) shows the power of dominant cultural repertoires and political and policy structures in shaping Muslims women's views of themselves. In her study of North African Muslim women's response to the French 'headscarf affair' she found older poorly educated women in France drew on traditional Islamic discourses from the Maghreb, while younger well educated Muslim women drew on French secularism to defend the headscarf as a matter of personal liberty and cultural expression.

For all the women in the study, Islam was a conscious site of memory and belonging—a 'second skin' through which their ethnic and religious identity was embodied and lived out through their subjectivity and sense of self (Mirza, 2013). Like the Muslim American women activists in Zahedi's study (2011) the women were constantly redefining themselves in relation to hegemonic Islamophobic and patriarchal discourses. In this context, Islam and being a Muslim meant different things to each woman. Amina used the physical space of the Mosque as her site of contestation. For Mehrunissa it was through her culture and food, and for Fatima it was her headscarf and Islamic practices. Brah (2005) talks about the ways in which transnational migration creates 'diaspora spaces' in new places of settlement. Here culture, class and communities become contested 'sites' which are reshaped when 'individual and collective memories and practices collide, reassemble and reconfigure' (Brah, 2005, p. 193).

The women could be seen to be dialogically constructing 'diaspora spaces' by both listening to and negotiating dominant external discourses about Islam and Muslims and then using them to re-construct their own shifting and contingent narratives of what it is to be a 'Muslim woman' when navigating and negotiating their space and place in British higher education.

SURVIVAL STRATEGIES: MUSLIMNESS, HOME
AND BELONGING

Working in academia, the three Muslim women live at the intersection of the race, religion, gender and class as it collides with hostile anti-immigrant British nationalism and globalised anti-Islamic discourses (Abbas, 2019; Boulila, 2019; EHRC, 2016; Ahmed, 2003). In these troubled diasporic spaces, the Muslim women in the university setting negotiated this disruption through a range of raced, classed and gendered identity strategies which they embodied through language and culture.

Amina who is of Canadian, Pakistani, Indian, British heritage sees herself as a *'worldly'* and *'nomadic'* academic. She is like a chameleon, a 'shape-shifter', with many layers of national and cultural identity that she employs simultaneously as the need arises in her research and teaching. However, it is within the negating discourse of multiculturalism and virulent discourses of Islamophobia that Amina's search for multiple and shifting identities must be located (Mirza, 2012). Anita Fábos (2012) argues the British discourse regarding the limits of multiculturalism has been framed in terms of home, family and belonging, which has striking implications for migrant and refugee women who are seen as embodying an 'unhomely' threat to Britishness. In her study of Muslim Arab Sudanese women in Britain, Fábos (2012, p. 224) talks about the impact these negative connotations have on the women. She explains, "The reactions to these ascribed identities include a distancing from the assumptions that Sudanese form part of the 'Black' community, development of strategies of belonging that rely on transnational networks, and a commitment to Islamic 'authenticity'". Resisting being 'named' by employing multiple identities that link outward towards a global transnational identity constitutes an embodied reaction to endemic racism and exclusion faced in Britain in general and on the campus in particular.

One such embodied act of resistance is to use powerful hegemonic symbols such as language to negotiate modernity. Fatima, who as a transnational academic speaks 3 languages fluently (Turkish, Dutch and English), expresses her determination to 'become' universal through speaking English. She explains "*English is the language where I express my universal identity. I mean, with English I can express my identity and share my thoughts and my ideas with this language and that gives me a refreshed feeling to know I know English*". (Fatima)

While Fatima is aware of colonial subjugation through language from her schooling 'back home', in her statement there is an implicit acceptance of the hegemony and power of English as a way to express herself and be understood as a transnational academic in British higher education. Franz Fanon (1990, p. 27) calls for the 'decolonising of the native intellectual' as a means to 'change the order of the world' in the wake of the violent colonial suppression and destruction of indigenous knowledges and culture in the Western Imperial project. Spivak (2014) describes the necessary process of decolonisation for 'Third world' Asian/Indian postcolonial intellectuals working in universities in the West, which includes strategically positioning themselves in the academy. As Mehrunissa explains, in British higher education it involves speaking the colonisers language, *"English speaking is more important than your own language, than your national language. Why?—Because here as in India, the communication, the mode of study is in English"*.

Though they all spoke English fluently, the women were still strongly rooted to their ethnic and cultural 'belonging' through a strong sense of place. They consciously created meaningful diasporic communities, across a number of nation-states which they recalled through gendered memories of childhood and family. These were strongly recalled through culturally specific smells, hearing, touch and particularly the taste of food. Fatima who feels most at home with friends and family in her home town in the Netherlands still holds on to emotional memories of growing up in Turkey.

I was born in a mountain village where the houses are situated very far from each other. And my mother used to live in this mountain with me. When the time comes, in spring time and they cut the grass and it dries and gives a smell, so if I smell this smell I immediately think of those villages and my mum. (Fatima)

Fatima's feelings of longing and belonging are embodied personal geographies that are shaped by people, place and time. Louise Ryan (2008, p. 300) in her study of working class Irish women nurses who came to Britain describes the 'emotional terrain of transnational journeys'. She argues that migrant women's emotional reactions are rooted in bodily processes, such as feelings of homesickness and the stoical need to conform to the ideal of the successful migrant. This insight into the 'psychic landscape' (Reay, 2005) of postcolonial transnational Muslim women academics reveals the ways in which the shared identification of race, religion, class and gender is embodied and lived out through a collective consciousness and memory.

Conclusion: "More than just a Nation"— Decolonising Race, Gender and Religion in Higher Education

When Mehrunissa declares 'this girl is a Nation', she is remarking on the ways in which she is so often reduced to the external discriminatory values embodied in her markers of race, gender and religion that precede her when she enters a room. However, the three transnational academic Muslim women in this study, Mehrunissa, Fatima and Amina, were much more than 'just a Nation'.

This chapter examines the personal costs and consequences for Muslim women working and studying in higher education in the Islamophobic spaces occupied by the postcolonial Muslim diaspora in Britain. As a Muslim female academic, to be in higher education is to be 'one in a million' (Mirza, 2017). You become an exotic token, an institutional symbol and a 'natural expert of all things to do with your race and religion'. This 'embodied' experience to be the holder of your 'nation' is something that many Muslim women recount in their careers in the academy (Razack, 2008; Ahmed, 2009). As a rare curiosity we are expected to share private information about ourselves while our white colleagues can opt for normative silence about theirs. For me, polite questions become microaggressions: "Where are you from", "How did you get your name", "Did your parents support you? Did your husband let you study?" These everyday microaggressions remind you of how you are 'seen' as 'out of place' and an oppressed 'other' and that your racialised Muslim female body is not perceived as a natural occupier of the white secular corridors of higher learning (Johnson & Joseph-Salisbury, 2018).

Like myself, the women in the study had evolved strategies for survival in white western higher educational spaces where their gendered, racially and religiously marked bodies were 'out of place' (Mirza, 2018a). They did so by engaging in embodied practices of contingent and reconfigured 'Muslimness' such as the wearing or not of the hijab, going to the Mosque, eating halal food, and other acts of gendered safety, resistance and accommodation. While Mehrunissa, Amina and Fatima were educated professionals with strong cross-national affiliations, they expressed a strong sense of being rooted in their ethnic cultures and religious identity through attachments to place, which was expressed through language, dialect, and rooted in food, memories and family. For them 'home' was powerfully recalled through 'other ways of knowing' which nurtured their souls (hooks, 1991).

In these decolonised spaces 'other knowledges' were 'felt' through their embodied sensory memories of childhood which were shaped by people and place and lived out through a spatially rooted sense of belonging to the 'land of their ancestors'. However dialogically, the women's embodied lived reality as raced and gendered Muslim women was also marked by the affective racist immigration and Islamophobic discourses of hate and fear in which they were now embedded as transnational female migrants living and working in Britain (Saeed, 2016; Boulila, 2019).

The framework of embodied intersectionality enables us to see not only how the women were constructed as recognisable visible Muslim others in discourse, but how that affective representation is signified and mediated by the body and experienced as a lived reality. The embodiment of power and disempowerment written through and within the sexed and raced body is particularly important if we are to understand how religious identity is performed, experienced and articulated through the women's subjectivity and sense of self.

Drawing on the embodied accounts of Fatima, Amina and Mehrunissa, the process of 'being and becoming' an intersectionally situated gendered, raced, religious and classed subject of discourse reveals not only the discursive effects of racist hegemonic power and white privilege—which can 'name' a Muslim woman as a 'nation'—but also highlights her embodied agency to consciously rename her identity as lived at the intersecting crossroads of her journey, as she moves in, and through the historically sedimented elite, white, male secular spaces of British higher education.

REFERENCES

Abbas, T. (2019). *Islamophobia and radicalisation: A vicious cycle.* Oxford University Press.

Abu-Lughod, L. (2002). Do Muslim women really need saving? Anthropological reflections on cultural relativism and its others. *American Anthropologist, 104*(3), 783–790.

Advance HE. (2021). Equality in higher education: Statistical reports 2021. Advance HE. advance-he.ac.uk.

Afshar, H. (2008). Can I see your hair? Choice, agency and attitudes: The dilemma of faith and feminism for Muslim women who cover. *Ethnic and Racial Studies, 31*(2), 411–427. https://doi.org/10.1080/01419870701710930

Ahmed, S. (2003). The politics of fear in the making of worlds. *International Journal of Qualitative Studies in Education, 16*(3), 377–398. https://doi.org/10.1080/0951839032000086745

Ahmed, S. (2009). Embodying diversity: Problems and paradoxes for black feminists. *Race Ethnicity and Education, 12*(1), 41–52. https://doi.org/10.1080/13613320802650931

Alexander, C., & Arday, J. (Eds.). (2015). *Aiming higher: Race, Inequality and diversity in the academy.* Runnymede Trust. https://www.runnymedetrust.org/uploads/Aiming%20Higher.pdf

Balzani, M. (2010). Masculinities and violence against women in South Asian communities: Transnational perspectives. In R. K. Thiara & A. K. Gill (Eds.), *Violence against women in South Asian communities: Issues for policy and practice.* JKP.

Boulila, S. C. (2019). *Race in post-racial Europe: An intersectional analysis.* Rowman & Littlefield.

Bourdieu, P. (1990). *In other words: Essays toward a reflexive sociology.* Polity Press.

Bradford, S., & Hey, V. (2007). Successful subjectivities? The successification of class, ethnic and gender positions. *Journal of Education Policy, 22*(6), 595–614. https://doi.org/10.1080/02680930701625205

Brah, A. (2005). *Cartographies of diaspora: Contesting identities.* Routledge.

Buitelaar, M. (2006). I am the ultimate challenge: Accounts of intersectionality in the life-story of a well-known daughter of a Moroccan migrant worker in the Netherlands. *European Journal of Women's Studies, 13*(3), 259–276. https://doi.org/10.1177/1350506806065756

Butler, J. (1993). *Bodies that matter: On the discursive limits of 'sex'.* Routledge.

Coene, G., & Longman, C. (2008). Gendering the diversification of diversity: The Belgium hijab (in) question. *Ethnicities, 8*(3), 302–321. https://doi.org/10.1177/1468796808092445

EHRC. (2016). *Healing a divided Britain: The need for a comprehensive race equality strategy.* Equality and Human Rights Commission London.

Emejulu, A. (2017). The university is not innocent: Speaking of universities. https://www.versobooks.com/en-gb/blogs/news/3148-the-university-is-not-innocent-speaking-of-universities

Fábos, A. (2012). Resisting blackness, embracing rightness: How Muslim Arab Sudanese women negotiate their identity in the diaspora. *Ethnicity and Racial Studies, 35*(2), 218–237. https://doi.org/10.1080/01419870.2011.592594

Fanon, F. (1986). *Black skin white masks* (3rd ed.). Pluto Books.

Fanon, F. (1990). *The wretched of the earth* (5th ed.). Penguin Books.

hooks, B. (1991). *Yearning: Race gender and cultural politics.* Turnaround Press.

Housee, S. (2004). Unveiling South Asian female identities post September 11: Asian female students' sense of identity and experiences of higher education. In I. Law, D. Phillips, & L. Turney (Eds.), *Institutional racism in higher education.* Trentham Books.

Jiwani, Y. (2006). *Discourses of denial: Mediations of race, gender and violence.* UBC Press.

Johnson, A., & Joseph-Salisbury, R. (2018). 'Are you supposed to be in here?' Racial microaggressions and knowledge production in Higher Education. In J. Arday & H. S. Mirza (Eds.), *Dismantling race in higher education: Racism, whiteness and decolonising the academy*. Palgrave Macmillan.

Khan, M. (2019). *It's not about the burqa: Muslim women on faith, feminism, sexuality and race*. Picador.

Killian, C. (2003). The other side of the veil: North African women in France respond to the headscarf affair. *Gender and Society, 17*(4), 567–590. https://doi.org/10.11770891243203253541

Ludhra, G., & Chappell, A. (2011). 'You were quiet — I did all the marching': Research processes involved in hearing the voices of South Asian girls. *International Journal of Adolescence and Youth, 16*, 101–118. https://doi.org/10.1080/02673843.2011.9748050

Mahmood, S. (2005). *The politics of piety: The Islamic revival and the feminist subject*. University Press.

Mani, L. (1989). Multiple mediations: Feminist scholarship in the age of multiple mediations. *Inscriptions, 5*, 1–23. https://doi.org/10.1057/fr.1990.26

Meetoo, V., & Mirza, H. S. (2007). 'There is nothing honourable about honour killings': Gender, violence and the limits of multiculturalism. *Women's Studies International Forum, 30*(3), 187–200.

Mirza, H. S. (2008). *Race, gender and educational desire: Why black women succeed and fail*. Routledge.

Mirza, H. S. (2009). Plotting a history: Black and postcolonial feminisms in 'new times'. *Race Ethnicity and Education, 12*(1), 1–10. https://doi.org/10.1016/j.wsif.2007.03.001

Mirza, H. S. (2012) Multiculturalism and the gender gap: The visibility and invisibility of Muslim women in Britain. In W. I. U. Ahmad & Z. Sardar (Eds.), *Britain's Muslims, Muslim Britain: Making social and political space for Muslims*. Routledge.

Mirza, H. S. (2013, January). 'A second skin': Embodied intersectionality, transnationalism and narratives of identity and belonging among Muslim women in Britain. In *Women's studies international forum* (Vol. 36, pp. 5–15). Pergamon.

Mirza, H. S. (2014). Decolonizing higher education: Black feminism and the intersectionality of race and gender. *Journal of Feminist Scholarship, 7*(7), 1–12.

Mirza, H. S. (2017). 'One in a million': A journey of a post-colonial woman of colour in the white academy. In D. Gabriel & S. Tate (Eds.), *Inside the Ivory tower, Narratives of women of colour surviving and thriving in British Academia*. Trentham Press.

Mirza, H. S. (2018a). Black bodies 'out of place' in academic spaces: Gender, race, faith and culture in post-race times. In J. Arday & H. S. Mirza (Eds.), *Dismantling race in higher education: Racism, whiteness and decolonising the academy*. Palgrave Macmillan.

Mirza, H. S. (2018b). Racism in higher education: 'What then, can be done?'. In J. Arday & H. S. Mirza (Eds.), *Dismantling race in higher education: Racism, whiteness and decolonising the academy*. Palgrave Macmillan.

Mirza, H. S., & Meetoo, V. (2018). Empowering Muslim girls? Post-feminism, multiculturalism and the production of the 'model' Muslim female student in British schools. *British Journal of Sociology of Education, 39*(2), 227–241. https://doi.org/10.1080/01425692.2017.1406336

Mirza, H. S. & Warwick, R. (2024). Race and ethnic inequalities—IFS Deaton review of inequalities. *Oxford Open Economics, 3*, i365–i452, odad026. https://doi.org/10.1093/ooec/odad026

Muslim Council of Britain. (2022). MCB census 2021. https://mcb.org.uk/wp-content/uploads/2022/12/MCB-Census-2021-%E2%80%93-First-Look.pdf

Nandi, A., & Platt, L. (2012). Developing ethnic identity questions for Understanding Society. *Longitudinal and Life Course Studies, 3*(1), 80–100.

Patel, P., & Siddiqui, H. (2010). Shrinking secular spaces: Asian Women at the intersect of race, religion and gender. In R. Thiara & A. Gill (Eds.), *Violence against women in South Asian communities: Issues for policy and practice*. JKP.

Razack, S. (2008). *Casting out: The eviction of Muslims from Western laws & politics*. University of Toronto Press.

Reay, D. (2005). Beyond consciousness? The psychic landscape of social class. *Sociology, 39*(5), 911–928. https://doi.org/10.1177/0038038505058372

Ryan, L. (2008). Navigating the emotional terrain of families "here" and "there": Women, migration and the management of emotions. *Journal of Intercultural Studies, 29*(3), 299–313.

Saeed, T. (2016). *Islamophobia and securitization. Religion, ethnicity and the female voice*. Palgrave Macmillan.

Scott, J. W. (2007). *The politics of the veil*. Princeton University Press.

Simmonds, F. (1997). My body myself: How does a black woman do sociology? In H. S. Mirza (Ed.), *Black British feminism*. Routledge.

Siraj, A. (2011). Meanings of modesty and the hijab amongst Muslim women in Glasgow, Scotland. *Gender, Place and Culture, 18*(6), 716–731. https://doi.org/10.1080/0966369X.2011.617907

Spivak, G. C. (2014). Questions of multiculturalism. In G.C. Spivak & S. Harasym. *The post-colonial critic: Interviews, strategies, dialogues*. Routledge.

Werbner, P. (2007). Veiled interventions in pure space: Honour shame and embodied struggles among Muslims in Britain and France. *Theory Culture and Society, 24*(2), 161–186. https://doi.org/10.1177/0263276407075004

Zahedi, A. (2011). Muslim American women in the post-11 September era. *International Feminist Journal of Politics, 13*(2), 183–203. https://doi.org/10.1080/14616742.2011.560038

Institutional and Policy Change
Geared Towards Religious Equity

Islamophobia's Past, Present, and Future: Insights and Reflections from Multi-generational Muslim Academics

Maisha Islam and Tariq Modood

INTRODUCTION

Detailed within this edited collection, the voices of Muslim students, early career, and seasoned academics are heard through autoethnographic, theoretical, and reflexive framings. Whilst varied in nature, the common thread underpinning their accounts are the ever-present manifestations of Islamophobia in their experiences. This points towards the capacity and strength of storytelling as a decolonial method to be optimised within research spaces, created at the intersection of a social, historical, cultural, political, personal, and intersubjective matrix (Sonn et al., 2013). Utilising such methods for researching resistance and 'civilised oppression' (i.e., the

M. Islam (✉)
University of Southampton, Southampton, UK
e-mail: m.islam@soton.ac.uk

T. Modood
University of Bristol, Bristol, UK

© The Author(s), under exclusive license to Springer Nature Switzerland AG 2024
A. Mahmud, M. Islam (eds.), *Uncovering Islamophobia in Higher Education*, Palgrave Studies in Race, Inequality and Social Justice in Education, https://doi.org/10.1007/978-3-031-65253-0_10

181

mundane yet deep inequalities experienced by minoritised groups) serves to awaken these injustices (Fine, 2006).

To exemplify the sustained marginalisation of Muslims within academia, this chapter comprises a conversational/narrative interview from two individuals who are striving to expose such inequities, yet, are differentially placed in their endeavours to do so. As a requirement of research integrity (Holmes, 2020), we make clear our positionality to alert readers of the lens we bring to the experiences described below. Professor Tariq Modood is a British-Pakistani male academic whose international reputation for contributing to the intellectual fields of political and sociological theory have seen him as a key pioneer in exploring majority-minority relations in Britain, where his analysis has largely centred British Muslims. In contrast, Maisha Islam is a British-Bangladeshi female, early career researcher, and doctoral student whose focus is primarily related to student experience, sense of belonging and student voice for Muslim students and students of colour in English HE. Although we represent two individuals at different career stages (i.e., with Tariq's career spanning over 45 years and Maisha's over 5) with differing social locations which have thus impacted our constructions of marginalisation, we use this as a strength in engaging with a collective reflexivity that exposes and explores the impacts and contemporary concerns related to Islamophobia in the British academy.

The conversational/narrative interview between multi-generational Muslim academics occupying English HE seeks to uncover the injustices that have been (and continue to be) felt. What can then be described as a version of storytelling, decolonial, critical race and feminist authors have long highlighted how this method is a powerful tool in constructing deeper and more nuanced understandings to power dynamics which are typically not privileged in knowledge production but expose hegemonic structures that sustain our subordination (Delgado, 1989; hooks, 1989; Tuhiwai Smith, 2021). The aim of the chapter and the utility of the stories told below are appropriately articulated by Mulvey et al. (2000), who note:

> Stories allow shifts across time and context, while facilitating contextualised, multilayered understanding of personal identities, social relationships, and cultural landscapes. Good stories paint pictures with details that actively engage listeners. The *best stories weave together past and present* [emphasis added], engage intellectually and emotionally, and connect personal, political, physical, and even metaphysical realms. (pg. 885)

It is here that we invite readers to listen and engage with the 'hidden transcript' (Scott, 1990) of the experiences felt by Muslim academics within a HE sector which strives to position itself as inclusive, diverse, and equitable, yet, often in performative and contradictory ways as detailed below (Ahmed, 2012).

20 July 2022: A Conversation Between Multi-generational Muslim Academics

Maisha Islam (MI):	Professor Modood, thank you so much for giving your time to talk about your experiences, reflections, and insights as a Muslim academic. Your long standing career and intellectual contributions will surely provide a nuanced exploration into Islamophobia in UK HE where we can begin to carve out progressive action for the current and future generations of Muslims to come. As a sociologist and political theorist by background, what does Islamophobia mean to you?
Tariq Modood (TM):	Thank you for providing the space to do so. For me, the root concept of Islamophobia is racialisation, a notion developed by sociologists to explain how it is that a population based on descent, identified usually, but not always, by physical appearance, can be made into a group by an 'outsider group' (Banton, 1967; Miles & Brown, 2004). Similar to how colonial Europeans constructed 'Black' individuals by appearance, rather than genetic biology (Banton, 1967; Miles & Brown, 2004; Tuck & Yang, 2012). I take this concept and build from it by theorising cultural racism. This not only describes how people are identified based on descent, but also based on their community, cultural identification, practices, and so on. For example, community structure, marriage, and religion (Modood, 2015). However, a particular kind of cultural racism can disproportionately focus on people's religion more than other identity markers—and for Muslims, this is very common. We regard this as Islamophobia which is the racialisation of Muslims and

is a standard form of racism in Western Europe and globally for Muslims (Meer & Modood, 2009). Often, people will discount religious discrimination as a form of racism, not understanding what religion has to do with race. Islamophobia can refer to people's beliefs or *perceived* beliefs, but it encompasses much wider concepts than this. The Spanish Inquisition and Bosnian genocide exemplify this. These events can be regarded as forms of Islamophobia as they involved ethnic cleansing of Muslims, but not just due to Islamic belief, rather racism against Muslims *as a people/membership of a community*. As such, one can be the object of Islamophobia simply through having a Muslim-sounding name or Muslim family background.

MI: Absolutely. Your concept of cultural racism has advanced an understanding of racism beyond the colour line to acknowledge the racialisation of Muslims in contemporary society. How do you believe this permeates into (UK) HE?

TM: Of course, in different ways but the most fundamental level is similar to how it is enacted in society. For example, variations of stereotypes about Muslims have evolved and have often been contradictory. Muslims were seen to be timid, passive, and non-participative (Brah, 1987); this has been overtaken by a perception of violence, aggression, and fanaticism (Abbas, 2001). Gendered stereotypes can also be understood along these lines, where men are more likely to be associated with the latter, whereas women are more likely to subject themselves/be subjected to obedience, conformity, and submission to community (Britton, 2019; Dwyer, 2000). These may well operate in our universities, affecting the experiences of students and staff. Islamophobia can also operate in a bias that (British) universities must be secular (Aune & Stevenson, 2017; Modood & Calhoun, 2015), in that religion should be practised privately, that is, invisible. This has led to terrible double standards in contemporary society, and especially in universities when other group identities are accepted and even encouraged. If the same principle were to apply to gender or race, one would be accused of sexism, transphobia, or racism. Whilst race, ethnicity, sexuality, etc., are publicly flourishing, being defended and promoted in (British) universities, Muslims do not benefit in the same way. I believe this to be Islamophobia as a form of double standards and discrimination.

Islamophobia also applies to the way we think about disciplinary knowledge, even in subjects related to the study of education. Nineteenth- and twentieth-century European Sociology, for example, created dominant forms of explanation on class, gender, and race. Introducing religion and religious identity, like I have, has been met with disdain (Modood, 1990a, 1990b). Religion only becomes an important feature of sociology *except and only to the extent* that it intersects with what is 'really important', for example, race, gender, class, power, or the economy, etc. Otherwise, religion by itself is seen to be an insignificant topic, unworthy of being central to a sociological inquiry or sociological theory. Muslims carrying out certain kinds of analysis, research, and theorising, can then find themselves marginalised, and that too acts as a form of Islamophobia in HE.

MI: Definitely, and it's one of the things I've really appreciated about your work, especially in making such arguments during a time where racial dualism (i.e., an assumption that society is racially divided into two groups—White and Black) was commonly accepted in Sociology (Modood, 1994). Following your last point, can you tell me about your own experiences of Islamophobia and being Muslim in (UK) HE?

TM: Well, prior to university, my school days in Northwest London were characterised by a lot of racist bullying, whereby South Asian students were the main victims. This was occurring at a time of a phenomenon that, rather distastefully, was/is called P*** bashing (Ashe et al., 2016; Iqbal, 2017). Being brown/Pakistani/Asian and having a 'funny culture' were the objects of cultural racism. As an undergraduate student, I was in a tiny minority of people who were not White, let alone Asian or Muslim. It's hard to recall what this was like as my experience as a minoritised student was quite marginal and not much dwelt on. My experience of racism as a Muslim really began in 1989 with the Satanic Verses affair.[1] Whilst I was against any violence against the author, Salman Rushdie, I argued in national media that Muslim grievances should be heard. The main issue was real anger and hurt; a sense of being violated in one's faith and one's religious feelings. However, this was lost in the threats of violence issued by the Ayatollah Khomeini.

MI: Could you tell me how the affair put Islamophobia and Islamic identity on the map, particularly as someone within (UK) HE?

TM: Well, as a public commentator on the matter, I took up my late father's advice of making it my mission to help the British society understand British Muslims *and* vice versa in the aftermath of the affair. In fulfilling this mission, I have lost many friends; White liberal friends who claimed I was defending violent Muslim fundamentalists. There are two experiences within academia which speak to the Islamophobia I have encountered. The first instance includes a book proposal I wrote in 1992, arguing how the Rushdie Affair signalled that the future of British minority-majority relations would be centred around Muslims, rather than solely on the Black-White divide. That book proposal was rejected 15 times before it was accepted and is an example of liberal Islamophobia. In the case of Salman Rushdie, I believe most publishers took his side and, therefore, did not want someone like me making a strong argued case against that position.

---

[1] The Satanic Verses affair (or Rushdie affair) relates to the release of a novel—*The Satanic Verses* (1988)—whereby author Salman Rushdie was criticised for portraying Islam and the prophet Muhammad (peace be upon him) in blasphemous ways. The novel sparked international outrage from Muslims, and most emphatically, led to a *fatwa* imposed upon Rushdie by Iran's Ayatollah Ruhollah Khomeini.

TM: The second instance took place at an international political science meeting in London during the mid-1990s when I was a junior researcher, attending the conference as an audience member. Following a paper discussing some aspects of democracy, a very senior political theorist started to bring Muslims into the conversation (despite the paper not being about Muslims at all). He made claims that Muslim-majority societies could not naturally become democracies; that they needed to be forced into democracy. He then turned to directly address me:

> *and Tariq, don't comfort yourself by thinking that I think this, and everyone else thinks something else. We all more or less think this, but I'm willing to say it out loud.*

That was a real stunning moment. He was one of the most senior political theorists around and he chose to single me out. I didn't know what to say or do, I was not delivering a paper or a discussant; he was so senior, and I was so junior. Luckily, one or two other more established academics came in, saying those remarks were not very productive and were unsure what they were based on. Whilst there was *some* public pushback, I feel I got a lot of support only *after* the seminar. A number of people came up to me and privately said how shocked they were at how I'd been treated. I have experienced this on a number of occasions when I've had to stand up for something or have been the object of an Islamophobic attack. On the whole, publicly, I have to look after myself, it is only afterwards that colleagues and other people offer private support.

MI: Thank you for sharing these experiences. They are truly unfortunate, and we know they are still being experienced by Muslim academics today. Did these experiences impact the way in which you could see yourself continuing in academia?

TM: I've experienced academic marginality because of Islamophobia, but also irrespective of it. I know a number of Muslim academics and we have often said that we were discovered as Muslims *as a result of* the Rushdie affair. We suddenly realised our place in British society and so discovered a social identity, a social location, and connection with fellow Muslims. Whilst I have described some very intense personal moments, where I did need support from people, I never once thought that I did not want to be an academic. My reaction was the opposite; I wanted to fight back intellectually. For example, arguing against racial dualism or how the term 'political blackness' did not serve Asian communities (Modood, 1994). Whilst I have attracted hostile arguments, it motivates me to point out inappropriate arguments and prove those arguments wrong. Universities, whilst not perfect, are much better than most places in society to have these debates; I have never wanted to leave academia, rather I want to intellectually fight back, create theories, do the research, write, and publish to promote perspectives so that the inadequacy, bias and frankly racism of normative views can be uncovered. Throughout my personal life and career, particularly in the 1990s and early 2000s, this has been met with intellectual disdain; that talking about inequalities for Muslims was not an important issue. However, I find this to be the case less now and see the intellectual climate changing, because people like me have persisted in trying to change it, bringing Muslim experiences into disciplinary focus.

Whilst being Muslim in academia can be an obstacle, it is also an advantage. I would never have been able to argue in relation to the issues around the Rushdie affair or develop the social science arguments from that had I not been Muslim. I'd have found it much more difficult. People also had to listen to me *because* I was a Muslim. Just like any minoritised identity, you can be put down because of it, but you can also argue with a certain authority which is difficult to dismiss.

MI: I really appreciate that empowered outlook. If we turn to intersectional minoritised identity, many of our contributors are Muslim women in academia. Where Muslim women are comparatively absent from public discourse, often spoken *about* rather than given a plat-

	form, I would be interested to hear what your gendered experience has been like as a Muslim male academic.
TM:	Yes, Maisha, that's really interesting because I'm not sure I really know how to answer that. Whilst I have written about gendered Muslim issues (Meer et al., 2010), I do not have a theorised gender self-perspective. Perhaps implying I have taken being a man for granted, or not been very conscious of that. I do however want to propose a gendered theory in relation to Muslim men. I sense that liberal institutions and civil society prefer Muslim women. Whilst I have not empirically investigated this, it seems that Muslim women are more likely to be found in the media, as politicians, and elected students' union officers than Muslim men. It seems to me that non-Muslims prefer to support and vote for a Muslim woman rather than a Muslim man.
MI:	Could you expand on this? We know that stereotypes about Muslim and South Asian men can and do permeate into HE, but do you have a specific sense as to why you think British society and universities are more likely to accept a Muslim woman than a man?
TM:	I believe a similar parallel can be made with Black women and Black men. I believe that British society feels slightly more threatened and afraid of Black men and Muslim men relative to Black women and Muslim women. That is with one significant difference, that Muslim women should not be 'too religious'. If they are (e.g., wear the hijab), they must then have a level of social skill to neutralise their religiosity as non-threatening. Whilst dress is a very significant tier, Muslim men have a higher hurdle to jump. This is not to say that Muslim women have a fairer fight, rather Muslim women in academia who can use their social and intellectual skills, abilities, and personality are more likely to find a door opening than Muslim men. This is merely my impression on the current landscape, and trying to gauge why it is that certain British institutions seem to be ones where South Asian and Muslim women are doing better than men.
MI:	This is indeed an interesting avenue for future research to explore. It resonates to your previous work whereby

you have argued that universities position themselves and hold a secular bias (Modood & Calhoun, 2015). How do you believe this relates to Islamophobia in HE?

TM: Whilst I am certainly fond of universities, there are aspects I want to see changed. When I received my first academic post in 1997, I could see that colleagues and the wider university community were very nervous to focus on religion as a theme, and especially Muslims. For example, I had seen requests for Muslim prayer spaces on campus denied based on a university having secular foundations. In these instances, I have highlighted how every academic year is opened by a Cathedral ceremony, that we have a Chaplaincy, that being secular does not negate the act of praying being possible. Whilst policies and procedures are beginning to change, there has been a lack of accommodation given to Muslim students in comparison to other student/staff experience measures. For example, sporting facilities have been prioritised for wellbeing purposes, counselling services are protected to safeguard mental health, and spaces to discuss women's issues are promoted. The same privilege has not been afforded to Muslims who request prayer spaces, an untenable position, especially now given that Muslim students from across the world form such a critical mass in British universities. Universities can position themselves as secular whilst still recognising a connection and duty to religious students and staff who are also entitled to having their needs and priorities met. They do not need to be inhospitable to Muslim (and other religiously minoritised) communities, rather just as they are making an effort to be hospitable for those of different genders, sexualities, or ethnicities, I argue that universities need to accommodate and embrace diversity, and see that religion is part of the diversity. It is also not a matter of a singular template for all identity recognitions, rather a real multi-recognising that different identities can operate and be recognised in different ways. However, it seems to me that often religion is the one thing made invisibilised, where all other identities are openly celebrated.

MI: This point also relates to how religion may be dispro-portionately marginalised in HE policy and practice. Whilst you have previously made clear your intention about staying on the periphery of these debates; that you want to influence these fields as an intellectual, not as a policy maker (Martínez, 2013), what do you think about current HE policy and the way in which it is impacting Muslim students and staff?

TM: For Muslims, the biggest single issue is the large shadow of the Prevent duty. Whilst I believe that most academics do not accept that duty, it does have a chilling effect on some Muslims in British universities. I am more con-scious of the equalities agenda and how this works in HE in regard to its hierarchical character. It is clear that in HE, gender has been the 'queen' of equality topics for decades (Bhopal & Henderson, 2019). Even when university managers were not discussing any other equal-ity issue, they would be talking about gender equality. We see with big initiatives like Athena Swan (Advance HE, 2023), initially just in STEM[2] but now expanded to other disciplines, advancing gender equality and not any other kind of equality. Coming down this 'equalities hierarchy', the next but more recent issue has been the International Holocaust Remembrance Alliance (IHRA) definition of antisemitism.[3] This has been a top-down imposition upon British universities, and by confusing criticism of Israel with antisemitism is a major attack on academic freedom and free speech, especially for sup-porters of the Palestinian cause like myself, is not a pro-ductive way of promoting equality and diversity (Modood, 2023a, b). The next rung down is anti-colour racism, especially after the Black Lives Matter movement in 2020 which has given a very big shove to universities

---

[2] Science, Technology, Engineering, and Maths.

[3] The IHRA defines antisemitism as "a certain perception of Jews, which may be expressed as hatred toward Jews. Rhetorical and physical manifestations of antisemitism are directed toward Jewish or non-Jewish individuals and/or their property, toward Jewish community institutions and religious facilities".

nationally and internationally (Dunn, 2020). Now, somewhere near the bottom is Islamophobia. Whilst universities do refer to it and say it is part of the equality and diversity portfolio, it has not gotten far in terms of prioritisation and resources. This may develop but will benefit from political effort on the part of Muslims, though this can make Muslims less popular if they are seen to be antagonistic.

Nevertheless, passionate and energetic activism in universities, such as has been utilised by other minoritised groups (Bovill et al., 2021; Rhoads, 2016), can create a space for Muslims in decision-making and consultative circles, in committees and in enactment of policies. I would argue that Muslims need to develop their own understanding and a programme of activity, but seek partnership with other groups of people, and partnership with the institution that they are trying to influence. Rather than make the institution something to oppose, seek to work from within. Ask for the space to work within the institution, ask for dialogue, committee formation, and policy initiatives; monitor them to develop progress over time. So, this is what I see developing in universities, and I would like Muslims to become less marginal to the equalities agenda, more participative and more respected as participants in it.

MI: I agree with that, but I know Muslim students and staff who are fighting to do this are constantly met with institutional barriers and come up against both covert and overt Islamophobia. I wonder if there is something to say about institutions driving this, to actively recognise, support, and welcome their Muslim students and staff as it then becomes an onerous task on our part.

TM: Yes, definitely but it is not an either/or. It is pressure group activity that gets an institution to attend to a particular problem. Leaving this solely to a senior/executive management team will likely not achieve a desired outcome, a certain amount of pressure from below is absolutely vital.

MI: And I would agree that a partnership approach is integral, particularly when advocating for certain spaces and provisions that you and similar others will be using...

TM: Or even understand. Initially, when these issues are first argued for or raised, there is usually insufficient understanding of what the issue is. For me, I believe Muslims need to drive forward their case for equality with an organised solidarity and, by being a part of a wider equalities coalition. Many Muslims already are active in anti-racist and pro-diversity activity. However, in forming coalitions, Muslims need to give their support to a wider coalition and to also expect support back from it.

MI: This chimes into previous advice you have given to younger generations of Muslims keen to enact change, stating that we should be generating work where the common good for Muslims also encompasses the common good for Britain (Modood, 2021). Could you speak to this more in relation HE?

TM: Having worked in the area of identity politics and specifically around British Muslim identities, I believe it important to recognise that difference must be integrated with commonality. In emphasising our differences, I have argued that we must equally attend to how we can be part of the whole British polity—thinking about what is good for Britain, as well as what is good for Muslims. We can apply this principle to equality in HE. Bringing difference and the common good together starts with rejecting an 'us versus them' dualism. Once this assertion is theoretically built in, it is difficult to undo, and actions or rhetoric end up being guided by it. This deepens divides rather than create grounds for common action, cooperation, and understanding. I am committed to an intellectual vision of multiculturalism that avoids this. Another way of avoiding a difference/common good division is to be committed to the flourishing of one's intellectual discipline(s). My own research areas of British Muslim studies, multiculturalism, and ethnic minority equalities have come through battle. This battle does not damage the discipline, rather the

opposite. I am seeking to improve my disciplines by pro-
posing ideas that are going to improve the quality of our
collective thinking and the direction of future research
and thinking. My concepts related to multiculturalism,
for example, are about thinking how Britain can be
changed for the better, in ways that Muslims and other
religious, ethnic, and racial minorities, can be a more
accepted and respected part of it.

MI: I think that is a great segue for our last question. What
would you say the future looks like for universities, and
higher education bodies and organisations that are seeking to improve the experiences, outcomes and successes
of Muslim students and staff?

TM: One thing that will be different for your/next generation, than it has been for me, is that there will be a critical mass of diversity of all kinds, including Muslims. This
creates quite a different physical and cultural university
experience. All kinds of institutional attention are being
given to minorities and equality at the moment, which
has only happened gradually across my life and career. I
would encourage the critical mass of Muslims that are
forming in British universities, not just students but also
PhD researchers, early career researchers and people
developing academic careers, to explore the Muslim
dimension. Not only in a discrete way, by which I mean
only being interested in Muslim issues, but how the
Muslim dimension connects to, for instance, British history, social theory, or our political system. While I am
committed to the project of rethinking Britishness in the
multiculturalist way, I believe one of the biggest projects
for our next generation is rethinking Britishness which
includes Muslimness. But beyond this, re-connecting
Muslimness as part of European identity, where Muslims
have been edited out despite our contribution to
Andalusia, Spain, Iberia, Sicily, the Balkans, and the
Ottoman and British Empires (Essa & Ali, 2012). The
revival of study of the ancient Greek and Roman texts,
and sciences and learning through the Arabs into Spain
was so significant to the development of modern Europe
because it was a platform out of which came the trans-

formation that Europeans themselves have always said has been historic and pathbreaking, namely the Renaissance and the big flowering of ideas and science that came after that. This is one of the biggest challenges for the new generation of Muslim researchers and scholars to rethink, that is, the edited-out parts of Islam and Muslims out of the subjects that they're studying, whether it's Education or Sociology or History or English Literature, or other languages and so on.

Finally, I would say that decolonisation has become a very big buzzword, yet, it seems that the content of this work is a very truncated version of decolonisation. If we accept that decolonisation is about the way in which the Global North has systematically excluded the Global South, not just economically and politically but also intellectually, then this needs to be reversed. How can we have a project of decolonisation that is so narrowly secular? One of the biggest differences between the Global North and Global South is the place of religion in society, people's identities, and their hopes for the future. Negating this implies a very 'Northern' perspective on the Global South. One of the challenges for your/next generation is that if we are to take decolonisation seriously, we must understand how the Global South understands itself and the place of religion—this differs quite significantly from the Global North.

CONCLUSION

Professor Modood's account, influenced by the complexities of his encounters as a Muslim academic, details the nuance of cultural racism in capturing the discrimination against Muslims, accounting for the evolving and contradictory ways in which Muslims are stereotypically perceived both within and outside of academia. His understanding of Islamophobia as a form of double standards, whereby it is exempt from public defence whilst all other identity characteristics are currently celebrated and promoted in universities, has been shaped by his experience within university spaces and in trying to broaden disciplinary perspectives using a religious lens. Therefore, we can regard Islamophobia manifesting within curricula, disciplines, and physical environments, inferring a need to broaden out concepts of how we decolonise which include reference to religion. Professor Modood's account also displays a lack of sympathy (historically) that has been given to Muslims, whereby allyship and public allyship are generally not proffered to Muslims within academia.

Despite such accounts, holding a religiously minoritised identity should be regarded as a double-edged sword—acting both as an obstacle for getting in and getting on in academia, and a unique distinction which differentiates our approach to research and social justice. We then recognise how positionality is difficult to argue against when advocating for religious equity, and that our form of storytelling has methodological benefit. Therefore, those committed to research on resistance/oppression must engage in cross-generational analytical spaces, as they build capacity to think critically, engage more rigorously, and enable a collective self-reflection which helps us to interrogate our framing of certain problems (Fine, 2006). For example, our account nodded towards further empirical research in relation to gender and theorising the experiences of Muslim men in academia, particularly their progression within HE.

Lastly, whilst there cannot be a hierarchy of oppression given that all forms of oppression arise from a similar hegemonic source (Lorde, 1983), we must acknowledge that awareness and importance of different equity-seeking groups has often prioritised other identity-markers (e.g., gender) over religion, and more so in relation to students than staff in UK HE (Deem & Morley, 2006). This does not infer that inequality for those groups (or indeed students) has disappeared but suggests a supposed construction of an 'equalities hierarchy' whereby religion is shunned from HE policy and practice (Aune & Stevenson, 2017) and that issues related to Islamophobia are found at the bottom of the rung (Modood, 2023a, b). Nevertheless, Muslim students and staff should continue employing an energetic activism and seek partnership with institutions to enact change, both within and outside of disciplinary spaces. This account also demonstrates and advocates for cross-generational work and for groups of Muslim students and staff to co-construct narratives of our resistance which thereby form community empowerment. In doing so, our stories become emergent and transformational to critique and counter the assertions so often made about our existence which not only generate self-agency but open listening, dialogue, and activism for those outside of our positionality too (Bell, 2020).

REFERENCES

Abbas, T. (2001). Media capital and the representation of South Asian Muslims in the British Press: An ideological analysis. *Journal of Muslim Minority Affairs, 21*(2), 245–257. https://doi.org/10.1080/1360200120092833

Advance HE. (2023). *Athena Swan charter.* https://www.advance-he.ac.uk/equality-charters/athena-swan-charter

Ahmed, S. (2012). *On being included: Racism and diversity in institutional life.* Duke University Press.

Ashe, S., Virdee, S., & Brown, L. (2016). Striking back against racist violence in the East End of London, 1968–1970. *Race and Class, 58*(1), 34–54. https://doi.org/10.1177/0306396816642997

Aune, K., & Stevenson, J. (2017). *Religion and higher education in Europe and North America.* Routledge. https://doi.org/10.4324/9781315623894

Banton, M. (1967). *Race relations.* Basic Books.

Bell, L. A. (2020). *Storytelling for Social Justice: Connecting narrative and the arts in antiracist teaching* (2nd ed.). Routledge.

Bhopal, K., & Henderson, H. (2019). Competing inequalities: gender versus race in higher education institutions in the UK. *Educational Review.* https://doi.org/10.1080/00131911.2019.1642305

Bovill, H., Mcmahon, S., Demers, J., Banyard, V., Carrasco, V., & Keep, L. (2021). How does student activism drive cultural campus change in the UK and US regarding sexual violence on campus? *Critical Social Policy, 41*(2), 165–187. https://doi.org/10.1177/0261018320913967

Brah, A. (1987). Women of South Asian origin in Britain: Issues and concerns. *South Asia Research, 7*(1), 39–54. https://doi.org/10.1177/026272808700700103

Britton, J. (2019). Muslim men, racialised masculinities and personal life. *Sociology, 53*(1), 36–51. https://doi.org/10.1177/0038038517749780

Deem, R., & Morley, L. (2006). Diversity in the academy? Staff perceptions of equality policies in six contemporary higher education institutions. *Policy Futures in Education, 4*(2), 185–202. https://doi.org/10.2304/pfie.2006.4.2.185

Delgado, R. (1989). Storytelling for oppositionists and others: A plea for narrative. *Michigan Law Review, 87*(8), 2411–2441.

Dunn, O. (2020). *UK universities' response to Black Lives Matter.* https://halpin-partnership.com/debate/halpin-sector-report-uk-universities-response-blm

Dwyer, C. (2000). Negotiating diasporic identities: Young British South Asian Muslim Women. *Women's Studies International Forum, 23*(4), 475–486.

Essa, A., & Ali, O. (2012). *Studies in Islamic civilisation: The Muslim contribution to the renaissance.* The International Institute of Islamic Thought. www.iiituk.com

Fine, M. (2006). Bearing witness: Methods for researching oppression and resistance - a textbook for critical research. *Social Justice Research, 19*(1), 83–108. https://doi.org/10.1007/s11211-006-0001-0

Holmes, D. G. A. (2020). Researcher positionality-a consideration of its influence and place in qualitative research-a new researcher guide. *Shanlax International Journal of Education, 8*(4), 1–10. https://doi.org/10.34293/education.v8i4.3232

hooks, b. (1989). Talking back. In *Talking back: Thinking feminist, thinking black* (pp. 5–9). South End Press. http://abacus.bates.edu/~cnero/rhetoric/hooks.pdf

Iqbal, K. (2017). *A biography of the word 'Paki': Racist incident in the workplace.* Independently published.

Lorde, A. (1983). There is no hierarchy of oppressions. *Interracial Books for Children Bulletin, 14*(3–4), 9.

Martínez, D. O. (2013). Intellectual biography, empirical sociology and normative political theory: An interview with Tariq Modood. *Journal of Intercultural Studies, 34*(6), 729–741. https://doi.org/10.1080/07256868.2013.846894

Meer, N., Dwyer, C., & Modood, T. (2010). Embodying nationhood? Conceptions of British national identity, citizenship, and gender in the "Veil Affair". *The Sociological Review, 58*(1), 84–111.

Meer, N., & Modood, T. (2009). Refutations of racism in the 'Muslim question'. *Patterns of Prejudice, 43*(3–4), 335–354. https://doi.org/10.1080/00313220903109250

Miles, R., & Brown, M. (2004). *Racism.* Routledge.

Modood, T. (1990a). Muslims, race and equality in Britain: Some post-Rushdie affair reflections. *Third Text, 4*(11), 127–134. https://doi.org/10.1080/09528829008576269

Modood, T. (1990b). British Asian Muslims and the Rushdie Affair. *The Political Quarterly, 61*(2), 143–160. https://doi.org/10.1111/j.1467-923X.1990.tb00806.x

Modood, T. (1994). Political blackness and British Asians. *Sociology, 28*(4), 859–876. https://doi.org/10.1177/0038038594028004004

Modood, T. (2015). Difference, cultural racism and anti-racism. In P. Werbner & T. Modood (Eds.), *Debating cultural hybridity: Multicultural identities and the politics of anti-Racism* (pp. 154–172). Zed Books.

Modood, T. (2021). Autobiography of first 45 years. *YouTube.* https://www.youtube.com/watch?v=aO1RQLhCqfwandab_channel=TariqModood

Modood, T. (2023a). Islamophobia, antisemitism and the struggle for recognition: The politics of definitions. In D. Feldman & M. Volocici (Eds.), *Antisemitism, Islamophobia and the politics of definition* (pp. 235–257). Palgrave Macmillan. https://doi.org/10.1007/978-3-031-16266-4_11

Modood, T. (2023b). Multiculturalism. *IPPR Progressive Review, 30* (2). pp. 77–83. https://doi.org/10.1111/newe.12350

Modood, T., & Calhoun, C. (2015). *Religion in Britain: Challenges for higher education.* http://www.tariqmodood.com/uploads/1/2/3/9/12392325/6379_lfhe_stimulus_paper_-_modood_calhoun_32pp.pdf

Mulvey, A., Terenzio, M., Hill, J., Bond, M. A., Huygens, I., Hamerton, H. R., & Cahill, S. (2000). Stories of relative privilege: Power and social change in feminist community psychology. *American Journal of Community Psychology, 28*(6), 883–911. https://doi.org/10.1023/A:1005120001986

Rhoads, R. A. (2016). Student activism, diversity, and the struggle for a just society. *Journal of Diversity in Higher Education, 9*(3), 189–202. https://doi.org/10.1037/dhe0000039

Scott, J. C. (1990). *Domination and the Arts of resistance: Hidden transcripts.* Yale University Press. https://www.jstor.org/stable/j.ctt1np6zz%0A

Sonn, C. C., Stevens, G., & Duncan, N. (2013). Decolonisation, critical methodologies and why stories matter. In G. Stevens, N. Duncan, & H. Derek (Eds.), *Race, Memory and the apartheid archive: Towards a transformative psychosocial praxis* (pp. 295–314). Palgrave Macmillan.

Tuck, E., & Yang, K. W. (2012). Decolonization is not a metaphor. *Decolonization: Indigeneity. Education and Society, 1*(1), 1–40.

Tuhiwai Smith, L. (2021). *Decolonising methodologies: Research and indigenous peoples* (3rd ed.). Zed Books.

CHAPTER 11

The Changing Landscape of Higher Education for British Muslims: Exclusion, Marginalisation, and Surveillance

Tahir Abbas

INTRODUCTION

The study of Muslims in higher education is a significant topic, given the continued exclusion, marginalisation, and bigotry faced by this population. In recent decades, the rise in Islamophobia and securitisation has compounded the difficulties Muslim students encounter (Gilks, 2020; Abbas, 2021). To address these issues and develop a more inclusive and equitable education system, it is essential to understand the experiences and needs of Muslim students in higher education. The evolution of Muslim students' experiences in the British higher education system has been diverse and multifaceted. Initially, Muslim students were perceived as a minority group within the education system and frequently faced discrimination from their peers and teachers (Gillborn, 1995). However, the perception of Muslim students has changed due to increased efforts

T. Abbas (✉)
Leiden University, Leiden, Netherlands
e-mail: t.abbas@fgga.leidenuniv.nl

towards diversity and inclusion and the growing number of Muslim students studying in the UK (Shah, 2006; Islam et al., 2018). Two forces are at play simultaneously: on the one hand, Islamophobia is increasing, and while there is greater appreciation for diversity in a broader sense, there appears to be a particularly negative focus on Islam and Muslims as the perpetual other.

The neoliberalisation of education is one of the most significant contributors to this transformation. Neoliberal policies prioritise market forces and competition, resulting in the marketisation of education (Munro, 2018). This shift has led to a greater emphasis on student satisfaction and employability than on critical thinking and knowledge development. It has had both beneficial and adverse effects on Muslim students. On the one hand, the increased focus on student satisfaction has led to more inclusion and support activities for minority groups, particularly Muslims. Universities have employed a more diverse faculty and implemented programmes such as safe spaces and support groups for Muslim students (Ellis, 2009; Miller, 2020). Nevertheless, Muslim students have been negatively affected by the neoliberalisation of education. Marketisation has reduced funding for some public institutions, causing budget cuts and a decline in education quality (McCaig, 2018). This has disproportionately harmed minority groups, such as young Muslims, who may not have the same access to resources and support as their wealthier peers (Scott-Baumann et al., 2020), as Muslims in higher education often herald from lower socio-economic backgrounds. In addition to the issues posed by neoliberalism, Muslim students in the UK higher education system have also faced obstacles related to securitisation. Following the 9/11 attacks and the rise of extremism, radicalisation, and terrorism, Muslim students have often been viewed as a threat to national security. This has led to increased surveillance and profiling of Muslim students and a greater emphasis on preventing radicalisation within universities (Abbas et al., 2023; Awan, 2012).

This securitisation of Muslim students has resulted in the erosion of civil liberties and the creation of an atmosphere of fear and suspicion. Muslim students have frequently felt targeted and discriminated against, negatively affecting their academic performance and mental health (Alharbi & Smith, 2018). Moreover, the securitisation of Muslim students has focused on preventing radicalisation rather than addressing the root causes of extremism and, in some cases, terrorism, such as poverty and inequality. Despite these obstacles, Muslim students in the UK higher education system have made significant progress in recent years. The increasing number of Muslim students studying in the UK has led to higher university representation and a stronger emphasis on this group's needs and experiences (Ahmad, 2001; Gholami, 2021). Furthermore, Muslim students have organised and advocated for their rights, resulting in increased support for their causes (Fetzer & Soper, 2005). Overall, the perception of Muslim students in the UK higher education system has evolved in a complex manner, influenced by both positive and negative factors. However, the neoliberalisation of education has had detrimental effects on education quality and accessibility. The securitisation of Muslim students has also led to discrimination and the weakening of civil liberties, among other significant repercussions. In terms of representation and campaigning for their rights, Muslim students have made progress despite these obstacles (Panjwani et al., 2017).

This chapter examines these themes in depth to demonstrate how racialisation and securitisation have created new challenges for British Muslims in higher education in the present moment. First, the consequences of how identities have evolved in the age of postmodernity and globalisation for British Muslims are examined. Second, the neoliberalisation of education is analysed in greater detail, focusing on the effects of being and becoming on the lived experience of British Muslims in higher education. The third section examines how securitisation has introduced a new dimension to othering and how this has generated new challenges despite policy thinking's claims to eradicate the threat of extremism and the repercussions it can have in specific circumstances. Finally, the concluding thoughts suggest that British Muslims are identifying a way forward based on the advancement of ethno-religious social capital, which serves as a resource against racism and othering despite these pervasive upheavals.

Muslim Students in the UK Higher Education System

Over the past half century, there has been a significant shift in defining groups, moving away from concepts such as people of colour, race, and ethnicity, and towards religion (Hall, 1992). Factors such as globalisation, migration, and the rise of identity politics have contributed to this change

(Grewal, 2005). Nonetheless, the particularisation of the religious category has had notable consequences, including the potential for an undue emphasis on religious norms, values, and identities as distinct and exclusive (Eisenstadt, 2000). This can lead to a narrow and reductionist perspective on religious groups, focusing mainly on their religion rather than their diversity and complexity as individuals. It might also result in a failure to acknowledge the intersections of identities, such as race, ethnicity, gender, and class (Crenshaw, 1989), neglecting the unique issues and experiences of religious groups who are likely members of multiple marginalised communities. Moreover, religious categorisation may have adverse effects on societal cohesiveness and the development of interfaith dialogue (Modood, 2007). It can establish a dichotomy between religious and non-religious groups, leading to a lack of appreciation and understanding of various religious traditions. Additionally, it can contribute to the formation of religious enclaves, in which religious groups are segregated from the larger population (Bhabha, 1994), having significant ramifications for social integration and the fostering of social cohesion.

The increasing globalisation and localisation of education have contributed to the trend towards the particularisation of the religious category (Ball, 2003; Eisenstadt, 2000). As education systems become more integrated, religion has been increasingly emphasised as a tool to classify and comprehend various communities (Modood, 2007). This is especially noticeable in the case of Muslim students, who have often been seen as a homogeneous group characterised solely by their religion. The growing emphasis on overseas students and cultural exchange has led to a greater appreciation of the richness and complexity of Muslim cultures and identities (Bhabha, 1994). This has resulted in an improved understanding and appreciation of different religious traditions and a more significant emphasis on the distinct cultural and social factors influencing Muslim students' experiences. However, the globalisation and localisation of education have also negatively affected Muslim students, such as through the homogenisation of Muslim students, who are frequently perceived to represent their entire culture and faith (Nurullah, 2008). This can result in a failure to understand the diversity and complexity of Muslim cultures and identities and the unique challenges and experiences faced by Muslim students in different regions of the world. It can also contribute to a restricted and reductionist view of Muslim students, focusing solely on their religion rather than the intersections of identity, including race, ethnicity, gender, and class.

Muslim students of colour often face prejudice and marginalisation within the higher education system due to their religion and race (Mirza, 2008). This can lead to a lack of representation and support, a decline in academic achievement, and a deterioration in mental health (Bloemraad, 2006; Kimura, 2014). However, the particularisation of the religious category can often conceal the experiences of Muslim students of colour, resulting in a failure to recognise the unique issues encountered by this group. The intersection of religion and gender for Muslim women is another example. Muslim women experience prejudice and marginalisation within the higher education system due to their religion and gender (Falah & Nagel, 2005; Avraamidou, 2020). This may involve the enforcement of traditional gender norms and expectations, as well as a lack of representation and assistance.

THE NEOLIBERALISATION OF EDUCATION

The neoliberalisation process has had a significant impact on the education system, affecting both localisation and globalisation (Ball, 2003). The emphasis placed by neoliberal policies on market forces and competition has led to the privatisation of education and the growth of for-profit organisations (Bourdieu, 2002). This has resulted in a variety of consequences and implications for Muslim students in the UK. One of the major benefits of neoliberalism is the increased focus on diversity and inclusion in education. As education has become more market-driven, institutions have had to compete for students, resulting in a greater focus on recruiting students from various backgrounds (Bourdieu, 2002). This has led to a deeper awareness of the experiences and needs of Muslim students and an increase in support and resources for this demographic. However, some argue that neoliberalism has benefited other marginalised groups, not specifically or intentionally Muslim students, who have been unintentional beneficiaries (Brown & Jones, 2013).

Nevertheless, neoliberalism has also had detrimental impacts on British Muslim students. The privatisation of education has led to rising tuition fees and increasing dependence on student loans, thereby exacerbating the financial burden of higher education. This has had an outsized impact on Muslim students, who often come from disadvantaged or low-income homes (Gosine & Islam, 2014). Some argue that neoliberalism has led to a decline in the quality of education, as organisations prioritise attainment over academic accomplishment (Klees, 2008). Despite the rhetoric and plans presented on paper, this may result in a lack of support and resources for students from disadvantaged backgrounds, including Muslim students, as well as a decline in academic performance and retention rates.

The marketisation of education is one of the most significant effects of neoliberalism on the educational system. Additionally, the privatisation of education has resulted in a greater focus on student satisfaction and employability than on the development of critical thinking and knowledge. The implications for Muslim students in the UK are both favourable and detrimental. On the one hand, the increased focus on student well-being has led to a rise in support and inclusion efforts for some minority groups, including Muslims, although much of this work is ongoing. Institutions have introduced programmes for Muslim students, such as safe spaces and support groups, and have hired more religiously and racially diverse staff, but it is unclear whether these are unintended consequences or a result of direct action (Kirton & Greene, 2021). Conversely, the focus on student satisfaction and employability has had a negative impact on British Muslim students. In universities' efforts to recruit a more diverse student body, the demand to conform to mainstream norms and beliefs has become one of the biggest barriers. This may lead to an inability to grasp the depth and complexity of Muslim cultures and identities, as well as the specific challenges and experiences Muslim students face. As institutions emphasise marketability and employability above academic accomplishment, a focus on student enjoyment may lead to a diminished emphasis on critical thinking and information acquisition. This may result in a narrow and reductionist view of education, with an exclusive focus on practical skills as opposed to wider intellectual development.

The Impact of Securitisation on Muslims in Higher Education Today

The process through which non-traditional security concerns are presented within the language and logic of security (Buzan et al., 1998) has ramifications for Muslim students. This process is known as the securitisation of higher education institutions. This chapter examines the influence that securitisation has had on Muslim students in higher education, looking at both the possible drawbacks and advantages to ensure that a fair view is presented. Stampnitzky (2014) notes that the manifestation of securitisation in higher education often takes the form of increasing surveillance and monitoring. According to Kundnani (2014), a widespread fear is that such a situation would increase racial profiling and stigmatise Muslim pupils. This would, in turn, generate an atmosphere of mistrust. In addition, research implies that the securitisation process has the potential to lower the educational performance of Muslim students, which contributes to inequity in the results of higher education. According to the findings of research conducted by Poynting and Perry (2007) on the experiences of Muslim students, heightened emotions of being surveilled and suspected have been brought about as a direct result of securitisation policies, which have led to an atmosphere of distrust. These emotions, when added to overt expressions of Islamophobia, lead to a climate that is unfriendly in educational institutions. Students have expressed that they get the impression that they are 'subjects of suspicion', which prevents them from participating fully in campus life. These kinds of circumstances might discourage potential Muslim students, leading to less diversity in educational institutions of higher learning. In addition, Amin (2012) believes that the subsequent stigma and distrust might have a negative impact on educational attainment. According to Masood, Okagaki, and Hossain's research from 2020, negative stereotypes and perceptions can cause psychological discomfort, which in turn can have an effect on academic achievement. The possibility of this outcome, which underlines the larger impact that securitisation has on educational equity, is cause for fear. Despite the fact that these findings bring up important questions, it is necessary not to portray an unduly simplified image of the consequences that securitisation has had on Muslim students. A few of the factors that go into determining how securitisation is experienced include the particular policies that are in place, the context of the institution, and the identity of the individual. According to Ahmed (2012), not all Muslims experience the securitisation process equally.

Certain academics maintain that the practice of securitisation, although posing a number of challenges, also offers a number of potential benefits. According to Morrison (2021), giving Muslim students more attention can help create awareness about the specific demands and issues they face, which might lead to reforms that improve inclusion and equality. These various experiences can be better understood within the framework of Tajfel's social identity theory (Tajfel, 1982). It is based on the premise that individuals acquire their sense of self-worth from their social identities, which can lead to in-group bias and discrimination. It is possible that negative preconceptions will be reinforced and divides will be created within the student body if security measures are prioritised with a focus on Muslim identity as a potential security risk. The extent to which a student's Muslim identity is front and centre in their lives and whether or not they have other, more positive social identities in their lives also influences how they would react to a scenario like this. In conclusion, the rising use of security measures at higher education institutions has major repercussions for Muslim students. These repercussions include an increase in distrust, the possibility of racial profiling, and a detrimental effect on educational outcomes. Nevertheless, this process is not consistent, and the particular impacts may vary depending on a number of different conditions. Even if securitisation has clear issues, it also has the potential to stimulate conversations about equity and diversity in higher education.

Concluding Thoughts

The neoliberalisation process has affected globalisation and localisation of education. As education systems become more interconnected, there has been increased emphasis on international students and the development of cultural exchange. However, globalisation and localisation have also had negative consequences for Muslim students in the UK. The securitisation of Muslim students, particularly following the events of 9/11 and the rise of terrorism, has resulted in increased surveillance and profiling of this group. This includes initiatives such as Prevent, aimed at preventing radicalisation on campuses (Home Office, 2023). The securitisation of Muslim students has had severe implications, including the erosion of civil liberties and the cultivation of a culture of fear and suspicion. Their academic performance and mental health have suffered as a result (Brown & Saeed, 2015). The perspective and management of Muslim students have been significantly influenced by counter-terrorism policy thinking.

As a South Asian Muslim man with a long-standing and successful career in various global higher education sectors, I have observed the historical framing of the evolving racialisation experienced by Muslim students and staff in the UK higher education system. The experience of being seen as a threat to social order is not new for South Asians and other minority groups in Britain. This sentiment has been present in British society for many years and is not unique to the higher education sector. The historical framing of this evolving racialisation in the higher education sector is complex and multifaceted. It can be traced back to the colonial era when Britain established its rule over South Asia and other parts of the world. The colonial legacy of racial and cultural superiority, perpetuating the myth of the 'white man's burden' continues to shape British society's perceptions towards South Asians and other minorities. Moreover, the rise of Islamophobia after the 9/11 attacks added another layer of complexity to the racialisation of Muslims in the higher education sector. The increasing surveillance and securitisation of Muslim students and staff contributed to a hostile environment that undermines their academic freedom and intellectual pursuits. However, it is essential to note that not all UK higher education institutions have been complicit in this historical framing of the racialisation of Muslim students and staff. Many institutions have taken steps to address issues of diversity and inclusion, such as implementing policies and practices to promote equality, diversity, and inclusion (EDI). The charter aims to address institutional and cultural barriers faced by staff and students from ethnic minority backgrounds, including South Asian Muslims. Similarly, the University of Sussex has established a 'Decolonising Sussex' initiative that seeks to challenge the legacies of colonialism in teaching, research, and the student experience. In conclusion, the historical framing of the evolving racialisation experienced by Muslim students and staff in UK higher education needs to be better understood. The issue is complex and multifaceted, requiring a comprehensive approach to address it. UK higher education institutions should prioritise equality, diversity, and inclusion (EDI) policies and practices to promote a more inclusive and diverse learning environment. By doing so, they can create an environment that is supportive of Muslims and other minority groups, contributing to a more equitable and just society.

The particularisation of the religious category has had significant repercussions, such as the potential for an overemphasis on religious norms, values, and identities as separate and exclusive, a failure to recognise the intersections of identity, and the negative effects on social cohesion and interfaith dialogue. To understand the effects of this transformation and address the challenges religious organisations face in contemporary society, further research is needed. Overall, the neoliberalisation process has had a substantial impact on the education system, affecting both localisation and globalisation. There have been both positive and negative consequences for British Muslim students, such as increased focus on diversity and inclusion, financial barriers, and a decline in educational quality, making further research necessary to understand the implications of neoliberalism and address the challenges Muslim students face in the higher education system.

The racialisation, marketisation, and securitisation of British Muslims in higher education point to a complex interplay of forces that shape the experiences and outcomes of these students. These processes together serve to single out Muslim students, placing them under scrutiny and creating unique challenges for their academic journeys and social experiences within the realm of higher education. Racialisation often leads to stereotyping, discrimination, and other forms of racial bias. For Muslim students, this may mean facing microaggressions, Islamophobia, and bias in the academic environment, leading to feelings of isolation and a hostile learning environment. The marketisation of higher education can exacerbate these challenges, as the drive for revenue generation and competition can overlook the need for inclusivity and equitable treatment of students. Higher education institutions, amidst competition, may neglect their social responsibility to foster an inclusive learning environment. This, in turn, can result in structural and systemic inequalities, impeding access and attainment for marginalised groups, including Muslim students. Securitisation, or the tendency to view certain groups as security risks, adds another layer of complexity to the issue.

The securitisation of Muslims in higher education in Britain has led to increased surveillance and profiling, contributing to an environment of mistrust. This not only inhibits the full participation of Muslim students in university life but may also indirectly impact their academic success. However, this complex scenario should not be accepted as a given. There is a critical need for universities to address these intersectional challenges by cultivating an inclusive academic culture, enhancing diversity training for staff, and implementing policies that challenge the racialisation, marketisation, and securitisation of their Muslim students. By acknowledging these issues, higher education institutions can work towards dismantling the barriers these processes create, enabling all students to thrive. In conclusion, the racialisation, marketisation, and securitisation of British Muslims in higher education is a deeply interwoven issue that requires a nuanced understanding and multifaceted approach to address effectively. Higher education institutions must take on the responsibility to challenge these practices, ensuring equal opportunities and fostering a safe and inclusive environment for all students.

REFERENCES

Abbas, T. (2021). *Countering violent extremism: The international deradicalization agenda*. Bloomsbury Publishing.

Abbas, T., Awan, I., & Marsden, J. (2023). 'Pushed to the edge': the consequences of the 'Prevent Duty' in de-radicalising pre-crime thought among British Muslim university students. *Race Ethnicity and Education, 26*(6), 719–734. https://doi.org/10.1080/13613324.2021.2019002

Ahmad, F. (2001). Modern traditions? British Muslim women and academic achievement. *Gender and Education, 13*(2), 137–152. https://doi.org/10.1080/09540250120051169

Ahmed, S. (2012). *On being included: Racism and diversity in institutional life*. Duke University Press.

Alharbi, A., & Smith, S. (2018). Muslim students' experiences in higher education: A qualitative study of challenges and coping strategies in the United Kingdom. *Education Sciences, 8*(3), 116.

Amin, K. (2012). The Effect of Islamophobia on the educational success of Muslim Americans. In *Issues in religion and education* (pp. 17–30). Brill.

Avraamidou, L. (2020). "I am a young immigrant woman doing physics and on top of that I am Muslim": Identities, intersections, and negotiations. *Journal of Research in Science Teaching, 57*(3), 311–341. https://doi.org/10.1002/tea.21593

Awan, I. (2012). 'I Am a Muslim Not an Extremist': How the prevent strategy has constructed a "suspect" community. *Politics & Policy, 40*(6), 1158–1185. https://doi.org/10.1111/j.1747-1346.2012.00397.x

Ball, S. (2003). The teacher's soul and the terrors of performativity. *Journal of Education Policy, 18*(2), 215–228. https://doi.org/10.1080/02680930 2000043065

Bhabha, H. K. (1994). *The location of culture*. Routledge.

Bloemraad, I. (2006). *Becoming a citizen: Incorporating immigrants and refugees in the United States and Canada*. University of California Press.

Bourdieu, P. (2002). *The state nobility: Elite schools in the field of power*. Stanford University Press.

Brown, K. E., & Saeed, T. (2015). Radicalisation and counter-radicalisation at British Universities: Muslim encounters and alternatives. *Ethnic and Racial Studies, 38*(11), 1952–1968.

Brown, L., & Jones, I. (2013). Encounters with racism and the international student experience. *Studies in Higher education, 38*(7), 1004–1019. https://doi.org/10.1080/01419870.2014.911343

Buzan, B., Waever, O., & Wilde, J. D. (1998). *Security: A new framework for analysis*. Lynne Rienner Publishers.

Crenshaw, K. (1989). Demarginalizing the intersection of race and sex: A black feminist critique of antidiscrimination doctrine, feminist theory and antiracist politics. *University of Chicago Legal Forum, 1*, 139–167. https://scholarship.law.columbia.edu/faculty_scholarship/3007

Eisenstadt, S. N. (2000). Multiple modernities. *Daedalus, 129*(1), 1–29. https://www.jstor.org/stable/20027613

Ellis, S. J. (2009). Diversity and inclusivity at university: A survey of the experiences of lesbian, gay, bisexual and trans (LGBT) students in the UK. *Higher Education, 57*(6), 723–739. https://www.jstor.org/stable/40269155

Falah, G. W., & Nagel, C. R. (Eds.). (2005). *Geographies of Muslim women: Gender, religion, and space.* Guilford Press.

Fetzer, J. S., & Soper, J. C. (2005). *Muslims and the state in Britain, France, and Germany.* Cambridge University Press.

Gholami, R. (2021). Critical race theory and Islamophobia: Challenging inequity in higher education. *Race Ethnicity and Education, 24*(3), 319–337. https://doi.org/10.1080/13613324.2021.1879770

Gilks, M. (2020). The security-prejudice nexus: "Islamist" terrorism and the structural logics of Islamophobia in the UK. *Critical studies on terrorism, 13*(1), 24–46. https://doi.org/10.1080/17539153.2019.1650874

Gillborn, D. (1995). *Racism and antiracism in real schools: Theory, policy and practice.* Open University Press.

Gosine, K., & Islam, F. (2014). "It's Like We're One Big Family": Marginalized young people, community, and the implications for urban schooling. *School Community Journal, 24*(2), 33–62.

Grewal, I. (2005). *Transnational America: Feminisms, diasporas, neoliberalisms.* Duke University Press.

Hall, S. (1992). The question of cultural identity. In S. Hall & P. du Gay (Eds.), *Questions of cultural identity* (pp. 1–17). Sage.

Home Office. (2023). *Prevent duty guidance: Guidance for specified authorities in England and Wales.* London: Crown Copyright.

Islam, M., Lowe, T., & Jones, G. (2018). A 'satisfied settling'? Investigating a sense of belonging for Muslim students in a UK small-medium Higher Education Institution. *Student Engagement in Higher Education Journal, 2*(2), 79–104. https://sehej.raise-network.com/raise/article/view/891

Kimura, M. (2014). Non-performativity of university and subjectification of students: The question of equality and diversity in UK universities. *British Journal of Sociology of Education, 35*(4), 523–540. https://doi.org/10.1080/0142569 2.2013.777207

Kirton, G., & Greene, A. M. (2021). *The dynamics of managing diversity: A critical approach.* Routledge.

Klees, S. J. (2008). A quarter century of neoliberal thinking in education: Misleading analyses and failed policies. *Globalisation, Societies and Education, 6*(4), 311–348. https://doi.org/10.1080/14767720802506672

Kundnani, A. (2014). *The Muslims are coming! Islamophobia, extremism, and the domestic war on terror*. Verso Books.

McCaig, C. (2018). *The marketisation of English higher education: A policy analysis of a risk-based system*. Emerald Group Publishing.

Miller, P. W. (2020). 'Tackling' race inequality in school leadership: Positive actions in BAME teacher progression–evidence from three English schools. *Educational management administration & leadership*, 48(6), 986–1006. https://doi.org/10.1177/174114321987309

Mirza, H. S. (2008). *Race, gender and educational desire: Why black women succeed and fail*. Routledge.

Modood, T. (2007). *Multiculturalism*. Polity Press.

Morrison, J. (2021). Student surveillance, (In)security and (In)equality in the age of Big Data. *Journal of Critical Education Policy Studies, 19*(1), 193–212.

Munro, M. (2018). The complicity of digital technologies in the marketisation of UK higher education: exploring the implications of a critical discourse analysis of thirteen national digital teaching and learning strategies. *International Journal of Educational Technology in Higher Education, 15*(1), 1–20. https://doi.org/10.1186/s41239-018-0093-2

Nurullah, A. S. (2008). Globalisation as a challenge to Islamic cultural identity. *International Journal of Interdisciplinary Social Sciences, 3*(6), 45–52. https://doi.org/10.18848/1833-1882/CGP/v03i06/52625

Panjwani, F., Revell, L., Gholami, R., & Diboll, M. (2017). *Education and extremisms: Rethinking liberal pedagogies in the contemporary world*. Routledge.

Poynting, S., & Perry, B. (2007). Climates of hate: Media and state inspired victimisation of Muslims in Canada and Australia since 9/11. *Current Issues in Criminal Justice, 19*(2), 151–171. https://doi.org/10.1080/1034532 9.2007.12036423

Scott-Baumann, A., Guest, M., Naguib, S., Cheruvallil-Contractor, S., & Phoenix, A. (2020). *Islam on campus: Contested identities and the cultures of higher education in Britain*. Oxford University Press.

Shah, S. (2006). Educational leadership: an Islamic perspective. *British Educational Research Journal, 32*(3), 363–385. https://doi.org/10.1080/014119 20600635403

Stampnitzky, L. (2014). Disciplining an unruly field: Terrorism experts and theories of scientific/intellectual production. *Qualitative Sociology, 34*, 1–19. https://doi.org/10.1007/s11133-010-9187-4

Tajfel, H. (1982). *Social identity and intergroup relations*. Cambridge University Press.

CHAPTER 12

Islamophobia in the Secular University: Understanding and Addressing the Muslim Student Awarding Gap

Reza Gholami

INTRODUCTION

This chapter is about the plight of students from Muslim backgrounds in higher education. As data from the UK's Higher Education Statistics Agency (HESA) have made painfully clear, Muslims are by some margin the lowest attaining—or lowest *awarded*—students in UK universities (Codiroli Mcmaster, 2020; Gholami, 2021); and given ample qualitative and anecdotal evidence, I suspect the same is true in many other countries across the global north. To be sure, the HESA data are disaggregated by religion, not just race/ethnicity, and as I will go on to argue, the 'religion issue' is important and warrants special attention. What should emerge from the following pages is that Muslim students' educational

R. Gholami (✉)
University of Birmingham, Birmingham, UK
e-mail: r.gholami@bham.ac.uk

© The Author(s), under exclusive license to Springer Nature
Switzerland AG 2024
A. Mahmud, M. Islam (eds.), *Uncovering Islamophobia in Higher Education*, Palgrave Studies in Race, Inequality and Social Justice in Education, https://doi.org/10.1007/978-3-031-65253-0_12

215

disadvantage has unique facets, and therefore addressing it cannot be done solely by falling back on familiar, and especially top-down, strategies. It requires careful analysis of the historical and current dynamics of Islamophobia and a willingness to resist intellectual and geographic parochialism.

A central component of such an analysis is a critical account of the role that political secularism and de-theologised Christian culture continue to play in Western politics and education. The chapter will demonstrate that in the era of counter-terrorism policies encroaching ever further into civic life, secularism functions almost counter-intuitively by 'religifying' people of Muslim backgrounds on one hand and *de-privatising* their putative religiosity on the other. Religification has several facets. It reduces the huge diversity of Muslim peoples to an orientalist, and needless to say illusory, vision of Islam, which is associated with extremism, irrationality, backwardness, misogyny, and so on. It also rests on the assumption that Christianity and Christian culture are somehow closer to, or more in harmony with, the proclaimed bedrocks of secular Western civilisation, such as Reason and Rationality (cf. Gray 2019). Moreover, it says something about how some Muslim people respond to their constant public vilification through intensified religiosity. In as much as university campuses are not separate from the wider world, these socio-political currents are operative in higher education too, especially in institutions that enjoy a reputation of prestige.

The chapter proposes two ways forward. First, despite recent arguments to the contrary by some commentators, I champion the importance of studying the unique dynamics of Islamophobia to better understand how racialisation and religification function in education within the broader context of secularism. Such an approach will not be content with reducing Islamophobia to traditional understandings of racism, although the latter is undeniably a key component. In turn, it will enable stakeholders to devise more effective solutions for the concrete outcomes and injustices of Islamophobia in education, such as the Muslim student awarding gap. Secondly, I argue that practical and political efforts to address the awarding gap are best mobilised under the umbrella of the decolonisation movement, which I see as the most viable and powerful due mainly to the fact that it is student led.

SECULARISM, RELIGIFICATION, AND ISLAMOPHOBIA

Asad begins his seminal study *Formations of the Secular* with the assertion that in a secular state, 'the law never seeks to eliminate violence since its object is always to regulate violence' (2003, p. 8). Asad is concerned with the way in which political secularism has developed through modern European history as a project that fuses together a liberalist ontology based on the notion of rational, autonomous individual citizenship with a globally oriented, nation-state driven, capitalist polity. Thus, secular governance is about putting into play particular understandings of law, economy, and discipline as a political strategy. The continuous attempt to define, problematise, and transcend religious and racial diversity—among other differences—is central to that project. It follows, therefore, that violence and inequity will not be eradicated but rather regulated and deployed to the extent deemed useful at any given time.

To see this in practice, we need only look at the ways in which categories of 'public' and 'private' are deployed in the spheres of law and policy making. Mahmood (2015) writes about how secularism has rendered religion a private matter and thus assigned to it a particular domain of authority and activity. In this configuration, religious authority is supposedly clearly distinguishable from state and legal authority and attends to 'private' matters such as the family, sexual relations, and gender hierarchies. Ostensibly, this leaves the modern citizen free to engage in public life (e.g., the law, commerce, politics, employment, education) without any reference to or influence by religion, thus guaranteeing the equality of citizens. However, secularism's relegation of religion to the private sphere does little to reduce the role that majoritarian religions continue to play in the social, political, and cultural life of nation-states. Consider, for example, the central function of Christian symbolism and culture—even if de-theologised—in Western public events, such as the coronation of Britain's King Charles the Third in 2023, or indeed the 2018 commemoration, attended by then British Prime Minister Theresa May, of the Manchester Arena bombing (BBC News, 2018). It would be an error to think of such events as having little or no socio-political relevance: apart from their very high public profiles, such events are key markers of national unity as well as being defining factors in international alliances with far-reaching *political* ramifications.

More importantly, although secular sovereignty has redefined religion as private and assigned to it 'non-political' functions (or in the case of

Laicist traditions tried to jettison it altogether), the secular state neverthe-less retains the power to problematise and castigate religions and religiosi-ties as it sees fit, potentially blaming them for all sorts of problems in public life while keeping its own power hidden. Mahmood (2015) gives the example of how Egyptian media discourse differently positions minori-tised and majoritarian religions, vis-à-vis family and gender laws, to pres-ent minority religious communities as a threat to public order, which may lead to increased inter-religious conflict between Muslims and Coptic Christians. But to take a more recent, and Western, example, since its inception, the UK's counterterrorism policy Prevent has gone well beyond notions of extremism and terrorism to problematise and vilify people of Muslim backgrounds as a general category. And since the policy became statutory in 2015, it has increasingly focused on tackling 'Islamist ideol-ogy', effectively opening the door to branding as extremist any expression of Islam or Muslimness the government and/or the majoritarian senti-ment might disagree with (cf. Gholami, 2022; Holmwood & O'Toole, 2018; Miah, 2017).

It is important not to lose sight of the fact that such policy manoeuvres are secular. That is, they work through the sort of political strategising mentioned above, and they put into play what Asad calls 'different struc-tures of ambition and fear' (2003, p. 7). In the case of Muslims in global north countries, the secular strategy, almost counter-intuitively, has been about *de-privatising* ideas of Islam and Muslimness. This 'making public' allows popular media and political discourses to manufacture and rational-ise their own version of Islam, one that in the post-9/11 world has been predominantly associated with extremism, irrationality, hatred of the West, misogyny, homophobia and so forth; and crucially one that Muslim peo-ples themselves have not had a say in. De-privatisation, in turn, allows Western governments to maintain a façade of neutrality and rationality, and to look as though they are 'dealing with' Islam and Muslims as just another piece of government business. According to this secular logic, there is not much practical difference between dealing with 'the Muslim issue' than with, say, the coronavirus pandemic: both are approached as objective threats to public safety and the government is discharging its duty to protect citizens in the most effective and efficient way possible. Yet, we know from numerous speeches and publications by senior figures in recent governments—including Boris Johnson, Michael Gove, and Dominic Cummings—as well as hundreds of allegations of Islamophobia against the British Conservative Party, that many politicians harbour deeply Islamophobic views.[1]

A useful way to articulate this mode of secular power is via the concept of religification, which is both about how a particular understanding of Islamic religiosity is manufactured by Islamophobic discourse and policy and then thrust upon the highly diverse peoples that may identify as Muslims, and about the ways in which some Muslims may respond to Islamophobia through intensified expressions of religious identity (cf. Ghaffar-Kucher, 2011; Gholami, 2021). Due to lack of space, I will concern myself mainly with the first element. In my view, what makes religification a powerful concept is its emphasis on religion, or rather the idea of being, or being seen to be, religious. This focus on religion and its relationship to secular governance has not been given enough attention in analyses of contemporary Islamophobia in general and Islamophobia in education specifically. However, in the post-9/11 world, and in the UK the post 'Trojan-Horse' context, Islamophobia has in the main been about the demonisation of Muslims along religious lines, i.e., the idea that Islam as a socio-spiritual system refuses to stay in the private sphere; that it inclines towards extremism; that it is inherently anti-western; and that it has an almost mesmeric grip on its adherents—'the Muslims'—who unlike people of European/Christian origin are incapable of exercising autonomy and critical thought and are therefore prone to violent extremism by way of their Islamic beliefs and practices (cf. Mamdani, 2002; Mahmood, 2015). As I will now go on to discuss, these representations of Islam-as-religion have become increasingly salient in education. Their normalisation is producing modes of educational inequity that cannot be easily framed and addressed by traditional approaches to race inequality.

---

[1] See for example: https://www.theguardian.com/politics/2020/mar/05/300-allegations-of-tory-islamophobia-sent-to-equality-watchdog (accessed 06/06/2023). It is important to note that Islamophobia exists in other political parties too. However, I am here concerned to illustrate the rationalisation and justification of Islamophobia through secular governance, a strategy that the Conservatives have deployed successfully since coming to power in 2010 and especially after the Trojan Horse affair in 2014. At the time of writing in 2023, the Conservatives are still in power.

THE POLITICS AND PRACTICE OF EDUCATION IN AN AGE OF ISLAMOPHOBIA

The issue of religification is well documented in secondary education in England and beyond. Vincent (2018) has shown how the teaching of Fundamental British values (FBV) is linked to a de-theologised and cultur-alised Christianity. This has happened alongside a repositioning of many South Asian students who have gone from being classified as studious and passive 'Asians' to being seen as 'Muslims' in need of surveillance and tutelage about the value of tolerance (ibid.). Beyond Britain, the tropes and dynamics of Islamophobia in education are surprisingly consistent. In Denmark, for example, where the state has effectively replicated the Prevent policy, Gilliam (2022) shows that Muslim students' inclusion in schools is dependent upon their ability and willingness to display a 'relaxed religiosity'. This assumes that Muslim religiosity, however it may manifest, is ultimately at odds with Danish values and culture, which, although offi-cially secular, have explicit and deep-running ties with the Lutheran Church, the Danish People's Church since 1849, and continually in receipt of public funds. The idea of 'relaxed religiosity', then, is defined in this secular, Christianised, and public context. Similarly, in South Korea, Kim and Kang (2022) have done research with 'progressive' high school students and found that many of them saw Muslim people as inherently irrational and prone to violence. As such, avoiding or excluding them would seem like a perfectly reasonable choice.

I would argue that the international consistency of Islamophobia in education results from the problematisation of Islamic religiosity as intrin-sically hostile to universalised notions of scientific and social progress, individual freedom, and economic prosperity. This vision of Islam has little basis in empirical reality; it is rooted in Orientalism and bolstered by counter-extremism policies and discourses whose most significant mecha-nism of delivery has been national education systems.[2] By purporting to address educational inequities related to minoritised populations under pre-existing policies, such as the Equality Act (2010) or the BAME[3] or EDI[4] agendas in the UK, and separately linking Muslims to issues of

---

[2] For the UK Government's most recent statistics, see: https://homeofficemedia.blog.gov.uk/2023/02/08/prevent-and-channel-factsheet-2023/ (accessed 01/07/2023)

[3] Black, Asian and Minority Ethnic.

[4] Equality, Diversity and Inclusion.

terrorism and national security, states have been quite successful in co-opting education systems to concretise and implement their Islamophobic agendas while avoiding accusations of Islamophobia. We have witnessed this in the way the Trojan Horse affair—at worst, an issue of educational leadership (see Cannizzaro & Gholami, 2018; Gholami, 2022; Holmwood & O'Toole, 2018)—was hijacked by right-wing politicians and media and became instrumental in making Prevent statutory, thus legally requiring teachers and university lecturers to look for 'signs of radicalisation' in their students; we have also seen it in how, since 2011, the UK government's definition of extremism[5] has been honed primarily through education policies such as the Teachers' Standards or the OFSTED framework (see Panjwani et al., 2018). A more brutal expression of such policies is the Chinese government's 're-education' of the Uyghur Muslim population: under the guise of counter-extremism, the Chinese government has embarked upon a terrifying campaign of making Uyghurs 'proper' Chinese citizens by forcibly 'educating' their Muslimness out of them (see Izgil 2023). In this way, over the last decade or so, the problematisation of Muslim beliefs and practices has increasingly become normalised in and through education.

In attending to the challenges that Muslim university students face, it is important to acknowledge this educational context and trace its manifestations on campuses. For universities are often thought of as somehow standing apart from these broader socio-political entanglements, perhaps by virtue of their being places of higher learning and sites of contested knowledges and student activism, or because of their reputation for 'left-wing' bias. Yet, there are at least three factors that point towards the normalised, if sometimes subtle, existence of Islamophobia on campuses in the UK and elsewhere in the global north. Firstly, and most importantly, there is the issue of counterterrorism policies, which of course operate in universities too. Previous academic and student-led research has often singled out such policies as decisive in how Muslim students fare at university. For example, a 2018 study by the UK's National Union of Students (NUS) presented first-hand evidence of Muslim students being anxious

---

[5] 'The vocal or active opposition to our fundamental values, including democracy, the rule of law, individual liberty and the mutual respect and tolerance of different faiths and beliefs. We also regard calls for the death of members of our armed forces as extremist.' https://report-extremism.education.gov.uk/#:~:text=The%20government%27s%20definition%20of%20extremism,our%20armed%20forces%20as%20extremist. (accessed 27/06/2023).

about being under suspicion and surveillance, and this had a direct impact on how they engaged in their classes and on their relationships with other students. Similarly, Stevenson's (2018) study found that Muslims can feel highly visible and monitored on campus, due to the ease with which they are often identifiable as Muslims. Secondly, as I have discussed elsewhere (Gholami, 2021), the ethos of most Western universities—and especially the 'elite' ones—has complex historical entanglements with both Christianity and secularism (see also Deslandes, 1998; Jouili, 2009; Reid, 2017). The upshot is that ideas of scientific/academic excellence are claimed as belonging primarily to the history of Western modernity in which secularism and Christianity are deeply enmeshed. Thus, religious, and especially Islamic, epistemologies and subject positions are placed in the realm of the magical, irrational, backward, and irrelevant. Simultaneously, there is in this narrative a sense that compared to other religions, Christianity is somehow closer to or more compatible with secular liberalism (see Gray 2019; Kitching & Gholami, 2023). As such, the spaces, ceremonies, and symbolisms of secular public universities in the global north have been and continue to be anchored in Christian traditions and can even be openly hostile towards Muslim religious and cultural demands (see Jouili, 2009).

The third important factor relates to the rise of what I see as a sinister right-wing movement against the so-called wokeism. As Davies and MacRae (2023) demonstrate, this anti-woke campaign has the backing of some senior academics[6] and generally attacks the intellectual traditions of historically oppressed people, including the Frankfurt School of Critical Theory and Critical Race Theory, as a way to supposedly prevent the erosion of Western civilisation by 'lefty loonies', multiculturalists, and the 'Wokerati'. As Gillborn et al. (2022) demonstrate, such far-right movements, which sometimes try to sneak a range of disturbing ideas such as Replacement Theory and Eugenics into the academic mainstream, comprise vast, though fluid, networks that span education, think tanks, and the government. They are also increasingly active on university campuses, for instance through events such as the 2015 'London Conference on Intelligence' held at University College London (UCL) and organised by James Thompson, who believes that intelligence is genetically determined, and that Black people are on average less intelligent than White people (ibid., p. 5). It is not surprising that within these groups and

[6] Such as political scientists Eric Kaufmann and Matthew Goodwin.

networks—which Gillborn et al., divide into three camps, the IQists, the Anti anti-racists, and the Authoritarian Educators—there are people with specifically Islamophobic ideas, such as Emil Kirkegaard who has written that Islamic countries on the whole have lower IQ (ibid., p. 6). The UK government's Higher Education (Freedom of Speech) Act, which received royal assent in May 2023, and its appointment of Arif Ahmed as the new director for freedom of speech and academic freedom in England, is likely to make these matters worse by identifying a problem that does not exist— i.e., that free speech is under attack in overwhelmingly 'leftist' universities—and thus opening the door for more extreme right-wing discourses on campuses.

Beyond 'Minding' the Gap

There is no doubt that racism is a key component of Islamophobia. The brown/black skin colour of the majority of Muslims in the UK, coupled with the fact that they are often easily identifiable through their style of clothing, marks them out as different and makes them prone to racist attacks. But the discursive content of these attacks, as we have seen, increasingly draws upon the vilification of Islam as a religion. Additionally, as alluded to above, there are institutional and policy modes of religification at play, which can often work subtly and implicitly, but nevertheless powerfully, to 'otherise' and ostracise Muslim students. Existing strategies, as I have shown elsewhere (Gholami, 2021), have not gone far enough in accounting for the sheer complexity of the issue. There seems to have been a tendency to view the problem as self-contained and without proper historical and political context. This approach has led to well-intentioned but ultimately futile 'best practice' recommendations, such as better reporting mechanisms and religious literacy training.

Institutions, meanwhile, seem to be outright impervious to the gravity of the issue. It should be obvious that since not all Muslim students are from racially minoritised backgrounds, and most in the UK are not international, the 'BAME' and 'Internationalisation' agendas will not be enough to guarantee the closing of the awarding gap. Similarly, institutions can say (and write) whatever they wish about their commitment to EDI, but as long as policies such as Prevent, as well as the ethos of institutions themselves, work to actively exclude Muslim students, equity remains a pipe dream. Furthermore, Sarah Ahmed (2006) has written convincingly about the way in which the production and circulation of EDI-related policy documents by institutions can come to replace actual equality and inclusion on campuses. This is in part because recognising inequality and committing to equality have become ends in themselves. On antiracism specifically, Ahmed writes: 'Being committed to antiracism can function as a perverse performance of racism: "you" are wrong to describe us as uncaring and racist because "we" are committed to being antiracist. Antiracism functions here as a discourse of organisational pride' (2006, p. 111). In recent years, the student-led decolonisation movement has gathered momentum across campuses in the UK and elsewhere. I see this movement as the most powerful and viable for addressing all sorts of educational injustices, including the Muslim awarding gap. I will come back to this below. But it is important to highlight here that although under pressure from students, universities have had to take decolonisation seriously, left to themselves they would probably do all they could to shirk their responsibilities, redefine the project, and perhaps even derail it altogether. Based on recent research in the UK, Shain et al. (2021) have summed up universities' responses to decolonisation so far as either rejection, reluctant acceptance ('OK, but we need more data...'), or strategic advancement (i.e., to be seen to be responsive, but ultimately opportunistic and tokenistic).

In my view, an effective strategy for addressing the Muslim student awarding gap must possess two core elements. Firstly, it must be based upon rigorous theories of racism *and* secularism. As for racism, I have suggested that Critical Race Theory (CRT) is useful because in addition to practical tools such as storytelling that are effective for anti-racist and alliance-building work, CRT offers incisive conceptual tools such as 'interest convergence' and 'interest divergence' through which students can ask the right questions of their institutions and hold them to account in the most effective ways.[7] In terms of theorising the secular, the sort of critical analysis advanced by Asad, Mahmood, and others is powerful for understanding how secularism works in the modern world. The concept of religification, I would argue, works well in this context because it can act as a bridge between contemporary dynamics of Islamophobia and the wider history and politics of secularism, including its institutional forms. Ultimately, we must work towards developing a 'critical secular studies' in education, a project I have been actively pursuing in recent years (see Gholami, 2018; Kitching & Gholami, 2023).

[7] Space does not permit me to offer a detailed discussion here. Please see Gholami (2021).

The second key element is about making sure that the practical aspect of addressing the awarding gap is genuinely student-led but that it is heavily invested in by institutions. The decolonisation movement provides an excellent umbrella under which this can be operationalised. As shown above, decolonisation cannot work through catch-all solutions or absolute notions of 'best practice'. Strategies that do are, I would argue, doomed to fail because they assume that all forms of prejudice or oppression with a racial/ethnic component are ultimately similar in that they are reducible to a generalised understanding of racism (cf. Patel, 2022). Thus, they are not only neglecting the sort of complexity this chapter has been concerned to foreground, but also giving *a priori* supremacy to secularist and liberalist modes of analysis. Instead, decolonisation ought to act as a broad framework under which specific forms and dynamics of prejudice are studied and appropriate solutions designed. In this way, the decolonisation movement can prevent itself from historical blindness. It is true that race, racism, and racialisation are central to the colonialist agenda, but so too are the systematic dismantling and delegitimisation of the cultures and knowledge systems, including religious/spiritual ones, of the global south, not to mention economic and environmental injustices. Decolonisation, then, frames and contextualises historical and extant social relations between the West and the non-West. It offers perspective and truth (both of which are in short supply these days). It compels us to address past injustices but also recognise current and future possibilities of injustice, and indeed of justice. It is about an absolute commitment to social justice that starts introspectively, reflexively, and works outwards.

Students have proven that they are excellent stewards of the decolonial legacy and outstanding practitioners and scholars of its politics. Conversely, institutions probably would sooner want that the whole thing just went away. This is why it is paramount that students retain leadership and ensure that mechanisms are put in place for continuity, consistency, and collaboration. Likewise, students must keep institutions' feet to the fire and demand rigorous research, action, funding, and accountability. Such work is beginning to proliferate (e.g., Islam, 2020), and it must be encouraged to grow and develop. Finally, where possible, students and institutions should open up spaces in which diverse local communities, including *diverse Muslim* communities, can engage as partners in teaching and research at the university. It is important to stress that the aim here is not to dismiss the achievements of Western sciences; nor to create an anti-scientific environment in which anyone can claim equal legitimacy for their assertion based purely on their identity or belief. On the contrary, the status of universities as places of scientific and scholarly rigour, free speech, equality, critical thought, and debate is sacrosanct and should be vigorously defended. The aim is perhaps to envision a future knowledge—a future epistemology—in which the Western/Non-Western binary has broken down.

Conclusion

This chapter has attempted to approach the issue, indeed the injustice, of the Muslim student awarding gap from a somewhat different angle. The awarding gap is part and parcel of the much bigger, and global, problem of Islamophobia, which can manifest differently in various national contexts—from Denmark to South Korea; from the UK to Japan; from Myanmar to India; from China to Australia. But it is also surprisingly consistent both in the way it problematises Muslim religious beliefs and in the way it often works through education. I have argued that understanding these dynamics is the necessary first step in addressing the injustices Muslims face in education. In turn, grappling with the complexities of Islamophobia leads us towards a critical analysis of political secularism and the ways in which it has worked to reshape the modern world, often under conditions of colonialism and imperialism, in economic, political, cultural, and epistemological terms.

To be sure, secularism is not 'the opposite' of 'religion'. The whole point is that contemporary concepts of religion and irreligion have been defined and universalised by secularism and its deployment of notions of public versus private, individual versus collective, and so on. Throughout colonial modernity, secularism has been a powerful tool for Western imperialists to establish and legalise the superiority of Western ideas, but crucially also to control populations and assign to them particular social positions. In the case of Muslim peoples, orientalist tropes made credible via academic/scholarly discourse have long cast them as backward, barbaric, and irrational. However, since 9/11, Muslims have been on the receiving end of increasingly draconian counter-extremism legislation which has not only subjected them to surveillance and biased policing, but also problematised and demonised their faith and beliefs. The power of secularism is most clearly visible in the fact that Muslim religiosity has been and continues to be very much a public issue, ostensibly because it is a matter of national security. At the same time, counterterror policies have

co-opted education systems into doing much of their work. The net outcome of this, as briefly explored above, is that 'Muslimness' has become a
highly fraught issue educationally: Muslim students learn that having
Islamic belief may cause them to be disliked and excluded; non-Muslim
students learn that it is okay to dislike and exclude Muslims. There are, of
course, also a host of related pedagogical problems, which it has not been
possible to explore in this chapter.

Addressing the Muslim student awarding gap is possible and in fact
quite feasible. But it will not be achieved by pitching our practical and
theoretical tents on familiar ground. As we saw above, there are numerous
reasons why existing strategies, even with the best of intentions, will fall
short of success. No matter how much we all may wish it were so,
Islamophobia and its manifestation in the awarding gap are not simple
phenomena and cannot be dealt with simplistically. There is, as mentioned,
the issue of secularism: its framing and de-privatisation of Islam, its relationship with Christianity, and its continued influence in institutional cultures. There is also the issue of counterterror policies, i.e., concrete,
secular political mechanisms that help to define 'Islam' and 'Muslims' and
legitimise their Islamophobic treatment. Therefore, I have argued for a
two-pronged strategy. Firstly, analyses of Islamophobia should start by
partially separating race and religion to understand their unique dynamics
and functioning. In this vein, the concept of religification, as part of a
wider critical secular studies, helps us to understand something about how
the aforementioned secular, historical, and political dynamics operate
socially (and sociologically) in day-to-day living. It also allows us to interrogate institutional forms of religious inequality. And as for race and racism, CRT, as mentioned, would be my preferred theory in this context.
Armed, then, with a more precise understanding, the second prong consists in ensuring that the practical and political elements on campuses are
led by students under the aegis of decolonisation, which has the capacity
to not only link the plight of specific groups of minoritised students to the
towering legacy of colonialism in higher education but is crucially also
highly active on campuses as a matter of course. Student-led decolonisation has become an inescapable fact for many Western institutions, who—
and I say 'who' because I want to draw attention to human
decision-makers—are finding that their power is not as un-checked as it
once was.

REFERENCES

Ahmed, S. (2006). The non-performativity of antiracism. *Meridians, 7*(1), 104–126. https://doi.org/10.2979/MER.2006.7.1.104

Asad, T. (2003). *Formations of the secular: Christianity, Islam, modernity.* Stanford University Press.

BBC News. (2018). Manchester attack: Hundreds gather to remember victims. *BBC News.* Retrieved July 16, 2023, from https://www.bbc.co.uk/news/uk-england-manchester-44197949.

Cannizzaro, S., & Gholami, R. (2018). The devil is *Not* in the detail: Representational absence and stereotyping in The 'Trojan Horse' news story. *Race Ethnicity and Education, 21*(1), 15–29. https://doi.org/10.1080/13613324.2016.1195350

Codiroli Mcmaster, N. (2020). Research insight: Religion and belief in UK higher education: Analysis of Higher Education Statistics Agency (HESA) student data for 2017/18. *Advance HE.* Retrieved April 17, 2020, from https://www.advance-he.ac.uk/knowledge-hub/research-insight-religion-and-belief-uk-higher-education

Davies, H. C., & MacRae, S. E. (2023). An anatomy of the British war on woke. *Race & Class, 0*(0). https://doi.org/10.1177/03063968231164905

Deslandes, P. (1998). The foreign element: Newcomers and the rhetoric of race, nation, and empire in 'oxbridge' undergraduate culture, 1850–1920. *The Journal of British Studies, 37*(1), 54–90. https://doi.org/10.1086/386151

Ghaffar-Kucher, A. (2011). The religification of Pakistani-American youth. *American Educational Research Journal.* Advance Online Publication. http://aer.sagepub.com/content/early/2011/08/02/0002831211414858

Gholami, R. (2018). New plan for RE needs to consider how secularism over two centuries fundamentally reshaped the world and helped plant the seeds of religious extremism. *UCL-IoE Blog.* https://ioelondonblog.wordpress.com/2018/09/28/new-plan-for-re-needs-to-consider-how-secularism-over-two-centuries-fundamentally-reshaped-the-world-and-helped-plant-the-seeds-of-religious-extremism/

Gholami, R. (2021). Critical race theory and Islamophobia: Challenging inequity in higher education. *Race Ethnicity and Education, 24*(3), 319–337. https://doi.org/10.1080/13613324.2021.1879770

Gholami, R. (2022). Reflections on the impact and legacy of 'Trojan Horse': An intersectional view. In C. Diamond (Ed.), *The Birmingham book: Lessons in urban education leadership and policy from the Trojan Horse affair* (pp. 289–313). Crown House Publishing.

Gillborn, D., McGimpsey, I., & Warmington, P. (2022). The fringe is the centre: Racism, pseudoscience and authoritarianism in the dominant English education policy network. *International Journal of Education Research, 115*. https://doi. org/10.1016/j.ijer.2022.102056

Gilliam, L. (2022). Being Muslim "without a fuss": Relaxed religiosity and conditional inclusion in Danish schools and society. *Ethnic and Racial Studies, 45*(6), 1096–1114. https://doi.org/10.1080/01419870.2021.1971733

Gray, J. (2019). Why the liberal West is a Christian creation: Christianity is dismissed as a fairy tale but its assumptions underpin the modern secular world, *The New Statesman*, https://www.newstatesman.com/culture/2019/09/why-the-liberal-west-is-a-christian-creation. (Accessed 27/09/2024).

Holmwood, J., & O'Toole, T. (2018). *Countering extremism in British schools: The truth about the Birmingham Trojan Horse affair*. Policy Press.

Islam, M. (2020). Building belonging: Developing religiously inclusive cultures for Muslim Students in Higher Education. *Advance HE:* https://www.advance-he. ac.uk/knowledge-hub/building-belonging-developing-religiously-inclusive-cultures-muslim-students-higher

Izgil, T. H. (2023). Let the Tragedy in My Homeland Be a Lesson, *The New York Times*, https://www.nytimes.com/2023/07/28/opinion/uyghur-china-internment-authoritarian.html. (Accessed 27/09/2024).

Jouili, J. S. (2009). Negotiating secular boundaries: Pious micro-practices of Muslim Women in French and German public spheres. *Social Anthropology, 17*(4), 455–470. https://doi.org/10.1111/j.1469-8676.2009.00082.x

Kim, G., & Kang, J. (2022). In-between the West and the other: Postcolonial contradictions in Korean Students' understandings of Islam. *Race Ethnicity and Education, 1–19*. https://doi.org/10.1080/13613324.2022.2154372

Kitching, K. & Gholami, R. (2023). Towards critical secular studies in education: Addressing secular education formations and their intersecting inequalities. *Discourse, Studies in the Cultural Politics of Education*. https://doi.org/1 0.1080/01596306.2023.2209710

Mahmood, S. (2015). *Religious difference in a secular age: A minority report*. Princeton University Press.

Mamdani, M. (2002). Good Muslim, bad Muslim: A political perspective on culture and Terrorism. *American Anthropologist, 104*(3), 766–775. https://doi. org/10.1525/aa.2002.104.3.766

Miah, S. (2017). *Muslims, schooling and security: Trojan Horse, prevent and racial politics*. Palgrave Macmillan.

Panjwani, F., Revell, L., Gholami, R., & Diboll, M. (2018). *Education and extremisms: Re-Thinking liberal pedagogies in the contemporary world*. Routledge.

Patel, P. (2022). The APPG, Islamophobia and Anti-Muslim racism. *Feminist Dissent, 6*, 205–229.

Reid, L. (2017). Navigating the secular: Religious students' experience of attending a Red-Brick University. In K. Aune & J. Stevenson (Eds.), *Religion and higher education in Europe and North America* (pp. 149–163). Routledge.

Shain, F., Yıldız, Ü., Poku, V., & Gokay, B. (2021). From silence to 'strategic advancement': Institutional responses to 'decolonising' in higher education in England. *Teaching in Higher Education, 26*(7–8), 920–936. https://doi. org/10.1080/13562517.2021.1976749

Stevenson, J. (2018). Muslim students in UK Higher Education: Issues of inequality and inequity. Bridge Institute for Research and Policy. Retrieved April 30, 2020, from http://azizfoundation.org.uk/wp-content/uploads/2019/04/Bridge-Higher-Education-report-2-FINAL.pdf

Vincent, C. (2018). Civic virtue and values teaching in a 'post-secular' world. *Theory and Research in Education, 16*(2), 226–243. https://doi.org/10.1177/1477878518774128

Utilising the Race Equality Charter to Embed Religious Equity for Muslim Students and Staff in Higher Education

Shames Maskeen

INTRODUCTION

Whoever among you sees evil, let him change it with his hand; if he cannot, then with his tongue; if he cannot, then with his heart—and that is the weakest of Faith. (Sunan an-Nasa'i, n.d.)

From a UK context, equality legislation and policies to address racial inequalities have existed for many decades. The *Race Relations Amendment Act* (2000) and subsequently The *Equality Act* (2010) require all public bodies, including universities, to tackle disadvantage and discrimination based on nine protected characteristics such as race including ethnicity, religion or belief, and sex. Many universities showcase their commitment to equality, diversity, and inclusion by providing public statements of commitment and working towards achieving equality charter marks (Ahmed,

S. Maskeen (✉)
Leeds Trinity University, Leeds, UK
e-mail: s.maskeen@leedstrinity.ac.uk

2012; Bhopal & Pitkin, 2020). Universities have often promised equality of opportunity for all. However, there have been student-led campaigns showing racial disparities in the HE sector, notably including the 'Why is my Curriculum White' movement (Peters, 2015). Furthermore, racial harassment has been highlighted as a common experience in HE, which is often intertwined with religious harassment (Equality and Human Rights Commission [EHRC], 2019a). However, in the executive summary of the same report, religious discrimination is not emphasised or given due regard other than one mention of antisemitism and Islamophobia respectively (EHRC, 2019b).

Despite decades of equality legislation and policies, Muslim students and staff do not have an equitable experience in comparison to their non-Muslim counterparts. Previous research has shown that Islamophobia exists in universities and Muslims experience racism based on their religious identities in HE (Islam & Mercer-Mapstone, 2021; Nojan, 2023; Stevenson, 2018). Whilst Islam is a religion, it has been argued that Muslims have become racialised (Garner & Selod, 2015; Mirza, 2013; Modood, 2005). Historically, categories of race have been derived from physical characteristics, where it has been suggested that the racialisation of Muslims is often related to their physical appearance (Garner & Selod, 2015). Muslim visibility, in particular men with beards or women wearing the hijab, plays a significant role in racial categorisation (Karaman & Christian, 2020; Selod, 2019). Despite undergoing racialisation, Muslim experiences have been under examined in HE due to secularism (Garner & Selod, 2015; Guest et al., 2020; Mirza, 2013; Modood, 2005; Stevenson, 2013). Therefore, there is a necessity to explore the racialisation of Muslims through an intersectional lens of race, religion, and gender (Mirza, 2013; Selod, 2019).

The Office for Students (OfS), as the regulator for English HE, requires that those universities charging higher tuition fees provide Access and Participation Plans which set out how they will improve equality of opportunity for under-represented students in HE (OfS, 2021). The OfS states that some Black, Asian, and minority ethnic students are disadvantaged in HE but does not currently consider Muslim students as a disadvantaged group (OfS, 2022). This is a significant oversight considering Muslim students are the second largest religious group in HE (Mcmaster, 2020), with a large proportion of Pakistani, Bangladeshi, African, and Arab students identifying as Muslim (Office for National Statistics, 2023). Thus, Muslims are more likely to be from racially minoritised backgrounds and will face intersectional barriers. For example, it has been well established that racially minoritised students are less likely to continue in HE and achieve a first/2:1 compared to White students (Advance HE, 2022). This chapter will demonstrate that the racial and religious experiences of Muslim students and staff cannot be considered separately and that utilising existing frameworks within HE can be a vehicle to bring these experiences into the fore.

THE RACE EQUALITY CHARTER (REC)

The REC, introduced in 2014, is a national scheme which was developed in response to addressing racial inequities in UK HE (Advance HE, 2019). It aims to improve the experiences, representation, progression, and success of racially minoritised students and staff (Advance HE, 2023a). The REC provides a framework for universities to identify areas of racial inequities and cultural barriers that exist through quantitative and qualitative data analysis, and for a subsequent action plan to be developed that addresses the issues identified. One of the guiding principles of the REC is acknowledging intersectionality. "Embracing intersectionality, from analysing data to developing actions, can better support institutions to tackle racism within the higher education sector" (Advance HE, 2023b, p. 12). A HE institution can choose which intersectional characteristics they focus on based on their specific context (Advance HE, 2023b). It has been argued that race, class, and gender are given precedence over religion (Barber, 2010). Therefore, it is likely that universities undertaking the REC may not consider religion in their data analysis and thus, fail in their duty to promote equal opportunity for all.

Whilst many universities have recognised the significance of the REC, it has been criticised for being performative, reinforcing White privilege and evidence has suggested it has made little difference to the lived experiences of racially minoritised students and staff (Bhopal & Pitkin, 2020). This may be in part due to some arguing that the award favours intent over action (Campion & Clark, 2022). At the time of writing, there are 101 REC members of which 44 hold a Bronze award and 2 institutions have achieved the Silver award (Advance HE, 2023c). Whilst the REC may be perceived as tokenistic, I argue here that if implemented correctly, it can empower racially minoritised Muslim students and staff to use it as a vehicle to drive change. This chapter explores how one university, Leeds Trinity University (LTU), utilised the REC to identify barriers facing racially minoritised Muslim students and staff, and developed actions that have resulted in transformational change.

BACKGROUND

LTU was established in 1966 as a Roman Catholic teacher training college and is underpinned by the values of the Catholic foundation. LTU is one of four Catholic universities in England alongside Liverpool Hope University, Newman University, and St Mary's University Twickenham. LTU was the first University in Yorkshire to achieve the REC Bronze award in November 2020. At the time of the REC application (academic year 2019/20), LTU had 3446 students and 423 staff members and is similar in size, student, and staff population with the other Catholic universities (Higher Education Statistics Agency, 2023a, 2023b). Muslim students at LTU were the second largest religious group after Christian students. Muslim students accounted for approximately 12% of the student population, with 81% of our Asian students stating their religious belief as Muslim, followed by Other (33%), Mixed (14%), and Black (8%) students. Whilst there were a relatively large proportion of Muslim students attending the university, there were few religious provisions in place to support these students. Muslim staff accounted for 1.7% of the staff population ($n < 10$), with most Muslim staff in professional service roles. There were no Muslim professors or professional support staff in senior grades, with only one racially minoritised Muslim staff member in a managerial position.

As is standard with the REC submission, an intersectional self-assessment team was formed and chaired by the Deputy Vice-Chancellor (DVC). The self-assessment team were to gather and interpret institutional data, in order to identify and develop an action plan to address racial barriers which formed the basis of the REC application. The team consisted of academics, professional support staff, and students in a range of different roles and levels within LTU. Seven members (32%) of the self-assessment team identified as Muslim. Our REC application covered several key priority areas identified through consultation with our racially minoritised students and staff. This included (1) increasing engagement with local racially minoritised communities, including Muslim organisations; (2) ensuring our staff were disclosing their protected characteristics; (3) eliminating disparities between racially minoritised and White applicants/staff in recruitment selection, retention, and career progression; (4)

eliminating discrimination, harassment, and microaggressions; (5) eliminating disparities between racially minoritised and White students/applicants in admission offers, continuation rates,[1] degree awarding,[2] and employability outcomes; (6) ensuring our marketing material was representative of LTU's ethnic and religious student body; (7) ensuring our curriculum, learning, teaching, and assessments are reflective of racial and ethnic diversity; and (8) ensuring our staff are confident in facilitating discussions around race and ethnicity.

METHODOLOGY

This research is a case study design which explored how LTU utilised the REC process to identify barriers facing racially minoritised Muslim students and staff. A case study design allows investigation into a particular phenomenon using multiple methods of data collection over a period of time (Yin, 2018). This research draws on primarily qualitative data gathered between May 2017 and March 2020, collected as part of the mandatory requirements set out by Advance HE (the organisation responsible for awarding RECs). The data was gathered in phases and at two time points. The first REC survey was conducted in 2017/18 and the second REC survey was carried out in 2020, with both surveys identifying racial barriers experienced by racially minoritised students and staff. The REC survey had a list of prescribed quantitative questions using a 7-point Likert scale (1 = strongly disagree and 7 = strongly agree) with the option for students and staff to add in open comments to provide context to their quantitative responses. The questions captured the diversity of the institution, the local population, and reporting of racial discrimination. Its recommendations are inclusive of institutional recruitment, academic progress, career development, future prospects, course content, academic support, and the Students' Union (Leeds Trinity Students' Union). These areas provide the race equality context of a HE institution. The REC survey employed at LTU, did not explore the data by religion due to the small number of Muslim staff ($n < 10$) and Muslim students ($n = 25$) completing the survey. Therefore, results at a more detailed level would

---

[1] Continuation rates refer to continuation from one year of study to the next (Advance HE, 2022).

[2] Degree awarding outcomes refers to the proportion of one group achieving a first/2:1 in comparison to another group (Advance HE, 2022).

not have been reliable. Moreover, the continuation rates and degree awarding outcomes of Muslim students were not analysed (the limitations of this are considered in the discussion section).

The REC survey was followed up by focus groups in 2018 and 2020 respectively. A qualitative approach allowed insights into participants' experiences, perceptions, and attitudes that were contextual to their lived experiences (DiCicco-Bloom & Crabtree, 2006). Twenty-seven Muslim students and five Muslim staff members participated across nine focus groups. All Muslim participants identified as being from a racially minoritised background. The focus group discussions were open ended with a particular emphasis placed on the lived experiences of racially minoritised students and staff and co-creating actions to improve their experiences at LTU. For the purposes of this chapter, the 2017/18 REC survey open comments and focus groups have been triangulated to identify barriers experienced by Muslim students and the second data collection phase in 2020 focuses on the impact of the implemented actions.

Reflexivity

As with most research, there is an ethical duty of researchers to make known vectors of their positionality which influence the way they approach, conduct, and disseminate their work (Berger, 2015; Gentles et al., 2014). I make clear here that as author of this chapter, I am a Pakistani heritage Muslim man undertaking a PhD at LTU. I am also a lecturer in Psychology and Associate Director of The Race Institute with lived experiences of racism and Islamophobia. I was employed as the operational lead for the REC and reported directly to Professor Malcolm Todd, the DVC. This role led to myself and the DVC engaging in reciprocal mentoring. The aim of the reciprocal mentoring programme is for senior leaders of an organisation (who are predominantly White and often not Muslim) to gain insight into the lived experiences and barriers facing racially minoritised staff. These roles have given me access to decision-making rooms, enabled me to share my lived experiences as a Muslim both studying and working in HE, and helped ensure the interplay of race and Islam is considered in LTU practices at both the individual and institutional level.

The theory of "satisfied settling" suggests that Muslims often unconsciously and, in some cases, consciously have accepted that their HE institution will not cater for their religious needs (Islam et al., 2019). Prior to engaging in reciprocal mentoring, "satisfied setting" was a view I held myself. I felt that LTU would not alter their provision to support the needs of Muslims. However, by developing a collegiate relationship and sharing of experiences, it has led the DVC to become aware of the discriminative everyday experiences of Muslim students and staff including Islamophobic microaggressions, importance of Halal catering, *Jummah* (Friday) prayers, and Ramadan practices. This relationship was enhanced further by the DVC sharing his experiences of leading a national project about teaching Islam in the Social Sciences. Prior to any actions being developed to support Muslims, there were discussions between the DVC and I to understand potential barriers for implementation and strategies to overcome obstacles. Furthermore, the DVC has personally led on implementing some of these actions. This visible leadership from the DVC has empowered Muslim students and staff to voice concerns and to ensure that LTU is supporting the religious needs of their Muslim students and staff.

RESULTS

This section summarises the initiatives that were developed and implemented at LTU in relation to the experiences reported by racially minoritised Muslims students and staff. First, the issue will be described and illustrated by utilising anonymised exemplar quotations and then the initiative will be presented. Three themes were developed from the data: (1) *a sense of belonging and social environment*, (2) *reporting and addressing religious microaggressions*, and (3) *creating safe spaces to discuss Islam.*

A Sense of Belonging and Social Environment

There was general agreement in the focus groups (conducted in 2018) that a sense of belonging was regarded as central to institutional culture and an inclusive environment. Muslim students and staff reported tensions between the experience the University promotes, such as valuing racial and religious diversity, and their actual experience, particularly in respect to the lack of religious provision provided. Discussion of social spaces was a consistent theme, with Muslim students identifying a lack of welcoming, vibrant, and inclusive social areas. In particular, the lack of an overt Halal catering in the canteen was highlighted as impacting Muslim students and staff desiring to use dining areas as a social space. Muslim students and staff also relayed that there was no on-campus provision for *Jummah*

(Friday) prayers and that this impacted their engagement with attending lectures which clashed during this time. This was a particular concern as there were no mosques in the immediate geographical area where LTU is located, with the closest being almost 5 miles away.

> *Being a Muslim, Friday prayers are important to not only me but Muslim students. If the University could arrange an Imam to come in and lead the prayers that would be great, as many students won't attend lectures on Fridays as they go for prayers.* (Muslim staff, REC focus group 2018)

These findings were relayed to the REC self-assessment team chaired by the DVC. The DVC personally led on implementing Halal food on campus and arranging an Imam for Friday prayers. There were minimal barriers due to the DVC's authority and seniority, making them a powerful ally working on behalf of Muslim students and staff. Following the implementation of Halal food and *Jummah* prayers, Muslim students and staff relayed that their sense of belonging was enhanced at LTU. Muslim students in the focus groups (conducted in 2020) reported that *Jummah* prayers helped them form friendships and that they were spending more time on campus. The inclusion of religious provision has also allowed the recruitment team at LTU to offer specific sessions aimed at Muslim students and parents to alleviate any concerns of accessing religious facilities. Furthermore, a new food policy implemented at LTU ensures that Halal food is now offered as standard unless requested otherwise for any internal events such as Open Days, graduation, and conferences. These initiatives have all contributed to a positive sense of belonging for Muslim students and staff.

> *The University providing Halal catering and not just a small stand, but an established brand has significantly increased my sense of belonging. There is also Friday prayers now which has helped me to remain on campus rather than having to travel to pray. I know this has increased Muslim students' sense of belonging.* (Muslim student, open comment REC survey 2020)

Further open comments from the REC survey (conducted in 2017/18) indicated that Student Union societies did not take into account ethnic and religious diversity of the student body. Muslim students in the focus groups (conducted in 2018) identified that the most proactive society was the Christian Union. Whilst this was not identified as an issue, it was contrasted with the lack of activity for other faith groups or interfaith activity. Whilst LTU had a high percentage of Muslim students, there was no Islamic Society, and many Muslim students relayed the need for one. In these focus groups, Muslim students reported that there had been several attempts to establish an Islamic Society; however, the society was never sustained for more than one year—as can be the case with student-led societies.

I think most Student Union societies, and this not specific to LTU, is around the drinking culture. I wanted to join one of the societies and students tried to make me join by promoting alcohol related activities. Also, there is no Islamic society which, considering there are a lot of Muslim students here, this should be a given. (Muslim student, REC focus group 2018)

Discussions with the Student Union suggested that there was a perception that all societies need the same level of support and as Muslim students had not relayed any issues, there was a perception that they did not need any support. This form of thinking is harmful as Muslim students in the focus groups (conducted in 2018) relayed contradicting statements and stated they asked for support but did not receive any response from the Students' Union. Therefore, as I had experience of studying in HE and access to decision-making rooms, I established the Islamic Society in 2020. Subsequently I have become the strategic advisor to the Islamic Society to ensure they are supported in having their needs met. This is one prime example that shows Muslim staff often have to carry out invisible work which is often unrecognised but makes a significant impact on the experiences of students (Ahmed, 2012). The Society, now in its fourth year of running, has become fully student led and has won several regional awards for charity fundraising.

Reporting and Addressing Religious Microaggressions

There was general acknowledgement in the focus groups (conducted in 2020) that Muslim students and staff were experiencing microaggressions and racism based on their race and religious identity. Most issues felt subtle with racially minoritised Muslims questioning whether the incident experience was race related or religiously related. It was reported in one of the focus groups (conducted in 2020) that a White member of staff once asked, "Where do Muslims come from?" to a Muslim staff member, reinforcing their feeling of being "othered". Muslim students reported experiencing religious microaggressions which were perceived as "minor" and as "banter". Both Muslim students and staff reported that it was difficult to report microaggressions and many did not want to take action. This was further problematic as Muslims staff in particular reported a lack of confidence that appropriate action would be taken if they reported religious discrimination. Thus, there was a need for LTU to be an anti-racist institution and that incidences of racism, including religious racism, would be taken seriously. Inspired by the work of the London Metropolitan University (Akel, 2021) and in consultation with the Islamic Society and staff via an open call led by the DVC, LTU endorsed the working definition of Islamophobia. "Islamophobia is rooted in racism and is a type of racism that targets expressions of Muslimness or perceived Muslimness" (All Party Parliamentary Group [APPG], 2018, p. 50). There was a conscious decision that this definition of Islamophobia had to explicitly mention racism as this would allow Muslims to ensure that any anti-racism discussion would also involve religious racism. It was also expected that accepting a definition of Islamophobia would increase students and staff confidence in reporting incidences of religious racism.

There have been many times when people have asked about views on terrorism. Just because I am Muslim, there is an assumption that somehow I agree with this. Also, when all the Shamima Begum stuff was occurring, other White students asked me about my views but when the New Zealand shooting in the Mosque happened, why weren't these same people asking me about my views on that. (Muslim student REC survey 2020)

Creating Safe Spaces to Discuss Islam

A recurring theme reported in the REC surveys (conducted both in 2017/18 and 2020) and focus groups (conducted both in 2018 and 2020) was a lack of social opportunities for Muslim students to engage with people who looked like them, and shared their perspectives, values, and outlooks. Some racially minoritised Muslim students (in the focus group conducted in 2020) discussed that it was "hard to fit in" and form friendships with White students, as activities revolved around drinking alcohol. Female Muslim students in particular relayed that many events were evening based which made it hard from them to attend due to parental concerns and gendered expectations. Muslim students commuting to

University also stated they did not engage in the more social aspects of university life due to little activities of interest being available.

> *I don't think there is a large amount of Asians, certainly on my course, which made me feel a little bit like I didn't belong. Student union events/socialising events don't take into consideration Asian religious beliefs/culture... there's too much focus on clubbing and nights out and that's not what everyone wants.* (Muslim student, open comment REC survey 2017/18)

To begin addressing this dearth, in September 2022, a year-long series of events to discuss Islam, the everyday lived experiences of Muslims and Islamophobia were developed in collaboration with the Islamic Society. These events ranged from workshops on the expression of anti-Blackness in the Muslim community, Islamic perspectives of mental health, reclaiming the narrative about Islamophobia and an Islamophobia Conference. Reclaiming the narrative about Islamophobia was an event delivered by a Muslim female poet and author Suhaiymah Manzoor-Khan. It was particularly noteworthy as the Vice Chancellor (VC) was in attendance and the experiences shared by Muslim staff and students led the VC to state that the university's Executive team will receive training in Islamophobia.

As part of Islamophobia Awareness month (held annually in the UK during November), a half day Conference on *Islamophobia: The Causes and Cures* was hosted at LTU. The aim of the conference was to raise awareness of the impact of Islamophobia on the everyday lived experiences of Muslims in HE and beyond. This Conference was open to students, staff, and those external to LTU. There was a clear message from the VC that Islamophobia exists and that as a senior leader, he was responsible and accountable for the experiences of Muslims at LTU.

Discussion

This chapter has explored that, when utilised effectively, the REC is an effective tool to promote race and intersectional equity for students and staff. The findings showed that the process of applying for the REC enabled individuals within LTU to develop personal agency and act as key change agents by identifying and more importantly implementing actions to create a more religiously inclusive university. Allyship and courageous leadership at an executive level amplified the voices of Muslims and ensured religious inclusivity is everybody's responsibility. The importance of psychological safety and spaces to discuss Islamophobia without fear of repercussions contributed to a positive sense of belonging. This discussion section sets out a number of ways universities undertaking their REC applications can ensure that it is not a performative gesture; that it can provide strategies to overcome barriers in implementing racial *and* religious practices.

Courageous Leadership and Psychological Safety

The results demonstrated that courageous leadership is crucial in making a real difference to the experiences of Muslims in all the initiatives implemented at LTU. Without powerful allies and a genuine commitment to race equality, the REC is nothing but a symbolic gesture. Leadership is crucial for the functioning and success of any organisation and the right leadership is the ability to put words into actions (Manzoor et al., 2019; Ndalamba et al., 2018). Whilst adopting the APPG working definition of Islamophobia can show that a HE institution acknowledges a problem, it will not eliminate Islamophobia. However, it can empower individuals to identify inconsistencies with the actions of universities (Ahmed, 2012). By acknowledging these systemic issues related to religion and Islam, initiatives to address identified issues can be implemented.

Every member of a HE institution has a role to play to embed racial and religious inclusivity; however, some actions are not possible without senior leadership support. Thus, it is vital that senior leaders such as Vice Chancellors openly discuss racial and religious inequities that exist in their universities as this will create a cultural requirement for others to discuss said inequalities (Ahmed, 2012). Where senior leaders acknowledge racial and religious barriers as a problem, it can lead to the development of psychological safety (Carmeli et al., 2010). Psychological safety is the perception of individuals to feel they can share their lived experiences in an environment without the fear of any negative consequences to their image or status (Ling et al., 2010; Carmeli et al., 2014; Chrobot-Mason & Aramovich, 2013). Psychological safety can be developed through creating safe spaces to discuss Islam and Islamophobia. This is particularly pertinent as Islamophobia and hate crimes against Muslim are underreported, with two in every three victims not reporting the incident (Copsey et al., 2013). Underreporting of religious discrimination may be due to a lack of confidence in reporting procedures, perceptions that incidents will not be taken seriously or the frequency of Islamophobia occurring (Copsey et al.,

2013; Shammas, 2017). Whilst universities may be attuned to racial discrimination, they need to be better equipped in recognising Islamophobia. By creating psychological safety, it may increase Muslim students and staff confidence in reporting religious discrimination.

Sense of Belonging

A positive sense of belonging has been defined as students and staff feeling valued, respected and accepted at their HE institution (Mahar et al., 2013; Strayhorn, 2019). Dynamism is a key component of sense of belonging and relates to temporary or permanent factors which restrict or influence individual interactions in students' social environment (Mahar et al., 2013). Therefore, sense of belonging can be associated with physical structures of an organisation. Prior to the implementation of Halal food, *Jummah* prayers, and establishment of the Islamic Society, Muslim students reported a lack of a sense of belonging. However, by embedding religious inclusivity into the physical structures of the University, it has enhanced Muslim students' sense of belonging on campus, helped them form friendships with like-minded individuals, and contributed to a sticky campus culture (Islam, 2021; Middha, 2022).

Research has shown the importance of religious provision, in particular Halal food and prayer spaces, on Muslim students' sense of belonging in HE (Islam & Mercer-Mapstone, 2021). Islamic Societies have also been shown to support the pastoral needs of Muslims students in HE as well as offer networking opportunities, conduct charitable work, and mobilise the needs of Muslims (Choudhury, 2017; Modood, 1996; Song, 2012). The success of the Islamic Society was partly due to a Muslim academic staff member becoming a strategic advisor to the society. Previous research has shown that racially minoritised staff have unequal distribution of responsibilities with additional burdens placed to meet the racial needs of students (Ahmed, 2012; Bhopal, 2023; Bhopal & Pitkin, 2020). These additional responsibilities are often rendered invisible. Thus, it is vital HE institutions pursuing the REC are not reinforcing structural racism by ensuring that racially minoritised staff are recognised and compensated for their involvement.

Data-Driven Approach

A limitation of this research is that quantitative religious data was not explored at LTU. This was partly due to the small number of Muslim students ($n = 25$) and staff ($n < 10$) completing the REC survey and therefore, the data would not have held a level of reliability. Furthermore, religious data is not routinely collected in HE (Mcmaster, 2020) and as it is not a standard practice across the HE sector, thus, comparisons between universities could not be made. On reflection, "satisfied setting" contributed to myself as the operational lead for REC not feeling confident to ask for institutional data such as degree awarding outcomes to be analysed by religion (Islam et al., 2019). The qualitative components of this research have demonstrated that the racialised experiences of Muslim students and staff cannot be considered separately. Therefore, if quantitative religious data cannot be analysed, then a qualitative approach exploring the intersections of race and religion should be carried out. By utilising quantitative and qualitative data, universities pursuing the REC can reach a consensus on the issues and take actions to improve the experiences of Muslims. By doing so, universities can be problem focused and solution orientated. Towards that end, it is not the job of Muslim students and staff to be solely left to tackle Islamophobia in HE.

CONCLUSION

This chapter has demonstrated that when utilised effectively, the REC has the potential to address racial and religious inequalities and make a real difference to the lived experiences of racially minoritised Muslim students and staff within universities. The REC process was a useful lever for LTU to begin having conversations about Islamophobia and to develop actions that have had some positive direct and indirect impact on the experiences on Muslim and non-Muslims. In order for transformational change to occur it is important there is an acknowledgement that Islamophobia exists and to understand the impact Islamophobia has on the experiences of Muslim students and staff.

It is the duty of every member of staff in the HE sector to improve the lives of those who study and work in universities. That said, some individuals will yield more power within their roles, and therefore, visible leadership at an executive level is vital in addressing Islamophobia and developing a culture that can create psychological safety and minimise the "satisfied settling" mindset some Muslim students and staff experience. Given the transformational change seen at LTU, I argue here that every HE institution should be mandated to engage through the REC process and that the OfS can support this mandate by requiring Access and Participation Plans to consider the needs of Muslim students. Sector bodies, such as Advance HE, also have a role to play in encouraging universities to develop their own actions that consider the intersectionality between race and religion. The REC is meaningless if leaders are not willing to listen to the people around them and recognise the context of their HE institution. To accomplish such a feat requires nothing short of courage and time.

REFERENCES

Advance HE. (2019). *Infographic: The story of the Race Equality Charter.* [Online]. Retrieved August 27, 2023, from https://www.advance-he.ac.uk/news-and-views/infographic-story-race-equality-charter

Advance HE. (2022). *Equality in higher education: Student statistical report 2022.* [Online]. Retrieved August 25, 2023, from https://www.advance-he.ac.uk/knowledge-hub/equality-higher-education-statistical-reports-2022

Advance HE. (2023a). *Race equality charter.* [Online]. Retrieved August 25, 2023, from https://www.advance-he.ac.uk/equality-charters/race-equality-charter

Advance HE. (2023b). *Updated race equality charter. Applicant information pack.* [Online]. Retrieved October 15, 2023, from https://connect.advance-he.ac.uk/topics/11602/media_center/file/1d5c676d-1403-4337-9c2a-f6bbe1100c8b

Advance HE. (2023c). *Race equality charter members.* [Online]. Retrieved October 15, 2023, from https://www.advance-he.ac.uk/equality-charters/race-equality-charter/members

Ahmed, S. (2012). *On being included: Racism and diversity in institutional life.* Durham Duke University Press.

Akel, S. (2021). *Institutionalised: The rise of Islamophobia in Higher Education.* [Online]. London Metropolitan University. Retrieved August 26, 2023, from https://repository.londonmet.ac.uk/6295/1/Institutionalised-the-rise-of-Islamophobia-in-Higher-Education.pdf

All Party Parliamentary Group. (2018). *Islamophobia Defined: The inquiry into a working definition of Islamophobia.* [Online]. Retrieved October 1, 2023, from https://static1.squarespace.com/static/599c3d2febbd1a90cffdd8a9/t/5bfd1ea3352f531a6170ceee/1543315109493/Islamophobia+Defined.pdf

Barber, K. (2010). Intersectional analyses of religion, paper presented at the *American Sociological Association Annual Meeting*. Hilton Atlanta and Atlanta Marriott Marquis, Atlanta, GA, 14 August 2010.

Berger, R. (2015). Now I see it, now I don't: Researcher's position and reflexivity in qualitative research. *Qualitative Research, 15*(2), 219–234. https://doi.org/10.1177/1468794112468475

Bhopal, K. (2023). 'We can talk the talk, but we're not allowed to walk the walk': The role of equality and diversity staff in higher education institutions in England. *Higher Education., 85*(2), 325–339. https://doi.org/10.1007/s10734-022-00835-7

Bhopal, K., & Pitkin, C. (2020). 'Same old story, just a different policy': Race and policy making in higher education in the UK. *Race Ethnicity and Education., 23*(4), 530–547. https://doi.org/10.1080/13613324.2020.1718082

Campion, K., & Clark, K. (2022). Revitalising race equality policy? Assessing the impact of the Race Equality Charter mark for British universities. *Race Ethnicity and Education., 25*(1), 18–37. https://doi.org/10.1080/13613324.2021.1924133

Carmeli, A., Reiter-Palmon, R., & Ziv, E. (2010). Inclusive leadership and employee involvement in creative tasks in the workplace: The mediating role of psychological safety. *Creativity Research Journal., 22*(3), 250–260. https://doi.org/10.1080/10400419.2010.504654

Carmeli, A., Sheaffer, Z., Binyamin, G., Reiter-Palmon, R., & Shimoni, T. (2014). Transformational leadership and creative problem-solving: The mediating role of psychological safety and reflexivity. *The Journal of Creative Behavior., 48*(2), 115–135. https://doi.org/10.1002/jocb.43

Choudhury, T. (2017). Campaigning on campus: Student Islamic societies and counterterrorism. *Studies in Conflict & Terrorism., 40*(12), 1004–1022. https://doi.org/10.1080/1057610X.2016.1253986

Chrobot-Mason, D., & Aramovich, N. P. (2013). The psychological benefits of creating an affirming climate for workplace diversity. *Group & Organization Management., 38*(6), 659–689. https://doi.org/10.1177/1059601113509835

Copsey, N., Dack, J., Littler, M., & Feldman, M. (2013). *Anti-Muslim hate crime and the far right*. [Online]. Teesside University. Retrieved November 28, 2023, from https://research.tees.ac.uk/ws/portalfiles/portal/8963116/Anti_Muslim_Hate_Crime_and_the_Far_Right.pdf

DiCicco-Bloom, B., & Crabtree, B. F. (2006). The qualitative research interview. *Medical Education., 40*(4), 314–321. https://doi.org/10.1111/j.1365-2929.2006.02418.x

Equality Act 2010. (c.15). [Online]. Retrieved August 28, 2023, from https://www.legislation.gov.uk/ukpga/2010/15/contents

Equality and Human Rights Commission. (2019a). *Tackling racial harassment: Universities challenged.* [Online]. Retrieved August 26, 2023, from https://

www.equalityhumanrights.com/sites/default/files/tackling-racial-harassment-universities-challenged.pdf

Equality and Human Rights Commission. (2019b). *Tackling racial harassment. Executive Summary*. [Online]. Retrieved August 26, 2023, from https://www.equalityhumanrights.com/sites/default/files/tackling-racial-harassment-universities-challenged.pdf

Garner, S., & Selod, S. (2015). The racialization of Muslims: Empirical studies of Islamophobia. *Critical Sociology., 41*(1), 9–19. https://doi.org/10.1177/0896920514531606

Gentles, S. J., Jack, S. M., Nicholas, D. B., & McKibbon, K. A. (2014). Critical approach to reflexivity in grounded theory. *The Qualitative Report., 19*(44), 1–14. https://doi.org/10.46743/2160-3715/2014.1109

Guest, M., Scott-Baumann, A., Cheruvallil-Contractor, S., Naguib, S., Phoenix, A., Lee, Y., & Al Baghal, T. (2020). *Islam and Muslims on UK University Campuses: perceptions and challenges*. [Online]. Durham University; SOAS; Coventry University; Lancaster University. Retrieved August 24, 2023, from https://eprints.soas.ac.uk/33345/1/file148310.pdf

Higher Education Statistics Agency. (2023a). *Who's studying in HE?: Student numbers*. [Online]. Retrieved December 1, 2023, from https://www.hesa.ac.uk/data-and-analysis/students/whos-in-he/numbers

Higher Education Statistics Agency. (2023b). *Who's working in HE?* [Online]. Retrieved December 1, 2023, from https://www.hesa.ac.uk/data-and-analysis/staff/working-in-he

Islam, M. (2021). *Building belonging: Developing religiously inclusive cultures for Muslim students in higher education*. [Online]. Advance HE. Retrieved October 1, 2023, from https://s3.eu-west-2.amazonaws.com/assets.creode.advancehe-document-manager/documents/advance-he/AdvHE_GPG_Winchester_Building%20Belonging_1649238306.pdf

Islam, M., Lowe, T., & Jones, G. (2019). A 'satisfied settling'? Investigating a sense of belonging for Muslim students in a UK small-medium Higher Education Institution. *Student Engagement in Higher Education Journal., 2*(2), 79–104. https://sehej.raise-network.com/raise/article/view/891

Islam, M., & Mercer-Mapstone, L. (2021). 'University is a non-Muslim experience, you know? The experience is as good as it can be': Satisfied settling in Muslim students' experiences and implications for Muslim student voice. *British Educational Research Journal., 47*(5), 1388–1415. https://doi.org/10.1002/berj.3733

Karaman, N., & Christian, M. (2020). "My hijab is like my skin color": Muslim women students, racialization, and intersectionality. *Sociology of Race and Ethnicity., 6*(4), 517–532. https://doi.org/10.1177/2332649220903740

Ling, B., Duan, J. Y., & Zhu, Y. L. (2010). Psychological safety in workplace: Conceptualization, antecedents and consequences. *Advances in Psychological*

Science., *18*(10), 1580–1589. https://journal.psych.ac.cn/adps/EN/Y2010/V18/I10/1580

Mahar, A. L., Cobigo, V., & Stuart, H. (2013). Conceptualizing belonging. *Disability and rehabilitation.*, *35*(12), 1026–1032. https://doi.org/10.3109/09638288.2012.717584

Manzoor, F., Wei, L., Nurunnabi, M., Subhan, Q. A., Shah, S. I. A., & Fallatah, S. (2019). The impact of transformational leadership on job performance and CSR as mediator in SMEs. *Sustainability.*, *11*(2), 436. https://doi.org/10.3390/su11020436

Mcmaster, N. C. (2020). *Research insight: Religion and belief in UK Higher Education.* [Online]. Advance HE. Retrieved October 2, 2023, from https://www.advance-he.ac.uk/knowledge-hub/research-insight-religion-and-belief-uk-higher-education

Middha, B. (2022). Urban food infrastructures: The role of inner-city universities. *Urban Policy and Research.*, *40*(3), 236–249. https://doi.org/10.1080/08111146.2022.2093181

Mirza, H. S. (2013). 'A second skin': Embodied intersectionality, transnationalism and narratives of identity and belonging among Muslim women in Britain. *Women's Studies International Forum.*, *36*, 5–15. https://doi.org/10.1016/j.wsif.2012.10.012

Modood, T. (1996). The changing context of 'race' in Britain: A symposium. *Patterns of Prejudice.*, *30*(1), 3–13. https://doi.org/10.1080/0031322X.1996.9970173

Modood, T. (2005). *Multicultural politics: Racism, ethnicity and Muslims in Britain.* University of Minnesota Press.

Ndalamba, K. K., Caldwell, C., & Anderson, V. (2018). Leadership vision as a moral duty. *Journal of Management Development.*, *37*(3), 309–319. https://doi.org/10.1108/JMD-08-2017-0262

Nojan, S. (2023). Racial-religious decoupling in the university: Investigating religious students' perceptions of institutional commitment to diversity. *AERA Open.*, *9*. https://doi.org/10.1177/23328584221121339

Office for National Statistics. (2023). *Ethnic group by religion.* [Online]. Retrieved September 2, 2023, from https://www.ons.gov.uk/datasets/RM031/editions/2021/versions/1/filter-outputs/217f1401-dab4-43d3-aa77-6c9382220c0c#summary

Office for Students. (2021). *Regulatory notice 1: Access and participation plan guidance.* [Online]. Retrieved October 6, 2023, from https://www.officeforstudents.org.uk/media/92d85140-2719-4af0-85c9-28ee1038c5e/regulatory_notice_1_access_and_participation_plans.pdf

Office for Students. (2022). *Our approach to access and participation.* [Online]. Retrieved October 19, 2023, from https://www.officeforstudents.org.uk/advice-and-guidance/promoting-equal-opportunities/our-approach-to-access-and-participation/

Peters, M. A. (2015). Why is my curriculum white? *Educational Philosophy and Theory., 47*(7), 641–646. https://doi.org/10.1080/00131857.2015.1037227

Race Relations (Amendment) Act 2000. (c.34). [Online]. Retrieved August 28, 2023, from https://www.legislation.gov.uk/ukpga/2000/34/notes/division/3#:~:text=place%20a%20duty%20on%20specified,discrimination%20by%20police%20officers%3B%20and

Selod, S. (2019). Gendered racialization: Muslim American men and women's encounters with racialized surveillance. *Ethnic and Racial Studies., 42*(4), 552–569. https://doi.org/10.1080/01419870.2018.1445870

Shammas, D. (2017). Underreporting discrimination among Arab American and Muslim American community college students: Using focus groups to unravel the ambiguities within the survey data. *Journal of Mixed Methods Research., 11*(1), 99–123. https://doi.org/10.1177/1558689815599467

Song, M. (2012). Part of the British mainstream? British Muslim students and Islamic student associations. *Journal of Youth Studies., 15*(2), 143–160. https://doi.org/10.1080/13676261.2011.630995

Stevenson, J. (2013). Discourses of inclusion and exclusion: Religious students in UK higher education. *Widening Participation and Lifelong Learning., 14*(3), 27–43. https://doi.org/10.5456/WPLL.14.3.27

Stevenson, J. (2018). *Muslim students in UK higher education: Issues of inequality and inequity.* [Online]. Bridge Institute. Retrieved August 27, 2023, from https://www.azizfoundation.org.uk/wp-content/uploads/2021/01/Bridge-Higher-Education-report-2.pdf

Strayhorn, T. L. (2019). *College Students' Sense of Belonging: A key to Educational Success for All Students* (2nd ed.). Routledge.

Sunan an-Nasa'I. (n.d.). *The book of faith and its signs.* [Online]. Retrieved October 3, 2023, from https://sunnah.com/nasai/47

Yin, K. R. (2018). *Case study research and application: Design and Methods* (6th ed.). Sage Publications.

CHAPTER 14

The 'New' Intersectionality of Disadvantage? British Muslim Students and the Widening Participation Agenda

Zain Sardar

INTRODUCTION

It is sometimes said that Muslims belong to cultures and societies that are moribund and have no vitality—no life of their own. Like ghosts they remain with us, haunting the present. (Sayyid, 2015)

This remark strikes me as a perfect description—and a common motif—of how British Muslim students sometimes feel on university campuses. In many respects they are invisible—their faith needs and identity are not codified in any widening participation schemes or in the Higher Education (HE) regulatory framework—and yet their presence—the haunting—has a persistent quality about it.

The persistence has much to do with what some widening access practitioners call 'hyper-diversification' (Atherton & Mazhari, 2019) and other

Z. Sardar (✉)
Aziz Foundation, London, UK
e-mail: z.sardar@azizfoundation.org.uk

© The Author(s), under exclusive license to Springer Nature   251
Switzerland AG 2024
A. Mahmud, M. Islam (eds.), *Uncovering Islamophobia in Higher Education*, Palgrave Studies in Race, Inequality and Social Justice in Education, https://doi.org/10.1007/978-3-031-65253-0_14

sociologists of religion identify as 'superdiversity' (Whitehead, 2012). The heterogeneity and relative youth of British Muslim communities, who are at the forefront of a demographic shift, mean that many more marginalised 'spectral bodies' are entering the HE system. This is corroborated by data released by the HE regulator (OfS, 2022b), which indicates there has been an increase of 50,000 British Muslims students between 2018 and 2021. Moreover, it is also reflective of wider social trends, confirmed by the publication of the latest census data reporting that British Muslims now make up 6.5% of the entire UK population (ONS, 2022; MCB, 2015). Indeed, this raises an urgent and perennial question, of whether we are experiencing a new species of 'multicultural drift' in HE? (Hall, 2019).

It is with this framing in mind that I briefly explore the short history of the widening participation (WP) and fair access agenda in HE, with its aim to advance social mobility and race equality for disadvantaged communities. Most significantly, this chapter is an attempt to bring WP into productive relation with well-established sociological studies of Islamophobia—inspired by sociologists such as Nasar Meer and Reza Gholami—that emphasise intersectional analysis and continuity with Critical Race Theory (CRT). Once I have contextualised WP, the majority of the chapter centres the voices of British Muslims and their experiences of higher education. It draws upon the testimonial evidence and autoethnographies of the Aziz Foundation's scholars and scholarship candidates, collated and analysed through internal research (Sardar, 2021a, 2021b).

Within British universities, it is increasingly becoming possible to use the machinery of recent regulatory developments to start de-institutionalising Islamophobia. The argument that Islamophobia is perceived to be a secondary form of racism, and that British Muslim claims appear to be uniquely exempt from policy considerations (made by APPG on British Muslims, 2019; Warsi, 2017; Mirza, 2012), can be countered in the HE sector. But it is contingent on the future of WP and how it comes to engage with British Muslims, their stories and impressions, and their academic success and progression, through its policy levers.

The current discussion is therefore intended to foreground a tantalising opportunity for a future-orientated sector to display some initiative, in developing a conjoined area of research and practice. It coalesces around two interlocking research strands: that is to say, (1) the hidden, shadow dynamic between ethnicity and faith—bracketed out in a sort of axiomatic manner by mainstream EDI frameworks—and (2) the extension of WP's mandate to the unfamiliar terrain of the PGT level. In factoring in the 'new' intersectionality of disadvantage (Nous Group, 2020, 2021) that informs the British Muslim student experience, therein lies a chance to reformulate engagement with marginalised cohorts, building 'intersectional inclusion' (Mirza, 2018) on university campuses.

THE WIDENING PARTICIPATION AGENDA IN HE

In mobilising higher education as a potential engine for social mobility, widening participation as an agenda was greatly advanced in the wake of the Dearing Report's findings into the future of the sector in 1997. Recommendations from the report were adopted in full, including making the mission to change the 'social mix' of those attending HE through the mechanism of access agreements a strategic policy aim (Dearing, 1997; Greenbank, 2006). Six years later saw the establishment of the Office for Fair Access (OFFA), the body with the powers of oversight and monitoring over access planning. Prior to this point, up until the late 1990s, according to Andrew Pilkington (2004, 2011, 2018), equal opportunities policy had a severely limited remit, confined to 'staffing issues' and predominantly centred on gender. The tectonic plates shifted in the conjunction of the late 1990s, with more defined public investment supporting widening access doubling from £400m to £800m over a period of two decades.

From 1997 onwards widening access was centred on initiatives targeting a "proportion of students from state schools and low-income backgrounds" (Pilkington, 2004; Madriaga, 2022). Ethnicity, let alone faith, did not figure as a protected characteristic that could act as a target for increasing access (Madriaga, 2022; Weekes-Bernard, 2010). The focus was also predominantly on the early stages of the student lifecycle, embodied in a range of initiatives and schemes, including outreach activity directed at local secondary schools, student ambassador programmes, greater work on accessible information, advice and guidance (IAG), as well as funding opportunities through scholarships and bursaries (Robinson & Salvestrini, 2020; Hancock & Wakeling, 2019; Greenbank, 2006; Weekes-Bernard, 2010).

At this stage, the agenda was a narrowly defined construction around 'access' or admissions, although it did steadily broaden out to include success and retention (Greenbank, 2006). Put otherwise, positionality and lived experiences—the particular ways in which certain groups experience their class position through the other elements of their identity—were not a due consideration in regulatory circles (Law et al., 2004).

From 2017, WP evolved via the new, longer-term Access and Participation Plans (APPs), operational from 2019. The idea behind their design is to enable universities to take a more strategic approach to widening access. Hence, institutions are encouraged to conduct an analysis of their own student populations, locating the equality gaps and, accordingly, setting their own targets in light of the evidence. Alongside this there remains a mandate in place covering certain key groups (Nous Group, 2021; OfS, 2022a), ensuring some uniformity across providers in tackling common access and progression issues.

A by-product of the new sectoral strategy, reported by the Nous Group in their review of APPs, is the increasing popularity amongst providers to assume an intersectional approach to access (UUK, 2021). This is also an outcome of a strengthening alignment of access with equality, diversity, and inclusion frameworks (Nous Group, 2020, 2021). The new mindset ushered in—of responsiveness to intersectional and marginalised students—is suggestive of the need to assume a more sophisticated and granular methodology in WP. This also plugs into a wider but closely associated discussion of gradually de-homogenising accepted terminology around 'BME' or 'BAME' in order to centre the lived experiences of discrete communities on campus (Singh et al., 2021).

With the genie now out of the bottle on intersectionality, institutions have, in theory, greater independence in exploring this relatively new terrain. Thus far, it has been the intersections of ethnicity and gender that have been uppermost in the minds of HEIs across the sector (Nous Group, 2020, 2021). This is indicative of an increasing appetite to reflect on the institutional inequalities that impact intersectional communities and accordingly work towards developing remedial and preventative interventions.

British Muslim Participation in Higher Education

The question now revolves around how the new opportunities opened up by modifications to the access regime can take into account the needs and claims of British Muslims, in the context of expanding participation from this demography. Indeed, at the undergraduate level 12% of the student body now identifies as British Muslim (OfS, 2022b).

In broad terms, there has been progress in that WP has become more differentiated over time in respect to the disadvantaged communities it targets. It has shifted to an approach encompassing a plurality of divergent groups, not solely defined by economic indicators, but by additional cultural and ethnic markers. This direction of travel is imputed, for example, by APPs now incorporating a list of underrepresented groups, including 'some BME communities', estranged students, and care leavers amongst others (OfS, 2022a; Nous, 2020, 2021).

In is also worth noting that in the current context—which is, debatably, more enlightened in the academy by CRT; influenced on the ground by mobilisations of activists around Black Lives Matter; and informed in civil society by a cross-section of British Muslim advocacy and representative groups pushing the APPG definition of Islamophobia (APPG on British Muslims, 2019; Bhatti, 2021; Elahi & Khan, 2017)—HEIs are being subsumed by 'liberal guilt' to structurally centre the EDI line of work (UUK, 2020). In this cultural shift, the concern raised by the sociologist Les Back that the government's WP direction of travel, while all well and good, did not include race as a significant criterion (Law et al., 2004) is now, perhaps, starting to be addressed (UUK, 2020, 2021; EHRC, 2019). WP has changed, but, critically, only in continuously transgressing thin notions of fair access in order to generate a stronger continuum with EDI.

Hence, my core argument is that while the logic of WP is progressively being extended to a further level of granularity, there is currently little movement to examine and, furthermore, incorporate the 'intersectional disadvantage' experienced by British Muslims. In engendering a new accessibility regime sensitive and receptive to intersectionality, the sense that faith is emblematic of a type 'false consciousness' in the secular space of the academy will have to be challenged. We can rather think of it as a form of 'ascendent consciousness' (Meer, 2010) that is emergent in different sites within the public realm and critical to driving a strand of civic duty (APPG on British Muslims, 2017, 2018), including within HE. Faith is a constitutive element of the 'new' intersectional disadvantage—now of much concern to university senior leaderships—and its salience as a marker of identity follows the trajectory of previous collective-forming mobilisations around race and ethnicity (Meer, 2010, 2012).

In seeking to comprehend the intersectional disadvantage of minoritised students, as very much part of the emerging agenda in HE, consideration of British Muslims will be pivotal. Yet HEIs have still to identify these communities of faith as integral to WP, constituting a form of policy exclusion. Thus, while the structural racism affecting the opportunities and life chances of Muslim students have been entrenched over some time, what makes this intersectional disadvantage 'new' is the degree to which this demography continue to be omitted from the evolving access framework I have attempted to trace.

Testimonies of Aziz Foundation Scholarship Candidates and Scholars

Interventions in the access regime are increasingly being influenced by charitable and community-based organisations, which form mutually beneficial collaborations with universities. One such organisation is the Aziz Foundation, which is an established grant-making body that runs a unique Masters scholarships programme, dedicated to British Muslim communities. A key part of its mission is to facilitate social mobility and widening access at the PGT level (Aziz Foundation, 2022). It has pursued these objectives since 2016 through awarding over 600 scholarships, geared towards enabling professional development and helping to realise career aims. In order to inform institutional approaches to EDI, it regularly surveys its scholarship candidates and scholars to better understand the challenges and aspirations of Muslims looking to undertake PGT study.

The research that I have conducted at the Foundation—utilising a rich stream of qualitative data drawn from focus groups and surveys—foregrounds the stories and personal narratives (which incorporates autoethnographic elements or 'counter discourses') of Muslim students and prospective Masters applicants. Annual surveys cover the academic experience, curriculum content, student support services, faith provision, and future expectations.

This data collection enables us to centre the testimonies of the Foundation's beneficiaries, shaping our programmes and building an evidence base supporting the idea that British Muslims ought to be more explicitly incorporated within WP strategies and frameworks.

Faith as Agency Bestowing

Common refrains from our survey respondents indicate that faith has significant force in bestowing and sustaining agency. For British Muslim students, it is core to their identity (Sardar, 2021b) and is commonly cited as a source of resilience and empowerment (Mirza, 2018) in navigating the institutional geography of the academy (Hopkins, 2011).

This is evident, in that the presence of adequate faith provision on university campuses can make an enormous difference to the quality of the British Muslim student experience. Hence comments, such as the ones below, are typical from scholarship candidates citing positive engagement with their institutions:

> *My university experience was a great one. One of the most significant things I really appreciated ... [is that] we had a wonderful prayer room, which was tranquil and calming. A great space to pray and reflect.*

> *They have provided me with the full support, especially as a British Muslim, the chaplaincy team are really helpful, they advise on spiritual and ethical concerns and when I started university they provided me with the information on where to pray.*

A sense of collective identity and belonging, for the many candidates we interview, revolves around faith services such as accessible prayer facilities and the chaplaincy, which have become hallmarks of the spatially inclusive campus (Islam et al., 2019; Islam, 2021). As such, EDI provision has an anchoring and orientating influence. The beneficial impact of this cannot be underestimated, as our own data management statistics indicate that 48% of our scholars are the first generation in their family into higher education (Aziz Foundation, 2022). In lacking the opportunities to draw upon family experiences in setting out expectations of campus life, British Muslims are more likely to rely on these student services to smooth the transition into university. And this is where, critically, there is an intersection between widening access and EDI provision.

In contradistinction, the agency-depleting structural challenges—as well as more overt ones—confronted by British Muslim students result in feelings of disorientation or 'dislocation' (Hall, 2019), as lived experiences and realities are seemingly discounted or belittled. This is indicated in such telling observations as the two presented below:

> *[S]taff did make derogatory comments towards Muslims, particularly those in higher positions of power i.e. Director of Admissions, and coordinator of student ambassadors. There was also a 'white-male' led culture which had the ability to make you feel isolated at times.* (Quoted in Sardar, 2021b)

[T]here was a conversation that occurred during a seminar that was particularly memorable ... someone mentioned the concept of God. To which the seminar leader reacted by saying 'who even believes in god anymore'. This was followed by laughter from the seminar leader and my class mates who I assumed were atheist. It was very uncomfortable occurrence. ... I did feel as if we were being shamed and ridiculed in a way.

The spectacle of Muslim staff members being disparaged has an 'isolating' and distancing effect in this account, diminishing the ability of the respondent to feel part of the campus community. What is also noteworthy here is the reference to a 'white-male led culture', which invokes what some Critical Race Theorists might call "normative whiteness" (Arday, 2019). In other words, there is a perception that the social norms of university life operate explicitly to consolidate existing hierarchies of power, with white men making up the majority of senior leaderships and setting the tone for campus culture. The consequence is to exclude minoritised communities.

We can also see a similar interaction in the testimony of the second respondent cited in this section. This recollection touches on a casual dismissal of theism by a seminar leader—'who believes in God anymore?' The lack of sensitivity in this clearly rhetorical question points to the type of uncontested secularism that manifests in academic settings (Gholami, 2021). The supportive laughter from seminar participants then marks out and emphasises the respondent as 'different'—'shamed and ridiculed'. These forms of 'othering' paint Muslims and communities of faith as somewhat primitive or anachronistic (Scott-Baumann et al., 2021; UUK, 2021; NUS, 2018). Both testimonies here show how Muslims are rendered conspicuous by being out of place and time, beyond or outside a given institutional culture (Mirza, 2018).

FEELINGS OF EXCEPTIONALISM

Amongst scholarship candidates, feelings of being treated differently by university administrators are frequently noted. There are instances cited of obstructionism in response to legitimate issues raised by Muslim students. This frustration is put succinctly by the comment that *"any small issues raised by Muslim students take a long time to resolve"*. To add to this, some candidates state they felt *"lost in the administrative process"*.

A recurring episode involves a scenario in which members of the university Islamic Society run into challenges when making bookings for events and meetings. One exemplar will suffice to illustrate the point:

> *There was one incident in which I felt was a case of indirect Islamophobia. ... This was an Open Mic Night we wanted to hold in collaboration with the wider ... Islamic Society. I was told to fill out two forms. ... I was then told that we had to pay because they deemed our proposed event to be a 'conference' where external speakers would be joining! None of this was on the booking form I sent.*

The claim here of 'indirect Islamophobia' goes beyond the notion that this may in fact be a benign misunderstanding or simple clerical error. This is perhaps due to the preconceptions that are encountered by Muslim students undertaking seemingly routine administrative tasks when liaising with university professional services staff. The mistaken idea that the respondent intended to host external speakers at a 'conference' speaks of subtle processes of securitisation; of an overly cautious means of engaging with Muslim students that considers them as a potential risk to be managed. Overall, there is a heightened climate of suspicion within higher education, informed by 'government directives' and monitoring around 'controversial speakers' (Scott-Baumann et al., 2021).

These types of experience feeds into the perception that accommodating the needs of Muslim students is far from a strategic priority for universities, and, in fact, catering for them represents a burden to be avoided. In the words of one respondent, there *"is an attitude of protecting one's image rather than fixing the problems that are discriminative towards Muslim students"*.

LACK OF INFLUENCE OVER RESEARCH AGENDAS

British Muslim students expressed their dismay at the inability to influence research agendas as academic staff displayed little interest in matters of faith and ethnicity when undergraduate students pursued related dissertation topics (Sardar, 2021b; Samatar & Sardar, 2023). To place this in context, British Muslim students are the smallest faith grouping at research-intensive universities (Mcmaster, 2020). And, as policy practitioners have noted, this not only has a significant impact on graduate outcomes, but it also reduces the influence British Muslims hold in public life through engagement with future decision-makers (Khan, 2010).

At the undergraduate level, final year projects or dissertations represent an important transition point to postgraduate research. That is because these projects shape formative experiences of research, and help to determine future areas of research. Hence, one graduate looking ahead to a Masters' degree states:

> *Representation in postgraduate degrees of professors and academic staff—[is]*
> *more important at [the] postgraduate stage as specialised research into a spe-*
> *cific topic shapes the majority of the postgraduate degree.* (Quoted in
> Sardar, 2021b)

A diversity of academic staff at the PGT level empowers students to explore research topics in the social sciences and humanities—particularly those students looking to tap into their own 'cultural capital'. Cultural capital can be thought of as 'high cultural knowledge', which could be embodied in access to one's own heritage and community through material culture ('books, photos' etc.). It could also be externalised through educational qualifications that recognises expertise developed in these areas. Predominately, though, it constitutes an 'investment' in the family (Vershinina et al., 2011).

As many of the Foundation's scholars have strong ties with their communities—with this shaping their practice and research—it becomes natural to harness this accumulated cultural capital for professional development purposes. Take this comment by a creative writer on what they expect from their postgraduate degree:

> *I expect to gain the skills and knowledge to be able to confidently teach writing*
> *to others, as a way to enable them to tell their own stories in an authentic way.*
> *I would like to bridge the gap between participatory story creation and story*
> *sharing through my wider community work. I would like the time to complete*
> *unfinished manuscripts of works that seek to connect people and places, and*
> *bring them to life through storytelling.*

Examples like this serve to show the virtuous cycle at the heart of some of our respondent's aspirations to pursue academic development. This creative writer identifies the furtherance of their vocation as fundamentally overlapping with the interests of his community, with their mission to help bring the community 'to life' through genuine, reciprocal engagement.

This could be seen as a form of community-based widening participation, breaking down barriers between communities and the academy.

However, a major concern is whether this cultural capital is convertible to social capital; major reports indicate this is seldom the case, hindering British Muslims' ability to gain a foothold in the labour market. Universities and employers do not always recognise the value and uses of cultural capital, and this can limit access to social and peer support networks that may aid in developing professional and academic credibility (Malik & Wykes, 2018; Citizens UK, 2017).

INTERSECTIONAL DISADVANTAGE

There is a double or triple penalty paid by Muslim students in higher education (Stevenson, 2018; Sardar 2021b) and beyond in the labour market, which I refer to as a type of 'intersectional disadvantage'. Put simply, in many testimonies we find that Muslim students and graduates feel that they are disadvantaged due to negative perceptions of their faith, in addition to being marginalised due to their ethnicity and gender. These modes of disadvantage combine to exacerbate each other.

The interrelation of these modes of disadvantage are laid bare in the anxieties that many students feel, in anticipating how these may play out to make realisation of future career prospects all the more challenging:

As a South Asian woman who visibly identifies as a Muslim—I feel like the narratives and stereotypes surrounding these layers of my identity may affect my job opportunities. (Quoted in Sardar, 2021b)

What is articulated here is how the respondent sees processes of racialisation unfolding in relation to how it targets markers or overlapping 'layers' of identity (i.e., South Asian/women/Muslim). The forms of prejudice she expects to encounter are themselves 'intersectional' in feeding off each other (Feldman & Allchorn, 2019). We also find in this statement reference to the construction of 'Muslimness' in wider society, through preconceptions and stereotypes of British Muslim communities that psychologically impacts Muslims even before they commence professional life. The fear here—and one echoed by many respondents—is that these intersectional prejudices are deeply embedded in the labour market and foreclose professional pathways. In particular, 'employment disadvantages' acutely affect Muslim women (as they display visible markers of their Muslimness), impacting self-esteem and creating a siege mentality (Shaw et al., 2016; Social Mobility Commission, 2017).

As I have stated above in my discussion of the evolution of the widening participation agenda, the traditional understanding of disadvantage is couched in socio-economic terms. However, to broaden out the analysis, with British Muslims the socio-economic dimension is conjoined with both ethnicity and faith. Hence, despite high educational aspirations amongst British Muslims (see the study commission by the Aziz Foundation: Kaur-Ballagan et al., 2018), financial barriers still stymie progression. This surfaces in the data, as there is a sharp decline in British Muslim progression from the UG to the PGT level, from 12% to 8%, a tendency which is not seen amongst students of Christian or non-faith background (OfS, 2022b). And while there are several factors involved here, one that we have not so far touched upon is the sensitivity around taking out interest-based student loans—which uniquely impacts British Muslims as one area where socio-economic disadvantage is intertwined with the practice of faith.

In the Foundation's scholarship interviews, we continually hear that while a Masters' degree is a necessity for career development and access to the professions, in financial terms it represents a 'luxury'. A luxury in the sense of Masters programmes being unaffordable and out of reach when a majority of our scholars have obligations to financially contribute to their family's household expenses (Samatar and Sardar, 2023; Aziz Foundation, 2022). But also, in the sense that many candidates see no clear grounds to take out the Student Finance postgraduate loan when they are interest bearing (Sardar, 2021b; Samatar & Sardar, 2023). In other words, if studying a Masters requires the violation of religious principles, it becomes a far less appealing prospect. This is communicated in concerns such as the one reproduced below:

> *[W]e now pay interest on our loans which conflicts with my religious beliefs. Although there are postgraduate loans available, I do not consider this a viable option for me so the cost of post graduate courses is a factor which potentially prohibits me from pursuing my studies if I am unable to obtain funding.* (Quoted in Sardar, 2021b)

Some interviewees reasoned——even while expressing regret—that they thought it permissible to access student finance loans at the undergraduate level; after all a first degree constitutes an entry level qualification required in many jobs. However, some scholarship candidates did not find a similar justification credible for PGT study, regardless of the importance they attached to their proposed programme of study. Many therefore state to us they would not study their chosen course if they were not awarded a scholarship.

THE FUTURE OF WIDENING PARTICIPATION

It is vital that we reflect upon the evolution of the WP framework, in light of the evidence and testimonies gathered by community-centred organisations such as the Aziz Foundation. There are several recommendations which universities ought to consider that flow from this, to inform strategic thinking on access and participation as they concern British Muslim students:

- The sector as a whole ought to reflect on how it engages British Muslims, using policy levers to build on UUK reports on racial harassment and Islamophobia (UUK, 2020, 2021). Acknowledgement of the intersectional disadvantage of British Muslims ought to be codified into the access framework.
- The regulatory extension of WP's mandate to the PGT level is overdue. This will have a great impact on dealing with the structural challenges encountered in the transition from UG to PGT study and is needed to help repair the pipeline between education and work (Samatar & Sardar, 2023), enhancing employability prospects or acting as a gateway into academia. Tackling the 'broken bridge' of PGT study (Hancock et al., 2017; Hancock & Wakeling, 2019) should be a sector-wide priority.
- Greater social impact can also be facilitated through consortiums of good practice and knowledge exchange focusing on the British Muslim learner; partnerships between universities and community organisations with specialist in-house knowledge—in a similar vein to the OfS-funded Yorkshire Consortium for Equity in Doctoral Education (YCEDE).
- HEIs ought to take the initiative in identifying British Muslims as a disadvantaged and/or underrepresented group, dependent on institutional context, in their own APPs. The Equality of Opportunity Risk Register (EORR) (OfS, 2022c) provides further chances to examine structural issues inhibiting access for these cohorts.

- HEIs need to be proactive in auditing the British Muslim student experience, putting aside reputational risk (Akel, 2021).

As we explained at the beginning of this chapter, British Muslims are occasionally seen as communities that assume a sort of spectral existence. They are subject to both hypervisibility through the tropes that (mis-) represent them and disappear into a shadowy form when it comes to codifications and formulas of access and participation. And yet, British Muslims are an essential part of the WP equation and will shape its future trajectory. The fair access agenda will need to grapple with the structural disadvantages confronting British Muslims to realise the 'promise' of social mobility, integrate intersectional inclusion, and ultimately come to terms with its ghosts.

References

Akel, S. (January 2021). *Institutionalised: The rise of Islamophobia in Higher Education.* Centre for Equity and Inclusion, London Metropolitan University.

All Party Parliamentary Group (APPG) on British Muslims. (2017, December). *A very Merry Muslim Christmas.* APPG on British Muslims.

All Party Parliamentary Group (APPG) on British Muslims. (2018). *Faith as the Fourth Emergency Service: British Muslim charitable contributions to the UK,* APPG on British Muslims.

All Party Parliamentary Group (APPG) on British Muslims. (2019). *Islamophobia defined: Report into the inquiry into Islamophobia/Anti-Muslim Hatred.* APPG on British Muslims.

Arday, J. (2019). Dismantling power and privilege through reflexivity: negotiating normative Whiteness, the Eurocentric curriculum and racial micro-aggressions within the Academy. *Whiteness and Education, 3*(2), 141–161. https://doi.org/10.1080/23793406.2019.1574211

Atherton, G., & Mazhari, T. (April 2019). *Working class heroes – Understanding access to higher education for white students from lower socio-economic backgrounds.* NEON.

Aziz Foundation. (2022). *Institutional partnership brochure.* Aziz Foundation. https://www.azizfoundation.org.uk/wpcontent/uploads/2024/04/Aziz-Foundation-PP-Brochure-UPDATED.pdf

Bhatti, T. (2021). *Defining Islamophobia: A contemporary understanding of how expressions of Muslimness are targeted.* MCB.

Bhopal, K., & Preston, J. (2012). *Intersectionality and "race" in education.* Routledge. https://doi.org/10.4324/9780203802755

Citizens UK. (2017). *The missing Muslims: Unlocking British Muslim potential for the benefit of all.* Citizens UK.

Dearing, R. (1997). *The dearing report: Higher education in the learning society.* HM Stationery Office. https://doi.org/10.4135/9781529714395.n139.

Elahi, F., & Khan, O. (November 2017). *Islamophobia: Still a challenge for us all.* Runnymede Trust.

Equality and Human Rights Commission. (2019). *Tackling racial harassment: Universities challenged.* EHRC.

Feldman, M., & Allchorn, W. (2019). *A working definition of Anti-Muslim hatred with a focus on hate-crime work.* Centre for the Analysis of the Radical Right.

Gholami, R. (January 2021). Critical race theory and Islamophobia: Challenging inequity in higher education. *Race, Ethnicity and Education, 24*(1), 319–337. https://doi.org/10.1080/13613324.2021.1879770

Greenbank, P. (2006, April). The evolution of government policy on widening participation'. *Higher Education Quarterly, 60,* 141–166. https://doi.org/10.1111/j.1468-2273.2006.00314.x

Hall, S. (2019). *Essential essays Vol. 2: identity and diaspora* (ed. Morley, D.). Duke University Press. https://doi.org/10.1515/9781478002710-toc.

Hancock, S. E., Ewart, A., & Wakeling, P. B. J. (August 2017). *Evaluation of the postgraduate support scheme 2015–16: Report to HEFCE.* HEFCE.

Hancock, S. E., & Wakeling, P. B. J. (2019, 22 March). *Progression to and Success in postgraduate study: Interim evaluation report.* University of York: Department of Education.

Hopkins, P. (2011, January). Towards critical geographies of the university campus: understanding the contested experiences of Muslim students. *Transactions of the Royal Geography Society, 36*(1), 157–169. https://doi.org/10.1111/j.1475-5661.2010.00407.x

Islam, M. (2021). *Building belonging: developing religiously inclusive cultures for Muslim students in higher education.* Advance HE.

Islam, M., Lowe, T., & Jones, G. (2019). A 'satisfied settling'? Investigating a sense of belonging for Muslim students in a UK small-medium Higher Education Institution. *Student Engagement in Higher Education Journal, 2*(2), 79–104. https://sehej.raise-network.com/raise/article/view/891

Kaur-Ballagan, K., Gottfried, G. K., & Mortimore, R. (2018, February). *A Review of Survey research on Muslims in Britain: Research report for the Aziz Foundation.* Barrow Cadbury Trust, The Joseph Rowntree Charitable Trust and Unbound Philanthropy, Ipsos Mori Social Research Institute.

Khan, O. (2010). *Self-respect and respecting others: The consequences of affirmative action in selective universities.* Runnymede Trust.

Law, I., Philips, D., & Turney, L. (2004). *Institutional racism in higher education.* Trentham Books.

Madriaga, M. (2022). Reframing race and widening access into higher education. *Higher Education*. https://doi.org/10.1007/s10734-022-00981-y.

Malik, A., & Wykes, E. (2018, October). *British Muslims in UK higher education: Socio-political, religious and policy considerations*. The Bridge Institute.

Mcmaster, N. C. (2020, March 17). *Research insight: Religion and belief in UK higher education*. Advance HE.

Meer, N. (2010). *Citizenship, identity and the politics of multiculturalism*. Palgrave Macmillan. https://doi.org/10.1057/9780230281202_2

Meer, N. (2012). Negotiating faith and politics: The emergence of Muslim consciousness in Britain. In I. U. Ahmad & Z. Sardar (Eds.), *Muslims in Britain: Making social and political space*. Routledge. https://doi.org/10.432 4/9780203121467-9

Mirza, H. S. (2012). Multiculturalism and the Gender Gap. In I. U. Ahmad & Z. Sardar (Eds.), *Muslims in Britain: Making social and political space*. Routledge.

Mirza, H. S. (2018). Black Bodies 'Out of Place' in Academic Spaces: Gender, Race, Faith and Culture in Post-race Times. In J. Arday & H. S. Mirza (Eds.), *Dismantling race in higher education: Racism, whiteness and decolonising the academy*. Palgrave Macmillan.

Muslim Council of Britain. (2015, January). British muslims in numbers: A demographic, socio-economic and health profile of Muslims in Britain drawing on the 2011 Census, MCB.

National Union of Students. (2018, March 18). *The experiences of Muslim students in 2017–18*. NUS.

Nous Group. (2020, October 23). *Effectiveness in implementation of access and participating plan reform: Part 1*. Office for Students.

Nous Group. (2021, March 11). *Effectiveness in implementation of access and participating plan reform: Part 2*. Office for Students.

Office for Students. (2022a). Access and participation plans. Retrieved February 04, 2022, from https://www.officeforstudents.org.uk/advice-and-guidance/promoting-equal-opportunities/access-and-participation-plans/

Office for Students. (2022b). Access and participation data dashboard. Retrieved February 04, 2022, from https://www.officeforstudents.org.uk/data-and-analysis/access-and-participation-data-dashboard/

Office for Students. (2022c). Equality of opportunity risk register. Retrieved February 05, 2022, from https://www.officeforstudents.org.uk/advice-and-guidance/promoting-equal-opportunities/equality-of-opportunity-risk-register/

ONS. (2022). Religion, England and Wales: Census 2021. https://www.ons.gov.uk/peoplepopulationandcommunity/culturalidentity/religion/bulletins/religionenglandandwales/census2021

Pilkington, A. (2004). Institutional racism in the academy: Comparing the police and university in Midshire. In I. Law, D. Philips, & L. Turney (Eds.), *Institutional racism in higher education*. Trentham Books.

Pilkington, A. (2011). *Institutional racism in the academy: A case study*. Trentham Books.

Pilkington, A. (2018). The rise and fall in the salience of race equality in higher education. In J. Arday & H. S. Mirza (Eds.), *Dismantling race in higher education*. Palgrave Macmillan. https://doi.org/10.1007/978-3-319-60261-5_2

Robinson, D., & Salvestrini, V. (2020, November). *Summary Report: Understanding the impact of interventions to address the inequalities in the student experience*. TASO.

Samatar, A., & Sardar, Z. (2023). *Transitions: British Muslims between undergraduate and postgraduate studies*. Foundation.

Sardar, Z. (2021a, November). *Catalysing institutional reform: Creating an inclusive learning environment for British Muslim students*. University of Exeter: Centre for Social Mobility.

Sardar, Z. (2021b, June). *Intersectionality of race and religion: Widening participation and the experience of British Muslim students at the PGT level*. Aziz Foundation.

Sayyid, S. (February 2015). *A fundamental fear: Eurocentrism and the emergence of Islamism*. Zed Books.

Scott-Baumann, A., Guest, M., Naguib, S., Cheruvallil-Contractor, S., & Phoenix, A. (July 2021). *Islam on campus: Contested identities and the cultures of higher education in Britain*. Oxford University Press.

Shaw, B., Menzies, L., Bernandes, E., & Baars, S. (December, 2016). *Ethnicity, gender and social mobility*. Social Mobility Commission.

Singh, G., Dixon-Smith, S., & DaCosta, C. (2021, April). *Beyond BAME: Rethinking the politics, application, and efficacy of ethnic categorisation*. https://pure.coventry.ac.uk/ws/portalfiles/portal/41898015/Beyond_BAME_final_report.pdf

Social Mobility Commission. (2017, June). *Time for change: An assessment of Government policies on social mobility 1997–2017*. The Stationary Office.

Stevenson, J. (2018, October). *Muslims students in UK education: Issues of inequality and inequity*. Bridge Institute.

Universities UK. (2020, November). *Tackling racial harassment in higher education*. Creative Commons.

Universities UK. (2021). *Tackling Islamophobia and anti-Muslim hatred: practical guidance for universities*. UUK.

Vershinina, N., Barrett, R., & Meyer, M. (2011, March). Forms of capital, intra-ethnic variation and Polish entrepreneurs in Leicester. *Work, Employment and Society, 25*(1), 101–117. https://doi.org/10.1177/0950017010389241

Warsi, S. (2017, March 30). *The enemy within: A tale of Muslim Britain*. Penguin.

Weekes-Bernard, D. (Ed.). (2010). *Widening participation and race equality*. Runnymede Trust.

Whitehead, L. (2012). *The Westminster faith debates: Seven debates on the place of religion in our public life.*, Religion and Society.

Yorkshire Consortium for Equity in Doctoral Education (YECEDE). https://ycede.ac.uk/

Conclusion: Entrenched Inequalities and Evolving Challenges: Harnessing Hope for Muslim Students and Staff in Higher Education

Maisha Islam

Whilst the UK HE landscape is predominantly characterised by marketisation and neo-liberalism (Molesworth et al., 2009; Tomlinson, 2017), its core purpose should always be understood through the lens of hope. In her book, Hope Circuits, Riddell (2024) asks 'What does it look like if we can build hopeful systems where individuals and communities flourish?' (pg. 10). Whilst the concept of hope may seem counter-intuitive to suggest, given the contributions offered here, this should be the question we return to. One would certainly not disagree with those academics, professional service staff, and students whose activism in areas related to religious (and other forms of intersectional) equity positions them at the opposite of hope. In countless ways, we see overt attacks on these efforts,

M. Islam (✉)
University of Southampton, Southampton, UK
e-mail: m.islam@soton.ac.uk

© The Author(s), under exclusive license to Springer Nature Switzerland AG 2024
A. Mahmud, M. Islam (eds.), *Uncovering Islamophobia in Higher Education*, Palgrave Studies in Race, Inequality and Social Justice in Education, https://doi.org/10.1007/978-3-031-65253-0_15

and individuals who work tirelessly and fiercely to advance equity and inclusion (Ahmed, 2007; Islam, 2023). At the time of writing (November 2023), this includes ministerial attacks on academics whose support for Gaza emerging out of the Israel-Hamas conflict (namely Israel's disproportionate retaliation on Palestinian civilians in response to the Hamas attack on October 7, 2023) have been misconstrued, misrepresented, and branded as 'extremist' (Coe, 2023). What is regarded as freedom of expression and diversity of thought for some is not a privilege granted to others against the backdrop of the current socio-political landscape—a sentiment which is sharply affecting Muslim students and staff.

The chapters within this edited collection must therefore be understood within a context whereby public advocacy on issues related to religious equity and inclusion for Muslims is becoming (yet has historically been) a risky and daring act (hooks, 1989). In these moments, it becomes integral to demonstrate academic activism and solidarity with those more susceptible to structural harm and violence. As such, this book represents an intentionality to seek out the voices of Muslim staff and students; recognising our claim to resist and re-exist (Irigaray et al., 2021) within the ivory tower of academia which has long done us a disservice. Acknowledging the pervasive nature of Islamophobia, this collection draws attention to how Islamophobia manifests within the micro- and macro-structures of universities. From learning and teaching spaces to Student Unions, and policy directives influencing how our oppression is (or rather is not) responded to. As such, this book should be useful to students, academics, professional service staff, and those working in higher education sector bodies.

Reflecting on our authors' contributions, four key themes are apparent—Gendered Islamophobia; Muslims as under-served and seen to be undeserving; the dynamic and fluid nature of Islamophobia; and Hope. Whilst there is overlap in these themes, and indeed in the messaging within individual chapters, these four themes represent our collective disruption and symbolise the burgeoning presence of Muslim academics, staff, and students in the sector. This chapter concludes with future directions and poses a series of reflexive questions for readers to consider, as we all play a part in enacting transformative disruption and change.

Gendered Islamophobia

Existing literature is extant with representations of Muslim girls and women, particularly in detailing their representation as oppressed victims but also dangerous by-products of their culture and gender which are harmful to their educational desires and labour market outcomes (Ali, 2003; Wilson, 2007, 2016). However, Muslim women's voices in this collection reveal the systemic inequalities operating within universities which are suppressing, silencing, and marginalising our existence. For example, the composite counter-stories in Chap. 3 reveal intimate experiences at a 'crossroad of complexity' from young, Somali, Muslim female doctoral students and early-career staff. From contradictions, empty actions, and disinterest from universities to understanding the intersections of race, gender, and religion, their narratives further evidence the additional labour and marginalisation experienced by Black Muslim women within HE (Johnson, 2020).

These narratives support the use of intersectionality and a Black feminist methodology in recognising the 'intersectional othering' that many Muslim women experience (see Chap. 9), despite universities claiming that equality, diversity, and inclusion (EDI) are amongst their current top priorities (WonkHE & Kortext, 2022). As a result, gendered Islamophobia transpires via marketised diversity over a genuine commitment towards eliminating bias and barriers to progression for Muslim women. In line with the work of Critical Race and Black feminist theorists, much of this is due to the overbearing presence of Whiteness, sexism, and colonialism, which many authors referenced within their accounts (see Chaps. 5 and 9). For Muslim women, this is evident in their bodies being seen as acceptable archetypes of Muslimness within university settings (see Chaps. 5 and 10), whilst simultaneously being subject to exceptionally high standards to prove our worth that non-Muslim/minoritised colleagues would not be expected to meet (see Chap. 8). It, therefore, seems that whilst universities perceive to welcome Muslim women (and other minoritised bodies) into the academy, they do little to personally confront and acknowledge the micro-aggressive and systemic harm they inflict upon us.

Whilst these experiences add to a limited body of literature about Muslim women's career experiences within HE, where traditionally undergraduate Muslim student experience is favoured (Asmar et al., 2004; Jamal Al-deen, 2019; Seggie & Sanford, 2010; Thompson & Pihlaja, 2018), there is an avenue which perhaps holds a larger dearth in existing literature related to gendered Islamophobia—the experience of Muslim male staff. Modood (see Chap. 10) draws attention to this by suggesting that Muslim males must jump higher professional hurdles in comparison to Muslim women to succeed in university spaces, perhaps due to the equally harmful stereotypes and representations Muslim men have been subject to, e.g., as terrorists, groomers, and anti-feminist (Britton, 2019; Mac an Ghaill & Haywood, 2015). Whilst this does not discredit the experiences and trauma that Muslim females encounter in academia, it raises an interesting intellectual avenue which can give further voice to Muslim male academics.

Overall, many women within this collection note how their struggles often remain unrecognised but are wagered against in efforts to showcase institutional diversity. This portrays a subtlety and contradiction to the harm and violence that they constantly experience. For example, Muslim female academics and early-career researchers here described battling accusations of bias due to the insider status of their research, whilst also being met with a constant expectation to undertake EDI work (see Chap. 7). This has obvious repercussions on the career trajectory of Muslim female researchers/academics and our ability to diversify the academy, particularly where such work has been attributed to academic burnout and epistemic exploitation (Berenstain, 2016; Decuir-Gunby, 2020). Overall, we see how the cultural, racial, gendered, and religious dynamics intersect within academic contexts, requiring Muslim women to juggle multiple identities and expectations, leading to internal conflict and negotiations/strategies of self that are largely navigated alone.

Under-served and Undeserving

What was particularly striking was the number of authors who resonated with the concept of 'satisfied settling' (Islam et al., 2019; Islam & Mercer-Mapstone, 2021) (see Chaps. 4, 5, and 13). It draws attention to the arguments made in Chap. 12 that there are unique experiences and barriers Muslim students encounter within HE, yet are passively acknowledged due to the influence of 'political secularism and de-theologised Christian culture'. Instead, issues related to Islam are treated as inherent threats, with representations continuing to be recycled by those within and outside of HE through a consistent demonisation of Muslims as a collective. This paints Muslim students and staff as a population which are undeserving of support. It is therefore unsurprising we see the existence of a Muslim student degree-awarding gap (Gholami, 2021), which needs to be more meaningfully addressed through a rigorous assessment of both racism *and* secularism. Indeed, the manifestation of a Muslim student-degree awarding gap highlights the positioning of Muslim students as an under-served and undeserving equity-seeking group within British HE, when existing practice has largely sought to understand issues related to degree-awarding gaps from a racialised perspective (Universities UK & National Union of Students, 2019).

Most practice related to eliminating the existence of degree-awarding gaps has also focussed on the learning and teaching sphere, e.g., the experiences of racially minoritised students within classroom settings (Bale et al., 2020; Claridge et al., 2018; Islam, 2021b) and pedagogical adaptions which support inclusive teaching practice (Arday et al., 2021; Cook-Sather et al., 2021; SOAS University of London, 2018). Whilst this progress must be celebrated, we see little disaggregation in literature which focuses on these experiences for Muslim students. For example, Chap. 2 notes the pedagogical violence Muslim female students experience whilst navigating the White atmosphere of the university. Using Bonilla-Silva's (2019) concept of the racial economy of emotions to capture the ambivalence experienced within these spaces, this chapter highlights how academic (and non-academic) spaces work to exclude religiously othered bodies. For example, students detailed the marginalisation, isolation, and epistemic violence they were made to experience in the classroom. The chapter describes however that incidental moments shared by staff and students (who were respectful of faith) can support Muslim students' existence, persistence, and resonance within White atmospheres.

Outside of curricula and university spaces, Muslim students are further seen to be undeserving of institutional and policy attention through their invisibility within the English HE regulatory framework. Focussing specifically on the widening participation (WP) agenda, Chap. 14 exposes a policy stance whereby Muslim students are uniquely exempt from consideration, despite showing gaps in accessing, succeeding within, and progressing from HE (Codiroli Mcmaster, 2020). Whilst policy levers have been used (and shown success) in supporting other disadvantaged groups who show similar trends, Muslim students remain absent within these discourses. If WP efforts (e.g., using Access and Participation Plans) factored in this 'new intersectionality of disadvantage' (i.e., recognition of faith as a factor of disadvantage alongside other forms of oppression), universities can better build a sense of inclusion which they so often preach.

Finally, similar to arguments made previously, Muslim (female) academics are being under-served by an academic environment marked by Whiteness, secularity, and minimal empathy. The raw autoethnographic account detailed in Chap. 8 leaves much food for thought and should be applauded for its honesty in highlighting the plight and unfair treatment of many brilliant Muslim (and other) minoritised academics in the sector (Arday, 2020; Bhopal et al., 2016). The experiences detailed demonstrate why religiously minoritised academics are under-represented or 'permanently precarious'—they are desperately trying to survive and compete with others who are not privy to the personal and professional burdens within our lives (such as unpaid caring responsibilities), though are made to believe that lack of permanency and 'success' is due to our shortcomings. Whilst academic precarity is a systemic issues affecting many given the period of financial challenge impacting the HE sector, we are reminded how this is further complicated due to religious, raced, and gendered harms. However, many of us rely 'on change to happen from within the institutions that continue to discriminate against us'.

THE DYNAMIC AND FLUID NATURE OF ISLAMOPHOBIA

It is commonly agreed within the social sciences that categories such as race, ethnicity, and gender are social constructs, i.e., they are concepts undergoing development in response to contextual factors (Haney Lopez, 2004; Lorber, 2018). Such claims are also applicable to the practice of Islamophobia as all chapters highlight the dynamism and fluid character it pertains to. This includes the intricacies and specificities of how Islamophobia manifests in the everyday lived experiences of Muslim students and staff—from being told that we should be grateful to be in universities and simply better exercise resilience in the face of institutional violence (see Chap. 3), to perceptions of research related to Islam and Muslims being considered intellectually unnecessary. The latter is an example proffered in Modood's reflections when describing early experiences of Islamophobia faced in trying to introduce religion as a vector of inequality within sociology and political theory, and a broader factor to consider in constructions of (cultural) racism (see Chap. 10).

Interestingly, the dynamic and fluid nature of Islamophobia is most apparent in how Muslims constantly face a double standard (in comparison to other marginalised groups) within HE spaces and rhetoric. Examples listed in this collection include the lack of provisions Muslim students are entitled to; disciplinary knowledge which rejects the worthiness of religion as sites for theorising and conducting research; and how elected Muslim student representatives are left unsupported when working in office. Chapter 4 highlights this under-recognised position of Muslim students navigating the terrain of Student Unions politics. Despite Student Unions being characterised by a liberal and progressive nature (Day & Dickinson, 2018), this chapter notes how Muslim sabbatical officers are still subject to Islamophobic tropes and increased scrutiny over their campaign preferences which tend to focus on religious-based politics and issues. Similar to the experiences described here by Muslim academics, the decline of Muslims taking up

sabbatical officer roles (which was once flourishing) is reflective of the symbolic violence and hegemony experienced when such positions are gained.
The fluidity of Islamophobia must therefore be looked at in tandem with the evolving British HE landscape which is (as previously mentioned) largely characterised by neo-liberalisation and marketisation. An often-understated change within this narrative of evolution is the securitisation of Muslim students which leaves them further disadvantaged. For example, many chapters reference the existence and detrimental impact of the Prevent duty (see Chaps. 3, 5, 8, 10, 12, and 14). Chapter 11 in particular highlights how the duty has led to increased surveillance and profiling of Muslim students, leading to a climate of suspicion and fear on campuses which invariably affects students' attainment and mental wellbeing. Existing research related to Prevent has demonstrated that this unfair targeting has created inhospitable social and intellectual climates (Awan, 2012; Kyriacou et al., 2017; NUS Connect, 2016) and so further implications can be drawn from this over-securitisation of Muslims on campus.

In sum, without acknowledging the changing nature of Islamophobia and how it responds to the socio-political context playing out within UK HE, limited progress can be made in better supporting Muslim students and staff. The intellectual and physical representation of Muslim students and academics (from within disciplinary perspectives to elected student representative roles) will consequently stagnate. Actively engaging with such discourses (e.g., research related to majority-minority relations mentioned in Chap. 10 or pro-Palestinian activism in Student Unions in Chap. 4) in psychologically safe spaces will allow a diversity of thought and stimulation of productive conversation around equity to flourish—an objective that is touted to be at the core of many universities' and Student Unions' missions.

HOPE

Recounting the message espoused earlier in this chapter, there are examples portrayed in this collection which describe various ways of stimulating productive activity for Muslim students and staff, leaving space for hope to flourish. This includes the utilisation of the Race Equality Charter to advance both racial and religious equity (see Chap. 13). As such, effective mobilisation of nationally recognised diversity awards can be used to promote university-wide embedded action, such as reviewing religiously competent report and support mechanisms or providing a safe space to discuss religious issues. This allows Muslim students and staff to benefit from an enhanced sense of belonging and social environment, as detailed elsewhere in existing literature (Abdulmula, 2021; Islam et al., 2019; Shaffait, 2019). Chapter 13 also sheds light on the importance of authentic change and engagement in implementing hope and trust in universities from the perspective of Muslim staff and students. It is reminiscent of how Gholami talks of an authentic decolonisation movement which is student led and seriously invested in by institutions to address the awarding gap (see Chap. 12).

I argue here that the single binding theme to all chapters within this collection should be seen through the lens of resistance—one which is both individually instigated and collectively embodied despite Muslim students and staff experiencing a nexus of oppressions. For example, Chap. 6 details how intentional pedagogical decisions can enable students' flourishment. Whether that may be motivation and inspiration to Muslim students who benefit from positive 'real-modelling' of Muslim academics, or non-Muslim students who can critically reflect on their cultural competencies. Decolonised curricula and inclusive pedagogical practice therefore actively supports learning gain (Florian & Linklater, 2010; Meda, 2020). Others also recognise the power of their presence in influencing students to be the next generation of Muslim academics (see Chapter "To be Muslim and Female in UK Higher Education: Reflections and Experiences"), suggesting that such actions support the academic pipeline for Muslims.

For Muslim students, their sense of hope is largely derived from their faith which is described as providing a 'bestowing and sustaining agency' (see Chap. 14), key to a sense of empowerment, identity, and belonging. With increasing Muslim representation within the UK HE student body, Muslim students' record of political activism which demonstrates an ethno-religious social capital should be celebrated (Franceschelli & O'Brien, 2014). This growing presence of Muslim staff and students alike is noted by Modood, whose 45-year+ career within academia describes an intellectual shift in the academic climate which is more open to acknowledging the religious-based inequalities discussed in this edited collection (see Chap. 10). As a result, whilst the experiences described by our fellow Muslim students and staff portray abject oppression, there are still examples of our re-existence (Achinte, 2008) within academia by using our Islamic identity as a form of capital and source of hope.

Future Directions

As this collection reifies the existence of a critical mass of Muslim academics, staff, and students working to bring religion and Islamophobia to the fore, core themes and recommendations across chapters suggest several avenues for colleagues within universities and higher education organisations to consider. These suggestions relate to institutional culture, academic knowledge, and policy provision but can be consolidated under the umbrella term of parity—namely in university-service provision, academic inclusion (related to both people and research agendas), and organisational policy (both at the local and national level). These are further expanded below:

University-Service Provision

Firstly, it was apparent across chapters (see Chaps. 2, 3, 10, and 13) that practical provisions for supporting Muslim students continue to be points of contention for universities to voluntarily integrate. However, existing research notes the importance of religious-based provisions for Muslim students to comfortably belong to academic and non-academic spaces (Chen et al., 2019; Cole & Ahmadi, 2010; Hopkins, 2011). This includes (but is not limited to) access to prayer rooms, Halal food, Muslim chaplains, considerations when observing Ramadan and non-alcoholic social events. Whilst it may seem that not implementing these would be non-consequential, providing these basic resources has been seen to support Muslim students' (and staff) sense of belonging. As has been asserted elsewhere, the link between sense of belonging and academic success should not be regarded as tenuous (Shalabi, 2014; Stevenson, 2018; Thomas, 2012). Rather, it should be seen as an integral area to invest in. This is reflected in existing practice to eliminate racialised degree-awarding gaps, and so similar provisions to meet the needs of Muslim students require closer consideration (see Chap. 12).

Furthermore, whilst universities may or may not wish to position themselves as secular institutions, they still hold a public sector duty to ensure that Muslim student and staff needs are being met as religion and belief is one of the nine protected characteristics under the Equality Act (2010). As part of this act, UK higher education institutions must offer equal treatment for people of different faiths and none. When this does not occur, Muslim students and staff are subject to indirect discrimination. Where similar efforts to create inclusive environments for other marginalised groups have been undertaken (e.g., providing gender-neutral bathrooms), these should also be extended to Muslims who demonstrate a constant negotiation of existence within university spaces.

Academic Inclusion

Secondly, many authors spoke about how their presence within academic settings was either covertly or overtly rejected and undermined. Whether it be through the White atmosphere of learning and teaching settings (see Chap. 2), the neglection of Black Muslim female experiences (see Chap. 3), of Islam within disciplinary debates (see Chap. 10), or the painstaking journey to overcome academic precarity (see Chap. 8), Islamophobia in these settings relates as much to intellectual disdain for Muslims/Islam as it does for the Muslim students and staff within these spaces. Academic inclusion must therefore relate to research agendas that are valued and the people we employ/provide opportunities to, to carry out research. Although the proceeding recommendation considers this at the organisational level, individuals within academia play an equally important role in ensuring this.

Islam (and religion at large) is relatively under-researched and under-theorised within academic literature (Aune & Stevenson, 2017). Whilst the academic climate is warming to the value of exploring these debates, aided by the growing presence of Muslim academics in national and international sectors (see the emergence of MusCrit[1] in America), there are still feats to climb to reach a level of academic parity. Some authors mentioned various academic avenues related to better establishing the role of religion in contributing to and advancing knowledge within multiple disciplinary debates. These included:

- A deeper investigation of gendered Islamophobia which focuses on male experiences in a more theorised description. Whilst our chapters have documented the institutional harm and violence experienced by Muslim women, it is unknown whether a similar or heightened perception of threat and difference is impacting Muslim men and their career progression in academia.
- Furthering discussions of decolonisation which include a religious dimension, recognising its significance and role within debates that currently acknowledge colonial harm across colour lines (see Chaps. 10 and 12). As measures to decolonise the curriculum are gaining traction within learning and teaching spaces, acknowledging the role

[1] MusCrit is described as a framework to explore the experiences of Muslim Americans, using a Critical Race Theory lens (see: Ali, 2022)

religion plays as part of colonialism becomes an important aspect to further research and give credence to.

- The utilisation and advancement of existing frameworks such as intersectionality, Black feminist methodologies, and Critical Race Theory to draw attention to the experiences of Muslim students and staff. Chapters 3, 4, and 9 expertly use these frameworks to communicate the harm and injustices experienced by Muslim students and staff and provide an example of how mixing and matching methodologies from other liberatory-based theories can bring attention to Muslim experiences (Schoonenboom, 2018).

As much of our academic research emerges out of collaboration, colleagues should consider where and how they might contribute and support these research avenues *with* Muslim researchers since these areas of investigation are yet to be appropriately considered.

Reflexive Questions to Support this Action:

1. How can I be an 'academic ally' in supporting the development of Muslim early-career and doctoral researchers whilst also recognising the contributions of existing Muslim researchers? Ghabra & Calafell (2018) demonstrate how allyship must be critically reflected upon to ensure academic alliances can be grounded in shared experiences of marginalisation.
2. Can I employ more conscious decision-making around collaboration partners, avenues for inter-disciplinary research, and citation practices which involve Muslim academics?
3. How can I begin to introduce religion and belief into curricula using a decolonial lens? Nye's (2019) work provides an exploration of how decolonisation efforts can be applied in the context of religion.
4. What opportunities can I provide for Muslim students to actively co-create visions of academic inclusion? Universities with student-staff partnership/student-led research programmes, such as the University of Leeds' Student Research Experience Placements, can leverage Muslim student voice and co-creation by creating projects which centre on religion and belief (Abdulmula, 2021).

Reflexive Questions to Support this Action:

1. Whilst it may be true that many universities offer religious-based provisions on campus, *management* of such provision is equally as important as the implementation of the provision itself. What mechanisms are available within your spaces for Muslim students and staff to suggest the effectiveness of having these provisions and whether they are appropriately meeting their needs?

To support an in-depth assessment of your current provisions for Muslim students and staff, use the reflective questions detailed in Islam's (2021a) report. Professional services staff may also take inspiration from Ali & Bagheri's (2009) case study about how they have created provisions and services to accommodate Muslim students' campus climate.

Organisational Policy

Finally, the role of universities and higher education policy/funding bodies should not be understated within endeavours to reach parity for Muslim staff and students via organisational policy. From shaping research agendas to implementing inclusive recruitment practices, measures required to support Muslim staff and students demand a step-change to occur at the structural level to enact an equitable level of inclusion. For universities, these can be leveraged as part of applications for nationally recognised diversity schemes such as the Athena Swan and Race Equality Charters which strongly encourage universities to take data-driven approaches to identify inequalities, promote career progression (see Chap. 8), and consider an intersectional lens (see Chap. 13) when supporting minoritised students and staff. As such, the notion of intersectionality must be extended to recognise the disadvantage faced by Muslims which acknowledges our gendered, classed, and racial representations intertwining with our religious identity. Similar considerations must also be taken on board by Student Unions and bodies such as the National Union of Students (NUS) more broadly. Although they should be commended for their values of democracy and activism, their treatment of Muslims within their organisations (see Chap. 4) describes further work needed to ensure the safety of Muslim officers and representatives. This is particularly pertinent to ensure given the ongoing violence in Gaza, where some student officers have been intimidated and suspended for their vocal pro-Palestinian support (Edwards, 2023).

For policy bodies and research councils, including those under UKRI[2], a focus on transforming academic/research culture is evidenced in the upcoming assessment of the Research Excellence Framework 2029 which includes an increased weighting to aspects related to people, culture, and research environment (Corner, 2022). Chapters within this collection have demonstrated how academic environments are epistemically harmful to Muslim researchers and academics. In supporting universities to demonstrate their effectiveness in meeting and developing a positive research culture, these organisations should consider how they can role model religiously aware behaviour and actions. For example, it has been established that research related to race is less likely to receive funding (Arday, 2017) and that principal investigators of funded projects are less likely to come from minoritised backgrounds (Adelaine et al., 2020). We can likely assume that these inequalities also manifest for Muslims. Recent funding competitions/calls demonstrate a focus towards equity and inclusion for policy organisations and funding councils (Hill & Turner, 2019; The Scottish Universities Partnership for Environmental Research, 2023). Simply put, these organisations hold immeasurable power to positively influence who and what is determined to be of 'positive impact', creating a ripple effect which can also influence universities' decisions to invest in certain areas. We must therefore consider how these interests can converge to benefit Muslim students and staff.

Our regulators and governmental bodies also play a role in shaping the outcomes and experiences of Muslim students and staff. For example, the use of Access and Participation Plans and broader WP agenda (see Chap. 14) have seen calls to better support students of colour, White working-class males, Gypsy, Roma, and Traveller communities and more

---

[2] UK Research and Innovation (UKRI) is a non-departmental governmental body, formed of nine organisations (seven of which are research councils) which often work closely with universities to foster research and development in the UK.

student groups based on national data which demonstrate their unequal access, participation and progression within HE. Positively, the Office for Students[3] Equality of Opportunity Risk Register has recently recognised religious groups at risk of not experiencing equality of opportunity. Muslim students specifically have been identified as being the most at-risk religious group related to experiencing insufficient personal support, cost pressures, and progression from higher education. Whilst data related to the outcomes of Muslim students has largely been absent, this demonstrates the significance of why we need to collect such data in a systematic way (Advance HE, 2018). As such, greater attention to inequities faced by Muslim students, supported by publicly available datasets from regulators, can empower universities to understand and subsequently tackle these issues.

Perhaps the most burgeoning policy directive which authors within and outside of this collection have repeatedly called for an overhaul of is the Prevent Duty which has been implemented without academic expertise and disproportionately targets Muslim students and staff. Policy development should therefore engage with the voices and experiences of minoritised communities to better understand and negate the detrimental consequences which can arise out of such legislation. Similarly, regulators and government bodies must also advocate for parity in recognising the disparities faced in the experiences of Muslim students and staff. For example, ministers have called upon universities to adopt the IHRA[4] definition of antisemitism (Adams, 2020; Parr, 2020), without due regard to or complete silence on encouraging universities to adopt definitions related to Islamophobia; only 21 UK HEIs (13%) currently adopt a definition of Islamophobia (National Secular Society, 2023), compared to the 119 that have adopted the IHRA definition (Union of Jewish Students, 2024).

---

[3] The Office for Students is the regulator for English higher education.
[4] International Holocaust Remembrance Alliance.

Reflexive Questions to Support this Action:

1. For those working in staff development departments (e.g., HR), how can systems be developed or made more resilient to better accommodate the career progression of Muslim staff? For example, reverse mentoring schemes have been adopted to benefit both junior and senior members of staff in professional development.
2. For those working in policy organisations or higher education sector bodies, how can funding and resources be utilised to better address inequities experienced by Muslim students? For example, the use of ring-fenced doctoral scholarships for ethnically minoritised student groups has been implemented to address the under-representation of these students within postgraduate research (University of Southampton, 2023).
3. For those working in policy development, how can you ensure that the voices of Muslims are present within policy documents which deal with our inequalities? For example, Universities UK has produced sector guidance on tackling Islamophobia by consulting with Muslim stakeholders (Universities UK, 2021).
4. For senior leaders, how can you advance conversations within your institutions related to adopting collectively agreed-upon definitions of Islamophobia? For example, London Metropolitan University became the first UK university to adopt the APPG[5] definition of Islamophobia, in consultation with students and staff (Akel, 2021).

Enacting Parity Using Values of Equity, Creativity, and Partnership

The preceding sections of this chapter have highlighted some measures which seek to ensure parity in service provision, academic inclusion, and organisational policy to better serve Muslim students and staff.

[5] All-Party Parliamentary Group.

However, we must recognise that in the journey towards equity, we consider the actors who are being compelled to act, stand for, and be 'diversity' (Ahmed, 2009). This collection demonstrates that for many Muslim students and staff, the boundaries of enacting positive change for our communities can be excessive and deficient. Importantly then, universities, higher education sector bodies, and policy organisations should utilise creativity and innovation to produce *real* change at all levels. For minoritised students and staff, we are too familiar with the performativity that accompanies the neoliberal and marketised version of diversity that many institutions feed into (Bhopal & Pitkin, 2020; Pathak, 2021). As a result, we must actively consider ethical rules of engagement to adopt if we are to achieve equitable outcomes for Muslim students and staff, i.e., how do we move away from an illusion of participation to progressive and collaborative institutions of change? (Arnstein, 1969).

Much of my work has centred on advocating for this using values which centre partnership and authentic engagement with religiously minoritised students and staff, influenced by the work of Critical Race theorists, Black feminists, and participatory methodologies (Islam, 2023; Islam & Valente, 2021). The value of employing social justice and liberatory frameworks within our efforts to support Muslim students and staff provides institutional actors with a recognition of the way inequality operates within HE. For example, De Bie et al. (2021) explicitly recognise the harm and violence under-represented students and staff experience as a starting point when adopting pedagogical partnership. The University of Westminster's Student Partnership framework also regards partnership to be a vehicle for social justice and transformational change and therefore centres love, trust, and co-creation between students and staff (Araneta et al., 2022). Indeed, universities, Student Unions, and students themselves should employ a trilateral partnership which utilises the strengths of all three parties to support tangible actions for Muslim students and staff (Islam et al., 2021). By centring these values of social justice and transformational change, we can subvert the power differentials at play which keep Muslim students and staff at the bottom of the rungs.

Reflexive Questions to Support this Action:

1. How can Muslim students and staff engaged in equity work be appropriately recognised, rewarded, and compensated? For example, are students being remunerated, and staff having this work factored into their workloads?
2. Do Muslim students and staff have safe spaces to engage in discussions related to religious equity? For example, through the development of communities of practice or student/staff networks?

CONCLUSION

In sum, this edited collection set out to uncover the low hum and deafening blare of Islamophobia manifesting within UK HE. In doing so, we share the heterogeneous voices of Muslim staff and students experiencing testimonial and epistemic injustice as part of their day-to-day experiences. Whilst diversity and inclusion agendas have been given a more prominent positioning within academia in recent decades (Koutsouris et al., 2022), many of our authors speak of an acute awareness of how this has not manifested in the same way for Muslim students and staff as it has done for other minoritised groups. Whilst progress for any minoritised group should be rightly celebrated, we hope to draw attention to an intersectional marginalisation which receives comparatively little attention.

Our aim is not only to contribute to academic literature related to Muslim staff and student experiences but also to support practitioners within and outside of universities who may work in areas related to EDI, WP, learning and teaching, and Student Unions. In doing so, we hope this collection further contributes to the existing body of work related to Islamophobia in HE but does so by appropriately considering a holistic lens, encompassing all spaces of the university to approach this systemic inequality. To end, a return to Riddell's (2024) hopes for a reconfigured HE should leave you, the reader, thinking about what role you will take if we are to create new paradigms and possibilities for Muslim students and staff within our university spaces:

'The work ahead constitutes a brand of hope that is inexorably difficult, unrelentingly hard. Birthing new paradigms is the work of hard hope. And it is, fundamentally, an act of love... Many of our existing systems have disconnections between institutional values and what we incentivize and reward' (pg. 10–11). However, 'the challenge ahead is understanding the forces that converge upon us in this moment, finding the tools necessary to build a new mindset, and creating an intentional community where we inspire a movement' (pg. 12). Let us take 'the tools and systems we have inherited and use them to renovate spaces for those who were never invited—or have been purposefully excluded—in the original conception of these organizations'. (Riddell, 2024, p. 45)

References

Abdulmula, H. (2021). *Faith and student success.* https://teachingexcellence.leeds.ac.uk/research/student-success-and-belonging-research-group/student-research-experience-placements/project-faith-and-student-success/

Achinte, A. A. (2008). nterculturalidad sin decolonialidad? Colonialidades circulantes y prácticas de re-existencia. In W. Villa & A. Grueso (Eds.), *Diversidad, interculturalidad y construcción de ciudad* (pp. 85–86). Universidad Pedagógica Nacional/Alcaldía Mayor.

Adams, R. (2020). Williamson accuses English universities of ignoring antisemitism. *The Guardian.* https://www.theguardian.com/education/2020/oct/09/williamson-accuses-english-universities-of-ignoring-antisemitism

Adelaine, A., Kalinga, C., Asani, F., Agbakoba Ngozika, R., Smith, N., Adisa, O., Francois, J., King-Okoye, M., Williams, P., & Zelzer, R. (2020). Knowledge is power—An open letter To UKRI. *Research Professional News.* https://www.researchprofessionalnews.com/rr-news-uk-views-of-the-uk-2020-8-knowledge-is-power-an-open-letter-to-ukri/

Advance HE. (2018). *Religion and belief: Supporting inclusion of staff and students in higher education and colleges.* https://www.advance-he.ac.uk/knowledge-hub/religion-and-belief-supporting-inclusion-staff-and-students-higher-education-and

Ahmed, S. (2007). 'You end up doing the document rather than doing the doing': Diversity, race equality and the politics of documentation. *Ethnic and Racial Studies, 30*(4), 590–609. https://doi.org/10.1080/01419870701356015

Ahmed, S. (2009). Embodying diversity: Problems and paradoxes for Black feminists. *Race Ethnicity and Education, 12*(1), 41–52. https://doi.org/10.1080/13613320802650931

Akel, S. (2021). *Institutionalised: The rise of Islamophobia in higher education.* http://repository.londonmet.ac.uk/6295/1/Institutionalised-the-rise-of-Islamophobia-in-Higher-Education.pdf

Ali, M. (2003). *Brick lane.* Black Swan Books.

Ali, N. (2022). Muscrit: Towards carving a niche in critical race theory for the Muslim educational experience. *International Journal of Research and Method in Education, 45*(4), 343–355. https://doi.org/10.108 0/1743727X.2022.2103112

Ali, S. R., & Bagheri, E. (2009). Practical suggestions to accommodate the needs of Muslim students on campus. *New Directions for Student Services, 125,* 47–54. https://doi.org/10.1002/ss.307

Araneta, K., Fraser, J., & Maawtk, F. (2022). *University of Westminster student partnership framework.* https://doi.org/10.34737/w0qz4

Arday, J. (2017). *Exploring black and minority ethnic (BME) doctoral students' perceptions of an academic career.* https://www.ucu.org.uk/media/8633/BME-doctoral-students-perceptions-of-an-academic-career/pdf/UCU_Arday_Report_-_June_20171.pdf

Arday, J. (2020). Fighting the tide: Understanding the difficulties facing Black, Asian and Minority Ethnic (BAME) Doctoral Students pursuing a career in Academia. *Educational Philosophy and Theory.* https://doi.org/10.108 0/00131857.2020.1777640

Arday, J., Zoe Belluigi, D., & Thomas, D. (2021). Attempting to break the chain: Reimaging inclusive pedagogy and decolonising the curriculum within the academy. *Educational Philosophy and Theory, 53*(3), 298–313. https://doi.org/10.1080/00131857.2020.1773257

Arnstein, S. R. (1969). A ladder of citizen participation. *Journal of the American Planning Association, 35*(4), 216–224. https://doi.org/10.1080/01944366908977225

Asmar, C., Proude, E., & Inge, L. (2004). 'Unwelcome Sisters?' An analysis of findings from a study of how Muslim Women (and Muslim Men) experience university. *Australian Journal of Education, 48*(1), 47–63. https://doi.org/10.1177/000494410404800104

Aune, K., & Stevenson, J. (2017). *Religion and higher education in Europe and North America.* Routledge. https://doi.org/10.4324/9781315623894

Awan, I. (2012). "I am a Muslim not an extremist": How the prevent strategy has constructed a "suspect" community. *Politics & Policy, 40*(6), 1158–1185. https://doi.org/10.1111/j.1747-1346.2012.00397.x

Bale, I., Broadhead, S., Case, K., Hussain, M., & Woolley, D. (2020). Exploring the black, Asian and ethnic minority (BAME) student experience using a Community of Inquiry approach. *Widening Participation and Lifelong Learning, 22*(1), 112–131. https://doi.org/10.5456/WPLL.22.1.112

Berenstain, N. (2016). Epistemic exploitation. *Ergo: An Open Access Journal of Philosophy, 3,* 569–590. https://doi.org/10.3998/ergo.12405314.0003.022

Bhopal, K., Brown, H., & Jackson, J. (2016). BME academic flight from UK to overseas higher education: Aspects of marginalisation and exclusion. *British Educational Research Journal, 42*(2), 240–257. https://doi.org/10.1002/berj.3204

Bhopal, K., & Pitkin, C. (2020). 'Same old story, just a different policy': Race and policy making in higher education in the UK. *Race Ethnicity and Education, 23*(4), 530–547. https://doi.org/10.1080/13613324.2020.1718082

Bonilla-Silva, E. (2019). Feeling race: Theorizing the racial economy of emotions. *American Sociological Review, 84*(1), 1–25. https://doi.org/10.1177/0003122418816958

Britton, J. (2019). Muslim Men, racialised masculinities and personal life. *Sociology, 53*(1), 36–51. https://doi.org/10.1177/0038038517749780

Chen, B., Tabassum, H., & Saeed, M. A. (2019). International Muslim students: Challenges and practical suggestions to accommodate their needs on campus. *Journal of International Students, 9*(4), 933–953. https://doi.org/10.32674/jis.v9i3.753

Claridge, H., Stone, K., & Ussher, M. (2018). The ethnicity attainment gap among medical and biomedical science students: A qualitative study. *BMC Medical Education, 18*(325). https://doi.org/10.1186/s12909-018-1426-5

Codiroli Mcmaster, N. (2020). *Research insight: Religion and belief in UK higher education.* https://www.advance-he.ac.uk/knowledge-hub/research-insight-religion-and-belief-uk-higher-education

Coe, J. (2023). Michelle Donelan writes to UKRI over "jobs for Hamas terrorist sympathisers." *WonkHE.* https://wonkhe.com/wonk-corner/michelle-donelan-writes-to-ukri-over-jobs-for-hamas-terrorist-sympathisers/

Cole, D., & Ahmadi, S. (2010). Reconsidering campus diversity: An examination of Muslim students' experiences. *The Journal of Higher Education, 81*(2), 121–139. https://doi.org/10.1080/00221546.2010.11779045

Cook-Sather, A., Addy, T. M., DeVault, A., Litvitskiy, N., DeVault, A., & Litvitskiy, N. (2021). Where are the students in efforts for inclusive excellence? Two approaches to positioning students as critical partners for inclusive pedagogical practices. *To Improve the Academy, 40*(1). https://doi.org/10.3998/tia.961

Corner, J. (2022). It's time to talk about research culture and the REF. *WonkHE.* https://wonkhe.com/blogs/its-time-to-talk-about-research-culture-and-the-ref/

Day, M., & Dickinson, J. (2018). *David versus Goliath: The past, present and future of students' unions in the UK.* https://www.hepi.ac.uk/wp-content/uploads/2018/09/HEPI-Students-Unions-Report-111-FINAL-EMBARGOED1.pdf

De Bie, A., Marquis, E., Cook-Sather, A., & Luqueno, P. L. (2021). *Promoting equity and justice through pedagogical partnership*. Stylus Publishing.

Decuir-Gunby, J. T. (2020). Using critical race mixed methodology to explore the experiences of African Americans in education. *Educational Psychologist, 55*(4), 244–255. https://doi.org/10.1080/00461520.2020.1793762

Edwards, A. (2023). Three King's College London SU officers suspended for showing solidarity with Gaza. The Tab. https://thetab.com/uk/kings/2023/12/07/three-kings-college-london-su-student-officers-suspended-for-showing-solidarity-with-gaza-34015 (accessed: 29 September 2024).

Florian, L., & Linklater, H. (2010). Preparing teachers for inclusive education: Using inclusive pedagogy to enhance teaching and learning for all. *Cambridge Journal of Education, 40*(4), 369–386. https://doi.org/10.1080/0305764X.2010.526588

Franceschelli, M., & O'Brien, M. (2014). "Islamic Capital" and Family Life: The Role of Islam in Parenting. *Sociology, 48*(6), 1190–1206. https://doi.org/10.1177/0038038513519879

Ghabra, H., & Calafell, B. M. (2018). From failure and allyship to feminist solidarities: Negotiating our privileges and oppressions across borders. *Text and Performance Quarterly, 38*(1–2), 38–54. https://doi.org/10.1080/10462937.2018.1457173

Gholami, R. (2021). Critical race theory and Islamophobia: Challenging inequity in Higher Education. *Race Ethnicity and Education, 24*(3), 319–337. https://doi.org/10.1080/13613324.2021.1879770

Haney Lopez, I. F. (2004). The social construction of race. In J. Rivkin & M. Ryan (Eds.), *Literary theory: An anthology* (2nd ed., pp. 964–974). http://www.blackwellpublishing.com

Hill, S., & Turner, N. (2019). *Access and success for black, Asian and minority ethnicity groups in postgraduate research study - Research England*. Research England. https://re.ukri.org/news-opinions-events/blog/access-and-success-for-black-asian-and-minority-ethnicity-groups-in-postgraduate-research-study/

hooks, b. (1989). Talking back. In *Talking back: Thinking feminist, thinking black* (pp. 5–9). South End Press. http://abacus.bates.edu/~cnero/rhetoric/hooks.pdf

Hopkins, P. (2011). Towards critical geographies of the university campus: Understanding the contested experiences of Muslim students. *Transactions of the Institute of British Geographers, 36*(1), 157–169. https://www.jstor.org/stable/23020847

Irigaray, H. A. R., Celano, A., Fontoura, Y., & Maher, R. (2021). Resisting by re-existing in the workplace: A decolonial perspective through the Brazilian adage "For the English to See". *Organization, 28*(5), 817–835. https://doi.org/10.1177/13505084211022666

Islam, M. (2021a). *Building belonging: Developing religiously inclusive cultures for Muslim students in higher education.* https://www.advance-he.ac.uk/knowledge-hub/building-belonging-developing-religiously-inclusive-cultures-muslim-students-higher

Islam, M. (2021b). *Disaggregating the BAME degree-awarding gap: Understanding and exploring the "Asian" student experience.* https://doi.org/10.13140/RG.2.2.19843.63525

Islam, M. (2023). Equality and diversity in our student engagement practice: Radical possibilities to reaching racial and religious equity in higher education. In T. Lowe (Ed.), *Advancing student engagement in higher education: Reflection, critique and challenge.* Routledge.

Islam, M., Burnett, T.-L., & Collins, S.-L. (2021). Trilateral partnership: An institution and students' union collaborative partnership project to support under-represented student groups. *International Journal for Students as Partners, 5*(1), 76–85. https://doi.org/10.15173/ijsap.v5i1.4455

Islam, M., Lowe, T., & Jones, G. (2019). A "Satisfied Settling"? Investigating a Sense of belonging for Muslim students in a UK Small-medium higher education institution. *Student Engagement in Higher Education Journal, 2*(2), 79–104. https://sehej.raise-network.com/raise/article/view/891/709

Islam, M., & Mercer-Mapstone, L. (2021). 'University is a non-Muslim experience, you know? The experience is as good as it can be': Satisfied settling in Muslim students' experiences and implications for Muslim student voice. *British Educational Research Journal, 47*(5), 1388–1415. https://doi.org/10.1002/berj.3733

Islam, M., & Valente, I. (2021). A critical dialogue reflecting on the potentials of black, Asian and minority ethnic student-staff partnerships. *Journal of Educational Innovation, Partnership and Change, 7*(1). https://doi.org/10.21100/JEIPC.V7I1.1037

Jamal Al-deen, T. (2019). Agency in action: Young Muslim women and negotiating higher education in Australia. *British Journal of Sociology of Education, 40*(5), 598–613. https://doi.org/10.1080/01425692.2019.1576120

Johnson, A. (2020). Throwing our bodies against the white background of academia. *Area, 52*(1), 89–96. https://doi.org/10.1111/area.12568

Koutsouris, G., Stentiford, L., & Norwich, B. (2022). A critical exploration of inclusion policies of elite UK universities. *British Educational Research Journal, 48*(5), 878–895. https://doi.org/10.1002/BERJ.3799

Kyriacou, C., Reed, B. S., Said, F., & Davies, I. (2017). British Muslim university students' perceptions of Prevent and its impact on their sense of identity. *Education, Citizenship and Social Justice, 12*(2), 97–110. https://doi.org/10.1177/1746197916688918

Lorber, J. (2018). The social construction of gender. In D. B. Grusky & S. Szelenyi (Eds.), *The inequality reader: Contemporary and foundational readings in race, class, and gender* (2nd ed., pp. 318–325). Routledge.

Mac an Ghaill, M., & Haywood, C. (2015). British-born Pakistani and Bangladeshi young men: Exploring unstable concepts of Muslim, Islamophobia and racialization. *Critical Sociology, 41*(1), 97–114. https://doi.org/10.1177/0896920513518947

Meda, L. (2020). Decolonising the curriculum: Students' perspectives. *Africa Education Review, 17*(2), 88–103. https://doi.org/10.1080/18146627.2018.1519372

Molesworth, M., Nixon, E., & Scullion, R. (2009). Having, being and higher education: The marketisation of the university and the transformation of the student into consumer. *Teaching in Higher Education, 14*(3), 277–287. https://doi.org/10.1080/13562510902898841

National Secular Society. (2023). Islamophobia definitions threaten free speech at 20+ universities. https://www.secularism.org.uk/news/2023/11/islamophobia-definitions-threaten-free-speech-at-20-universities

NUS Connect. (2016). *Preventing prevent.* https://www.nusconnect.org.uk/campaigns/preventing-prevent-we-are-students-not-suspects

Nye, M. (2019). Decolonizing the study of religion. *Open Library of Humanities, 5*(1). https://doi.org/10.16995/olh.421

Parr, C. (2020). More universities adopt IHRA antisemitism definition. *Research Professional News.* https://www.researchprofessionalnews.com/rr-news-uk-universities-2020-12-more-universities-adopt-ihra-antisemitism-definition/

Pathak, P. (2021). Prefiguring the anti-racist university: A systems change approach to the race equality charter. *IMPact, 4*(2), 1–16.

Riddell, J. (2024). *Hope Circuits: Rewiring Universities and Other Organizations for Human Flourishing.* McGill-Queen's University Press.

Schoonenboom, J. (2018). Designing mixed methods research by mixing and merging methodologies: A 13-step model. *American Behavioral Scientist, 62*(7), 998–1015. https://doi.org/10.1177/0002764218772674

Seggie, F. N., & Sanford, G. (2010). Perceptions of female Muslim students who veil: Campus religious climate. *Race Ethnicity and Education, 13*(1), 59–82. https://doi.org/10.1080/13613320903549701

Shaffait, H. (2019). *Inclusivity at university Muslim student experiences.* https://www.kcl.ac.uk/geography/assets/kcl-sspp-muslim-policy-report-digital-aw.pdf

Shalabi, N. (2014). Toward inclusive understanding and practice of diversity: Directions for accommodating Muslim and other religious minoritized students on university campuses. *Journal of Critical Thought and Praxis, 2*(2) https://doi.org/10.31274/jctp-180810-19

SOAS University of London. (2018). *Decolonising SOAS: Learning and teaching toolkit for programme and module convenors.*

Stevenson, J. (2018). *Muslim students in UK higher education: Issues of inequality and inequity.* Bridge Institute for Research and Policy. https://www.azizfoundation.org.uk/wp-content/uploads/2021/01/Bridge-Higher-Education-report-2.pdf

The Scottish Universities Partnership for Environmental Research. (2023). *Diversity, equity, and inclusion.* https://superdtp.st-andrews.ac.uk/diversity-equity-and-inclusion/

Thomas, L. (2012). *Building student engagement and belonging in Higher education at a time of change: Final report from the what works? student retention & success programme.* https://www.heacademy.ac.uk/system/files/what_works_final_report_0.pdf

Thompson, N., & Pihlaja, S. (2018). Temporary liberties and uncertain futures: Young Female Muslim perceptions of life in England. *Journal of Youth Studies, 21*(10), 1326–1343. https://doi.org/10.1080/13676261.2018.1468021

Tomlinson, M. (2017). Student perceptions of themselves as 'consumers' of higher education. *British Journal of Sociology of Education, 38*(4), 450–467. https://doi.org/10.1080/01425692.2015.1113856

Union of Jewish Students. (2024). *IHRA campaign.* https://www.ujs.org.uk/ihra_campaign

Universities UK. (2021). *Tackling Islamophobia and anti-Muslim hatred: Practical guidance for UK universities.* https://www.universitiesuk.ac.uk/what-we-do/policy-and-research/publications/tackling-islamophobia-and-anti-muslim

Universities UK, & National Union of Students. (2019). *Black, Asian and minority ethnic student attainment at UK universities: #ClosingTheGap.* https://www.universitiesuk.ac.uk/policy-and-analysis/reports/Documents/2019/bame-student-attainment-uk-universities-closing-the-gap.pdf

University of Southampton. (2023). *Black futures scholarship.* https://www.southampton.ac.uk/study/fees-funding/scholarships/competitive-postgraduate/black-futures

Wilson, A. (2007). The forced marriage debate and the British state. *Race & Class, 49*(1), 25–38. https://doi.org/10.1177/0306396807080065

Wilson, E. (2016). *"Traditionally submissive Muslim women" say who us?* BBC. https://www.bbc.co.uk/news/blogs-trending-35403106

WonkHE, & Kortext. (2022). *Leaders of learning and teaching survey.* https://wonkhe.com/wp-content/wonkhe-uploads/2022/02/Wonkhe-Kortext-LT-leaders-survey-Feb-22.pdf

Index[1]

A

Academic career, 44, 125, 133, 194
  freedom, vii, 66, 191, 209, 223
  marginality, 126, 187
Access and Participation Plans (APPs),
  50, 232, 245, 254, 255, 263,
  273, 281
Activism, 46, 59, 65–66, 127, 192,
  196, 221, 269, 275, 276, 281
Agency, 43, 79, 89, 110, 112, 143,
  163, 164, 166, 170, 175, 241,
  256–258, 276
Alcohol, 19, 26, 31, 63, 106, 147,
  155, 239, 240
  drinking culture, 63, 239
Alienation, 20, 23
Ally/allyship/advocates, 47, 47n11,
  49, 50, 104, 109, 127, 196, 238,
  241, 279, 282
Ambivalence, 18, 24–25, 31, 273
Anti-Blackness, 34, 48, 241

Antisemitism, 59, 65–66, 70, 156,
  191, 191n3, 232, 282
Athena Swan Charter, 112, 280
Attainment, 3, 49, 88, 125, 205, 207,
  210, 275
Awarding gap, 18, 36–38, 36n2, 50,
  81, 215–227, 272, 276

B

Belonging, 3, 7, 10, 31, 35, 39, 41,
  45–48, 59, 63, 78, 79, 82, 83,
  86, 88, 89, 105, 122, 125–127,
  162, 169, 171–173, 175, 182,
  222, 237–239, 242, 243,
  257, 275–277
Black Asian and Minority Ethnic
  (BAME), 36n2, 37, 48, 81–84,
  98, 100, 101, 103, 106,
  108–111, 163, 220, 223,
  232, 254

[1] Note: Page numbers followed by 'n' refer to notes.

Black feminist theory, 7
Black (Muslim) women, 7, 33–51, 271
Black students, 37, 39, 46, 47n10, 48

C
Capital, 9, 169, 276
    cultural, 82, 260, 261
    economic, 82
    socio, 61, 106, 203, 261, 276
Career development/progression,
    110, 122, 129, 148, 234, 235,
    278, 280, 283
Christian culture, 9, 216, 272
Civil liberties, 202, 203, 208
Class, 8, 19, 23, 26, 27, 37, 48, 60,
    62, 79, 101, 102, 106, 111, 129,
    164, 165, 171–173, 185, 204,
    222, 233, 254, 258
    poverty, 202
    socio-economic disadvantage, 262
    working-class, viii, ix, 7, 60, 61, 78,
        81, 85, 98, 100, 102, 104,
        144, 173, 281
Colonialism, 48, 209, 226, 227,
    271, 279
Counter-narratives, 5, 6, 33–51
Counter-terrorism, 9, 216, 218
Critical Race Theory (CRT), 6, 34,
    62, 222, 224, 227, 252, 255,
    278n1, 279
Cultural racism, 183, 184, 186,
    195, 274

D
Dearing Report, 253
Decolonial/decolonisation/
    decolonise(ing), ix, 31, 46, 99,
    122, 173, 181, 182, 195, 196,
    216, 224, 225, 227, 276,
    278, 279

Diaspora, 106, 148, 161, 165, 174
Discrimination, vii–ix, 4, 18, 34, 36,
    39n5, 40, 45, 62, 67, 79, 99,
    124, 132, 133, 145, 147, 149,
    155, 156n3, 163, 167, 169, 184,
    185, 195, 201, 203, 207, 210,
    231, 232, 235, 240, 242,
    243, 277
Doctorate, 98
Double standards, 2, 184, 185,
    195, 274
Duoethnographic approach, 8

E
Early career, 6–8, 121–135, 148, 181,
    182, 194, 271, 272, 279
    academics/researchers/scientists,
        viii, 3, 4, 6–10, 18–25, 28,
        33–36, 41, 42, 44, 47–50, 57,
        59, 60, 66, 77–79, 82, 97, 98,
        100–109, 111–113, 121–135,
        143–153, 155–157, 161–163,
        165, 168, 171–174, 181–196,
        202, 205–210, 221–223,
        222n6, 226, 234–236, 243,
        252, 256, 258–261, 269, 270,
        272–283, 285
Empowerment, 10, 103, 196,
    257, 276
Epistemological, 18, 22, 26–27, 226
Equalities hierarchy, 191, 196
Equalities Impact Assessments
    (EIA), 153
Equality, diversity & inclusion (EDI),
    8, 41, 43, 48, 49, 79, 82–85, 89,
    101, 110, 112, 209, 220, 223,
    252, 254–257, 271, 272, 285
Eurocentric curriculum, 8, 21, 102
Exclusion, vii, 18, 36, 44, 63, 99–101,
    124, 126, 163, 172,
    201–210, 256

F

Freedom of speech, 2, 223
Fundamental British values
    (FBV), 1, 220

G

Gendered Islamophobia, 7, 10,
    270–272, 278

H

Harassment, 3, 36, 99, 126, 232,
    235, 263
Hate crimes, 2, 3, 112, 242
Hijab/hijabi/headscarf, 27, 35, 40,
    41, 43, 48, 57, 57n1, 59–61, 67,
    79, 81, 82, 85, 87, 102, 103,
    123, 124, 124n1, 126, 128, 131,
    162, 165, 166, 169–171, 174,
    189, 232
Hypervisibility, 143–157, 264

I

Identity, viii, 3, 5, 7–11, 23, 24, 34,
    35, 37, 40, 41, 48, 49, 51, 57,
    60–61, 63–65, 77–89, 98, 99,
    102, 103, 123–129, 131–135,
    145, 153, 154, 156, 162–167,
    170–172, 174, 175, 184–190,
    192, 195–196, 203, 204,
    207–209, 219, 226, 239, 251,
    254–257, 261, 276, 280
    formation/politics/recognition, 8,
        63–65, 102, 127, 135, 190,
        193, 203
IHRA Definition of antisemitism,
    65–66, 191
Imposter syndrome, 8, 58, 60, 61,
    100, 102, 104–106,
    112, 147–152

Inclusivity, 26, 33, 88, 134, 135,
    210, 241–243
Institutionalisation, 5
Intersectionality, 8, 34, 36, 48, 50,
    60–61, 97–113, 126, 127,
    162–164, 175, 233, 245,
    251–264, 269, 271, 273,
    279, 280
    communities prejudice, 261
    identities, 34, 48, 51, 60–61, 102,
        164, 188
    inclusion, 253, 264
    intersectional–disadvantage, 34,
        251–264, 273, 280
Islamic Society (ISOC), 35, 101, 104,
    239–241, 243, 259
Islamophobic tropes, 63–65, 274
Isolation, 18, 28–29, 59, 71, 122,
    132, 133, 210, 273

M

Marginalisation, 2, 35, 40, 43, 127,
    132, 155, 182, 201–210, 271,
    273, 279, 285
Marketisation, 78, 83–85, 89, 144,
    202, 206, 210, 269–286
Media, 1–3, 40, 65, 66, 78, 99, 106,
    132, 186, 189, 218, 221
Memory, 166, 171, 173–175
Mental health/fatigue, 3, 42, 50, 59,
    70, 88, 98, 108, 112, 122, 127,
    132–134, 144, 145, 190, 202,
    205, 208
Mentoring, 82, 112, 129, 236, 283
Microaggressions, 3, 8, 21, 35, 38,
    40–44, 49, 100, 102, 104, 107,
    110, 112, 147, 153–156, 174,
    210, 235, 237, 239–240
Minority-majority relations, 186
Misogynoir, 7, 34, 43n7
Multicultural drift, 252

Multiculturalism, 83–85, 163, 172, 193, 194
Multiple identities, 37, 40, 99, 134, 172, 272
  Muslimness, 170
  students, 37
  women, 37, 134, 272

N
Narrative interview/method, 9, 164–167, 182
National Union of Students (NUS), 3, 36, 58, 59, 65, 67–71, 123, 221, 258, 272, 275, 280
Neoliberalism, 9, 144, 202, 205, 206, 209, 269–286

O
Office for Students (OfS), 50, 81, 232, 245, 252, 254, 255, 262, 263, 282, 282n3

P
Palestine/Gaza, 2–4, 19, 48, 65, 156, 270
Parentification, 106
Partnership, 10, 36, 58, 192, 193, 196, 263, 279, 283–285
Pedagogic violence, 18–31
Positionality, 78, 97–99, 102, 182, 196, 236, 253
Postcolonial, 8, 126, 161, 162, 165, 167, 173
Precarity, ix, 122, 143–152, 274, 278
Prevent, 4, 9, 46, 88, 100, 129, 151, 155, 191, 207, 208, 218, 220–223, 225, 275
Psychological safety, 242–244

R
Race Equality Charter (REC), 7, 9, 101, 112, 231–245, 275, 280
Racial economy of emotions, 18, 20, 25, 273
Racialisation, 4, 40, 167, 183, 184, 203, 208–210, 216, 225, 232, 261
Radicalisation, 202, 208
Ramadan, 101, 102, 105, 147, 237, 277
Religification/religifying, 216–220, 223, 224, 227
Religious equity, 9, 196, 231–245, 270, 275, 285
Resistance, 6, 21, 89, 124, 151, 164, 165, 170, 172, 174, 181, 196, 276
Resonance, 7, 23, 30, 31, 273
Rushdie affair, 186, 186n1, 188

S
Sabbatical officer(s)/student officer, 6, 7, 57–71, 274, 275
Safe space(s), 8, 69, 70, 110, 144, 157, 202, 206, 237, 240–242, 275, 285
Satisfied settling, 85, 236, 245, 272
Second skin, 167, 169, 171
Secular/secularism, 9, 20–22, 26, 48, 62–64, 87, 147, 153, 155, 174, 175, 184, 190, 195, 215–227, 232, 255, 258, 272, 277
Securitisation, 47, 201–203, 206–210, 259, 275
Senior leaders/leadership, viii, 5, 9, 60, 70, 236, 241, 242, 255, 258, 283
Social psychology, 99

Stereotypes, 24, 43n7, 63, 71, 80,
    132, 134, 151, 153, 184, 189,
    207, 261, 271
Student loans, 205, 262
Student-led, 58, 221, 224, 225, 227,
    232, 239, 279
Superdiversity, 252
Surveillance, 4, 41, 43, 48, 88, 124,
    125, 128, 201–210, 220, 222,
    226, 275
Survival, 8, 127, 151, 161–175

T
Tokenism/tokenistic, 8, 38,
    100, 102, 104, 110, 112, 124,
    224, 233
Transnational, 8, 161,
    165–167, 171–175
Trojan Horse, 219, 219n1, 221

U
UK Research and Innovation (UKRI),
    124, 281, 281n2
Union of Jewish Students
    (UJS), 65, 282

V
Veil, 40, 78, 162, 166, 167, 169–171

W
White atmosphere, 7, 18–31, 273, 278
White privilege, 149, 163, 175, 233
White supremacy, 47, 47n11,
    63, 64, 79
Whiteness, vii, 34, 39, 44, 83, 85, 100,
    112, 145, 162, 164, 271, 273
Widening participation (WP), 10,
    251–264, 273, 281, 285

GPSR Compliance

The European Union's (EU) General Product Safety Regulation (GPSR) is a set of rules that requires consumer products to be safe and our obligations to ensure this.

If you have any concerns about our products, you can contact us on ProductSafety@springernature.com

In case Publisher is established outside the EU, the EU authorized representative is:

Springer Nature Customer Service Center GmbH
Europaplatz 3
69115 Heidelberg, Germany

Batch number: 07936080

Printed by Printforce, the Netherlands